PENGUIN BOOKS

DOCTORING THE MIND

D1390056

Richard Bentall has held chairs in
sities of Liverpool and Manches
Clinical Psychology at the Unive
internationally for his research into the causes and treatment of
severe mental illness, his previous book, *Madness Explained:
Psychosis and Human Nature* won the British Psychological
Society Book Award for 2004.

RICHARD P. BENTALL

Doctoring the Mind

Why Psychiatric Treatments Fail

PENGUIN BOOKS

This book is dedicated to
Sarah Butler
sister and friend

PENGUIN BOOKS

Published by the Penguin Group
Penguin Books Ltd, 80 Strand, London WC2R 0RL, England
Penguin Group (USA) Inc., 375 Hudson Street, New York, New York 10014, USA
Penguin Group (Canada), 90 Eglinton Avenue East, Suite 700, Toronto, Ontario, Canada M4P 2Y3
(a division of Pearson Penguin Canada Inc.)
Penguin Ireland, 25 St Stephen's Green, Dublin 2, Ireland (a division of Penguin Books Ltd)
Penguin Group (Australia), 250 Camberwell Road, Camberwell, Victoria 3124, Australia
(a division of Pearson Australia Group Pty Ltd)
Penguin Books India Pvt Ltd, 11 Community Centre, Panchsheel Park, New Delhi – 110 017, India
Penguin Group (NZ), 67 Apollo Drive, Rosedale, North Shore 0632, New Zealand
(a division of Pearson New Zealand Ltd)
Penguin Books (South Africa) (Pty) Ltd, 24 Sturdee Avenue, Rosebank, Johannesburg 2196, South Africa

Penguin Books Ltd, Registered Offices: 80 Strand, London WC2R 0RL, England

www.penguin.com

First published by Allen Lane 2009
Published in Penguin Books 2010
2

Copyright © Richard P. Bentall, 2009
All rights reserved

The moral right of the author has been asserted

Printed in England by Clays Ltd, St Ives plc

978-0-141-02369-4

www.greenpenguin.co.uk

Penguin Books is committed to a sustainable future
for our business, our readers and our planet.
The book in your hands is made from paper
certified by the Forest Stewardship Council.

Contents

List of Illustrations

Photographic acknowledgements are given in parentheses.

List of Figures

Acknowledgements

As usual I must thank my numerous postgraduate students and colleagues in clinical psychology and psychiatry for stimulating my thinking about the issues discussed in the following chapters. Of my current and recent postgraduates, I would like to mention Eve Applegate, Hazel Dunn, Paul French, Becca Knowles, Sara Melo, Michael Moutoussis, Justin Thomas, Alisa Udachina and Filippo Verase. Of my colleagues I would like to mention, in clinical psychology, Tony Morrison, Mike Jackson, Steve Jones, John Read and Sara Tai, in biomedical statistics Graham Dunn, Chris Roberts, Paula Williamson and Gill Lancaster, and, in psychiatry, Shôn Lewis, David Kingdon, David Linden, Richard Morriss, Jan Scott and Richard Drake (who, I guess, would disagree with much of what I have written but who seem to be relaxed about collaborating with someone who has one foot in the antipsychiatry camp). I would also like to thank my assistant Hanneke Booij for keeping me organized during my first extremely busy year at Bangor. A special mention should also be given to Pete Saunders of PCCS Books (a small publishing house specializing in books about psychotherapy) for alerting me to the contribution of Carl Rogers, which has almost been forgotten by most clinical psychologists. Self-evidently, none of these people should be held in any way responsible for any errors I have made. Perhaps one of the greatest joys of an academic life is that it allows one to work in friendly cooperation with talented people whose views on important issues are often completely different from one's own.

I would like to thank my wife Aisling, a clinical psychologist who works in an early intervention service, for her support and for endless discussions about service users, their problems and their aspirations.

I would also like to thank my children Fintan and Keeva for putting up with my occasional grumpiness during the writing of this book. My sister and brother-in-law Deirdre and Steven O'Connor are to be thanked for wining and dining me while I was welded to my laptop during visits to Mullingar. My good friend and collaborator Charles Fernyhough is to be thanked for coming up with the title of the book after a mere second of thought; I had been struggling with the problem for months. I would also like to thank the helpful and constructively critical team at Penguin Books, especially Helen Conford, who has the patience of several saints.

Finally, I must offer my thanks to the numerous service users who have taught me most of what I know about psychosis, and especially those who have consented to me including their (necessarily heavily disguised) stories in these pages. I suspect that the time we have spent together has often been of more benefit to me than to them.

Richard Bentall
November 2008

Preface: Rational Antipsychiatry

Several years ago I was invited to give a talk at a conference held for the lay people and professionals who sit on the British National Health Service's numerous research ethics committees. These committees, which meet in every corner of the country, are responsible for regulating the conduct of medical research. Any investigator who wishes to carry out a study in the NHS is required to submit detailed plans to the local committee, which will then debate the merits of the proposed investigation, ensure that any risks to patients are outweighed by likely benefits, and make sure that that all those participating freely consent to doing so.

I had been invited to talk at the conference because the organizers thought that, during two decades of work as a clinical psychologist* studying severe mental illness, I was likely to have gained some insights into the specific problems encountered when trying to conduct research with psychiatric patients. The conference was scheduled to take place in the city of Chester, about 20 miles from my home, so I had reluctantly agreed to give my talk early on a Saturday morning, a time I normally prefer to spend with my family. As I made my way to the conference venue my mind was focused on a less cerebral

---

* The differences between the profession of clinical psychology (to which I belong) and the profession of psychiatry will be discussed at length as we proceed. Suffice it to say for the moment that psychiatrists first of all obtain a degree in medicine before receiving further training in the treatment of mental illness. Clinical psychologists, on the other hand, first of all receive a scientific training in psychology (the science of mind and human behaviour) before going on to take an advanced training (a taught doctorate in Britain and the United States) in the use of psychological techniques in the assessment and treatment of mental illness and other clinical conditions.

purpose – I had discovered that the film *ET* was going to be shown at a local cinema later in the morning and that, if I managed to leave promptly after my talk, I would be able to take my 5-year-old twins to see it.

When I arrived I found about a hundred delegates sitting behind long tables draped in white cloth. They looked like fairly ordinary folk and I reminded myself that they would be from a variety of backgrounds; quite a few doctors no doubt, a few professional philosophers, as well as many people from other walks of life. They were listening respectfully to a smartly dressed young surgeon who, from his position on the podium, was enthusiastically berating them. Although I had missed the first few minutes of his talk, his theme seemed to be that, by requiring the detailed scrutiny of every aspect of a proposed project, a process that could take many months, ethics committees were in danger of preventing vital research from happening at all. (Anyone who has tried to conduct research in the NHS is likely to have some sympathy with this position although, of course, this is not to suggest that research projects should not be subject to detailed independent review.)

Like the surgeon who preceded me, I wanted to say something about the increasing difficulties I was encountering when carrying out my research. However, I also thought that an audience of ethics committee members would appreciate hearing a talk that was thought-provoking, and which would stimulate debate. I therefore decided to challenge the widespread assumption that many psychiatric patients are unable to understand the purpose of research, and are therefore unable give meaningful consent. I began by listing some of the terrible abuses that had been perpetrated against psychiatric patients during the middle decades of the twentieth century – for example, the way in which they had been incarcerated in large asylums and subjected to cruel and ineffective treatments such as the prefrontal leucotomy (a crude brain operation). I suggested that these abuses had been possible because patients' objections had been systematically ignored on the grounds that their mental illness disqualified them from offering a reasoned opinion about their treatment. I then went on to describe some recent psychological research which showed that even severely ill patients are usually capable of reasoning about their experiences.

I concluded that ethics committees should trust psychiatric patients and recognize their right to autonomy (that is, their prerogative to decide what is in their own interests; a fundamental right according to medical ethicists[1]), adding that patients would almost certainly get better treatment if clinicians dealt with them in the same way.

After my closing words, I took a deep breath and waited for questions. My mind was still focused on the problem of escaping as quickly as possible. As I smiled benignly at the audience, a middle-aged man rose at the back of the conference hall, and began to speak, 'Professor Bentall has told us that he is a scientist,' he began in an amiable enough tone of voice. He paused for effect, and then his tone suddenly darkened. 'But he is not!' he thundered. 'Nothing that Professor Bentall has said – not a single word – is true. We have been forced to listen to a wild, antipsychiatric rant!'

I was a bit stunned. I was used to being challenged politely, and on particular points ('I would like to disagree with what you said about the effectiveness of antipsychotic medication', perhaps) but I could not remember any previous occasion on which someone had tried to rubbish everything that I had said in a single sentence. Trying to gather my thoughts, and still mindful of the fact that I needed to get away as quickly as possible, I asked the speaker – presumably a psychiatrist – to identify any particular observation I had made that he thought was inaccurate. There then followed a slightly rambling intellectual tussle as, to the likely confusion of nearly everyone present, we debated whether schizophrenia is a genetically determined brain disorder. Eventually, our debate was interrupted by the chairman, who wanted to introduce the next speaker.

As I hurried away from the podium two people spoke to me. The first was the next speaker, another smartly dressed doctor, who, passing in the opposite direction, whispered, 'Blimey, that was exciting!' The second was a middle-aged woman, who chased after me and stopped me at the door. 'Ignore that fool!' she said, her eyes flooded with tears. 'My husband has been mentally ill for twenty years. Nothing they have done has ever helped him. You're the first person I have heard who has ever given me any hope.'

On the distinction between antipsychiatry and being against psychiatrists

As my experience at the conference demonstrates, debates about the causes and treatment of mental illness can provoke powerful emotions, perhaps because they are not mere intellectual games but affect the lives of real people. The heat in these debates has often been stoked by professional rivalry between different groups of mental health professionals. For example, psychiatrists (who are trained in medicine before going on to specialize in the treatment of the mentally ill) often (but not always) assume that mental illness is the consequence of some kind of genetically determined brain disease, and therefore often use drugs as their first line of treatment. On the other hand, clinical psychologists (who are first trained in the science of psychology before going on to learn how to apply psychological technique to clinical problems) usually (but not always) start from the assumption that mental illness is caused when normal psychological processes are placed under intolerable stress, and advocate the use of psychological treatments (with few exceptions, they are not licensed to prescribe psychiatric drugs).

As psychiatry is the older of the two professions and clinical psychology is a relative newcomer, it is the medical approach that has taken precedence in the mental health services of most countries of the world. However, as we shall see, throughout the history of psychiatry there have always been people who have opposed the medical approach, sometimes meekly but often with great energy. This opposition has come, not only from other mental health practitioners such as clinical psychologists, but often from within psychiatry itself. For example, during the 1960s and 1970s it was dissident psychiatrists such as Thomas Szasz[2] and Ronald Laing[3] who formed the core of what was known as the *antipsychiatry movement*, which, perhaps because it chimed with the anti-authoritarian spirit of the times, enjoyed widespread support amongst the chattering classes.

Of course, there have never been any anti-oncologists, anti-cardiologists, anti-gastroenterologists or even anti-obstetricians. Psychiatry has therefore been unique in the extent to which it has generated both fascination and mistrust amongst intelligent people. Perhaps this is because, alone among the medical specialities, it has the power to compel people to receive treatment, and because some of the treatments inflicted on the mentally ill have seemed more terrifying than madness itself. Perhaps it is also because the human sciences of psychology and sociology seem to offer an obvious alternative to the medical way of thinking about human distress, leaving a suspicion that much of what passes for medical science in the field owes more to Frankenstein than to Louis Pasteur or Alexander Fleming.

The movement failed to achieve its aims, partly because it was unable to propose a convincing and workable alternative to traditional psychiatric care but also because startling advances in the neurosciences led to renewed enthusiasm for the medical approach to mental illness. Roll the clock thirty years onwards and we arrive at a time when a psychiatrist arguing with a clinical psychologist can use the term 'antipsychiatry' as a kind of sneer, a single word that can be deployed to signify that any opposition to conventional psychiatric thinking is crazy and as outdated as luxuriant moustaches and multi-coloured flared jeans. What has been lost in all this is that it might be possible to be rationally antipsychiatric, that conventional psychiatry might reasonably be criticized, not on hard-to-define humanistic grounds (although these are important) but because it has been profoundly unscientific and at the same time unsuccessful at helping some of the most distressed and vulnerable people in our society. This is the main argument of this book.

Of course, one difficulty in making this argument is that it provokes defensiveness in even the most forward-thinking of psychiatrists. Responding to a highly critical history of the profession by the American journalist Robert Whitaker,[4] a British doctor of my acquaintance (whom I would count as on the side of the angels), remarked that he felt as bruised as a sinner who had been denounced by a strident evangelical preacher. This kind of response reflects an understandable difficulty in distinguishing between being *antipsychiatry* and being *against psychiatrists*. It is logically possible to object to much of the theory of medical psychiatry and to exclusively biological treatments for psychiatric disorder, while at the same time recognizing that even the most conventionally minded psychiatrists usually want the very best for their patients, and that there are many amongst their number who, sometimes despite their training, are highly skilled and empathetic clinicians. It is also possible to object to conventional psychiatry while recognizing that some of its most influential opponents today, just as in the 1960s and 1970s, are psychiatrists themselves. Rather than dispensing with psychiatrists, perhaps we need more psychiatrists who are better trained, and who are better able to help their patients.

The purpose of this book

One important difference between the 1970s and today is that we now know much more about psychiatric disorders. Far from shoring up the medical approach, however, recent scientific research shows that it is fatally flawed. As a consequence, a new picture of mental illness has begun to emerge. In my previous book, *Madness Explained: Psychosis and Human Nature*, I tried to describe this new picture in detail. My aim was to show how modern research was leading to a coherent understanding of madness that is dramatically different from that found in even the most recent textbooks of psychiatry. In the process, I found it necessary to explain what was wrong with some very widely accepted theories of mental illness, but I avoided launching an all-out assault against conventional psychiatric treatment. Anticipating criticism from my medical colleagues, I made sure that the relevant evidence was meticulously referenced, with the consequence that the book was long – 512 pages followed by another 110 pages of notes. On the whole, it was well received (it won the British Psychological Society Book Award in 2004). However, its length may have prevented the dissemination of its ideas as widely as I would have liked.

This book tackles some of the same themes but is shorter and therefore (I hope) more accessible. However, it differs from its predecessor in some important respects. It focuses much more on the stories of patients, and is also much more concerned with the effects of different kinds of treatment, which were not discussed at any length in the previous book. I argue that many of these treatments are nowhere near as powerful as is often believed, and that their effects have been exaggerated by skilful pharmaceutical industry marketing.

An important theme I have tried to address throughout, and which I entirely neglected in *Madness Explained*, is the crucial importance of relationships in psychiatric care. After adopting a technical, bio-medical approach to mental illness during the 1980s, psychiatry (especially in the United States but also in Britain to some extent) decided that talking to patients is not very important. The result is a style of care that many patients find coercive and dehumanizing. Ironically (although perhaps not to the surprise of many outside psychiatry), the research evidence shows that warm, collaborative relationships, far from being dispensable, are the key to success in psychiatric care. Hence, if psychiatric services are to become more genuinely therapeutic, and if they are to help people rather than merely 'manage' their difficulties, it will be necessary to rediscover the art of relating to patients with warmth, kindness and empathy.

For those readers who would like a more detailed outline of the contents of *Doctoring the Mind* I proceed as follows. In Chapter 1, I ask whether there is any evidence that psychiatry has made a positive impact on human welfare. Surprisingly, it seems that there is not. For example, whereas the recent history of physical medicine has been marked by dramatic breakthroughs, leading to measurable improve-ments in the likelihood of surviving life-threatening diseases, there is no evidence of similar advances in our ability to treat severe mental illness. This leads me to ask why psychiatry has failed when other branches of medicine have been so successful.

The historical section of the book, which occupies the next three chapters, explains how the current ineffective approach to psychiatric care has evolved. Whereas the historical chapters in *Madness Explained* focused exclusively on the development of theories of psy-chiatric classification, in this book I focus much more on the evolution of different kinds of psychiatric treatment. Of course, any history must be selective, emphasizing some events and neglecting others in an attempt to weave a coherent narrative. For obvious reasons, I have tried to provide an antidote to the kind of Whig history contained in books such as Michael Stone's *Healing the Mind*,[5] and Edward Shorter's *A History of Psychiatry*,[6] which, despite having many strengths, inaccurately portray the glorious present as the culmination of centuries of steady scientific progress. Along the way, I consider the impact of the creation of the new profession of clinical psychology at the end of the Second World War, which has been completely overlooked by conventional histories. (A psychiatrist reviewing *Madness Explained* argued that naked professional rivalry had undermined its arguments.[7] This observation made me think carefully about how I portrayed the relationship between clinical psychology and psychiatry in this book. However, in the end, it seemed to me that ideological and professional conflict between the two professions has been a historical reality and so I decided that it was pointless to pretend otherwise.) After describing how the discovery of chlorpromazine prompted renewed optimism in biomedical approaches to mental illness, I explain how the emergence of the new technologies of neuro-imaging and molecular genetics has reinforced the modern view that psychiatric disorders are genetically determined brain diseases that must be treated with drugs.

The next three chapters deal with some myths about the nature of severe mental illness that underpin current psychiatric practice. Chapter 5 is the only chapter that overlaps considerably with *Madness Explained*, and considers the value of psychiatric diagnoses. In Chapter 6, I review what the current evidence tells us about the genetic and environmental determinants of psychosis, contrasting theories that locate the causes of illness within the person with those that locate them in the world. A particular target of my critique is the statistical measure of *heritability*, which is often cited by those who believe that psychiatric disorders are genetic diseases. This is probably the most technically demanding chapter in the book but I hope that I have explained the relevant concepts in a way that will be easily followed by the intelligent lay reader. In Chapter 7, I consider whether and to what extent psychiatric disorders can be said to be caused by brain disease. It turns out that this question is much more easily addressed if we attempt to explain particular kinds of complaints (symptoms) such as hallucinations and delusions, rather than meaningless diagnostic categories such as 'schizophrenia'. The picture that emerges is much more consistent with the idea that severe mental illnesses are influenced by the social environment, than with the idea that they are genetically determined disorders of the brain.

The following three chapters consider the effectiveness of modern psychiatric therapies. I begin by describing the emergence of the evidence-based medicine movement, which has led to widespread faith in the randomized controlled trial (RCT) as a measure of treatment effectiveness. Focusing on antidepressants, I show how the pharmaceutical industry has systematically distorted RCT data to promulgate a wildly over-optimistic impression of what psychiatric drugs can do. In Chapter 9, I extend this analysis by showing that the evidence in favour of antipsychotic drugs is much less compelling than is usually supposed, and that psychiatrists have been blinded to the adverse effects of these drugs in much the same way that they were blind to the effects of the crude brain operations and other extreme remedies used in the middle years of the twentieth century. Unfortunately, as we discover in Chapter 10, this does not mean that drug therapies can be entirely replaced by psychological treatments. Although the last decade has shown growing enthusiasm for one particular type of psychological treatment for severe mental illness – cognitive behaviour therapy (CBT) – the evidence that any one type of therapy is better than any other is by no means clear-cut. This observation provokes two kinds of responses. Some hardline biological psychiatrists have concluded that CBT is just some form of elaborate placebo but a better conclusion is that it is the quality of the therapeutic relationship that determines outcome. Hence, by paying attention to this relationship, and placing it at the centre of psychiatric practice, we can see a way to develop services that are more humane and effective. As much as psychiatric services today are an improvement on those of the past, it is because they are kinder and more respectful of the needs of patients, rather than because of the availability of new therapies.

This conclusion leads me to the last chapter, in which I address what is to be done to improve psychiatric services in the future. It will be no surprise that I think that they need to be much less medically orientated, but perhaps a disappointment to some of my colleagues that I do not see the solution as a full-scale takeover bid by Clinical Psychology Inc. Indeed, I argue that it is the engagement of patients in the design and development of services that is most likely to lead to lasting improvements.

PART ONE

AN ILLUSION OF PROGRESS

I

A Smashing Success?

If there is one central intellectual reality at the end of the twentieth century, it is that the biological approach to psychiatry – treating mental illness as a genetically influenced disorder of the brain chemistry – has been a smashing success.

Edward Shorter, *A History of Psychiatry*

A dank smell pervades the small, windowless interview room whenever Peter comes to see me. I have been trying to help him for too long; the six-month period during which a clinical psychologist would normally expect to see a client passed more than a year ago. Always, it seems, we are about to make an important breakthrough.

Our meetings, first thing in the morning, always begin with the same ritual. Checking his watch as I rush through the door of the community mental health centre after my long journey from home, Peter looks at me scornfully, then cracks a smile and says, 'Hello mate!' Occasionally, he tries to hug me, but I discourage him from doing so, more because I worry about his poor hygiene than for fear of violating a professional boundary. He will not see me later in the day, when his hallucinatory voices often begin to torment him, driving him back to his small, untidy flat, where he uses loud music to drown them out.

A tall, likeable man in his early thirties, he might look handsome if only he could clean himself up and do something about his burgeoning stomach. His difficulties, told to me with the precision of a man who has repeated his story many times, began more than thirteen years before we met. Happily employed on a production line and the father

3

of a baby girl, his settled life was abruptly shattered when his girlfriend announced that she no longer wanted to live with him and had found another lover. Ejected from the family home, he was forced to move into a gloomy bed-sit, sank into depression and stopped turning up for work. Eventually he lost his job and became homeless. It was while sleeping rough on the streets that he began to hear voices, which he attributed to former friends who wished to hurt him. 'Offer him out!' they would say; 'Order him out!' which he took to mean that they wanted to take him somewhere to beat him up.

There is no record of mental illness in Peter's immediate family. Although he was sexually abused by his stepfather when he was 10 years old, apart from a few drunken brushes with the police during adolescence, there was no other indication in his earlier life that he was destined to become a psychiatric patient. On the positive side, unlike many patients with similar difficulties, he has managed to re-establish a network of friends, and enjoys warm relationships with his mother and sister. He is also on good terms with his now-teenage daughter, whom he sees regularly. Thanks to generous social security allowances he is stuck in the benefit trap: he currently has more than enough money to meet his needs and fears he will lose out if he attempts to return to work.

The original referral letter from Peter's psychiatrist, noting that his symptoms had persisted despite more than a decade's treatment with medication, asked if I could try cognitive behaviour therapy, a form of psychological treatment, to help him with his voices. Despite scepticism in the past about the value of psychological treatment for patients with severe mental illness, recent studies have shown that this kind of therapy can sometimes help people like Peter.[1] In our first few months together I followed the usual protocol for this kind of treatment, asking him to keep records of when his voices came and went away, questioning him about potential triggers and investigating how his beliefs about his voices might be making them more persistent. Like many patients with voices, Peter believed that they were omniscient and omnipotent,[2] and I did my best to challenge his belief that they were irresistibly powerful. He also believed that other people could hear his voices and might attack him as a consequence, so I suggested a 'behavioural experiment' in which he attempted to record his voices with a tape recorder. Observing that he was invariably very tense, and that his anxiety on anticipating the voices seemed to provoke them, I also taught him some simple relaxation techniques. Gradually, over a period of about a year, this approach seemed to work. Peter's diary indicated that he was hearing the voices less frequently. Whereas he was previously experiencing them on a daily basis, he eventually achieved an all-time record of thirteen days without them. He began to think about the future, discussed the possibility of voluntary work and arranged to move to a more pleasant neighbourhood.

Just as I began to contemplate a discharge letter to Peter's psychiatrist, which would have quietly boasted about what we had achieved together, things took a dramatic turn for the worse. Arriving to see me for what was planned to be one of his final sessions, he was agitated and paranoid, his eyes flickering from side to side as he told me that his voices had kept him awake for the past two nights. At the end of the session, I watched him scan his environment nervously, before mustering the courage to step out into the street. I immediately telephoned his community psychiatric nurse, a warm, supportive woman who soon afterwards went to visit him in his new flat. Her efforts to calm him were fruitless. Within a few days he was admitted to hospital for more intensive treatment.

Psychiatric wards are often frightening places. The local psychiatric unit, built about twenty years ago in the grounds of a District General Hospital and alongside a busy motorway, has long, narrow corridors and looks shabby and impersonal. The patients' bedrooms are dark and claustrophobic. The communal areas, the dining rooms and lounges where patients sit passively watching daytime television, smell of sweat. The nurses seem to hide away in their nursing offices, gazing out at the patients through windows of toughened glass. On the open wards, where patients can come and go as they please, some make use of the occupational therapy facilities elsewhere in the hospital, others disappear on home leave so that their capacity to live in the real world can be tested, and still others languish in silent contemplation, waiting for their drugs to take effect. On the locked wards, where the more agitated patients are contained, there is a palpable atmosphere of menace, punctuated by cries and occasional violent acts by the most disturbed patients who have yet to succumb to the sedating effects of their medication. It was on just such a ward that I found Peter, cowering in his room, too frightened to come out for fear that the other patients would assault him. It was difficult to work out the extent to which his fear was justified by his new circumstances and to what extent it was a product of his imagination.

On questioning Peter, the cause of his sudden relapse quickly became obvious. Buoyed by our success together and, unknown to me or anyone else on the clinical team, he had suddenly stopped taking his drugs. Moving home, at the best of times a stressful experience, had taken its toll. While he remained in hospital it seemed impossible to do anything particularly therapeutic. Until he was released, re-medicated, some weeks later, I was reduced to dropping by occasionally to engage him in friendly conversation, in the hope of showing him that I had not forgotten him.

Although I continue to see Peter, I cannot do so indefinitely. Recently we have been experimenting with a new strategy, inspired by studies which show that Buddhist meditation techniques are useful for patients who have not responded to more traditional forms of psychotherapy.[3] I have taught him to spend brief periods sitting in silence, directing his attention towards his breathing and noticing when his thoughts wander elsewhere. Most people find that these exercises help them develop some detachment from thoughts that are distressing and preoccupying. In the hope of addressing his fear of his voices, I have had Peter repeat the words, 'Offer him out, order him out,' over and over to himself before beginning the exercises. Over the last few months, the frequency of his voices has again decreased and he is now spending many days without them. Is it working? Is this the method we have been searching for? Peter is increasingly optimistic, and I want to be optimistic too, but experience has taught me that confidence is often a misleading sentiment. Sometimes I feel as if I am only pretending to be useful.

What is psychosis?

Peter was diagnosed as suffering from *schizophrenia*. According to the textbooks, patients with this disorder typically suffer from *auditory hallucinations* (voices of people who are not actually present) and *delusions* (bizarre and irrational beliefs that are resistant to counter-argument). Many patients also become *thought disordered* on occasion, speaking incoherently, especially when distressed. In addition to these *positive symptoms*, so called because they are normally absent in healthy people, many patients also suffer from *negative symptoms*, so called because they seem to reflect a loss of normal ability. These include apathy, *anhedonia* (the inability to experience pleasure) and emotional flatness.

Schizophrenia is usually considered to belong to a family of illnesses in which the patient, when most severely ill, seems to loose touch with reality. These disorders, which roughly correspond to the popular understanding of madness, are collectively known as the *psychoses*, and are the most severe type of mental illness. They are often contrasted with the *neuroses* (more common and less severe types of mental illness in which the individual, although very anxious or depressed, is aware of being ill, and does not experience hallucinations and delusions) and the *personality disorders* (lifelong dysfunctional patterns of relating to other people).

The other main type of psychosis is *bipolar disorder*, which is also sometimes known as *manic depression*. In this condition the sufferer experiences episodes of profound depression and also episodes of either *mania* (periods of uncontrollable excitement and irritability, often accompanied by disordered thinking and delusions about special powers, spectacular wealth or a special mission in life) or *hypomania* (a less extreme mood state characterized by euphoria, excitement and impulsive behaviour). Current diagnostic systems now distinguish between *bipolar 1 disorder*, in which patients experience both depression and mania, and *bipolar 2 disorder*, in which depression and hypomania but not mania are experienced. In both cases, episodes of extreme mood are typically interspersed by periods of *remission* or relatively normal functioning. *Unipolar depression* (depression in the absence of a history of mania), when very severe, can also be accompanied by psychotic symptoms, for example auditory hallucinations that are highly critical of the patient or delusions that the individual is guilty of some kind of terrible crime. The term *psychotic depression* is sometimes used to describe this kind of condition.

Without a doubt, the psychoses have a profound impact on the human world. The number of cases of schizophrenia dealt with by psychiatric services is difficult to gauge because definitions of the disorder have varied from study to study, but estimates of the number of new cases each year from different parts of the world range between around 7 to 40 new cases per 100,000 people[4] and the figures reported for bipolar disorder are not dissimilar.[5] The number of people who receive a diagnosis of schizophrenia at any time in their lives is certainly above 0.5 per cent[6] and, again, about the same estimate has been reported for bipolar disorder.[7] Taking a broader perspective, it has been calculated that the lifetime risk of suffering from any kind of psychotic disorder may be as high as 3 per cent.[8] As the current population of Britain is about 60 million people and that of the United States is about 300 million, this means that as many as 1.8 million British citizens and as many as 9 million US citizens may be affected. Extrapolating to the whole world, about 200 million people currently living on the earth are likely to suffer from psychosis at some point in their lives. That is a very large number of people.

The impact of these conditions on quality of life can be gleaned from the fact that, in the developed world, about 5 per cent of schizophrenia patients[9] and over 7 per cent of bipolar patients commit suicide[10] and many more attempt it. The inability to work or pursue a career is also common. In a recent study of schizophrenia patients in six European countries,[11] 41 per cent were judged to be severely disabled when first assessed. Fifteen years later, 25 per cent were still badly disabled. For about two-thirds of these patients their close relationships were affected (many remaining without partners) and about the same proportion were unable to function effectively in the workplace. Once more, a similar picture is evident with respect to bipolar disorder. It has been estimated that a young adult receiving the diagnosis in the United States can expect to lose, on average, nine years of life, twelve years of normal health and fourteen years of employment.[12] To add to this catalogue of misery, the psychoses are also the source of great fear in ordinary people. Selective reporting in the mass media has created the impression that schizophrenia, in particular, is associated with a tendency towards extreme, random violence.[13]

It is, of course, true that psychotic patients, in the grip of their delusions, sometimes commit terrible crimes, although fortunately this happens only rarely. In Britain, a charitable organization called the Zito Trust was set up in 1994 following the senseless slaying of Jayne Zito's husband Jonathan by Christopher Clunis, a psychiatric patient. On 17 December 1992 Clunis walked up to Zito as he stood waiting for a train at the Finsbury Park Tube station and stabbed him without warning. An official inquiry following the killing revealed that Clunis was well known to local psychiatric services, having been seen by no less than forty-three psychiatrists in five years, and that he had not been detained in hospital despite committing a number of random assaults in the weeks preceding Zito's death. Against the background of this and similar incidents, many psychiatric services have seen their main role as containment. Surveys carried out in Britain and the United States reveal the widespread use of both informal and formal coercion in the management of people with psychotic illnesses.[14] In Britain and some parts of the United States new legislation allows psychiatrists to compel patients to take their medication on the threat of being detained in hospital if they do not.

Not surprisingly, the financial burdens associated with the psychoses are huge, but vary according to local economic and political conditions. The annual cost of caring for people diagnosed with schizophrenia in the United States has recently been estimated as $22.7 billion[15] and in Britain it has been estimated to be £2.2 billion.[16] However, these direct costs are sometimes dwarfed by the indirect costs accrued through, for example, loss of economic productivity by patients and their carers. The true annual cost of schizophrenia has therefore been estimated at $62.7 billion in the United States and £4 billion in Britain. In many ways, it seems, psychosis is a problem for all of us.

Given these human and financial costs, it is imperative that we bring whatever resources we can muster to address the problems that severe mental illness create for us. We need to find ways of helping those suffering from psychosis to overcome their difficulties, in an attempt to relieve them of their delusions and hallucinations and return them to a full role in society. We need to find ways of supporting their carers – often parents – so that they are not crippled by the emotional and financial burden of looking after their disturbed and often disturbing loved ones. We need to find ways of protecting society from any risks associated with psychosis and we must do all of this cost-effectively, within the constraints of the limited budgets available to fund modern psychiatric services.

The medical treatment of severe mental illness

The majority of people who experience psychological problems never receive treatment from psychiatric services. Many people suffering from the less severe neurotic disorders choose to endure them, hoping that they will feel less anxious and depressed with the passage of time, or after their circumstances change and life becomes less stressful (the majority of people whose symptoms meet current criteria for major depression recover within a few months[17]). If the symptoms persist, the chances are that any treatment received will be managed by a family doctor, who may prescribe antidepressant medication, or refer the patient to a counsellor or clinical psychologist with whom he can discuss his difficulties. However if, like Peter, a patient has the misfortune to experience the more serious symptoms of psychosis, he will very likely find himself in the care of psychiatric services, and the treatment he receives may stretch over a very long time.

Patients can enter into psychiatric treatment by a number of pathways.[18] Although the exact steps that lead to the involvement of psychiatric services may vary from place to place, the following routes are fairly typical. Very often a family doctor will decide that the symptoms experienced by a patient are much too serious to be managed by a non-specialist, and will arrange for an appointment with a psychiatrist. Sometimes the first contact with the psychiatrist will occur after some kind of crisis, for example after a person suffering from delusions and hallucinations is taken to an accident and emergency clinic by a worried friend or relative. Occasionally, law enforcement agencies are involved; in most countries the police have powers to detain someone who is behaving in a frightening and erratic way, pending a psychiatric examination. However it happens, the psychiatrist usually follows a pattern of working that is similar to that followed by her colleagues in other branches of medicine. First, the patient's symptoms are assessed so that the psychiatrist can make a diagnosis. (As there are no biological tests for psychiatric disorder, the assessment is by means of a detailed cross-examination – known as a *mental state examination* – during which the patient is questioned about unusual beliefs, experiences and feelings.) Then, once the diagnosis has been made, a course of treatment is decided on.

If the patient's behaviour is thought to constitute a risk to himself or others (for example, if he appears to be suicidal, explosively angry or dangerously impulsive), he will usually be admitted to a psychiatric ward, where he will stay until his symptoms improve sufficiently for the psychiatrist to chance discharging him back into the community. If necessary, and if she cannot persuade the patient to enter hospital voluntarily, the psychiatrist may use special legal powers (*sections*, in the jargon of British mental health legislation*) to compel the patient to stay on the ward. The main treatment offered during the stay will usually be psychiatric drugs, although other methods such as group discussions and occupational therapy (in which the patient is encouraged to engage in various meaningful and stimulating activities) may also be offered. During this period the patient will usually be seen by the psychiatrist fairly infrequently, perhaps once a week for ten minutes or so, during which time the patient's symptoms will be assessed to try and determine whether the treatment is having the desired effect. If the patient's stay extends beyond a few weeks, more formal case conferences will sometimes be held, at which the psychiatrist, nurses and other mental health professionals will meet to discuss the patient's progress and to determine whether any change in the treatment is merited. Sometimes these discussions will take place behind closed doors but usually the patient will be called into the meeting so that he can express his own view about how things are going. This can be a stressful experience as the patient may find himself sitting in front of a row of professionals, almost as if he were attending

* This term refers to the various sections of the relevant mental health legislation.

a job interview. If he is very anxious to leave the ward, he may be guarded about his symptoms, aware that words that are not carefully chosen may be interpreted by the psychiatrist as evidence that he is not fit to go home.

Following discharge from the hospital, or from the outset if hospitalization is deemed unnecessary, the patient's treatment may follow a number of courses. In the best of circumstances, the patient will respond well to the medication as his progress is monitored by the psychiatrist every few months, and eventually the psychiatrist will decide that the treatment is no longer necessary. However, it is more likely that the psychiatrist will decide that the patient should continue to take medication – for years or perhaps even decades – to ensure that the symptoms do not return. Under these circumstances, one of the main purposes of the regular but infrequent psychiatric appointments will be to persuade the patient to continue taking his drugs, despite any unpleasant side effects they cause. Patients often discontinue their medication and sometimes, like Peter, they do this without informing the psychiatrist, fearing that announcing their decision will provoke an unfavourable response. This fear is often well founded: if non-compliance is suspected, the psychiatrist may resort to a number of strategies to ensure that the medication continues to be taken. One approach involves arranging regular visits from a community psychiatric nurse (CPN), who will spend time getting to know the patient, offering emotional and practical support on a day-to-day basis, and encouraging the patient to keep on taking his tablets. Another approach is to prescribe a long-lasting *depot medication*, which is injected into the patient's buttock every few weeks, though this approach can be undermined by the patient simply refusing to turn up for his appointment at the depot clinic or being elsewhere when the CPN arrives with her syringe. One consequence of this is that psychiatric care often becomes adversarial, a battle of wills between the psychiatric team and the patient.

I am sure that some mental health professionals will object that the above characterization of how psychiatric services work is something of an over-simplification. Of course, policies and procedures vary from place to place. Some psychiatrists take an interest in psychotherapy, and some services employ clinical psychologists or specially trained nurses who can provide psychological treatments to the severely mentally ill. Nonetheless, official guidelines for the treatment of psychosis in Britain[19] and the United States[20] emphasize the importance of drug treatments. The global market for antipsychotic medication is currently about $15 billion per year.[21] Between 1997 and 2004 the number of US citizens receiving these drugs rose from 2.2 million to 3.4 million and expenditure on them tripled.[22] In Britain, in the period between 1991 and 2001, antipsychotic drug prescriptions for patients living in the community increased by a (less dramatic) 23 per cent; interestingly, this seems to be mostly accounted for by individual patients being kept on drug treatments for longer, rather than by an increase in the number of patients receiving medication for the first time.[23] The use of less powerful drugs for people with less severe psychiatric conditions has risen even more sharply.[24] Recently there has been a move to encourage patients with psychosis to take medication as early as possible in the belief that a delay in treatment will lead to a poor outcome (we shall consider the evidence for this claim later).[25] At the time of writing, specialist early intervention services are being rolled out throughout the NHS and the most widely used measure of their effectiveness is their ability to reduce the duration of untreated psychosis (DUP), defined as the interval between the onset of symptoms and first treatment with antipsychotic drugs. Some psychiatrists are now even advocating that people should be given antipsychotics if there is a high risk that they will develop a psychotic illness in the future.[26]

Of course, most people drawn to work in psychiatry are kind and caring and only want the very best for their patients. Often they become upset and frustrated when patients fail to benefit from their efforts. They pursue a medical approach, in which social and psychological therapies, if they are used at all, are seen as secondary to drug treatment, because they genuinely believe that this is the best way of helping their patients.

The main assumption behind this approach is that psychosis is a disease of the brain, an idea that has been dominant in psychiatric circles for more than a century, and which continues to be promulgated in texts written for trainee mental health professionals, books authored by psychiatrists and psychologists for the general reader,[27] and advice given to patients and carers by clinicians, pharmaceutical companies[28] and various other organizations which insist, for example, that 'schizophrenia is a treatable medical condition'.[29] The meaning of the patient's symptoms, and the context in which they have occurred, are therefore seen as irrelevant, and efforts made by the patient to discuss them, and to have his story heard, are often discouraged.[30] If the patient objects to this approach, he risks being described as *lacking in insight*, where insight is defined as 'The correct attitude to morbid change in oneself.'[31] As a lack of insight is regarded as a symptom of psychosis in its own right,[32] any attempt made by the patient to challenge the medical approach or question its underlying assumptions is often seen as further evidence that the patient is ill and therefore as an indication that more vigorous treatment is required.

In later chapters, I shall show that the scientific foundations of this approach are extremely shaky. However, I shall first try to address a question that is of more immediate importance to patients and those who care for them: does the medical approach really work? In asking this question, I am not concerned with the effectiveness of particular treatments (I shall get to them later) but instead with the broad impact that psychiatric services have on society.

We can find out whether this impact has been positive by addressing three sources of evidence. First, we can try to determine whether there have been advances in the medical treatment of mental illness that have led to demonstrably improved prospects for psychotic patients living today compared to the past. Second, we can consider whether psychotic patients living in countries with well-resourced psychiatric services fare better than similar patients in countries in which such services are absent. Finally, we can look at what happens to patients when conventional psychiatric services are suspended.

Has there been progress in the treatment of mental illness?

Without a doubt, the last century saw fantastic improvements in the ability of doctors to treat physical illnesses (although, as we shall see later, the extent to which these improvements have impacted on public

health have been questioned – it is sometimes claimed that improvements in nutrition and hygiene have been more important). The
medical journalist James Le Fanu[33] recently chronicled twelve definitive moments in the history of medicine, in which these kinds of
advances occurred. Alexander Fleming's discovery in 1928 that penicillin could kill bacterial infections is perhaps the best-known entry
on Le Fanu's list but other, less well-known advances are equally
deserving of our attention and admiration. During the Copenhagen
polio epidemic of 1952, for example, the anaesthetist Bjørn Ibsen
observed that many afflicted children were dying because they were
too weak to breathe, and experimented with simple artificial ventila-
tion techniques (initially, he employed teams of medical students
working in shifts to mechanically pump air into his patients' lungs, a
procedure which was continued until the children had recovered
enough strength to breathe for themselves). The survival rate of polio
victims treated in Ibsen's hospital leapt from about 10 per cent to
approximately 70 per cent.

Only one of Le Fanu's definitive moments concerned psychiatry: the
accidental discovery (by a French naval surgeon) of the first effective
psychiatric drug, now known as chlorpromazine, which was introduced in the early 1950s. Two Nobel Prizes have been awarded for
improvements in psychiatric treatment but in the cool light of history
it is easy to see why these do not appear in Le Fanu's list. The first
was given in 1927 to the Viennese psychiatrist Julius Wagner-Jauregg,
who developed a method for treating patients with general paresis of
the insane (the final stage of syphilis, in which the brain becomes
infected). Wagner-Jauregg infected his patients with malaria and the
febrile illness that followed apparently arrested, or even sometimes
reversed, the progress of the disease.[34] Wagner-Jauregg's therapy
(which in any case was given for a condition which would now be
regarded as neurological rather than psychiatric) was controversial in
its time, and faded from use after the Second World War. The second
was awarded to the Portuguese neurosurgeon Egas Monitz for the
development of the prefrontal leucotomy, a brain operation in
which the nerve fibres leading from the frontal regions of the brain to
more posterior regions are crudely sliced. The widespread use of the
prefrontal leucotomy is now regarded as a dark episode in the history

of psychiatry. Certainly, with the possible exception of the discovery of chlorpromazine, the kinds of advances in therapeutic technology that have marked the progress of modern medicine have been denied to psychiatric services.

The improvements in mortality brought about by breakthroughs in the treatment of physical disease have been documented in large-scale surveys. The US Centers for Disease Control have estimated that 64 per cent of adults whose cancers were diagnosed between 1995 and 2000 survived at least five years after receiving their diagnosis, compared with about 50 per cent of those whose cancers were diagnosed between 1972 and 1976; the comparable improvement in children was from 54 to 79 per cent.[35] Similarly, the UK Office of National Statistics has reported improvements in five-year survival rates between 1971 and 1995 for most types of cancer.[36] Clearly something important has been happening in the field of cancer treatment. Nor are these kinds of improvements confined to the field of therapeutic oncology. British data on coronary heart disease indicates that the proportion of people surviving more than four weeks after a heart attack has been improving by a rate of approximately 1.5 per cent a year since the late 1960s.[37] Comparable data for psychiatric problems are difficult to come by, but as far as they are available, they tell a different story.

The lack of evidence of improving outcomes for patients suffering from severe mental illness was first highlighted by psychiatrist and anthropologist Richard Warner, in his seminal 1985 book *Recovery from Schizophrenia: Psychiatry and Political Economy*.[38] Warner was able to identify sixty-eight American and European studies in which patients diagnosed with schizophrenia were followed up and their outcomes measured, finding no evidence of an overall improvement since the first decades of the twentieth century. Importantly, Warner observed that there was no indication that outcomes had been affected by the introduction of chlorpromazine and the other antipsychotics, but there was some evidence of the importance of economic circumstances – patients recovered less well during periods of economic recession than during periods of economic boom.

A subsequent paper by American psychiatrist James Hegarty used a sophisticated statistical technique known as *meta-analysis* to consider all available data on the recovery rates of schizophrenia patients published between 1895 and 1992.[39] He found evidence of modest improvements in outcomes between the middle of the twentieth century and the early 1980s, and a worsening of outcomes afterwards. Although this pattern is consistent with Warner's suggestion that recovery rates are affected by the vibrancy of the labour market, Hegarty argued that the main factor responsible for these differences was changes in the way in which schizophrenia was diagnosed. Between the early years of the twentieth century and the 1970s there was a tendency to give the diagnosis to an ever-widening group of patients, including many suffering from relatively mild conditions. After this time, when psychiatrists became concerned about the reliability of their diagnoses, the way that the term 'schizophrenia' was used was tightened up, so that only more severely afflicted patients were included. Overall, the findings do not suggest that patients' lives have been transformed by the introduction of new psychiatric treatments.

A different way of assessing the impact of modern psychiatric treatment has recently been suggested by Robert Whitaker, an American investigative journalist who has an interest in mental health issues. Whitaker has shown that, although the number of psychiatric beds occupied in the United States has declined since the early 1950s, nearly every other metric used to measure the number of people suffering from severe mental illness has shown a dramatic increase.[40] Taking data collected by the US Department of Health and Human Services, Whitaker found that 1,028 'patient care episodes' per 100,000 population were recorded in 1955, the approximate date that chlorpromazine became widely available, but that in 2000 this number had risen to 3,806 per 100,000, a nearly fourfold increase. Of course, it might be argued that this increase has been the consequence of the better and earlier detection of mental illness, in which case it might be expected that the number of people who are psychiatrically disabled would have decreased as a consequence of more efficient treatment. Because people with severe mental illness are now, in the main, cared for in the community, whereas, before the advent of chlorpromazine, they were more often hospitalized, Whitaker used hospital bed utilization prior to 1955 and social security disability payments in the more recent decades to calculate an – admittedly crude – estimate of the proportion of the population affected. On this measure, the number of mentally ill people in the United States rose from 3.38 per 1,000 in 1955 to 19.69 per 1,000 in 2003, an approximately sixfold increase.

A comparable analysis of the impact of psychiatric treatment in Britain has been reported by psychiatrist David Healy and historian Margaret Harris, using data from North Wales.[41] The population of this area, mainly rural with low incomes, has remained stable from the end of the nineteenth century until the present day, and, for much of that time, has been served by a single psychiatric unit, the North Wales Hospital in Denbigh. By examining the detailed records kept at the hospital, Healy and Harris were able retrospectively to diagnose patients treated in 1896 and trace their psychiatric careers, comparing them with those treated a century later. They found that, although patients in the modern period typically enjoy much shorter stays in hospital, they are also admitted more frequently than in the past. Astonishingly, when they totalled bed occupancy, by taking into account the many admissions of modern patients and also the fact that many now spend long periods of their lives living in hostels rather than in hospital, they found that it was greater in 1996 than 1896.

The causes of these changes are undoubtedly complex. Although researchers within mainstream psychiatry have also noted this 'epidemic of mental illness',[42] they would not agree with Robert Whitaker's conclusion that modern psychiatric treatment actually makes patients *worse* than they would be if left alone. However, interpreting the evidence cautiously, it seems fair to say that there are no grounds for believing that advances in psychiatric care have led to improvements in the mental health of the industrialized nations.

The best psychiatry in the world?

Comparative studies of health care outcomes in different countries confirm what might be expected from common sense: that the prospect of recovering from serious physical disease is better in countries that have comprehensive and widely available medical services than in countries that do not. For example, a recent report on global cancer statistics, published by the International Agency for Research on Cancer,[43] found striking but expected differences in outcome between the industrialized countries and the developing world.

In the late 1960s the World Health Organization (WHO) initiated a project, known as the International Pilot Study of Schizophrenia (IPSS), to determine the extent to which schizophrenia could be found outside the industrialized nations. I have already noted that this diagnosis has been used in different ways at different times. In the light of this problem, a major aim of the study was to determine whether a universal, culturally invariant form of the disease could be discovered. Another aim was to investigate the extent to which psychiatrists in different parts of the world, in their local practice, defined it, and hence diagnosed it, in different ways.

In nine countries – Colombia, Czechoslovakia (now the Czech Republic), China, Denmark, India, Nigeria, the former Soviet Union, Britain and the United States – project psychiatrists recruited a total of 1,202 patients who had recently been admitted to psychiatric services and their initial observations were reported in 1973.[44] After analysing their data, and with great excitement, the investigators announced that patients meeting a narrow definition of schizophrenia, agreed in advance of the study, could be found in every country. In retrospect, this 'discovery' seems to have been inevitable, as the psychiatrists who were looking for patients had this concept in their minds. However, it seemed that psychiatrists in the United States and the Soviet Union had a much broader local concept of schizophrenia – and hence were willing to diagnose many more patients as schizophrenic – than psychiatrists elsewhere. (It subsequently emerged that the Soviet definition of schizophrenia was so broad that it encompassed political dissent; many intellectuals who disagreed with the Communist government found themselves consigned to asylums and being forcefully treated with chlorpromazine or similar drugs.[45])

The most important study finding emerged later, from a five-year follow-up which aimed to discover what happened to the patients.[46] This revealed that those in the developing countries had done much better than those in the industrialized world. For example, whereas 27 per cent of patients in the developing nations experienced only one episode of illness followed by complete recovery, this was true of only 7 per cent of the patients from the industrialized nations. By the end of the follow-up period, 65 per cent of the patients in the developing countries were judged to have either mild or no impairment in social functioning compared to 56 per cent of the patients in the industrialized countries.

This finding was so striking that WHO set up a further, more ambitious study on the Determinants of Outcome of Severe Mental Disorders.[47] A team of more than a hundred psychiatrists tried to identify people with severe mental illness in ten countries. Efforts were made to interview people who might not be known to psychiatric services, for example by contacting traditional healers who worked outside the medical system in developing countries. In the two-year follow-up data from the study, 37 per cent of patients from the developing countries suffered one episode followed by complete recovery, compared with only 16 per cent of patients from the developed world. Nearly 16 per cent of patients in the developing countries showed impaired social functioning throughout the follow-up period, whereas the corresponding figure for the developed countries was nearly 42 per cent. Subsequent studies have confirmed that patients in the developing world are much more likely to recover from severe mental illness than patients in the richer countries, well served by psychiatrists and clinical psychologists.[48]

The same attention has not been devoted to the outcome of less severe psychiatric disorders, so any conclusions about these must be tentative. However, some information about depression is available from surveys conducted for the Global Burden of Disease study, which was launched by the WHO in the early 1990s. The aim of this study was to determine the extent to which different parts of the world were being burdened by different kinds of mental and physical illness. An initial report published in 1996 astonishingly concluded that unipolar (simple) depression was the fourth leading medical cause of burden, responsible for 3.7 per cent of disability-adjusted life years (years of active life lost because of disability or premature death).[49] Clearly, if this estimate is correct, the world is in the midst of an epidemic of depression of startling proportions, itself hardly an indication that medical psychiatry is having a positive impact. (An obvious alternative explanation is that the depression measured in these studies is not a simple medical disease, but encompasses a broad spectrum of human misery.[50])

In a more recent report, data from a variety of sources was compiled to compute estimates of burden in the year 2000.[51] The authors of the report noted a large difference in the proportion of burden attributed to depression in rich countries (8.9 per cent of all disability-adjusted life years) and poor (4.1 per cent). However, these figures are all relative to the total burden of disability and, as the authors point out, could be accounted for by the high levels of physical disability caused by poor nutrition and hygiene in the poorer nations. An indication of the absolute levels of disability associated with depression in different parts of the world can be gleaned only by detailed inspection of the data tables, which show the highest rates in North America and the lowest rates in Africa.

Doing without medical psychiatry

Because the findings from historical and cross-cultural studies are open to various interpretations, the evidence they provide about the human and social impact of modern psychiatry is far from conclusive. An experiment in which conventional treatment is suspended would surely be better. Fortunately, such an experiment has been conducted in the United States. Its instigator was Loren Mosher, an American psychiatrist who was once a leader of his profession, but who eventually became so alienated from it that, in 1998, he made public an angry letter of resignation from the American Psychiatric Association. In the letter, he stated: 'The major reason for this action is my belief that I am actually resigning from the American Psychopharmacological Association.'[52]

After graduating in medicine from Harvard, Mosher took a research position with the US National Institute of Mental Health (NIMH), where, at the age of 34, he became chief of its new Center for Studies of Schizophrenia, a position he held for twelve years.[53] During his tenure of this key post, he founded and edited *Schizophrenia Bulletin*, still one of the foremost journals for psychosis researchers.

In the summer before he became chief of the Center, Mosher

travelled to London and visited Kingsley Hall, a therapeutic community created by Ronald Laing, a dissident British psychiatrist who had become highly critical of his own profession. Laing argued that psychosis could sometimes be a healing, transcendental experience and that sufferers, if provided with appropriate support, might be able to find a pathway through their madness, emerging at the other end as stronger, more creative individuals.[54] Mosher was intrigued although not entirely won over by Laing's ideas, but dismayed by the chaotic way that they were being realized. Kingsley Hall, where a small group of people with psychosis were supported without drug therapy, was dirty, its budget was disorganized and the gathering and preparation of food was, at best, haphazard. Correctly, as it turned out, Mosher anticipated that the residents would soon find themselves in conflict with the local community. Returning to the United States, he wondered what would happen if a more orderly version of Kingsley Hall was created. His new position at NIMH placed him in unique position to address this question.

Mosher found a rambling, two-storey house in a poverty-stricken area of San Jose, California. With a capacity for six residents and two full-time staff, supported by part-time workers and voluntary assistants, the house, known as Soteria (Greek for 'deliverance'), was opened for business in April 1971. The participants in the experiment were young people attending psychiatric emergency services in the San Francisco Bay area. To take part they had to be unmarried and suffering from their first or second episode of psychosis. Mosher assigned half to conventional treatment in local psychiatric wards, where they received medication, and half to Soteria.† At Soteria, the staff, who had no formal training in psychiatry or psychology, worked in 24-hour and 72-hour shifts, and therefore lived with the residents. Except in emergencies, drugs were not used during the first six weeks of a resident's stay. The main working principle of Soteria was

† In an initial group of 79 people, this assignment was based on the availability of beds in the different units. However, Mosher then investigated a second cohort of 100 people who were randomly assigned to the two conditions. This distinction is important because random assignment is considered to be essential when an experiment of this kind is carried out. However, no important differences were observed in the results obtained from the two studies.

described by Mosher as *interpersonal phenomenology*, by which he meant that the staff endeavoured to be with the residents, 'getting themselves into the residents' shoes', in a gradual, non-intrusive way while attempting to develop a shared understanding of their psychotic experiences. As far as possible, the staff tried to tolerate any eccentric behaviour. Rules were few. Violence was prohibited, as were illicit drugs and sexual relationships between the residents and staff. Visits from outsiders were rare and agreed in advance by the residents. On average, the residents stayed five months, although most were substantially better by the end of six weeks.

The Soteria project soon became a source of conflict between Mosher and his superiors at NIMH. They reacted to early news that the residents were doing well by questioning whether the project was being conducted in an unbiased way (no malpractice has even been demonstrated and Mosher's approach seems to have been scrupulously scientific). Eventually they demanded that someone else take over the day-to-day running of the project. Mosher acceded to these demands but his relationship with his employers continued to deteriorate, no doubt partly because of the increasingly uncompromising way that he criticized conventional psychiatric treatment. Eventually, marginalized and removed from his position as chief of the Center for Studies of Schizophrenia, Mosher left NIMH in 1980. Although initial results of the Soteria experiment were published immediately, it took more than two decades for all the data from the project to be properly analysed.

Early publications describing what happened during the first six weeks showed that both the Soteria patients (of whom only 24 per cent received medication) and the conventionally treated patients experienced equal and significant improvements in their symptoms. The results from two-year follow-up interviews with the participants,[55] published much later, found that 43 per cent of the Soteria residents had still not received psychiatric drugs, and that, if anything, there was evidence of modest superiority for the Soteria approach compared with conventional treatment. Those participants who were subsequently judged to meet a tighter definition of schizophrenia that was later introduced by the American Psychiatric Association were judged to have done especially well. An attempt to replicate the project in Berne, Switzerland, produced broadly comparable results.[56]

1. Soteria House

The Soteria project was a far from perfect investigation of whether conventional psychiatry is helpful to people with severe mental illness. Although the care of patients was mostly left in the hands of people who were not psychiatrically qualified, and who used kindness, tolerance, and common sense when deciding what they should do, some residents did receive drugs. But the project undoubtedly succeeded in demonstrating that many people with severe mental illness do at least as well with much reduced exposure to conventional psychiatric treatment than they typically experience. Some, it seems, can do well with no psychiatry at all.

Psychiatry is not working

The evidence on the global impact of medical psychiatry points to a series of startling conclusions. More than a century of endeavour has not led to improvements in outcomes for patients with severe mental illness. People experiencing psychotic symptoms in countries with few mental health professionals do better than patients in countries with well-resourced psychiatric services. Reducing mentally ill patients' exposure to biomedical psychiatry certainly does them no harm, and may even do them some good. Any claim by modern mental health professionals to have contributed to human well-being therefore looks tenuous, at least as far as the treatment of the psychotic disorders is concerned. And yet, as the epigraph to this chapter indicates, many apparently well-informed observers have assumed otherwise.

Inevitably we are led to a series of pressing questions. How did the biomedical approach become so dominant in psychiatry, and why has it persisted? What are the assumptions behind this approach and are they supported by scientific evidence? Do the research findings collected using such dazzling technologies as functional magnetic resonance imaging and the methods of molecular genetics really support the idea that mental illness is a genetically influenced disorder of the brain? And what of the evidence on the effectiveness of psychiatric drugs? When answering these questions, we shall see that vested interests have often played a greater role in maintaining the biomedical approach than rational argument, that the objections made by patients to cold and ineffective treatments have more often been ignored than heeded, and that there has been a proliferation of systematic misinformation about the effects of some of the most widely used psychiatric treatments.

2

The Appliance of Science: The Emergence of Psychiatry as a Medical Discipline

> History . . . is, indeed, little more than the register of the crimes, follies, and misfortunes of mankind.
>
> Edward Gibbon, *The History of the Decline and Fall of the Roman Empire*

Although the idea that mental disorders are diseases of the brain can be traced back to before the Christian era, the profession of psychiatry as we now know it became firmly established as a sub-speciality of medicine only in the middle years of the nineteenth century.[1] Despite the rapid advances in the biomedical and psychological sciences that have occurred since then, many of the assumptions about mental illness made by Victorian psychiatrists continue to guide the practice of mental health professionals today, and hence it is important to understand what these assumptions are and how they arose.

The most important practitioners of the new discipline lived and worked in the German-speaking countries of Europe (the first university department of psychiatry was opened in Berlin in 1863). In a short paper published in 1898, the Swiss-born neuropathologist-turned-psychiatrist Adolf Meyer reflected on this time and observed:

The tendency of the day was to make as much progress as possible in the more promising field, namely, in the anatomy of the nervous system and pathology of nervous diseases . . . practically all the clinicians who were professors of psychiatry in the German universities and elsewhere were far more interested in these anatomical problems, and the medical public also looked upon the alienist rather as a research man in neurology than a real student of mental diseases.[2]

Meyer had originally intended to specialize in neurology but would eventually become one of the most influential psychiatrists in the United States. He had migrated to America in 1892, and had obtained his first paid employment there in May of the following year, when he had taken the position of pathologist at an asylum in the small town of Kankakee, 60 miles south of Chicago. Although he had continued his studies in neuroanatomy (it is said that he was partially responsible for American neurologists and psychologists adopting the white rat as their standard laboratory animal[3]), his despair at the poor quality of the services offered to the patients at the hospital had quickly prompted him to become involved in their care. A shy man who was warmly remembered by those who worked under him,[4] he developed a common-sense approach to psychiatry and believed that it was impossible to understand his patients' symptoms without first understanding their life histories. His approach has been described as *psychobiological*, in the sense that it attempted to integrate findings from a wide range of disciplines, ranging from the social sciences to neurology. After his appointment as director of the Pathological Institute of the New York State Hospitals in 1902, Meyer's ideas about the causes and treatment of psychiatric disorders became well known and highly respected throughout the United States and eventually also in Britain.

In his short paper of 1898, Meyer expressed the opinion that Emil Kraepelin, who was then based at the University of Heidelberg, was the most important German psychiatrist working at that time. However, he probably did not imagine that Kraepelin's ideas would have an even greater impact than his own on the way psychiatrists worked a century later. Today it is sometimes claimed that Kraepelin is a more important figure in the history of the profession than Freud, who was born in the same year. Indeed, by the early years of the twenty-first century, many psychiatrists had become 'eager to enshrine Kraepelin as their historical lodestar – as a new, post-Freudian "father" of clinical psychiatry'.[5]

Building the intellectual foundations of psychiatry

Heidelberg is a modestly sized city located in the federal state of Baden-Württemberg in the south-west of Germany, where the River Neckar leaves a narrow valley in the Odenwald hills before reaching across the Rhine valley towards Mannheim, 20 miles away. It is dominated by a dark and imposing medieval castle on one side of the valley, which looks down over the old town centre, home to the University of Heidelberg, one of the oldest academic institutions in Europe. Kraepelin was appointed professor of psychiatry at the university in 1891, when he was just 35 years old, by which time he had already established for himself a reputation as a leader in his field. His first textbook, *A Compendium of Psychiatry*, had been published in 1883, when he was 27. It was this book, revised throughout his life (the final edition, ten times larger than the first, was published a year after his death, in 1927) that was to provide the intellectual foundations of modern psychiatric theory and research.

Those who knew Kraepelin described him as aloof and obsessional. He was a lifelong campaigner against the evils of alcoholism, a fierce German nationalist and admirer of Bismarck, and wrote dreadful poetry in support of his social and political opinions. And yet his scientific interests were wide-ranging. Following his experiments with caffeine and morphine he became recognized as a pioneer of the science of *psychopharmacology* (the study of the psychological affects of drugs). Although he had a deep interest in psychology, he rejected Freud's theory of psychoanalysis* on the grounds that it was too subjective, advocating instead the experimental methods and objective tests which he had learned about during a period of study in Leipzig with Wilhelm Wundt, the director of the world's first experimental psychology laboratory. With his older brother Karl, a distinguished

* The term *psychoanalysis* refers to the particular psychological theories developed by Freud, and also to the particular kind of psychotherapy he developed. A *psychoanalyst* (analyst for short) is therefore someone who practises this kind of therapy. Some people train in psychoanalysis after first qualifying as psychiatrists, psychologists or social workers. The rules for admission to training vary between different training institutes.

2. Emil Kraepelin (1856–1926), psychiatrist, scientist
and German nationalist

botanist, Kraepelin travelled to Java to see whether the forms of
mental illness suffered by the indigenous population were the same as
those observed in the psychiatric hospitals of Europe. (He concluded
that they were, although 'The relative absence of delusion among the
Javanese might be related to the lower stage of intellectual development attained, and the rarity of auditory hallucinations might reflect
the fact that speech counts far less than it does with us and that
thoughts tend to be governed by sensory images'.)[6] He can therefore
be credited as one of the founders of the sub-discipline of *cross-cultural
psychiatry*.

From the beginning of his career, Kraepelin accepted that psychiatry
needed 'a profound and deep union with general medicine' and that
'above all the medical, somatic side of our science . . . has comprised
the point of departure for psychiatric research'.[7] However, he was
highly sceptical about the work of many of his peers, who tended
to speculate about the causes of psychiatric conditions solely on the
basis of their anatomical observations, and whose research made
no connection with the actual clinical phenomena observed in the

asylums. He therefore argued that psychiatric research should begin with the detailed examination of patients supported by the results obtained from simple psychological tests.

Kraepelin's overarching ambition was to discover a workable diagnostic system that would allow his fellow psychiatrists to describe and make sense of the myriad problems they encountered in their clinics. He hoped that he would be able to achieve this aim by studying his patients' symptoms and the way that they developed over time, arguing that symptoms which tended to occur together and which also followed a characteristic course (for example deteriorating, fluctuating or improving as the months went by) should be grouped under a single diagnosis. He assumed that, on further investigation, each diagnosis would then be shown to correspond with a specific type of pathology in the brain, which in turn would have a specific aetiology.

In order to discover meaningful clusters of symptoms it was necessary for Kraepelin to study large numbers of patients. By 1896 he had collected information on more than a thousand cases, whose details he recorded on file cards, but he lamented that these were not enough to serve his purpose.[8] Through the successive editions of his *Compendium*, which he renamed *A Textbook of Psychiatry for Physicians and Students*, he grouped and then regrouped together conditions that other researchers had considered separate diseases. In this way, he was led to the distinction, for which he is most remembered today, between the two most serious and disabling forms of mental illness: *dementia praecox* and *manic depression*. Although the term dementia praecox was eventually replaced by the term *schizophrenia* (introduced by the Swiss psychiatrist Eugen Bleuler in 1911), these diagnostic concepts are still widely used by psychiatrists today.[9]

According to Kraepelin, dementia praecox (literally 'senility of the young') was a disease that typically struck in adolescence or early adulthood, which usually involved hallucinations and delusions, and which almost always had a deteriorating course – patients rarely if ever got better. He assumed that it was the product of 'a tangible morbid process in the brain', leading to problems of attention and memory, and eventually to intellectual deterioration. This morbid process was in turn, he believed, almost certainly caused by some kind of autointoxication (poison secreted within the body), most likely from the gonads, which explained why the illness often took hold soon after puberty.[10]

Kraepelin hoped that his account of dementia praecox would eventually be proved by pathological research. After moving to the University of Munich in 1902, he asked a junior colleague, Alois Alzheimer† to examine the brains of deceased patients. He was disappointed when Alzheimer was unable to report anything abnormal but his belief that there must be some kind of cerebral degeneration underlying the disorder remained unshaken.

By contrast, manic depression seemed to have a much more favourable outcome. Under this diagnosis Kraepelin included not only patients who experienced episodes of mania and depression (who would today be described as suffering from bipolar disorder), but also patients who experienced episodes of depression in the absence of mania; what we now call unipolar depression. About half of the patients that Kraepelin diagnosed as manic depressive were judged to recover completely after a single episode.

When evaluating Kraepelin's work it is important to remember that, before his ideas became widely accepted, there was no agreement about the classification of psychiatric disorders, their causes or how they should be named. Indeed, it has been said that no self-respecting psychiatrist of the late nineteenth century could manage without his very own diagnostic system.[11] As a consequence, communication between researchers in different clinics and universities was almost impossible. How was a psychiatrist working in, say, Edinburgh, to know that he was studying the same kind of patients as his rival in Boston?

It was because British psychiatrists were well aware of this problem that they welcomed the clarity brought by Kraepelin's diagnoses. The sixth edition of the *Textbook* appeared in English translation in 1902, and the concept of dementia praecox was vigorously debated in British journals and at medical meetings over the following few years, until it became widely accepted.[12] Adolf Meyer cautiously introduced

† Alzheimer was eventually to become famous for identifying the form of senile dementia that now bears his name. Actually, it was Kraepelin who realized the significance of the observation, and who insisted that the disease be known by Alzheimer's name.

American psychiatrists to Kraepelin's ideas at about the same time and the first detailed discussions of dementia praecox appeared in American medical journals in the early years of the new century.[13] The American public became aware of the diagnosis in 1907, when it was touted as a possible explanation for the behaviour of the millionaire Harry Thaw, who had sensationally murdered the well-known architect Stanford White during an altercation at a party in New York. Although sexual jealousy was probably the real motive for the crime (Thaw's wife had previously been White's mistress), experts testifying on Thaw's behalf at the subsequent trial successfully argued that he had been suffering from a madness that had been smouldering in his brain since puberty.

Of course, Kraepelin's methods (unlike those eventually advocated by Meyer) did not require practitioners of psychiatry to get to know their patients very well, a characteristic of his approach that no doubt suited his temperament. Instead, as his detailed case studies reveal, patients were considered as bearers of symptoms rather than as people with histories and stories to tell.[14] This is not to indicate that he was indolent in his efforts to understand the individual case. Indeed, he sometimes went to prodigious lengths in order to justify his diagnoses: while visiting the Department of Psychiatry at Heidelberg a few years ago, I was able to examine one of his handwritten reports, penned for the purposes of a court case. It ran to more than a hundred pages.

Life in the asylums

During the Victorian period the developed world had seen a steady increase in the number of people seeking treatment for mental illness. In many countries, a dramatic increase in the number of asylum beds had been required in order to accommodate this apparent epidemic of insanity. In the United States in 1843 the social reformer Dorothea Dix had presented a *Memorial* to the Legislature of the State of Massachusetts, describing 'the present state of insane persons confined within this Commonwealth, in cages, closets, cellars, stalls, pens . . . naked, beaten with rods, and lashed into obedience',[15] provoking the creation of a system of state asylums. Two years later, Parliament in

London had passed the County Asylum Act, requiring local authorities to establish a similar network of asylums across Great Britain.[16]

Some indication of the quality of routine psychiatric care at the time that Kraepelin and Meyer were working can be gleaned from a letter written by Miss Edilla D to her parents, describing her experiences in the Royal Edinburgh Asylum in 1898.

I feel I cannot stand this place a minute longer and soon I shall lose the brains I had, and not be able to interest myself in others and everything that goes on in the world. The monotony and routine simply drives me wild . . . I feel I shall go on degenerating in this environment into an animal that only lives to eat.

The letter was one of more than a thousand intercepted by the hospital staff and filed in the patients' medical records, from where they were disinterred a century later by Edinburgh psychiatrist Alan Beveridge.[17] According to Beveridge's account, the documents discovered in this treasure-trove, which were addressed not only to friends and relatives but also to staff, were written by the patients for a variety of reasons:

To understand their predicament, to make sense of their distress, to complain, to get out, to communicate with the outside world, to plead their sanity, to condemn the Asylum, to criticize other inmates or to express affection for them, to appeal to Clouston [the medical superintendent] or to ask him to intervene over some grievance. Patients wrote on headed notepaper, on postcards, on scraps of paper, on pages torn from magazines, on wrapping paper, on old letters, on envelopes and even on toilet paper.

Thomas Clouston, who was in charge of the Royal Edinburgh Asylum between 1873 and 1908, was one of the most respected British psychiatrists of his day. The institution over which he presided was divided into two sections, one for private patients and the other for paupers. Most of the residents, whether wealthy or destitute, had been admitted against their will, usually with the connivance of their families and often by subterfuge. (Several of the letters record the ruses used by families to coax them through the asylum gates.) As Clouston believed that madness was caused by a loss of self-control, once inside, the patients found themselves submitted to a regime of 'discipline, order, a life under medical rule', which began at 6.00 a.m. and ended promptly and without argument at 8.00 p.m. They also had to endure large but barely edible meals, as Clouston believed that stoutness was conducive to mental health.

Although some patients proclaimed their gratitude for the treatment they received from him, the majority recorded their resentment. The letters complain of ill-treatment by some of the attendants, of fear of other patients, of boredom, of the paradox of being required to behave reasonably in an unreasonable environment, and perhaps most of all, of the sheer injustice of being wrongfully confined. They also revealed the patients' impressions of their doctor:

I solemnly state that Dr Clouston has never conversed with me five minutes on an end, either publicly or privately, at any time in Morningside Asylum. How then can the Doctor know that I am insane? It can't be from personal observation. The few minutes he ever saw me were not of the slightest value in forming a correct general inference.

And:

I challenge the whole attitude of mind of Dr Clouston in his estimate of the insanity of those in his charge . . . They are always watching for evidence to justify detention. All your rational conduct, all the evidence of sanity makes no impression on their mind, is quickly or immediately forgotten. While the slightest mistake, the slightest momentary forgetfulness, the slightest ebullition of temper is carefully noted, is always treasured up and will be remembered against you months or even years afterwards.

Many of the asylums established during this period grew very large indeed, often catering for thousands of patients. The largest were in the United States. For example, by the early decades of the twentieth century New York State was caring for its expanding population of mentally ill patients in six overcrowded psychiatric hospitals, and the state authorities decided to solve the problem of managing such large numbers by moving everyone to a single, purpose-built facility, the Pilgrim State Psychiatric Hospital on Long Island. The hospital welcomed its first residents in 1931.[18] With an eventual population of 14,000 patients, it became the largest psychiatric institution in the world. As well as facilities for the patients, the hospital boasted a bakery, a laundry, fire and police departments, a power plant, a church with a cemetery, a post office, a farm, and its own station on the Long Island Railroad. Doctors and their families lived in a small, purpose-built community close to but separated from the hospital.

Extreme remedies

Confronted with such huge numbers, practitioners of asylum psychiatry were not afraid to borrow the very latest ideas from physical medicine. A striking example can be found in the work of Dr Henry Cotton, who was appointed medical director of the New Jersey State Hospital at Trenton in 1907, at the tender age of 30.[19] At the time, the idea that disease was caused by infectious agents constituted the very cutting edge of medical science, and so it was only natural to wonder whether mental illnesses could be caused in the same way, perhaps by toxins pouring into the brain after entering the blood from reservoirs of infection elsewhere in the body. With the tacit support of Adolf Meyer (by then, director of the prestigious Phipps Clinic at Johns Hopkins University, a model psychiatric hospital that had been created with generous funding from the wealthy financier Andrew Phipps), Cotton decided to use surgery to eliminate all possible sources of infection from the body. Recruiting surgical and medical specialists, and installing operating theatres and X-ray machines in his hospital, he began to experiment by removing teeth, at times claiming that as many as 85 per cent of his patients were cured in this way. If removing all the patient's teeth did not work, then the tonsils would follow. If the patient still failed to respond, the testicles, ovaries, gall bladder or even the colon might be the next target of surgical intervention. It was only when Meyer demanded a review of the hospital's procedures that the true horror of what was happening became apparent. In an age before antibiotics as many as 45 per cent of those receiving invasive surgery died either on the operating table or soon afterwards.

Fortunately, surgical intervention for focal sepsis was not widely used as a psychiatric intervention outside New Jersey. Unfortunately, *electroconvulsive therapy* (ECT), the *prefrontal leucotomy* and *insulin coma therapy*, which all involved direct assaults on the brain, were more widely adopted. The first of these began its life in Hungary, during the 1920s, where Ladislaus von Meduna attempted to use chemicals, such as camphor and metrazol, to induce epileptic-like seizures in his patients on the mistaken assumption that epilepsy and schizophrenia are incompatible conditions.[20] However, chemical methods proved highly unreliable, and both the doctor and the terrified patient would often have to wait for many minutes before discovering whether a convulsive episode would occur. The earliest use for this purpose of much more easily controlled electricity is attributed to Ugo Cerletti and his junior assistant Lucio Bini, psychiatrists working at the University of Rome. After observing the use of electric shocks to stun animals in local abattoirs, Cerletti and Bini first attempted their new treatment on a 39-year-old engineer from Milan, who had been picked up by the police after wandering around a railway station in a confused and hallucinated state, and who, Cerletti decided, was suffering from schizophrenia. After receiving his first shock one April morning in 1938, the patient stiffened, and began to sing loudly. On overhearing Cerletti and Bini discuss whether they should try again with a more powerful shock, 'All at once, the patient, who evidently had been following our conversation, said clearly and solemnly, without his usual gibberish: Not another one! It's deadly!'[21] Nervous but undaunted, Cerletti increased the voltage and pressed on. The patient convulsed and stopped breathing for forty agonizing seconds, after which he sat upright and uttered a profound sigh. When Cerletti asked, 'What happened to you?' he answered, 'I don't know. Maybe I was asleep,' demonstrating for the first time the effect of electroshock on short-term memory.

By the early 1940s, electroshock machines had been installed in most asylums in Britain and North America but the treatment could prove hazardous. As patients convulsed, they would sometimes break limbs or suffer spinal fractures. Restraints and the physical exertions of nurses holding on to arms and legs were often ineffective at preventing injuries of this kind. The solution to this problem was first proposed by the American neurosurgeon Walter Freeman, who suggested that patients should be first given the muscle-relaxing drug curare. Before the end of the decade, patients awaiting ECT were being prepared for their ordeal by the administration of the safer muscle relaxant succinylcholine together with methohexital sodium, a short-acting general anaesthetic, making the procedure much less dangerous and more easily tolerated. Muscle relaxants and anaesthetics are always used when ECT is administered today. Although as a consequence ECT has undoubtedly been transformed into a physically safe procedure, we shall see later that its effectiveness as a treatment for mental illness remains, at best, unclear.

Freeman was to have a starring role in the development of perhaps the most frightening of the early physical treatments, the prefrontal leucotomy. This surgical procedure involved making crude incisions through the skull to sever the frontal lobes of the brain from the posterior regions. The operation was first performed in 1935 by the Portuguese neurosurgeon (and one-time Minister for Foreign Affairs) Egas Monitz[22] after he attended a conference in London, at which he learned about the effects of experimental surgery on the brains of primates. It was for this innovation that Monitz was rewarded with perhaps the least deserved Nobel Prize of all time. Freeman, an evangelical practitioner of the technique, travelled around the United States during the 1950s in a van he nicknamed 'the lobotomobile' so that he could demonstrate the procedure to doctors working in the state hospitals.

Freeman's version of the operation involved stunning the patient with electroshock before using a hammer to tap an ice-pick-like instrument placed above the eyeball and against the orbital bone behind. After inserting the ice pick through the bone and into the brain, he would move it from side to side in order to produce the desired lesion. Eventually, Freeman came to see his operation as a method of treating all manner of ills. Consider, for example, his treatment of Howard Dully, who was operated on by Freeman when he was just 12 years old, after his stepmother complained that he was defiant.[23] Freeman's medical notes of 30 November 1960 recorded that

Mrs Dully came in for a talk about Howard. Things have gotten much worse and she can barely endure it. I explained to Mrs Dully that the family

3. Walter Freeman changes Howard Dully's mind

should consider the possibility of changing Howard's personality by means of transorbital lobotomy. Mrs Dully said it was up to her husband, that I would have to talk with him and make it stick.

In a further note, dated 3 December 1960, Freeman added: 'Mr and Mrs Dully have apparently decided to have Howard operated on. I suggested [they] not tell Howard anything about it.'

In a way Dully was lucky, being surprisingly unaffected by what was done to him and able, in later life to tell his tale.[24] A few patients appeared to obtain relief from their turbulent emotions but many suffered a variety of disabilities, some losing the ability to care for themselves altogether, and others dying as a consequence of the damage inflicted on their brains. Possibly Freeman's most famous victim was Rosemary Kennedy, sister of the future President John F. Kennedy. Her unruly behaviour during adolescence created problems for her distinguished family, who sought the opinions of a series of psychiatrists before finding their way to Freeman's consulting room. Operated on in 1941, a woman who had perhaps suffered from mild intellectual impairment, but who could read and write, was left incontinent and able to utter only a few words. She remained in institutional care for the rest of her life.

Freeman conceded that about a quarter of his patients were left with the intellectual capacity of a household pet, but argued that

THE APPLIANCE OF SCIENCE

We are quite happy about these folks, and although the families may have their trials and tribulations because of indolence and lack of cooperation, nevertheless when it comes right down to the question of such domestic invalidism as against the type of raving maniac that was operated on, the results could hardly be called anything but good.[25]

Like ECT and the prefrontal leucotomy, insulin coma therapy was also invented on the basis of reckless extrapolation from recent developments in physical medicine. In 1927, just five years after researchers at the University of Toronto discovered insulin, Manfred Sakel first administered the hormone to drug addicts who were withdrawing from opiates, and noted that it made them calmer and more cooperative. Encouraged by this observation, Sakel, a Polish neurophysiologist and psychiatrist working in Vienna, began to administer insulin experimentally to patients with other kinds of difficulties. By the early 1930s he was using it to induce a coma in schizophrenia patients.

Psychiatric hospitals in Britain and the United States quickly established specialist insulin coma therapy units. In a typical unit,[26] patients would be woken early in the morning, dressed in cotton shirts and long drawers, and taken to the ward, where they would be assigned a bed. After their blood pressure and heart rate had been checked, they would receive an intramuscular injection of insulin in the buttock or shoulder. Over the next forty-five minutes or so, as their brains were starved of glucose, they would gradually fall asleep and then into one of two kinds of coma. In the wet form, the patient sweated profusely whereas, in the dry form, the skin became hot and the patient's muscles twitched. As time passed, the patient's breathing would become more laboured, the pupillary response to light would be lost, and occasional spasms of the main body muscles could be observed. The patients would be monitored in the deepest stage of coma for as long as an hour before being slowly revived with glucose, usually administered through a thin rubber tube placed through the nose and into the stomach. Becoming conscious, the patients' responses would be slow, their speech slurred, but within fifteen minutes they would be able to recognize the nurses and doctors attending them. As the patients very often soiled themselves, they would be led off to be showered, and then given a hearty breakfast – the procedure usually left them ravenously hungry.

Again, almost miraculous rates of improvement were claimed for insulin therapy. Sakel estimated that as many as 88 per cent of his patients responded well to it. Again, like the surgical removal of hypothetically infected organs and the leucotomy, the procedure carried a high risk; somewhere between 1 and 10 per cent of patients died because of it. It was not until a young psychiatrist, Harold Bourne, published a critical review of the therapy in the British medical journal the *Lancet* in 1953, that the flimsy evidence in its favour became apparent.[27] For many weeks after Bourne's article appeared some of the most prominent members of the British psychiatric establishment wrote angry letters to the journal, accusing him of youthful intemperance, lack of experience and selective reporting of the evidence.[28]

The absence of alternatives

Of course, those doctors who defended the physical treatments were not monsters. For the most part they wanted the best for their patients and believed that they were observing miraculous recoveries when previously there had been no hope. They were propelled forwards in their actions by a powerful idea: that psychiatric disorders are brain diseases which can be easily distinguished from the ordinary miseries of life by means of the diagnostic framework developed by Kraepelin. They were no doubt also motivated by desperation. After all, there were few alternatives to the physical therapies in the early and middle years of the twentieth century.

At the time, the only widely recognized non-physical approach to mental illness was psychoanalysis. This type of psychotherapy had become established as the gold-standard treatment for the less severe psychiatric disorders after 1909, when Freud gave a celebrated series of lectures at Clark University in Massachusetts.[29] Although Adolf Meyer has often been credited for encouraging this development, in fact, he was quite ambivalent about Freud's theories, which were consistent with his ideas about the psychological causes of mental illness, but which placed too much emphasis on sexuality for his liking.[30] However, psychoanalysis seemed unlikely to be of benefit to the kinds of patients living in the asylums for at least two reasons. First, many psychoanalysts, including Freud, were sceptical about its value for patients with psychosis, who, they believed, suffered from rigid defences and could not form a sufficiently close relationship with the therapist.[31] More importantly, outside a few expensive private institutions such as the Chestnut Lodge hospital in Rockville, Maryland (named after the many chestnut trees in its sumptuous grounds), psychoanalysis was impossible to deliver on a mass scale because it required several meetings with a therapist every week, often over a period of years. This made the treatment prohibitively expensive, especially in America where, against Freud's own wishes[32] but at Meyer's insistence, psychoanalysis was seen as a medical treatment that could only be delivered by a qualified doctor.

Of the treatments described in this chapter, only ECT survives today as a rarely used and controversial therapy for depression which, depending on the commentator, is either the most powerful psychiatric treatment ever discovered – the penicillin of psychiatry[33] – or a traumatizing and ineffective procedure that causes permanent brain damage.[34] The others are now, for the most part, considered historical embarrassments that are best forgotten. Their significance lies not only in what they tell us about the conditions endured by those lost within the asylum system, but in what they tell us about the evolution of ideas in psychiatry. Looking at photographs of leucotomy operations, ECT suites and insulin coma wards, one is struck in each case by the sight of physicians gathered together and bending over their supine patients. Dressed in their white coats, they are archetypal practitioners of medical science. Indeed, there can be little doubt that the physical therapies were a means by which psychiatry attempted to claim a place at the high table of medicine. This struggle for recognition has been an enduring theme throughout the history of the profession. Only the tools with which this struggle has been fought have changed.

3

Therapeutic Innovation at the End of the Asylum Era

A feature of the interplay between psychiatrist and patient is that if the patient's part is taken out of context, as is done in the clinical description, it might seem very odd. The psychiatrist's part, however, is taken as the very touchstone for our common-sense view of normality. The psychiatrist, as ipso facto sane, shows that the patient is out of contact with him. The fact that he is out of contact with the patient shows that there is something wrong with the patient, but not with the psychiatrist.

R. D. Laing, *The Politics of Experience and the Bird of Paradise*

Psychiatric patients receiving treatment at the beginning of the twenty-first century are no doubt fortunate that their doctors no longer resort to psychosurgery or insulin coma therapy, and use ECT only sparingly. Most of the treatments that are used instead were developed during a time of intense innovation that followed the Second World War. The discoveries of this period therefore shaped the way that psychiatry is practised throughout the world today. They also revealed a dialectical tension that has been a constant theme in the history of mental health care, between those who have sought technical remedies for psychiatric problems and those who have argued that empathy and warmth are the most powerful therapeutic tools available to the clinician.

In most countries, the appearance of the new therapies coincided with the end of the asylum system. After increasing from a few thousand in the 1860s to more than 150,000 in the early 1950s, the psychiatric hospital population in Britain fell steadily in the second half of the century, dropping to about 60,000 at the beginning of the final decade. This was not because fewer people were seeking treatment but because the patients who were admitted to hospital were being discharged more quickly.[1] In 1961, the Minister of Health, Enoch Powell, announced the British government's intention of phasing out the county asylums altogether. A similar pattern was followed in the United States where, in 1963, President Kennedy signed the Community Mental Health Act into law and, for the first time, states were provided with the federal funding required to establish local mental health centres. As a consequence, the number of psychiatric hospital residents plummeted even more dramatically than in Britain, from more than half a million in 1950 to just over 60,000 in the mid-1990s.[2]

Various names have been given to this trend, but the most common is *deinstitutionalization*, a term that implicitly acknowledges the harm that long-term incarceration did to those contained within the asylum walls, some of whom should never have been there in the first place (in the early 1970s, a series of articles in the *Guardian* newspaper exposed the scandal of old women still held in British asylums, who had been admitted as teenagers after they had given birth to illegitimate children[3]). The forces behind this process have been much debated,[4] but some were undoubtedly financial; taxpayers were increasingly reluctant to pay for the huge costs of running large psychiatric hospitals which required patients to be fed, watered and housed, often indefinitely. A system in which patients lived in the community, only returning to psychiatric wards during periods of crisis, promised to be much cheaper.[5]

Equally important was growing public awareness of the way that the asylum system was destroying lives. During the Second World War the shocking conditions in the large American asylums were exposed by conscientious objectors serving in the Civilian Public Service, a government-recognized organization funded by religious groups opposed to the war. Many had been assigned to work as psychiatric hospital attendants as an alternative to military duties. Their observations, which included accounts of routine violence directed at patients by paid attendants, were eventually publicized in an article in *Life* magazine.[6] Newspaper exposés and campaigns run by organizations such as the National Council for Civil Liberties did their bit to reveal similar cruelties in Britain. These concerns were amplified in popular culture, by films such as Ken Loach's *Family Life* (1971) and by books such as Ken Kesey's *One Flew Over the Cuckoo's Nest* (1962) and Robert Pirsig's *Zen and the Art of Motorcycle Maintenance* (1974), which portrayed apparently sane misfits (a pregnant teenager, a petty criminal and a misguided philosopher respectively) being robbed of their identities by biological psychiatrists brandishing leucotomy knives and ECT machines.

Today it is often claimed that the availability of new drug therapies also played an important role in establishing psychiatric treatment in the community, and that, without crucial advances in pharmacology, the closure of the asylums would not have been possible.[7] The new drug treatments, it is argued, have allowed people with psychosis to live relatively normal lives whereas previously they would have required residential care. This claim is not merely historical but is part of the rhetoric used to justify the continuing priority given to drugs today.

The first drug that worked

Many historians trace the modern era of psychiatry to a single event, which led to a resurgence of interest in biological therapies just when enthusiasm for them was waning.[8] In the first half of the twentieth century, asylum doctors had used a wide range of medicines, for example bromides and barbiturates to quell agitation and stimulants for patients who were depressed and stuporous, but none had been shown to have lasting effects on the behaviour of patients. The breakthrough came in the form of a drug that is now known as chlorpromazine which, when it was introduced in the early 1950s, was quickly shown to have effects that appeared to be both specific and enduring. Ironically, perhaps, the person who took the first steps in bringing the drug into psychiatry was not a psychiatrist, but a colourful and energetic French naval surgeon named Henri Laborit. (In later life, Laborit went on to become a successful popular science writer, campaigned against the Paris–Dakar rally because he abhorred competitions, and played a starring role – as himself – in Alain Resnais's 1980 film *Mon oncle d'Amérique*.)[9]

4. Henri Laborit (1914–1995)

In 1949 Laborit, then in his mid-thirties and stationed in Tunisia, was looking for ways of preventing surgical shock, a condition involving a sudden loss of blood pressure which sometimes caused patients to die on the operating table. Believing that shock might be triggered by an extreme histamine reaction, he began experimenting with synthetic antihistamines belonging to a family of chemicals known as the phenothiazines, provided to him by Rhône-Poulenc, a leading pharmaceutical company. He noticed that some of the compounds he was investigating appeared to have profound effects on the central nervous system, making his patients more tolerant of pain and indifferent to their surroundings, and sometime inducing an unusual state of sedation he described as 'euphoric quietude'.

Laborit passed on his observations to Paul Charpentier, a chemist working for Rhône-Poulenc, who synthesized further compounds in the hope of capitalizing on these 'secondary effects'. Simone Courvoisier, a physiologist working for the company, developed a method of screening the new substances for their psychological properties. Placing rats in a box with a vertical rope, she sounded a bell while administering an electric shock through the floor of the box. The rats quickly learned to climb the rope, even when the bell was rung in the absence of shock – a phenomenon now known as *conditioned avoidance*. When the rats had been injected with the more potent of the new compounds, they no longer climbed the rope on hearing the bell alone, but tried just as vigorously to escape the shock once it had been administered. The drugs seemed to stop the rats from avoiding the shocks, but they had no effect on the extent to which they were experienced as unpleasant. This property was eventually used as a method of identifying promising compounds before they were selected for testing on patients.

In 1951 Rhône-Poulenc released the most potent of Charpentier's new drugs, then labelled 4560RP, to a small number of French psychiatrists. By this time Laborit had transferred to the Val-de-Grâce Hospital in Paris, and was trying to find out if cooling his patients would protect them against the physical stress of surgery. As 4560RP was known to inhibit the body's ability to regulate temperature, he tried administering it to his anaesthetized patients before packing them in ice. However, he remained convinced that it had more potential as a psychiatric treatment.

On 9 November 1951 Laborit persuaded a psychiatrist friend, Dr Cornelia Quarti, to agree to an intravenous injection of 4560RP in order to experience its psychological effects. Quarti's initial reaction was unfavourable – she felt profoundly depressed and nearly fainted. However, after about two hours she began to experience a state of 'euphoric relaxation', which was encouraging enough to justify an experiment with a patient. Two months later a Val-de-Grâce psychiatrist, Colonel Joseph Hamon, administered 4560RP in combination with a barbiturate to a severely manic patient who had failed to respond to electroconvulsive therapy or pentothal (an anaesthetic then sometimes used to treat extreme excitement). The patient's response was remarkable, and twenty days after his first dose on 19 January 1952 he was judged 'fit for normal life'.

Later that year, a series of experiments with 4560RP carried out at the St Anne's Psychiatric Centre in Paris provoked the interest of psychiatrists working elsewhere in the world. The experiments were conducted by Jean Delay, one of the most respected French psychiatrists of the day, and his junior colleague Pierre Deniker. Delay had first heard of 4560RP from Deniker's brother-in-law, an anaesthetist who had tried to replicate Laborit's experimental use of the drug during surgery. Initially, Delay and Deniker planned to use ice packs to cool patients who had been administered 4560RP, following Laborit's idea that this would increase their tolerance of stress. However, when the hospital pharmacy ran out of ice packs, the nurses went ahead and gave the drug without them. Quickly overcoming their amazement that cooling was unnecessary, Delay and Deniker went on to give 4560RP – soon to be renamed chlorpromazine – to a number of (mainly manic) patients, allowing them to carry out a more rigorous evaluation of its effects. They quickly decided to call the drug a *neuroleptic*, a word derived from Greek and meaning 'to clasp the nerves', and this term was used to describe all drugs belonging to the same general class until the 1990s, when the term *antipsychotic* became more widely adopted.[10]

An undignified dispute between Laborit and Delay and Deniker about who should be credited for chlorpromazine's introduction was probably the only reason that no one received a Nobel Prize for its discovery.[11] First marketed in the United States as a treatment for nausea, it came to the attention of North American psychiatrists only after a French-speaking Canadian psychiatrist working in Montreal, Hans Lehmann, was given one of Delay and Deniker's papers by a Rhône-Poulenc representative. Lehmann read it while soaking in the bath one afternoon and, the very next day, tried the drug out on some of his patients.[12] (He had trouble publishing the results of his hastily organized trial, because critics judged them too good to be true.) Studies later conducted in the United States by the National Institute for Mental Health established that, although it had a sedative effect at high dose, chlorpromazine's impact on psychotic symptoms, especially hallucinations and delusions, was not related to this effect: patients given an equally sedating dose of barbiturate did not improve in the same way.[13] Further investigation suggested that it was an effective prophylactic agent, which could be given to patients who had been discharged from hospital, to prevent them from becoming ill again.[14] By this time, in the early 1970s, chlorpromazine was widely seen as a specific treatment for schizophrenia, despite the fact that early French studies had all indicated that it was particularly effective with patients suffering from mania.

The discovery of chlorpromazine stimulated intense activity in the pharmaceutical industry, which grasped, for the first time, that serious amounts of money could be made from the development of drugs for psychiatric disorders. Almost immediately after chlorpromazine was introduced in the United States, meprobamate or Miltown, the first 'minor tranquilizer' became available for the treatment of anxiety, extending the reach of the new discipline of clinical psychopharmacology beyond the asylum to the outpatient clinic. Although it was initially a huge success in terms of sales, and in convincing the public of the acceptability of drug treatments for less serious psychiatric problems, later studies raised doubts about whether Miltown was more effective than ordinary sedatives.[15]

Meprobamate was in turn followed by the first antidepressants, which were stumbled upon by drug companies searching for new antipsychotics. The person who initiated this development was Roland Kuhn, like Laborit an outsider, who was working at the state psychiatric hospital in Münsterlingen in Switzerland.[16] Given samples of G22355, a chlorpromazine-like compound that had been synthesized by the Swiss pharmaceutical giant Geigy, Kuhn was disappointed to discover that it had no effect on his patients' hallucinations and delusions. However, he was struck by the fact that the patients receiving it sometimes appeared less miserable. After administering it to three profoundly depressed patients he became convinced that it was a completely new kind of therapy. The pharmaceutical industry was slow to recognize that there was a market for treatments of depression,[17] but eventually G22355 was sold as imipramine, and became recognized as the first of a new class of medicines, the tricyclic antidepressants. Although now less popular than the more recently discovered *selective serotonin re-uptake inhibitors* (SSRIs), imipramine is still in use today.

A final accidental discovery which seemed to complete the biological psychiatrist's armoury was a drug that appeared to stabilize the mood swings of patients diagnosed as suffering from bipolar disorder (manic depression). The person who was most responsible for this innovation was again an outsider, John Cade, the medical superintendent of the Repatriation Mental Hospital in Bundoora, Australia, whose observations took some years to reach the ears of the psychiatric establishment.

Cade, like Kraepelin before him, believed that mental illness might be caused by autointoxication and set out to test this theory by injecting guinea pigs with urine from his patients. It was while conducting these experiments that he noticed that lithium carbonate, which he mixed with the urine in an attempt to make it more tolerable when injected, seemed to make the animals lethargic and relaxed. Although reported in a paper published in the *Medical Journal of Australia* in 1949, Cade's subsequent observation that lithium carbonate reduced the excitement of manic patients went unnoticed until much later, and the drug only became widely used in the 1970s. Its slow introduction reflected not only the fact that Cade was a relative nobody, hailing from a remote region of the world, but also the pharmaceutical industry's reluctance to invest in a compound that is abundant in nature, impossible to patent, and therefore difficult to turn into profit.[18]

The clinical psychologist arrives

The revolution in psychopharmacology sparked by the discovery of chlorpromazine overshadowed other developments in psychiatric care which were arguably just as important, but which have been neglected by historians. One such innovation of the post-war period was the creation of a completely new kind of mental health professional.

Before the war, psychology was a non-applied, scientific discipline. A handful of psychologists worked in child guidance clinics and an even smaller number worked in hospitals, but most were based in university departments, where they studied normal mental processes and the behaviour of laboratory animals.[19] Determined efforts to recruit psychologists into clinical roles began in Britain and North America only when it was recognized in both countries that insufficient numbers of doctors were either available or willing to work in the asylum system.

In Britain, formal training in clinical psychology began cautiously in 1948, when Aubrey Lewis, professor of psychiatry at the London University Institute of Psychiatry (based in the Maudsley Hospital), introduced a thirteen-month course for psychology graduates.* The person he chose to lead the programme was Hans Eysenck, a German-born refugee from Nazism who, during the war, had worked at the Mill Hill Emergency Hospital, a vacant school in a North London suburb to which large sections of the Maudsley had been evacuated to avoid the worst of the bombing.[20] Lewis and the other medical practitioners at the Institute anticipated that the psychologists trained by Eysenck would provide them with the results of psychological tests, in much the same way that laboratory technicians provided biochemical test results to physicians. To many psychologists, however, this emphasis on assessment seemed to lead to a kind of black comedy, in which psychiatrists asked for tests they did not understand, which they often failed to use, or which they interpreted in the wrong way.[21] The frustration felt by the psychologists, who believed that they could do much more to help their patients, would eventually lead them to develop completely novel kinds of therapy.

In the United States, the birth of the new profession occurred with more fanfare. During the Second World War more than four hundred psychologists had been inducted into psychiatric teams in the American armed forces, where they had worked out their roles without any formal training, many practising psychotherapy with injured and traumatized soldiers returning from the battlefields of Europe and the Pacific.[22] Following this precedent, government agencies funding the large asylums began to wonder whether they could use psychologists to remedy the shortfall in medical psychiatric staff. In the summer of 1949, at the instigation of the Veterans' Administration (responsible for providing health care to ex-servicemen and their families) and the United States Public Health Service, seventy-three American and Canadian delegates gathered at Boulder, Colorado, to formulate a national strategy for teaching clinical skills to psychology graduates.[23] Those delegates who had been expecting a lazy sojourn in the Rocky Mountains were disappointed. That they were able to emerge, after two weeks of exhaustive debate, with an agreement on how training should proceed was largely due to the efforts of David

---

* A three-year doctoral-level qualification for clinical psychologists was eventually established in Britain in the 1990s.

Shakow, a psychologist who had begun work at the Worcester State Hospital, Massachusetts, in 1932, where he had developed a clear vision of what appropriately trained psychologists might do. Inspired by Shakow, the delegates proposed that the new professionals should be 'scientist-practitioners', competent in both research and therapy. A doctoral-level qualification was therefore assumed to be a minimum requirement from the start. Shortly afterwards, American clinical psychology programmes admitted their first students. Some indication of the remarkable way in which the profession expanded in America during its early years is provided by the fact that, by the mid-1950s, about half of the psychology graduate students in the United States were specializing in clinical psychology.[24]

Newly qualified clinical psychologists working in the asylums for the first time were dismayed by what they found there. Arriving at a large American institution in the late 1960s, Brian Hopkins recorded his impressions:

Twenty-eight hundred people live in several old buildings. Unless drastic changes occur, most of these 'miserables' will live the rest of their lives inside these buildings with only an occasional trip home for Christmas or a family visit with a picnic lunch on the hospital grounds . . . If you were sent to this institution, you would probably live for a while as a recently admitted patient in one of the relatively new buildings. The odds are about two to one that you will somehow be discharged from the hospital within six months . . . Many patients never get out the first time. If you have remained in the admitting area for a few weeks or months but a physician judges that you are still behaving so abnormally that society would not tolerate you, it is likely that you will be moved to continuing treatment. Here, the building is much older. The ceilings are fourteen feet high and the light from the occasional sixty-watt bulb doesn't go far. You live with fifty other crazy people. Unusual, often bizarre behavior occurs everywhere. Fights are frequent. One man spends much of the time cursing loudly to the heavens. Another masturbates several times a day but there is no privacy to shield his behavior. Many just sit and stare and sleep.[25]

Although Hopkins was able to present carefully recorded evidence of substantial improvements in his patients, he found that the hospital management was indifferent to his efforts. A suggestion that he might teach some of his techniques to hospital attendants was especially resisted; it seemed that awarding a supervisory role to a psychologist would threaten the authority of the medical staff, many of whom visited the wards for only a few minutes every week. Grumbling about these difficulties to a friendly attendant who had worked at the hospital for decades, Hopkins was advised, 'Don't worry, Dr H., the first twenty years at the hospital are the hardest.'

The psychologist as engineer

Reluctant to accept the role of the meter reader, administering pointless psychological tests at the whim of the psychiatrists, the newly qualified clinical psychologists on both sides of the Atlantic busied themselves trying to develop their own distinctive therapeutic methods. Although a few dabbled in psychoanalysis, most channelled their effort into one of two novel but apparently incompatible approaches, either drawing on specialist knowledge obtained from the psychological laboratory, or exploring the therapeutic value of supportive human relationships.

Although he never practised as a psychotherapist, Hans Eysenck championed the first approach, which had the virtue of according the psychologist a unique kind of expertise. By the early 1950s he had fallen out with his medical colleagues at the Institute of Psychiatry, partly because he had rejected psychoanalysis, the only type of psychotherapy they were prepared to recognize. He regarded Freud's theory of the human mind as a pseudoscience,[26] and provocatively used statistical evidence to suggest that psychoanalytic therapy was no more effective than leaving patients to their own devices.[27] He was much more impressed by the ideas of pre-war experimental psychologists, particularly those of the American John Broadus Watson,†

† An enthusiastic promoter of the idea that psychology should address real world problems, Watson had obtained permission from Adolf Meyer to set up a laboratory at the Phipps Clinic. There, he had set out to demonstrate that psychiatric disorders are the product of conditioning by the simple method of deliberately inducing a disorder in a previously healthy individual (J. B. Watson and R. Rayner (1920),

who had proposed the doctrine of *behaviourism* while working at Johns Hopkins University between 1907 and 1920. According to this doctrine, psychologists should abandon the study of subjective mental states in favour of the study of observable behaviour (although Watson had been careful to add that, '*saying* is doing – that is, *behaving*. Speaking overtly or to ourselves [thinking] is just as objective a type of behaviour as baseball.'[28]) In the clinical domain, this doctrine carried the implication that psychologists should pay little attention to how their patients felt and instead focus on what they did. Phobias were therefore redefined in terms of excessive avoidance behaviour, and obsessional disorders in terms of ritualistic behaviours such as persistent hand-washing.

With Eysenck's encouragement, psychologists at the Institute began to develop what eventually became known as *behaviour therapy*. The assumption behind this approach was that mental illness might be eradicated by establishing new responses to the stimuli that were the source of the patient's distress. An early behaviour therapy technique, known as *systematic desensitization* (actually first suggested by a South African psychiatrist, Joseph Wolpe, who had been experimenting along similar lines[29]), involved training anxious patients to relax while imagining progressively more challenging confrontations with frightening stimuli.[30] The idea was that the feeling of relaxation would eventually displace the fear provoked by the phobic object. Desensitization proved to be so quick, reliable and effective that it is still today regarded as the treatment of choice for simple phobias.

Although there was a continuous exchange of ideas between British and American psychologists, many Americans who followed the technical path took their inspiration, not from Watson, but from a later

---

'Conditioned emotional reactions', *Journal of Experimental Psychology*, 3: 1–14). The victim of this now notorious experiment was a nine-month-old boy, Little Albert. With his student (and lover) Rosaline Rayner, Watson had first shown that Albert was untroubled by a tame white rat, before proceeding to frighten the poor boy with a loud noise whenever he attempted to stroke it. Pretty soon, Albert had become phobic not only of the rat but also of other furry objects. Watson's career came to an abrupt end, not, as might be expected, as a consequence of this fairly blatant form of child abuse, but because of a sexual scandal (his affair with Rayner was reported to the university authorities and Meyer, who held strong views about such matters, was either unable or unwilling to protect him from dismissal).

5. B. F. Skinner (1904–1990)

experimental psychologist, Bhurrus F. Skinner. Skinner had turned to psychology only after convincing himself that he lacked the talent to become a novelist. A quiet and modest family man from the small town of Susquehanna in Pennsylvania, he spent most of his working life at Harvard University, where he developed a sophisticated version of the behaviourist philosophy. In his research, he investigated how entirely new behaviours could be established in animals by a process that he called *operant conditioning*, which involved the careful use of *reinforcing stimuli* (rewards, in ordinary language) to 'shape' behaviour. Skinner was influential, partly because of his inventiveness and experimental rigour, but also because he was able to articulate a powerful utopian vision about how his discoveries might be used to create a better world. He eventually achieved his ambition to become a novelist in 1948, when he published *Walden Two*, which described a society in which benign and clever psychologists manipulated reinforcements to maximize the happiness and well-being of the citizens.[31]

Like Eysenck, Skinner was not a therapist. However, his ideas had obvious implications for the practice of clinical psychology and, when realized by his disciples working on psychiatric wards, the result was a new kind of case report, which was often accompanied by graphs:

The S [subject; a patient who had been mute since hospitalization nineteen years previously] was brought to a group therapy session with other chronic schizophrenics (who were verbal), but he sat in the position in which he was placed and continued the withdrawal behaviors which characterized him. He remained impassive and stared ahead even when cigarettes, which other members accepted, were offered to him and were waved before his face. At one session, when E [the experimenter] removed cigarettes from his pocket, a packet of chewing gum accidentally fell out. The S's eyes moved towards the gum and then returned to their usual position. This response was chosen by E as one with which he would start to work, using the method of successive approximations ... [The report goes on to describe experiments in which this method had been used to 'shape' the behaviour of laboratory pigeons.] The S met individually with E three times a week ...

Weeks 1, 2. A stick of gum was held before S's face, and E waited until S's eyes moved towards it. When this response occurred, E as a consequence gave him the gum. By the end of the second week, response probability in the presence of the gum was increased to such an extent that S's eyes moved towards the gum as soon as it was held up.

Weeks 3, 4. The E now held the gum before S, waiting until he noticed movement in S's lips, before giving it to him. Toward the end of the first session of the third week, a lip movement spontaneously occurred, which E promptly reinforced. By the end of this week, both lip movement and eye movement occurred when the gum was held up. The E then withheld giving S the gum until S spontaneously made a vocalization, at which time E gave S the gum. By the end of this week, holding up the gum readily occasioned eye movement toward it, lip movement, and a vocalization resembling a croak.

Weeks 5, 6. The E held up the gum, and said, 'Say *gum, gum,*' repeating these words each time S vocalized. Giving S the gum was made contingent upon vocalizations increasingly approximating *gum*. At the sixth session (at the end of week 6), when E said, 'Say gum, gum,' S suddenly said, 'Gum, please!' This response was accompanied by reinstatement of other responses of this class, that is, S answered questions regarding his name and age.[32]

[The report goes on to explain how the treatment was continued until the patient began to initiate conversations with staff.]

Notice that, following the terminology of the animal laboratory, the patient is described as a *subject* (S) and the therapist an *experimenter* (E).

Not only could new or long-lost behaviours be established in this way, but undesirable behaviours could be abolished by identifying the responsible reinforcing stimuli and removing them, a process known as *extinction*. For example, Teodoro Ayllon and Jack Michael, working at the Saskatchewan Hospital in Canada,[33] described their treatment of a woman, Helen, who, for more than three years, had annoyed nurses and other patients with 'psychotic talk' about her illegitimate child and men who were pursuing her. Over a five-day observation period, Ayllon and Michael noticed that some nurses listened to her in an effort to get to the root of the problem, whereas others feigned interest by nodding or making vague comments such as 'I understand', before attempting to change the subject. The nurses were instructed to ignore the 'psychotic' talk but to pay attention to 'sensible' talk. Over the following weeks, the proportion of Helen's speech that was classified as psychotic dropped from 91 per cent to below 25 per cent, only to rise again to around 50 per cent after a social worker took an interest in her story.

It is hard not to be curious about what had happened to Helen before her admission to hospital. For example, had she ever given birth to an illegitimate child, which, at that time, would have been a cause of great shame? Ayllon and Michael's paper is silent on this question, because they did not consider it relevant to their goal of changing Helen's verbal behaviour. (A very small number of psychologists persist with this attitude today.[34]) If there is an impression that their methods of *behaviour modification* were similar to those that might be used to train a dog, it is because they were so. Nonetheless, the psychologists who chose to work in this way were often successful in changing the conduct of patients who had languished in the asylum system for decades; after all, eliciting speech from a man who had been mute for nearly twenty years is an achievement that should not be dismissed lightly.

The high-water mark of behaviour modification was reached in the mid-1960s when Ayllon with his colleague Nathan Azrin,[35] by then working at the Anna State Hospital in Illinois, devised a *token economy system*, in which all of the chronically institutionalized patients on a ward were rewarded with plastic tokens that could later be exchanged for goodies such as sweets or cigarettes. This approach was eventually to become surprisingly complex, requiring meticulous records of the patients' behaviour and nurses who had been specially trained to administer the tokens exactly as required.[36] Charts kept in the ward office would document how the chronically institutionalized residents responded, as they gradually relearned self-care skills, for example how to wash and dress themselves properly, that they had slowly forgotten during their decades in the hospital. Overseeing it all, the supervising clinical psychologist would be a regular visitor to the ward, checking that everything was running smoothly and offering encouragement to the staff.

The revolutionary zeal of the behaviour modifiers seemed to be supported by numerous case studies, which documented dramatic changes in the behaviour of individual patients.[37] Even more compelling evidence eventually emerged from a five-year study in Illinois, funded by the National Institute of Mental Health, in which 102 highly disturbed and institutionalized patients were randomly assigned to a token economy programme, milieu therapy (a supportive but less structured ward environment) or standard psychiatric care.[38] The patients recruited to the study had been in hospital for an average of seventeen years, all had received many years of drug treatment, and a large proportion had received multiple series of ECT or insulin coma therapy. By the end of the project, 97 per cent of the patients treated on the token economy programme had been discharged into the community, compared to 71 per cent of the milieu patients and just 45 per cent of those receiving standard hospital care. Careful examination of the data revealed that these differences could not be explained by the new drugs that were available. In fact, the token economy patients actually received less medication than the patients receiving the other treatments.

Harnessing the therapeutic relationship

Not surprisingly, behaviour modification appealed to psychologists of an intellectually muscular, scientific disposition (indeed, many described themselves as *behavioural engineers*). The alternative approach to dealing with the problems of psychiatric patients that emerged in the early years of American clinical psychology reflected a very different view of the psychologist and his relationship with the patient. And yet, as a person, its author was remarkably similar to Skinner.

Carl Rogers was the shy son of a well-off Midwestern farming family, who drifted into psychology after abandoning his plans to become a priest.[39] In 1928 he began working in a child guidance clinic run by the Rochester Society for the Prevention of Cruelty to Children (where he avoided opposition from psychiatrists by insisting that he worked only with children 'who fall within the "normal grouping" and are not definitely abnormal'). At this time, before the formal establishment of the profession of clinical psychology, Rogers sometimes described himself as a psychologist, sometimes as a child welfare worker, and sometimes even as a 'social economist'. It was partly because the psychologists at the nearby University of Rochester could see no merit in what he was doing ('[They] made it clear that the work I was doing wasn't psychology, and they had no interest in my teaching in the psychology department') that he moved to the State University of Ohio, in 1940, where he first saw adult patients, university students referred for treatment because of various emotional difficulties that were affecting their academic performance. (The term *counselling* was used for this kind of work, again because psychotherapy was at the time seen as a medical treatment that could be carried out only by doctors. In fact, Rogers was harassed by doctors throughout his career, at one point receiving a letter from the head of the Department of Psychiatry at the University of Chicago, who accused him of practising medicine without a licence.)

During these early years Rogers experimented with psychoanalytic methods, attempting to offer his patients' interpretations of their introspections in the hope that this would inculcate insight and thereby

6. Carl Rogers (1902–1987)

promote emotional change. However, he gradually became convinced that this strategy often provoked negative reactions, and sometimes even outright resistance, so that a much less direct approach was required. It seemed that many of the people he was struggling to help already had the capacity to improve their lives, which just needed to be released in the context of a supportive therapeutic relationship. The therapist's task, on this view, was to demonstrate understanding of the patients' position, by reflecting back the patient's thoughts and feelings. This idea became the foundation stone of what was eventually to be called *client* (*or person*) *centred psychotherapy* (the patient being renamed the client in order to emphasize his equal status with the therapist).

Rogers' approach has often been parodied, most famously when Massachusetts Institute of Technology computer scientist Joseph Weizenbaum designed a primitive computer program called ELIZA‡ (named after the character Eliza Doolittle in George Bernard Shaw's *Pygmalion*) which mockingly simulated client-centred therapy by using a few stock phrases and rearranging the words said to it by the

‡ Working versions of ELIZA can be found at numerous websites. Exchanging messages with one version led to the following dialogue: *E:* Hello, I'm ELIZA. *R:* Hi. I'm Richard. *E:* Do you think it is normal to be Richard? *R:* I hope so. *E:* Okay, tell me more. *R:* I'm writing a book about psychiatry. *E:* Did you come to me because you're writing a book about psychiatry? *R:* Yes, I wanted to find out what it's like to receive therapy from a dumb computer. *E:* What do you think? *R:* I don't think it's helping me very much. *E:* Don't you think it's helping you very much? *R:* Actually, it's making me quite depressed. *E:* Say, do you have any psychological problems?

'patient'.[40] However, despite Rogers' strong humanistic orientation, he was also committed to the scientific development of psychological treatment, and he introduced three innovations that were remarkable when judged by the standards of the day.

First, he recognized the importance of documenting exactly what happened in the psychotherapy session. Accordingly, he recorded his treatment sessions with the primitive devices available at the time (beginning with 78 rpm wax phonographic discs, each capable of recording three minutes of conversation), had the recordings laboriously transcribed, and then made them available for others to study. His books were therefore replete with verbatim accounts of his attempts to help his patients.

Second, when analysing these records Rogers realized that the *process* of psychotherapy could not be taken for granted, and that research was necessary in order to identify the essential ingredients that promoted a successful outcome. Before this time, the psychoanalysts had written about the importance of *transference* (the tendency of the patient to develop strong feelings for the therapist) and also the *therapeutic alliance* (the willingness of the patient and therapist to work together on the basis of a shared understanding of the patient's problems) but had not attempted to study these constructs scientifically. Rogers and his colleagues devised ways of coding their transcripts so that they could test hypotheses about the relationships between what the therapist did and how the patient responded. The effort required for this detailed work was enormous. For example, during a prolific period of work at the University of Chicago between 1945 and 1957, Rogers and his colleagues published a long series of studies on a group of twenty-five patients and twenty-five untreated controls. They estimated that it took approximately seven hundred hours to collect, code and analyse the data from a single patient receiving forty hours of therapy.[41] This was the beginning of what is now known as *psychotherapy process research*, a field that continues to be vibrant today.

Rogers eventually came to emphasize the importance of three qualities of the effective therapist that, he believed, virtually guaranteed that the patient would find treatment beneficial. First, according to Rogers, the therapist must demonstrate an *empathetic understanding* of the patient's frame of reference; he must show that he knows how the patient experiences the world. Second, it was necessary to show *unconditional positive regard* towards the patient; that is, to treat the patient with respect no matter what he said or did. Finally, the therapist must demonstrate *congruence* (sometimes called *genuineness*), by which Rogers meant that 'It is important for the therapist to be what he is in contact with the client. To the extent that he presents an outward façade of one attitude or feeling, while inwardly or at an unconscious level he experiences another feeling, the likelihood of successful therapy will be diminished.'[42] (Anyone who has attempted to carry out therapy on a cold Friday afternoon after the end of a busy week will understand just how difficult it can be to realize these qualities.)

Following an essay published in 1957, these became known as the *necessary and sufficient conditions*.[43] According to Rogers, if these conditions exist, 'No other conditions are necessary' and 'the process of constructive personality change will follow'. To emphasize this point, he went on to add:

It is *not* stated that these conditions apply to one type of client, and that other conditions are necessary to bring about psychotherapeutic change with another type of client ... It is *not* stated that these ... conditions are the essential conditions for client-centred therapy, and that other conditions are essential to other types of psychotherapy ... It is *not* stated that psychotherapy is a special kind of relationship, different in kind from all others which occur in everyday life ... It is *not* stated that special intellectual professional knowledge – psychological, psychiatric, medical, or religious – is required of the therapist ... Intellectual training and the acquiring of information has, I believe, many valuable results – but becoming a therapist is not one of those results. It is *not* stated that it is necessary for psychotherapy that the therapist has an accurate psychological diagnosis of the client.

To psychologists and psychiatrists who liked to revel in their technical expertise this was a claim that was not only profound, but also unsettling to the point of seeming dangerous.

Rogers' final and least successful innovation was to recognize that psychological treatment must be shown to be effective. Therefore, soon after leaving Chicago for the University of Wisconsin in 1957, he devised one of the first rigorous clinical trials in the field. Convinced that his person-centred approach would be helpful even to patients with severe mental illness, he persuaded his colleagues in the university's department of psychiatry that the study should be conducted with people diagnosed as suffering from schizophrenia, exactly the same kinds of patients that the behaviour modifiers were trying to work with in the asylum wards. A group of thirty-two patients at the Mendota State Hospital (sixteen long-stay patients and sixteen who had been at the hospital under eight months), together with sixteen 'normal' controls, were selected for the study, half in each group being randomized to client-centred therapy.¶

Unfortunately, although the study was undoubtedly groundbreaking in conception, it proved to be one of the most frustrating experiences in Rogers' long career. Rogers and his team had little experience in psychiatric hospitals, and struggled to adapt their therapy to the needs of patients who were often extremely withdrawn. More disastrously, a serious dispute erupted between members of the research team, apparently precipitated by one of their number, Charles Traux, who wanted to keep much of the project data for his own personal use. When pressure was put on Traux to release the data (this was a time before complex data sets could be copied onto CDs or emailed from one person to another), he responded by calling the police and reporting that it had been stolen. At this point, to the exasperation of the rest of the team, Rogers' warm, generous attitude became his undoing; instead of firing Traux he continued to try to reason with him. The task of restoring the data, together with protracted discussions about who should be included on the final author list (often conducted via lawyers' letters), ensured that the findings did not appear until 1967, five years after the last data point had been collected.[44] When they did, the results could not be called anything but disappointing – overall, there were few differences between the patients who had received therapy and those who had not.

¶ It is not clear why the healthy control group was recruited. Apparently many did not feel that they needed therapy.

The two psychologies confront each other

It was perhaps inevitable that the leaders of the two great traditions in mid-twentieth-century American psychology would be asked to debate their ideas. Skinner and Rogers met, first, at the American Psychological Association annual convention in September 1956, then at a specially arranged meeting of the American Academy of Arts and Sciences in December 1960, and lastly for a more intimate, two-day exchange of opinions at Ripon College in Wisconsin in June 1962. Given the sort of people that they were, it is perhaps unsurprising that the meetings were characterized not only by profound disagreements about human nature, the way forward for psychology, and the implications of behavioural science for society, but also by mutual respect, warmth and humour that was, at times, self-parodying. (Skinner kicked off the 1962 meeting by ruefully observing, 'I always make the same mistake! When debating with Carl Rogers I always assume that he will make no effort to influence the audience. And then I have to follow him and speak to a group of people who are very far from free to accept my view.')

There were points of agreement. Both recognized the importance of fostering human creativity, and applying ideas from psychology to the problems of society. However, whereas Rogers saw psychology as a tool for fostering personal growth and individual autonomy, Skinner wanted to create planned environments that would optimally shape behaviour. Rogers feared that Skinner's attempt to develop a tech-nology of behavioural control would, if successful, create powerful tools that might be exploited by an unscrupulous tyrant. Skinner replied that introducing behaviour modification into all spheres of social life would make it possible to create a world in which 'there is food, clothing and shelter for all, where everyone chooses his own work and works for only four hours a day, where music and arts flourish, where personal relationships develop under the most favourable of circum-stances, where education prepares every child for the social and intel-lectual life before him'. He then asked rhetorically, 'What is wrong with it? Only one thing: someone "planned it that way".'

So who had the strongest arguments? In terms of the empirical evidence, it seemed that the Skinnerians had a good case. They had pulled off the difficult trick of getting severely disabled patients out of hospital, a goal that Rogers and his colleagues had failed to achieve. However, further reflection suggests a conclusion that is more complex and which has profound implications for the way in which psychiatric treatment is delivered today.

In 1966 Charles Traux (the man who Rogers believed had sabotaged his schizophrenia study) published a paper entitled 'Reinforcement and non-reinforcement in Rogerian psychotherapy', in which he presented an analysis of one of Rogers' own therapy transcripts.[45] It seemed that, whenever the patient said something positive or optimistic, Rogers responded with warmth and empathy, whereas negative or pessimistic statements were greeted with silence. According to Traux's analysis, Rogers had been unconsciously reinforcing positive thinking in his patient. Rogers' positive regard, it seemed, far from being unconditional, was really quite contingent. He had been doing behaviour modification on the sly.

But this kind of argument could be played out both ways. Working on a token economy ward during the late 1970s, British psychologists Roger Baker and John Hall noticed that the requirement to give out tokens was taking the nurses out of their offices and changing the way that they related to their patients.[46] What if the tokens were not given contingently but at regular intervals in the day, but the nurses still spent time talking with the patients whenever they did something useful? Amazingly (or so it seemed to those in the behaviour modification camp), the patients did just as well. It seems that the most powerful reinforcing stimulus available to a human being is not a token that can be exchanged for goodies, but the warm and empathetic attention of another human being. Arguably, if modern psychiatric staff could just recognize this simple truth and put it into practice, the quality of the care they provide would improve dramatically.

The impact of innovation

The idea that the new therapies which emerged after the end of the Second World War contributed to the demise of the asylum system has been attractive to many commentators, perhaps because it is concordant with the assumption of inexorable progress from a barbaric and pre-scientific era to the present golden era of rational psychiatric treatment. Conventional histories usually award the lion's share of credit to chlorpromazine and the other new psychiatric medicines. It is certainly true that, at the beginning of the 1970s, biological-orientated psychiatrists could look back with some satisfaction on the preceding two decades, a period which had provided them with apparently effective remedies for schizophrenia, bipolar disorder, anxiety and depression, the four main afflictions encountered in their practice. However, we shall see later that many of these remedies are not as effective as typically supposed. In some countries, notably Japan, the asylum populations continued to increase long after the discovery of chlorpromazine.[47] In Europe and North America, on the other hand, the political determination to close the large psychiatric hospitals seemed to emerge independently of any therapeutic innovation, whether biological or psychological.

The impact of the new profession of clinical psychology is just as difficult to gauge, partly because it has yet to attract the attention of disinterested historians. After completing his schizophrenia trial, Rogers abandoned his efforts to demonstrate that psychotic patients could be healed by mere exposure to his necessary and sufficient therapeutic conditions. In the 1970s he drifted away from the field of psychiatry altogether, and became a leading light of the human potentials movement, offering encounter groups to healthy people seeking enlightenment and personal growth. As for the token economies, although they were widely used throughout the English-speaking world, they eventually went the way of the leucotomy and insulin coma. By the mid-1980s, one prominent American clinical psychologist was moved to lament that schizophrenia had become behaviour modification's 'forgotten child'.[48]

Defenders of behaviour modification programmes now point to the very high rates of discharge from hospital achieved by patients passing through them.[49] It might also be argued that the programmes created a new optimism about what patients might achieve, and that psychiatric rehabilitation programmes throughout the world make pragmatic use of some behaviourist principles, even today. Detractors argue that the skills obtained by patients were not sustained once they were living in the community and that, after discharge, it was probably the new drugs that kept them out of hospital.[50] Any attempt to interpret the evidence is made all the more difficult by the fact that many early behaviour modification programmes look ethically troubling when judged by modern standards. (Although Skinner argued passionately against the use of punishment in behaviour modification programmes, the psychologists working on the NIMH Illinois study reported that they were only able to suppress aggressive behaviour by confining violent patients to *time out from reinforcement* – solitary confinement in ordinary language – for seventy-two hours, a practice that is inconsistent with current ideas about human rights.) In any case, it was virtually impossible to run a token system outside the controlled environment of a ward. By the late 1970s, therefore, many within the behaviour modification movement were experimenting with new therapeutic techniques that were more suited to the problems of patients who could come and visit them in their offices. Consistent with Watson's assertion that thinking 'is just as objective a type of behaviour as baseball', these new methods focused on what was at first termed 'covert behaviour' – the patients' thoughts and feelings. Eventually, this approach evolved into what is now known as *cognitive behaviour therapy* (CBT), a type of psychological treatment that attempts to help patients achieve emotional stability by finding more rational and adaptive ways of thinking.

Insane places

The early clinical psychologists probably had their greatest impact when they joined the clamour of voices raised against the horrors of the asylum system. Adding to this cacophony, in 1972 an American psychologist, David Rosenhan, reported one of the most notorious experiments ever conducted in the history of psychiatry.[51] His paper, which was published in the prestigious journal *Science*, had the arresting title, 'On being sane in insane places.'

The study was inspired by a lecture Rosenhan attended given by the radical Scottish psychiatrist Ronald Laing. During the lecture, Laing denied that psychiatric diagnoses were objective descriptions of diseases analogous to those treated in physical medicine. Reflecting on this claim, the psychologist wondered whether there was any empirical way of testing the objectivity of psychiatrists' judgements.

With seven others (two psychologists, a graduate student, a paediatrician, a psychiatrist, a painter and a housewife), he refrained from showering, shaving or brushing his teeth for five days. The 'pseudo-patients' then rang various psychiatric hospitals to request appointments. When interviewed by the hospital psychiatrists, they complained of hearing voices saying the words, 'Empty', 'Hollow' and 'Thud'. All were admitted for periods ranging between seven and fifty-two days, and seven were diagnosed as suffering from schizophrenia. As planned beforehand, immediately after arriving on the wards, they told the staff that their voices had gone away and then made every effort to behave as normally as possible.

The experiences of the pseudo-patients would have seemed familiar to the residents of the Royal Edinburgh Asylum three-quarters of a century earlier. The nurses and psychiatrists they encountered seemed unable to recognize that they were well. Part of the problem seemed to be that the staff were reluctant to get to know the inmates at all; psychiatrists approached by the pseudo-patients moved on with their heads averted on 71 per cent of occasions, made eye contact on only 23 per cent of occasions, and paused to chat on only 6 per cent of occasions. To make matters worse, the staff interpreted everything the pseudo-patients did in the light of their diagnostic presuppositions. A pseudo-patient waiting outside a cafeteria half an hour before it opened (there was nothing else to do) was described by one psychiatrist as having an 'oral acquisitive syndrome'. When observed making notes, another was said to exhibit obsessive writing behaviour. Only the other patients seemed to recognize that the researchers were not who they pretended to be, some making remarks such as 'You're not crazy. You're a journalist or a professor ... checking up on the hospital.' When the pseudo-patients were eventually released, those diagnosed as schizophrenic were not said to have recovered but to be 'in remission'.

After Rosenhan's results became widely known, the psychiatric staff at a reputable teaching hospital claimed that similar mistakes would not be made at their institution. Rosenhan rose to the challenge and told them that he would send one or more pseudo-patients to the hospital over the following three months. During this time, 41 out of 193 patients were judged to be impostors by a least one member of staff; in fact, Rosenhan did not send a single pseudo-patient to the hospital.

The 'Insane places' experiment could not have been published at a worse time for psychiatry. Its reputation at an all-time low, it was struggling more than ever to hold itself up against the other medical specialities. Meanwhile, as if sensing its weaknesses and contradictions, its enemies were gathering around it.

4

Dissent and Resolution:
The Triumph of Biological Psychiatry

Formerly, when religion was strong and science weak, men mistook magic for medicine; now, when science is strong and religion weak, men mistake medicine for magic.

Thomas Szasz, *The Second Sin*

Rosenhan's 'On being sane in insane places' paper was published at a difficult time for psychiatry, which in the early 1970s felt under attack from all directions. Not surprisingly, it did nothing to improve relationships between psychiatry and clinical psychology. In Britain, simmering disputes about the extent to which the work of psychologists should be supervised by psychiatrists eventually led the psychologists to leave the large asylums and set up their own independent outpatient clinics.[1] In the United States, rivalry between the two professions was even more intense, and psychologists sometimes found it expedient to resort to the courts in order to claim their right to practise psychotherapy, to work as independent practitioners in hospitals, or to diagnose psychiatric disorders.[2]

However, perhaps the biggest threat faced by psychiatry at this time came, not from outside the profession, but from within its own ranks. David Cooper,[3] a South African-born psychiatrist living in London, coined the term *antipsychiatry* in the mid-1960s in order to express his objection to the kind of dehumanizing treatment he saw being offered to severely ill patients in the large mental hospitals. The idea of a movement explicitly opposed to the aims of conventional psychiatry quickly caught the imagination of an emerging counter-culture eager to spurn anything that seemed old fashioned or illiberal. By the mid-1970s, antipsychiatric ideas were being espoused not only by dissident psychiatrists but also by sociologists, philosophers, and other intellectuals clamouring to establish their anti-Establishment credentials.[4] Whether or not there really was an antipsychiatry *movement* as such, however, is still debated.[5] Certainly, the antipsychiatrists had no agreed manifesto, nor any umbrella organization to which it was possible to gain membership. Those who were identified with the term expressed a wide range of views, and appeared to have in common only their objection to the asylums and biological treatments.

For the British public, the archetypal antipsychiatrist was Ronald (R. D.) Laing, the man whose lecture had inspired Rosenhan's experiment.[6] Born in Glasgow in 1927, Laing began his career as a conscripted psychiatrist in the British Army, where he found conversation with some of his psychotic patients more congenial than the company of his fellow officers. On completing his military service, he worked for a while at Gartnaval Hospital in Glasgow, with a group of psychiatrists who were interested in psychoanalytic theories of schizophrenia. However, it was only after moving to work at the Tavistock Clinic in London that Laing wrote the book that was to make him famous.

The Divided Self,[7] published in 1960, combined dense existential theorizing with psychotherapeutic insights to provide a dazzling account of the inner world of the psychotic patient. Although it was presented as a serious study of schizophrenia, it was widely read (or at least, was claimed to be read) by many outside psychiatry. Within a few years it was followed by other books, including *Sanity, Madness and the Family*,[8] which explicitly rejected the medical approach to mental illness, and which claimed to show how psychosis could arise understandably as a reaction to victimization within the nuclear family. (Reading Laing's case studies, it was hard not to be convinced that the many parents of mentally ill adolescents were almost monsters. Not surprisingly, this portrayal was very hurtful to many people who were unfortunate enough to have children with psychosis, and sometimes led them to be sympathetic to medical approaches which located the 'blame' for psychiatric disorders in genes, biochemistry and defective brains, rather than human relationships.[9])

Laing's views were attractive to many people who barely under-

7. Ronald Laing (1927–1989)

stood them because they seemed to chime with the spirit of the times. His rejection of orthodoxy appealed to a generation of young adults who, in the early 1970s, were embracing new freedoms and rejecting parental authority, and whose attitudes towards life were shaped by pop music and opposition to the war in Vietnam. Although he was undoubtedly a talented and empathetic observer of disturbed minds, as he embraced his unexpected celebrity, his ideas became increasingly chaotic and inconsistent. In *The Politics of Experience*,[10] he argued that psychosis could be both a rational reaction to an irrational world and a positive, transcendental journey. Consistent with this last idea, he helped found an organization, the Philadelphia Association, which established a series of therapeutic communities, the most famous of which was located in a community centre called Kingsley Hall in East London. The residents of the community were free to be mad without molestation, and were encouraged to pursue whatever therapeutic pathways they found most helpful. Such was the community's reputation that it briefly became a popular port of call for touring intellectuals. An account of the psychotic journey of one its residents, *Mary Barnes*, was eventually published as a best-selling book[11] which was

8. Thomas Szazs (1920–   )

in turn transformed into a West End play by the radical playwright David Edgar.

In the United States, the person most associated with antipsychiatry (although he objected to the term) was following a very different agenda. Thomas Szasz,[12] a Hungarian-born psychiatrist and psychotherapist worked at the State University of New York at Syracuse, was (and still is) a political and moral libertarian. Troubled by the fact that psychiatric patients can be compelled to receive treatment against their will, he argued for the separation of psychiatry and the state. Unlike Laing, he offered few insights into the experiences of patients or recommendations about how they might be better helped. Nor, for that matter, did he object to psychiatry between consenting adults. In his most important publication, a 1960 paper entitled 'The myth of mental illness',[13] Szasz claimed that the very idea of mental illness is incoherent because the term 'illness' implies physical pathology whereas no pathology could be found in the brains of psychiatric patients. (Indeed, he suggested, should a specific lesion ever be found to cause psychosis, madness would then become a neurological condition.) The idea of mental illness seems nonetheless compelling, he argued, because it allows psychiatrists to perform a kind of moral sleight of hand, removing misfits from society on the dubious grounds that they are ill.

Laing and Szasz differed not only in their opinions, but also in their personalities. Laing was impetuous and drank far too heavily for his own good (on the eve of a 1978 debate with Carl Rogers in London, he tried to get the ever-optimistic American psychologist to acknowledge the dark side of human nature and, frustrated at 'the California nice guy bullshit' he got in response, goaded one of Rogers' colleagues by spitting in her drink[14]). Szasz, by contrast, has a reputation for being charming and courteous, even when debating with opponents, and his criticisms of psychiatry are reasoned and logical, which may help to explain why they continue to be debated more than forty years after the publication of his most famous work.[15] Despite these differences, however, Laing and Szasz were often erroneously perceived as sharing a common ideology, and their ideas fuelled widespread concern about the ethics of psychiatric treatment amongst educated people on both sides of the Atlantic. The suspicion was raised that psychiatry might have more to do with the control and regulation of behaviour than with healing.

Not surprisingly, less radical psychiatrists in Britain and the United States were not pleased by these kinds of criticism. Some marshalled evidence in the hope of demonstrating that the biological therapies were not as irrational and dehumanizing as the dissidents suggested. (In Britain, a defence of psychiatry along these lines turned its smooth-talking author, the Irish psychiatrist Anthony Clare,[16] into a media celebrity.) Other psychiatrists reacted more emotionally, and demanded that the antipsychiatrists be punished for their opinions.[17] Clinical psychologists, meanwhile, mostly watched the growing conflict with a mixture of amusement and embarrassment, delighted at the discomfort of their medical colleagues, but worried about the implications of antipsychiatry for science-based treatments such as behaviour therapy.

In the end, it was not opposition from organized psychiatry that prevented the antipsychiatry movement from achieving its goal of a liberal revolution in mental health care. Rather, it was the inability of leading figures in the movement to establish a workable alternative to conventional treatment. Laing's approach floundered because he had neither the organizational skills necessary to sustain Kingsley Hall as a working project, nor the diplomatic skills required to ensure that it was acceptable to ordinary people living in the neighbourhood. By the time the project closed in 1970, the building had become dilapidated to the point of being uninhabitable. Its main legacy was its inspiration of Loren Mosher's much better organized Soteria project, which I described in Chapter 1.

After the collapse of Kingsley Hall, Laing flirted with various New Age psychotherapies and continued to write, but his later books had none of the fire of his earlier publications. His profession exacted its revenge in 1987, when the medical authorities persuaded Laing to voluntarily remove his name from the register of medical practitioners, after threatening him with disciplinary action on the grounds that his alleged alcoholism made him unfit to practise. Shortly afterwards, after finishing a lecture on Buddhism to an audience in New York, he responded to a question about his battles with the psychiatric establishment, by remarking that he had perhaps been too forthright. He added that the establishment would say to him, 'Ronald, we agree with you, but you shouldn't talk like this in front of the children, those outside the cloth.'[18] Within a year, he was struck down by a heart attack while playing tennis at Saint-Tropez. His last words as he lay dying were, 'Doctor, what fucking doctor?'

In the end, antipsychiatry had a lasting impact in only one country. In 1978, a dissident psychiatrist, Franco Basaglia, persuaded the Italian government to pass Law 180, which made new admissions to the large psychiatric hospitals illegal. The results were controversial. In the following decade many Italian doctors lamented that the jails had become repositories for the seriously mentally ill, and that they found themselves 'in a state of psychiatric-therapeutic impotence when faced with the uncontrollable paranoid schizophrenic, the agitated-meddlesome manic, or the catatonic'.[19] Their complaints were seized upon by psychiatrists elsewhere, eager to demonstrate the folly of abandoning traditional methods. Gradually, however, an effective network of smaller community mental health clinics evolved to replace the old system.[20]

The new biological psychiatry

Ironically, perhaps, most conventional psychiatrists agreed with Szasz that physical pathology is the hallmark of disease.[21] At the time that 'The myth of mental illness' was published, however, no conventional psychiatrist felt able to rise to the paper's obvious challenge because, in 1960, no evidence of pathology in the brains of psychotic patients had been discovered. Shortly afterwards there was a rapid acceleration in research into the biology of mental illness which led to renewed confidence in the medical approach.

Much of this research was prompted by the discovery of the new drugs such as chlorpromazine and imipramine, which not only appeared to be effective therapies, but which also seemed to offer new ways of understanding the brain. By figuring out how these drugs worked, researchers reasoned, it should be possible to identify what is wrong with the brains of mentally ill patients. This was the origin of the chemical-imbalance explanation for mental illness, an idea that was to prove more potent in the minds of ordinary people than anything dreamed up by the antipsychiatrists. To understand the logic of this idea, it is first necessary to understand something about how the brain works.

The brain consists of about one hundred billion *neurones* or electrically excitable cells, which are connected together in circuits of almost baffling complexity. The computations carried out by these circuits sustain our thoughts, feelings and behaviour. Each neurone consists of three main components: a cell body, a tree-like structure of dendrites that receives stimulation from other neurones, and an axon which projects forwards and stimulates the dendrites of other neurones further along the circuit. The neurones do not actually touch each other; rather the axon of one neurone comes very close to the dendrite of the next at a special junction, known as a *synapse*. Each neurone may be connected to thousands of others in this way. When a pre-synaptic neurone fires, it secretes a chemical, known as a *neurotransmitter*, into the synaptic cleft. This binds to a *receptor* on the next dendrite of the post-synaptic neurone in the circuit, causing it to become electrically excited in turn. Complex biochemical processes are then involved in the *re-uptake* of the neurotransmitter from the synaptic cleft, so that it is cleared from the synapse in preparation for the next time that the pre-synaptic neurone fires.

When the post-synaptic neurone is stimulated by a neurotransmitter arriving at a receptor, an electrical potential is created inside the cell. These potentials (summed from several firings of the same pre-synaptic neurone, or from a number of pre-synaptic neurones firing at approximately the same time) determine whether the post-synaptic neurone in turn fires, discharging an electrical spike along its axon and releasing its neurotransmitter. It is by interfering with this process that psychiatric drugs affect thinking, emotions and behaviour.

One of the most influential and enduring chemical imbalance theories of mental illness is the *dopamine theory of schizophrenia*,* which arose from efforts to understand the therapeutic action of chlorpromazine and the other antipsychotics. In the late 1950s a Swedish pharmacologist named Arvid Carlsson discovered that dopamine is an important neurotransmitter secreted by neurones located in areas in the mid-brain such as the nucleus accumbens and the striatum. (For this achievement, Carlsson won the 2000 Nobel Prize for medicine.) At about the same time, psychiatrists in Britain observed that drug abusers who took large quantities of amphetamine, a chemical that stimulates the release of dopamine at the synapse, sometimes experienced an acute psychotic state in which they became paranoid and experienced visual hallucinations.[22] It was not long afterwards that researchers in the United States found that all of the antipsychotic drugs blocked a specific type of dopamine receptor, known as the D_2 receptor, and that their potency correlated with the extent to which they did this.[23] Putting all these jigsaw pieces together led to an inescapable conclusion: too much dopamine at the synapse causes schizo-

---

* At the time that the dopamine theory was proposed it had already been forgotten that the antipsychotics were effective in the treatment of mania. Carlson later said that theory should have been named the dopamine theory of *psychosis* rather than the dopamine theory of *schizophrenia*.

phrenia, whereas blocking dopamine receptors transmission in the mid-brain helps patients recover from their symptoms.

A similar line of reasoning led to the suggestion that depression might be caused by an imbalance in the neurotransmitter serotonin (or 5-hydroxytryptamine, 5-HT for short).[24] For example, it was discovered that reserpine, a drug used to treat hypertension but which sometimes caused depression as a side effect, caused a depletion of serotonin at the synapse. On the other hand, a class of drugs known as the monoamine oxydase inhibitors, which prevented the re-uptake of serotonin, appeared to be effective antidepressants, and evidence soon emerged that imipramine and the other tricyclic antidepressants worked in a similar way. Together, these discoveries seemed to suggest that depression is the consequence of a serotonin deficiency.

In fact, both the dopamine and the serotonin theories were based on indirect evidence, often from animal experiments, mainly the effects of drugs on the brains of animals that could be killed for the purposes of science. Researchers realized that direct observation of abnormal biochemistry in the brains of living patients would be necessary to firm up their theories. Obtaining this evidence proved difficult because the brains of patients could not be observed directly and, in any case, the drugs the patients were by then inevitably receiving interfered with the very biochemical processes that researchers wanted to study. Although some evidence has emerged to support the role of dopamine in psychosis, direct support for the serotonin hypothesis has remained elusive to this day.[25] Nonetheless, the chemical imbalance theory of depression has continued to be enthusiastically promoted in drug advertisements (sometimes targeted directly at consumers rather than professionals: 'Celexa helps to restore the brain's chemical balance by increasing the supply of a chemical messenger in the brain called serotonin') and by the popular press.[26] Perhaps this is partly because the idea is so easy to understand, but it is also because this type of explanation for mental illness serves the interests of biological-orientated psychiatrists and drug companies very well.

Psychiatrists would probably have been discouraged by the slow progress of research into the biochemistry of mental illness had other evidence implicating biological processes not become available. In an influential series of studies published in the mid-1970s, American investigators Seymour Kety, a psychiatrist, and David Rosenthal, a psychologist, used Denmark's unusually detailed adoption records to trace children who had been given up for adoption at an early age by mothers who had been diagnosed as suffering from schizophrenia. They reported that these children were more likely to develop schizophrenia than the adopted-away children of women who were not mentally ill. As the index children had not been raised by their biological mothers, it looked as though the only way the illness could be passed from generation to generation was via genes, an observation that seemed to sound the death knell for accounts of psychosis, such as Laing's, which located the cause of madness in dysfunctional family relationships. In a parallel investigation, Kety and Rosenthal also identified adults with a diagnosis of schizophrenia who had been adopted early in life, and worked backwards to trace their biological parents, reporting that they also were more likely to be psychotic than the biological parents of healthy adult adoptees.[27] Believing that these findings constituted conclusive proof that schizophrenia is a hereditary condition, Kety felt able to proclaim, 'If schizophrenia is a myth, it is a myth with a strong genetic component.'[28]

It was soon after this discovery that in the late 1970s new methods of imaging the living body became available. These would eventually revolutionize medical diagnostics. The earliest method was *computerized axial tomography* (CT), invented by Godfrey Hounsfield, a self-taught electronic engineer who worked for the EMI record company in Britain. Hounsfield realized that, by taking X-ray images from many different angles, it should be possible to use computer software to integrate the information obtained in order to create a composite picture showing a cross-section of the body. In 1976, three years before Hounsfield received a well-deserved Nobel Prize for his invention, the first attempt to use CT scanning to image the living brains of psychotic patients was reported by Eve Johnston and Tim Crow, psychiatrists working at Northwick Park Hospital in London.[29] Their observation that the ventricles (fluid-filled cavities) in the centre of the brain were much larger in schizophrenia patients than in healthy adults appeared to provide conclusive evidence that the brains of patients were different – perhaps as a consequence of some kind of degenerative process – from the brains of ordinary people.

The neo-Kraepelinian revolution

This inexorable advance of biological research into mental illness seemed to offer hope to those psychiatrists who wanted to restore their tarnished image and reclaim psychiatry's rightful place alongside the other specialities of medicine. An influential group of psychiatrists in the United States who sought this goal acknowledged their ideological debt to Emil Kraepelin and self-consciously styled themselves as *neo-Kraepelinians*. Among their number was Robert Spitzer, who had started his career intending to become a psychoanalyst, but who, in the early 1970s, had fallen under the influence of his more biologically orientated colleagues at Columbia University in New York. Spitzer recognized that the lack of clear criteria for defining the major psychiatric disorders was an impediment to the development of a rational biomedical approach to treating mental illness, and played a leading role in what was perhaps the neo-Kraepelinians' main achievement: the creation of a new approach to psychiatric diagnosis, which was described in the third edition of the American Psychiatric Association's *Diagnostic and Statistical Manual* (*DSM*), published in 1980.[30] This development was of enormous significance, and will be discussed in detail in the next chapter.

Another influential member of the movement was Samuel Guze of the University of Washington, who, in a 1989 journal editorial, famously argued, 'There can be no such thing as a psychiatry that is too biological.'[31] Also important was Nancy Andreasen of the University of Iowa, a former Shakespeare scholar who had started a second career in medicine after experiencing complications during the birth of her first child, and who was eventually to become editor in chief of the prestigious *American Journal of Psychiatry*. In 1978, Gerald Klerman, a neo-Kraepelinian psychiatrist working at Yale University, wrote a manifesto for the movement, in which he outlined its fundamental tenets.[32] This had nine propositions, but three were particularly important. Klerman asserted that 'there is a boundary between the normal and the sick' (either you had a mental illness or you did not); that 'there are discrete mental illnesses. There is not one, but many mental illnesses'; and that 'the focus of psychiatric physicians should be particularly on the biological aspects of mental illness'. These, of course, were exactly the same assumptions that Kraepelin had made when beginning his studies of mental illness in the final decades of the nineteenth century.

Psychotherapy, in the neo-Kraepelinian world-view, was to play a relatively minor role in the treatment of mental disorders, and was perhaps to be administered by ancillary professionals who would help patients cope with their difficulties until their medical treatment had taken effect. Neuroscience was the core discipline relevant to psychiatry, and psychology and the social sciences were considered to be of peripheral interest. Young psychiatrists were told that they should pay more attention to developments in molecular genetics than to the talking therapies. Not surprisingly, the therapeutic relationship was relegated in importance. Of course, psychiatrists would have to be civil to their patients, but healing was to be achieved by manipulating neurotransmitters, not by understanding and interpreting the patients' thoughts and feelings. In a book called *The Broken Brain*,[33] written for a lay audience and published in 1984, Nancy Andreasen suggested that psychiatric treatment sessions in the future might be much briefer than in the past. Psychiatrists would no longer need to spend long periods getting to know their patients. Instead, treatment would involve assessing patients' symptoms and then adjusting their medication:

As the fifteen-minute appointment replaces the fifty-minute hour for many patients, they may actually find it preferable after they recover from their initial surprise. Briefer appointments are a more efficient and economical way of providing psychiatric care for a larger number of people ... Much of the time, fifteen minutes is long enough for doctor and patient to talk to one another about the patient's symptoms and how they are affecting his personal life.

The strange case of Rafael Osheroff

Just as the beginning of the modern era in psychiatry was marked in the minds of many psychiatrists by Laborit's discovery of chlorpromazine, so, too, it seemed that the hope that psychotherapy would be helpful to the severely mentally ill was crushed by a single event. In

1988 the Chestnut Lodge hospital in Maryland, which prided itself on using intensive psychoanalysis to treat even the most severely disturbed patients, was forced to settle a lawsuit lodged by a psychotically depressed physician, Dr Rafael Osheroff, to whom the hospital had denied drug treatment.[34] One of the expert witnesses who had been prepared to testify on behalf of Osheroff was Gerald Klerman, the author of the neo-Kraepelinian manifesto. In 1990 he wrote an account of the case, and attempted to identify the lessons that might be learned from it.[35]

According to Klerman, Osheroff had been admitted to Chestnut Lodge after the New Year holiday in 1979, following a two-year history of anxiety and depression. During this period he had been prescribed antidepressants by Dr Nathan Kline, an internationally respected psychopharmacologist who was later also willing to testify on Osheroff's behalf. After his admission, Osheroff was offered psychoanalysis four times a week but continued to deteriorate, losing 40 pounds (18 kilos) over a period of seven months. Although he developed severe insomnia and became increasingly agitated, he was not given any medication. Pacing up and down all day, his feet became so swollen and blistered that they required medical attention. In response to complaints from Osheroff's family over the treatment he was receiving, the Chestnut Lodge psychiatrists reviewed their treatment plan but decided to persevere as they had started. Eventually, at the family's insistence, the long-suffering doctor was transferred to a different hospital, the Silver Hill Foundation in Connecticut, where he was given a combination of antipsychotics and tricyclic antidepressants. Osheroff's reaction to his new treatment was so dramatic that he was discharged from hospital only three months later. Although he was eventually able to go back to work, during his period in Chestnut Lodge he had lost a lucrative medical practice, his standing among his medical colleagues and the custody of his two children from his second marriage (his third marriage and his relationship with his third child survived). In his lawsuit he claimed that many of the consequences of his illness could have been avoided had Chestnut Lodge offered him drug treatment.

The gaps in this narrative are as fascinating as the story. Why did the case receive so much publicity and why was it accorded such significance? (I am inclined to believe that Osheroff had a reasonable complaint but, to Klerman, the lawsuit must have seemed an unmissable opportunity to promote the chemical-imbalance explanation of mental illness.) Did Osheroff suffer from any kind of stress, either before the onset of his initial symptoms or immediately before his admission to Chestnut Lodge? (According to another account, by psychiatrist Alan Stone, difficulties in Osheroff's third marriage – to a medical student who he had wedded after a whirlwind romance – contributed to the doctor's depression.[36]) Why had his symptoms worsened so dramatically over the New Year period? Was it possible that the Silver Hill Foundation psychiatrists were successful, not only because they were prepared to use medication, but also because they declined to use a type of treatment (psychoanalysis) that is stressful, and hence potentially harmful, to the sensitive patient? We shall probably never know the answers to these questions.

Not surprisingly, given his neo-Kraepelinian credentials, Klerman thought that the case highlighted the importance of making the 'correct' diagnosis. Although all the doctors who saw Osheroff recognized that he was depressed, the Chestnut Lodge physicians diagnosed him as suffering from 'narcissistic personality disorder'. In Klerman's opinion, he actually suffered a major depressive episode with melancholia, a condition that, he argued, is peculiarly responsive to biological therapies such as drugs and ECT.

The Osheroff case was reported in newspapers and debated in psychiatric journals,[37] and was widely seen as marking the demise of an outdated and unscientific approach to severe mental illness. As Klerman pointed out, one reason why it had this impact was that it followed the publication of a series of clinical trials which seemed to show that psychotherapy had little to offer the psychotic patient. One of these was Carl Rogers' study, discussed in the last chapter.[38] Another, a large study carried out at the Camarillo State Hospital in California, compared five treatments: psychotherapy alone, antipsychotic medication, psychotherapy plus drugs, ECT and a control condition (no drugs, psychotherapy or ECT), finding that drugs and ECT accelerated the rate at which patients could be discharged from hospital but that psychotherapy had little or no impact.[39] Yet another study, published a few years after the Osheroff case was settled, found no evidence that intensive psychoanalytic therapy was more effective than simple counselling about everyday difficulties.[40] In the same year, a Chestnut Lodge psychiatrist, Thomas McGlashan, completed a long-term follow-up study of psychotic patients treated at the institution and could find no evidence that they had benefited from their lengthy psychoanalytic treatment.[41] For McGlashan, who had invested considerable time and energy in training to be a psychoanalyst, this was a turning point in his career. Later in his life he became a strong advocate of drug treatments, arguing that antipsychotic drugs should be given to people who seemed to be at risk of severe mental illness, before they had the opportunity to become ill.[42]

Replicating Rosenhan

By the end of the twentieth century the idea that the severe psychiatric disorders are genetically determined brain diseases had become so widely accepted that anyone challenging it was in danger of being branded a heretic. This was especially so in the United States, where even psychologists (who are obliged to give *DSM* diagnoses in order to obtain payment from their patients' medical insurance schemes) have long been encouraged to embrace the medical approach.[43] One ironic consequence is that American psychologists have recently sought the right to prescribe drugs.[44] Following a US Department of Defense demonstration project during the 1990s, in which a small number of clinical psychologists working in the military were taught to prescribe, new laws that allow appropriately trained civilian psychologists to use drugs have been introduced in New Mexico and Louisiana and are pending in several other states.

Of course, this challenge to psychiatry's monopoly is being vigorously opposed by the American Psychiatric Association which, according to its website, represents 'more than 36,000 physician leaders in mental health'. An indication of how American psychiatrists now see themselves was, until very recently, available on the Association's home page,† where the browser was greeted with a sequence of photographs, presumably chosen to represent the work of the profession. One showed

† The images were removed in the summer of 2008.

four relaxed, ordinary people, perhaps a family that has received successful treatment, smiling at the camera. The remaining three showed psychiatrists standing in line, studying CT images of a patient's brain, and sitting at a table in earnest discussion. Incredibly, most of the doctors in the photographs were wearing white coats or surgical scrubs. Clearly, the Association was trying to project an image of clinical professionalism, to make yet another stab at claiming its place at the high table of medicine. But a white coat has no obvious function for a doctor who is never in physical contact with patients, and the wearing of surgical gowns is even more absurd. The only psychiatrists who have ever needed scrubs were those who carried out prefrontal leucotomies, a procedure which the profession has been in a hurry to forget.

This vision of psychiatry's identity has not gone unchallenged in the United States, where some members of the profession have objected that the biomedical approach has led their colleagues to neglect their patients' life histories, to ignore patients' understanding of their problems, to take symptoms out of context, and thereby to misclassify the ordinary miseries of life as mental illness.[45] Perhaps they are making some headway. In 2005 even the American Psychiatric Association's president was moved to lament, 'As a profession, we have allowed the biopsychosocial model [of mental illness] to become the bio-bio-bio model.'[46] Some indication of how this way of doing psychiatry is experienced by patients can be gleaned from a recent attempt to replicate Rosenhan's famous experiment, reported by American writer and clinical psychologist Lauren Slater. In her book *Opening Skinner's Box*,[47] Slater describes how she forsook her personal hygiene for several days before presenting herself at nine psychiatric emergency rooms in New York State. On each occasion she complained of hearing a voice saying, 'Thud'. Like Rosenhan and his colleagues before her, she denied experiencing any other symptoms.

Slater's story has been disputed as implausible by some commentators.‡ However, according to her account, the nursing and medical

‡ The accuracy of Slater's testimony has been challenged, most notably by Robert Spitzer. In her book, Slater quotes Spitzer as boasting that modern psychiatrists would never be fooled by pseudo-patients. The subsequent vitriolic and amusing correspondence between them is available at http://taxa.epi.umn.edu/slater/letters/ (accessed 2 February 2008).

staff who assessed her had either never heard of Rosenhan's study or, if they had, they had forgotten about it. Slater was treated courteously but, after waiting an average of two and a half hours before seeing a duty psychiatrist, was interviewed for no longer than twelve and a half minutes. The doctors who questioned her made no attempt to explore her background except to enquire about her religious beliefs. They offered various diagnoses to account for her symptom, most often 'depression with psychotic features', and then prescribed either antidepressant or antipsychotic medication. To be fair, Slater's observations were not entirely negative. Comparing her experiences with Rosenhan's, she says:

No one even thought about admitting me. I was mislabelled but not locked up. Here's another thing that's different: every single medical professional was nice to me. Rosenhan and his confederates felt diminished by their diagnoses. I, for whatever reason, was treated with palpable kindness. One psychiatrist touched my arm. One psychiatrist said, 'Look, I know it's scary for you, hearing a voice like that, but I really have a feeling that the Risperdal [an antipsychotic] will take care of this immediately' . . . One psychiatrist, upon handing me my prescription, said, 'Don't fall through the cracks, Lucy [Slater's pseudonym for the purposes of the exercise]. We want to see you back here in two days for a follow-up. And know we're here twenty-four hours a day, for anything you need. I mean that. ANYTHING.'

In Britain, the situation is a little different. The presence of a growing cadre of psychologists within the National Health Service has ensured that psychological treatments for severe mental illness have never been entirely off the agenda, and a small number of psychiatrists have also played a significant role in promoting talking therapies. Relationships between the two professions have improved in recent years and psychiatrists and psychologists often work well together. Nonetheless, drugs continue to be the main treatment offered to people with severe mental illness, and, if they are available at all, psychological therapies are usually considered to be 'adjunctive' (that is, additional to and less important than medication). Even in Britain, it seems that Andreasen's fifteen-minute psychiatric interview has come to pass. When a research group at University College London recently observed psychiatrists at work,[48] they found that they reviewed their patients' symptoms, tried to assess whether the medications they had prescribed were helpful, and discussed daytime and social activities, living arrangements, finances and contacts with other mental health professionals. When the patients, in turn, made repeated efforts to discuss the meaning of their experiences, the psychiatrists 'hesitated, responded with a question rather than with an answer, and smiled or laughed (when informal carers were present), indicating that they were reluctant to engage with patients' concerns about their psychotic symptoms'. The interviews were, for the most part, polite but discordant conversations, in which the participants failed to communicate effectively because they had different agendas. They were usually terminated when the psychiatrist felt that an agreement to continue taking medication had been secured.

Of course, this emphasis on drugs reflects the assumptions about mental illness made by Kraepelin and other psychiatrists at the end of the nineteenth century and carried forward into the present by the neo-Kraepelinians and their successors. If severe psychiatric disorders really are genetically determined diseases of the brain, it makes sense for services to focus their efforts on providing medical remedies for the underlying pathological processes. However, if this understanding of mental illness is flawed, the approach to treatment that follows from it will be flawed also.

PART TWO

THREE MYTHS ABOUT
MENTAL ILLNESS

5

People or Plants? The Myth that Psychiatric Diagnoses are Meaningful

> The wit of man has rarely been more exercised than in the attempt
> to classify the morbid mental phenomena covered by the term
> insanity. The result has been disappointing.
>
> Daniel Hack Tuke, writing in 1892

Andrew's letter, asking for my help, arrived on my desk out of the blue. Enclosed was a copy of a letter he had received from his psychiatrist, which read as follows:

Dear Mr ——

Further to our recent letter about your illness, I am writing to confirm that my colleague Dr —— shares my opinion about your diagnosis. On this basis, a revision of your diagnosis is not possible. You are, of course, at liberty to seek a private psychiatric opinion. For the record, your diagnosis is one of paranoid schizophrenic illness currently in remission, with PTSD related to a traumatic experience in childhood.

Yours sincerely,

Dr ——

A couple of weeks later, Andrew visited my office, accompanied by an elderly minder from the Royal British Legion (a voluntary organization that looks after the interests of veterans). Leaving his companion on a seat in the corridor outside, he entered and sat down, dropping a heavy file on my desk. He was, I guessed, in his early thirties, and was neatly dressed in a grey shirt with tie and a black corduroy jacket. Even before the introductions were over I could see that he was an angry man. He fidgeted constantly and words rushed out of his mouth as if he had been struggling to contain them.

With hardly a pause for breath, he explained how he had found me from a newspaper article I had once written about the problems of psychiatric diagnosis. He went on to say that I was perhaps the only person in the world who could help him and, on hearing this, I smiled nervously, knowing that his faith in my abilities was unlikely to be realistic. As if to emphasize this faith, and despite being repeatedly invited to use my first name, he insisted on calling me 'Professor'. Struggling to keep up as he told his story, I jotted a few notes on a writing pad, my efforts to slow him down all being futile. Eventually, after about half an hour, he seemed spent and stumbled to a halt.

'Well, Professor,' he said. 'Can you do something for me?'

Briefly summarized, his story was as follows. At the age of 15, he had been run over by a bus and had been badly injured. Following a long period in hospital, he had continued to experience troubling flashbacks of the accident and difficulty sleeping, and had been referred to a clinical psychologist. The psychologist had concluded that he had been suffering from post-traumatic stress disorder (PTSD, a diagnosis used to describe the psychological symptoms that typically occur after a traumatic event). As if fearing that I might not believe him, Andrew took the psychologist's report from his file and thrust it across the table towards me.

After struggling through his school examinations, Andrew had decided to join the British Army and, coming from an Irish family, had been advised to join the Royal Irish Regiment (which, according to its publicity, welcomes recruits from both the United Kingdom and the Irish Republic). This proved to be a spectacularly bad piece of advice because the regiment, based in Northern Ireland, a province that has been wracked by sectarian tensions for as long as anyone can remember, is mainly composed of Protestants. Andrew, who was a Catholic, had been badly bullied by his fellow soldiers.

After enduring this treatment for some months, he had eventually complained to the Royal Military Police (reaching into his file, he pulled out a thick pile of correspondence from the Army Special Investigation Branch). As a consequence, he had been withdrawn from his infantry duties and made to endure the humiliation of working as a waiter in the officers' mess. Eventually, it had been decided that he should be discharged from the army on psychiatric grounds and a subsequent legal tussle over his pension rights had led to the diagnostic dispute that was now the subject of our meeting.

According to Andrew, his pre-existing PTSD was exacerbated by the bullying he received, in which case he should be entitled to a substantial army pension, whereas, according to the psychiatric assessment commissioned by the army, Andrew's delusions of persecution warranted a diagnosis of paranoid schizophrenia, a problem that was probably genetic in origin and which certainly could not be attributed to what had happened to him while serving. Andrew's distress and anger at this injustice, compounded by legal negotiations with the army that had stretched over several years, had prompted his family doctor to refer him to a civilian psychiatrist, who had agreed with the army psychiatrist's opinion.

I asked Andrew how he would describe his difficulties, given his absolute conviction that he was not suffering from paranoid schizophrenia. Interestingly, he did not seem to doubt that he is suffering from *something*. 'Well,' he said, 'first I was nearly killed by the bus and that gave me PTSD. Then I was bullied in the army, and that turned my PTSD into a persecution mania.'

'That seems like a pretty good theory to me,' I found myself replying.

The personal and political significance of psychiatric diagnoses

In the last chapter, we saw that modern biological psychiatrists assume that psychiatric disorders can be classified into a discrete number of diseases analogous to those encountered in physical medicine; in the words of Klerman's neo-Kraepelinian manifesto, 'there is a boundary between the normal and the sick' and 'there is not one, but many mental illnesses'.[1] Andrew's anxiety about his diagnosis reminds us that this assumption may have important consequences for both clinicians and patients. For the clinician, classifying the patient's experiences under a diagnosis may seem to be an important first step, required in order to make sense of the patient's difficulties, to predict how the illness will develop in the future and to determine which treatment is most likely to be effective. For the patient, on the other hand, being diagnosed will often evoke some kind of emotional response, especially if the diagnosis seems to be a prophecy of doom or carries some kind of stigma.

Other implications of the way psychiatric disorders are classified extend well beyond the clinic. Researchers use diagnoses to select and define the patients they are studying. In a typical experiment, a group of patients with the diagnosis of interest, say schizophrenia, is compared with healthy individuals and possibly (in order to control for non-specific factors such as the experience of disability or hospitalization) with a group of patients who have been diagnosed with some other kind of disorder, say depression. This strategy cannot hope to yield meaningful information unless the patients with the diagnosis of interest have something in common that distinguishes them from those in the control conditions.

Governments use diagnoses to compile information about the health needs of populations, and to plan the delivery of medical services. (Countries within the European Union use the tenth edition of the World Health Organization's *International Statistical Classification of Diseases and Related Health Problems*[2] for these purposes.) Diagnoses are also used by regulators, for example, the United States Food and Drugs Administration (FDA), who require pharmaceutical companies to specify the conditions which their products can be used to treat. By extending the licence of a medication to a new diagnosis, companies can sometimes, at a stroke, generate vast increases in their profits. When GlaxoSmithKline persuaded the FDA to recognize the antidepressant paroxetine (Paxil or Seroxat) as a treatment for social phobia, for example, the price of stocks in the company soared overnight.[3]

Because of these enormous implications, it is important that any widely used system of psychiatric classification provides a realistic and meaningful framework for understanding the problems that patients bring to the clinic. If they do not, their utility in determining treatment must be suspect, research that makes use of them is undermined, and the decisions made by health ministers and drug licensing authorities are exposed as arbitrary. This question of *diagnostic validity*, then, lies at the heart of modern psychiatric theory and impacts, directly and indirectly, on the well-being of patients and society.

How psychiatric diagnoses were invented

Although modern clinicians tend to use terms such as 'schizophrenia' and 'bipolar disorder' as if they refer to naturally occurring categories, in much the same way that biologists distinguish between mammals and fish, the diagnostic concepts now used to describe psychiatric patients were invented, not discovered. As we saw in Part One of this book, they date back to the efforts of nineteenth-century German psychiatrists who, quite reasonably, presumed that scientific progress in their field would not be possible unless the bewildering symptoms they observed in their clinics could be properly described. Foremost among those who attempted to solve this problem was Emil Kraepelin, who first proposed the distinction between dementia praecox and manic depression.

Kraepelin is now revered, almost as the Darwin of his field. But although his approach to describing and understanding psychiatric disorders has become widely accepted by psychiatrists in the English-speaking world, his diagnostic concepts have not survived without revision. The first important amendment to his system was introduced in 1911 when Eugen Bleuler,[4] a Swiss psychiatrist, objected to the term 'dementia praecox', believing that the condition was neither a dementia (intellectual deterioration was not inevitable) nor praecox (it was possible to develop the condition in middle age or later life). An empathetic and workaholic clinician, Bleuler spent many hours getting to know his patients, and struggled to understand their inner life. He suggested the alternative name *schizophrenia* for the disorder, by which he meant, not a split personality, but a condition in which the various mental functions had become disconnected from each other, resulting in subtle disruptions of emotion and cognition. According to Bleuler, the hallucinations and delusions experienced by schizophrenia patients were not primary but accessory symptoms which developed as a consequence of these underlying difficulties. In formulating this account, he credited not only Kraepelin, but also Freud for enlarging the range of concepts available to psychiatric researchers.

The translation of this account into the modern concept of schizophrenia was largely brought about by Kurt Schneider,[5] one of Kraepelin's successors at Heidelberg. In the 1950s Schneider suggested that a number of *first rank symptoms* could be used to identify the disorder. These were all forms of hallucinations (e.g. hearing voices arguing) or delusions (e.g. passivity delusions, in which the patient believes that feelings, impulses or actions are caused by other people) and were chosen because they were easy to spot during a clinical interview. Although it was never Schneider's intention to dispute Kraepelin's view that intellectual deterioration was the central feature of disorder, his approach to diagnosing the condition became so influential that modern textbooks and diagnostic manuals all define schizophrenia in terms of what we now call positive symptoms.

The concept of *manic depression* went through a similar series of transformations. The most important revision of Kraepelin's account of this condition occurred when, just after the Second World War, the German psychiatrist Klaus Leonhard[6] argued that it is important to distinguish between mood disorders characterized by recurrent depressive episodes, and those in which patients also experience episodes of mania (periods of intense euphoria, excitement and irritability, often accompanied by delusions and hallucinations). In modern systems of psychiatric classification, the term *unipolar depression* is often used to describe the first type of illness, whereas the term *bipolar disorder* is used to describe the second. Bipolar disorder is often further subdivided into bipolar 1 disorder (in which the patient experiences periods of depression and periods of mania) and bipolar 2 disorder (in which the patient experiences depression and hypomania, but never full-blown mania).

These developments were paralleled by an increasingly refined approach to describing the less severe psychiatric disorders, *the neuroses*, which were subdivided into the anxiety disorders (specific phobias, generalized anxiety disorder, obsessive compulsive disorder) and minor (non-psychotic) depression. Hence, by the second half of the twentieth century a consensus had begun to emerge amongst psychiatrists in Europe and North America about the best way to describe the problems experienced by their patients. However, as many psychiatrists were beginning to realize, achieving agreement about the conceptual framework around which a scientific approach to psychiatry could be built was not the same thing as ensuring that these concepts were always used consistently.

The mass production of psychiatric diagnoses

A profound difference between psychiatry and other branches of medicine concerns the way in which diagnoses are made. In most medical specialities, doctors make extensive use of physical investigations (for example, biochemical tests or X-ray images of hidden regions of the body) when deciding what their patients are suffering from. However, objective measures of this kind are simply not available to mental health professionals. Even formal psychological tests have proved to be of little utility in aiding the diagnostic process. Instead, clinicians must base their judgements on accounts of the patient's behaviour and experiences, either offered by the patient during a clinical interview or by informants such as friends and relatives. One problem this creates is the increased opportunity for subjectivity and confusion. Mindful of this problem, researchers have responded by developing increasingly rigorous definitions of different diagnoses, and also detailed guidance about how clinicians should interrogate their patients.

The earliest attempts to write down precise criteria for different diagnoses were made in the first decades of the twentieth century, and further attempts were made sporadically over the following fifty years. Whereas the development of the diagnostic concepts during the nineteenth century had been largely a German enterprise, much of this work was carried out in the English-speaking world, especially in America. A watershed in this process was reached in 1980, when the American Psychiatric Association published the third edition of their *Diagnostic and Statistical Manual (DSM-III)*.[7] The psychiatrists who introduced this manual were our old friends the neo-Kraepelinians. The man who chaired the *DSM-III* task force, and who took on the formidable task of coordinating the large number of committees which were convened to draw up criteria for the different disorders, was Robert Spitzer. He and the other neo-Kraepelinians had two main motives for designing and introducing the manual, one honourable and the other perhaps less so.

On the honourable side, the neo-Kraepelinians were concerned about the inconsistent ways in which psychiatric diagnoses were employed. In the terminology of psychometrics (the science of the measurement of human behaviour), a diagnosis can be said to be reliable if different clinicians, working independently, can agree about who should receive it. However, studies available at the time showed that psychiatrists often disagreed about which patients merited which diagnoses,[8] so that whether a patient was described as schizophrenic or manic depressive would often depend on which doctor happened to be attending a clinic on a particular day. A related problem was the discovery, in a series of landmark studies carried out in the 1970s, that psychiatrists in the United States and Russia were approximately twice as likely to diagnose their patients as schizophrenic than their colleagues in Britain and elsewhere in Europe.[9] Clearly, scientific progress in psychiatry was not going to be possible if the schizophrenia patients studied in one part of the world were different from the schizophrenia patients studied in other countries. The neo-Kraepelinians' less honourable motive concerned the perceived status of the psychiatric profession.[10] As described in the last chapter, in the United States and elsewhere in the 1970s psychiatry was held in low esteem compared to the other medical specialities, and was under threat from clinical psychologists and the antipsychiatrists. The creation of a universal standard for medical-style psychiatric diagnoses was likely to solve both of these problems at a stroke, enabling psychiatric research to flourish while at the same time reasserting the dominant role of medicine in the care of the mentally ill.

When creating *DSM-III*, the neo-Kraepelinians sought to minimize the possibilities for disagreement between clinicians by devising detailed checklists (arrived at by consensus in the various task force committees, rather than on the basis of research) of the conditions (mainly symptoms) that must be met for each diagnosis. The resulting manual therefore had a Chinese-menu-like appearance. In field trials conducted with draft definitions, groups of clinicians attempted to use the proposed criteria and then checked the extent to which they agreed. Disputes about some diagnoses, notably post-traumatic stress disorder (included after Vietnam veterans, who wanted to have their sufferings acknowledged, lobbied the American Psychiatric Association) and homosexuality (excluded following lobbying by gay rights organizations, but only after lengthy arguments about whether same-sex sexual interest is an illness) were more political than scientific. However, at the end of the day, Spitzer declared that the reliability problem had at last been solved.[11]

Whether or not this was indeed the case would, of course, depend not only on the availability of precise diagnostic rules, but also on whether psychiatrists were consistent in the way they questioned their patients. In parallel to the development of *DSM-III*, therefore, efforts were made to develop *structured interview schedules*, which included lists of questions that should be asked during diagnostic interviews. Spitzer and his colleagues published their Structured Clinical Interview for *DSM-III-R* (SCID) in 1992.[12] It was preceded by the widely used Positive and Negative Syndromes Scale[13] (often employed in drug trials because it enables clinicians and researchers to rate not only the presence of positive and negative symptoms but also their severity) and followed by the Schedules for Clinical Assessment in Neuro-psychiatry[14] (a broad-ranging diagnostic interview developed by the World Health Organization). To many people working in the field of mental health, these advances appeared to put psychiatry on a rational footing, and offered the hope that there would at last be genuine progress in understanding the causes of mental illness.

Spurious precision

The designers of *DSM-III* were aware that clinicians might occasionally agree with each other by chance, rather than as a consequence of the principled application of their diagnostic criteria. Even before the development of the manual, researchers studying the reliability of psychiatric diagnoses realized that simple measures of agreement between clinicians could be misleading for this reason. Imagine, for example, that two psychiatrists each randomly assign (perhaps by tossing coins) two diagnoses – say schizophrenia and bipolar disorder – to a group of 100 patients. Under these circumstances they would accidentally agree in about fifty cases. However, if they instead included a third diagnosis their level of chance agreement would drop to about a third. To allow for this problem, Spitzer[15] introduced a statistic, *kappa*, which measures agreement above chance level. A kappa value of 0 indicates agreement at chance, and a value of 1 indicates perfect agreement. It became accepted that a kappa value of 0.7 was adequate for most purposes and studies prior to *DSM-III* rarely obtained values that approached this level.

Despite the claims by Spitzer and others that *DSM-III* had solved the reliability problem, the data from the published field trials revealed that this magic threshold was rarely obtained.[16] Moreover, these trials were often unrealistic because the clinicians taking part in them usually received special training in the *DSM* system. They were also allowed much longer to interview patients than would be common in ordinary psychiatric practice, often using the specially designed structured interview schedules which, even today, are rarely employed except in research projects. That these schedules introduced a level of spurious precision was demonstrated in an Australian study, in which four different interview schedules were employed to give *DSM* diagnoses to a group of fifty patients; when any two methods were compared kappa values varied between 0.53 and 0.67 and perfect agreement between the methods was achieved for only just over half the patients.[17]

A further complication is that *DSM-III* is not the only diagnostic manual. When designing it, Spitzer and his colleagues took as a model a set of Research Diagnostic Criteria (RDC), which had been previously developed and informally circulated for the purposes of comparing patients in different research centres. *DSM-III* has received one major revision and two less substantial revisions, resulting in *DSM-III-R* (revised *DSM-III*), *DSM-IV*, and *DSM-IV-TR* (*DSM-IV* with text revision) manuals,[18] and planning is well under way for *DSM-V*. The World Health Organization's *International Classification of Diseases*, currently in its tenth edition (*ICD-10*),[19] uses detailed checklists like the *DSM*s, but differs from them in detail. Add to the mix various less widely used diagnostic systems, and it is

DSM-III definitions of schizophrenia

SCHIZOPHRENIA

A   At least one of the following during a phase of the illness:

1. bizarre delusions (content is patently absurd and has *no* possible basis in fact), such as delusions of being controlled, thought broadcasting, thought insertion, or thought withdrawal.
2. somatic, grandiose, religious, nihilistic or other delusions without persecutory or jealous content
3. delusions with persecutory or jealous content, if accompanied by hallucinations of any type
4. auditory hallucinations in which either a voice keeps a running commentary on the individual's behaviour or thoughts, or two or more voices converse with each other
5. auditory hallucinations on several occasions with content of more than one or two words, having no apparent relation to depression or elation
6. incoherence, marked loosening of associations, markedly illogical thinking, or marked poverty of content of speech if associated with at least one of the following:
   (a) blunted, flat, or inappropriate affect
   (b) delusions or hallucinations
   (c) catatonic or other grossly disorganized behaviour.

B. Deterioration from a previous level of functioning in such areas as work, social relations and self-care.

C. Duration: Continuous signs of the illness for at least six months at some time during the person's life, with some signs of the illness at present. The six-month period must include an active phase during which there were symptoms from B, with or without a prodromal or residual phase.

easy to agree with British psychiatrist Ian Brockington who, when discussing contemporary approaches to diagnosing schizophrenia, complained that confusion about the diagnosis had been replaced by 'a babble of precise but different formulations of the same concept'.[20]

Brockington's own research in the 1980s starkly demonstrated this problem. Examining the symptoms of a group of patients at the Netherne Hospital in London, he found that the number suffering from schizophrenia ranged from 163 (using pre-*DSM-III* American criteria) to 19 (*DSM-III*), depending on the definition of schizophrenia employed.[21] In a more recent study of more than 700 British patients diagnosed using the RDC, *DSM-III-R* and *ICD-10* systems, the number of schizophrenia patients varied between 268 and 387, and the number of patients with bipolar disorder ranged between 6 and 66.[22] If we accept Gerald Klerman's assertion that an accurate diagnosis is a prerequisite for deciding on effective treatment, the alarming implication of this level of disagreement is that treatments are often being decided arbitrarily.

Multiplying diagnoses

Poor reliability is not the only problem affecting modern diagnostic systems. The assumption that there are discrete types of mental illness implies that patients should rarely meet the criteria for more than one diagnosis. For example, if, as most epidemiologists suppose, approximately 1 per cent of the population has schizophrenia,[23] a similar proportion has bipolar disorder,[24] and the two conditions are unrelated, only an unfortunate one in ten thousand (1 per cent of 1 per cent) should be afflicted by both diseases. However, soon after Kraepelin first made the distinction between dementia praecox and manic depression, it became apparent that many patients, perhaps the majority of those suffering from psychosis, experienced symptoms of both conditions. Following a suggestion first made by the American psychiatrist Jacob Kasanin in 1933,[25] these patients are now usually described as suffering from *schizoaffective disorder*, which is listed as a separate illness in both the *DSM* and *ICD*.

Research involving the statistical analysis of symptom data has shown that these patients fall midway along a continuum that runs from 'pure' schizophrenia to 'pure' bipolar disorder,[26] suggesting that there are no clear boundaries between these conditions. However, an illusion that they are separate is reinforced by arbitrary exclusion rules contained in the *DSM* system that prevent a patient from being assigned one diagnosis if they already meet the criteria for another. For example, *DSM-IV* states that patients may not be diagnosed as suffering from schizophrenia if they also meet the criteria for schizoaffective disorder, major depression or mania.

The US Epidemiological Catchment Area (ECA) study, conducted in the late 1980s, was one of the first large-scale population studies of psychiatric disorders. The researchers carrying out the study approached approximately 18,000 randomly selected urban-living American citizens and asked them to agree to a psychiatric interview.[27] A major finding from the study was that all psychiatric symptoms, including those of psychosis, are much more common than might be thought from considering people who are actually receiving psychiatric treatment; it seems that only a proportion of those who meet the criteria for any diagnosis come to the attention of psychiatric services.

In order to investigate the extent to which people met the criteria for more than one diagnosis – a phenomenon known in psychiatric jargon as *comorbidity* – the ECA research team decided to suspend the *DSM* exclusion rules. When they did this, they found that, on average, the odds that any two diagnoses would occur together was twice what would be expected by chance. Someone who met the criteria for schizophrenia had a forty-six-times greater than chance probability of also meeting the criteria for mania and a fourteen-times greater than chance probability of also meeting the criteria for depression. Amazingly, the ECA researchers concluded that, 'The most likely explanation for co-occurrence is that having one disorder puts the affected person at risk of developing other disorders', thereby showing how difficult it was for them to think outside the box provided by their psychiatric training; surely the real reason why patients meet the criteria for more than one diagnosis is that the diagnoses do not pick out discrete diseases after all.

Comorbidity is not a problem unique to the psychoses. In the case of the less severe neurotic disorders it is also very common for patients to meet the criteria for more than one diagnosis.[28] Indeed, studies of both population samples and patients receiving psychiatric treatment show that anxiety and depression, the two main types of non-psychotic disorders, almost always occur together.

Correlations between symptoms

One of the principal methods used by Kraepelin to classify psychiatric disorders was to observe the extent to which different symptoms occurred together. He assumed that commonly co-occurring symptoms would be caused by a common underlying pathology of the brain and would, in turn, prove to have a common aetiology. Although Kraepelin kept detailed records of his patients' symptoms in the hope of verifying his diagnostic intuitions, formal mathematical methods for analysing this evidence were not available at the time he was working.

In the 1920s psychologists in the United States, for example Charles Spearman, began to develop statistical methods for investigating groups of correlations, in particular a set of methods that are collectively known as *factor analysis*. These techniques (which, before the age of the digital computer, would typically require many weeks of calculation by a team of clerks, simply to carry out a single analysis) were initially used to analyse the results of questionnaires and IQ tests. (It was in this way that Spearman convinced himself that a single ability, known as 'g' or general intelligence, was responsible for human performance on a wide range of intellectual tests.) Shortly afterwards a psychologist called Thomas Moore first used the method to analyse the symptoms of psychiatric patients.[29] According to Kraepelin's theory, factor-analysing the symptoms of patients diagnosed as suffering from schizophrenia should yield a single factor, indicating that all the symptoms tend to occur together. In fact, Moore found eight factors. One corresponded to hallucinations and delusions, suggesting that these positive symptoms typically co-occur. However, there were two types of depression, two types of mania, and separate factors of disinhibited behaviour, catatonic behaviour and cognitive dysfunction.

After a long period of neglect this method of looking at symptom data became popular again in the late 1980s, by which time computers had rendered the necessary calculations painless. An early and highly influential paper of this period, published by the British psychiatrist Peter Liddle,[30] reported three distinct clusters of schizophrenia symptoms – positive symptoms (replicating Thomas Moore's first factor), negative symptoms and symptoms of cognitive disorganization. One possible interpretation of this finding is that the psychiatric phenomena subsumed within the diagnosis of schizophrenia correspond to three relatively independent types of abnormality, perhaps with different causes. Perhaps we need three theories of schizophrenia, not just one.

The flurry of further studies that were conducted following this landmark publication either reported similar three-factor solutions, or more complex solutions in which one or more of Liddle's factors were subdivided into different groups.[31] Some studies even reported similar findings when bipolar patients were considered alone, or when all psychotic patients were included together.[32] No study has *ever* yielded a single schizophrenia factor consistent with Kraepelin's original description of the disorder and, when both psychotic and mood symptoms are included in the analyses, perhaps the most convincing models include five factors: positive symptoms, negative symptoms, symptoms of cognitive disorganization, negative mood and mania.[33] That these findings have not impacted on clinical practice illustrates the difficulty of supplanting clinical tradition and medical folklore with research-based knowledge. (Although some researchers are arguing that a dimensional classification system should be included in the next revision of the *DSM*, I have never seen this type of assessment attempted in a clinic.)

The predictive validity of psychiatric diagnoses

These debates about correlations between symptoms would perhaps seem academic if they did not have a direct impact on the way that psychiatry is practised in the clinic. From both the patient's and the clinician's perspective, the main purpose of a diagnosis is to predict the patient's prospects and the likely effects of treatment. According to Kraepelin's account of the distinction between dementia praecox and manic depression, recovery is all but impossible with the former diagnosis but quite common with the latter. I have occasionally witnessed well-meaning psychiatrists who are convinced by this idea telling patients diagnosed with schizophrenia that they will never get better, in the mistaken belief that it is best to discourage them from having unrealistic expectations. Not surprisingly, the patients hearing this news often feel crushed.

At first sight, research into the long-term outcome of psychiatric disorders seems to provide some support for this approach, as patients with a diagnosis of bipolar disorder, *on average*, do better than those who are diagnosed as suffering from schizophrenia.[34] However, patients in both groups have a wide variety of outcomes, varying from complete recovery to lifelong illness.[35] In the case of schizophrenia, as a rough rule of thumb, about one-third of patients in the industrialized nations completely recover, about one-third remain ill and about one-third have intermediate outcomes, often living quite well for most of their lives but occasionally experiencing episodes of illness. When I am asked by patients about their prospects, my own strategy is to explain these findings. After all, unless there are very compelling reasons to do otherwise, when talking to patients a clinician's default option should always be the truth.

As we saw at the beginning of this book, the proportion of patients having a good outcome is greater in the developing world than in the rich, developed nations.[36] This difference may reflect the different kinds of stress experienced by patients in industrialized and non-industrialized economies. A further complication is that most long-term studies of psychiatric disorders have suffered from what the British psychiatrist Tim Crow[37] has described as the fallacy of the excluded middle – the tendency to examine only those patients who clearly meet the criteria for either schizophrenia or bipolar disorder while ignoring the larger number of schizoaffective patients suffering from both types of symptoms. When these patients are included, it appears that they have average outcomes that are worse than those of patients with 'pure' bipolar disorder but better than those with 'pure' schizophrenia.[38] Hence, instead of two different groups, one with typically poor outcomes and the other with typically good outcomes, there appears to be a schizoaffective continuum, with average outcomes looking worse towards the schizophrenia end, but with enormous variability at any point along the way.

The ability of diagnoses to predict response to treatment is even less impressive. Following the discovery of chlorpromazine, it became widely accepted that antipsychotic drugs are effective treatments for schizophrenia, even though the first clinical trial of this kind of medication demonstrated its effectiveness in patients suffering from mania. The later introduced mood-stabilizing drugs, notably lithium carbonate, are regarded as effective in the treatment of bipolar disorder. However, in the only published experiment in which psychotic patients were randomly given an antipsychotic medication, lithium carbonate, both or neither, diagnosis did not predict treatment response although symptoms did; hallucinations or delusions, whatever the diagnosis of the patient, tended to improve when patients took the antipsychotic drug, whereas mood problems, again irrespective of diagnosis, tended to improve in the patients taking the mood stabilizer.[39]

Today it is widely recognized that antipsychotic drugs are useful in the treatment not only of patients diagnosed as suffering from schizophrenia, but also patients diagnosed as suffering from bipolar disorder. Not surprisingly, this has led some investigators to wonder belatedly whether common biochemical processes underlie these different diagnoses.[40] Ironically, this development suggests that the continuing disagreements about definitions of schizophrenia and bipolar disorder may not be so disastrous after all; if the same drugs work for everyone the diagnosis given to the patient has virtually no implications at all.

The boundary between the 'normal' and the 'sick'

The evidence we have considered so far suggests that it is not possible to divide people with severe psychiatric symptoms into discrete groups as required by the *DSM* and other modern diagnostic systems. However, as we have also seen, these systems assume not only that boundaries can be drawn between different disorders, but also that a clear boundary exists between mental health and mental illness. In the last twenty years evidence that calls this assumption into question has provided a final reason for rejecting the conventional approach to psychiatric classification.

Some of the most challenging research that addresses this issue has been carried out by Marius Romme, a Dutch psychiatrist, who in the late 1980s was working at the department of psychiatry at the University of Maastricht. Romme was asked to help a 38-year-old woman who was suffering from severe auditory hallucinations, and whose voices gave her orders, forbade her from doing things and generally dominated her life.[41] Although antipsychotic drugs reduced her anxiety, they did not affect the frequency of her voices and, in any case, she often avoided taking the medication because she found its sedative effect intolerable. After several years of treatment the woman began to talk of suicide, and Romme feared that she was about to take 'a road with no turning point'.

Unexpectedly, the woman suddenly became much happier and more optimistic. This change happened after she had read an unusual and controversial book, *The Origins of Consciousness in the Breakdown of Bicameral Mind*, written by a reclusive American psychologist called Julian Jaynes.[42] The book presents the startling thesis, based on an analysis of the language of the *Iliad*, that the ancient Greeks were not conscious in the same way that modern humans are. According to Jaynes, because the ancient Greeks had no sense of 'I' with which to locate their mental processes, their inner thoughts were perceived as coming from the gods, which is why the characters in the *Iliad* find themselves in frequent communication with supernatural entities. Jaynes's theory (which is not taken seriously by modern classicists) therefore implies that hearing voices was once a normal experience. On discovering this theory, Romme's patient decided that she was probably an ancient Greek rather than a schizophrenic, and this belief made her much less frightened of her voices.

Thinking that his patient might be able to communicate effectively with other people hearing voices, Romme persuaded her to appear on a popular television programme. After the broadcast, he was contacted by about 450 voice-hearers. To his astonishment, about a third of these people did not seem to be troubled by their experiences, and many had avoided contact with psychiatric services altogether. When Romme compared 'healthy' hallucinators with psychiatric patients, the main differences seemed to be that the non-patients believed themselves to be stronger than their voices, whereas the patients believed that their voices were omnipotent and threatening.[43] These findings are in agreement with other studies, which have shown that it is not hallucinations per se that usually cause distress, but voice-hearers' negative interpretations of their experiences.[44]

Romme and his partner, Sondra Escher, have formed Resonance, a society which runs frequent conferences and workshops designed to help people with hallucinations accept and tolerate their voices. They have worked tirelessly to disseminate their approach throughout Europe,* and have inspired people who hear voices to form self-help groups in many countries. For example, the Hearing Voices Network in Britain[45] aims to give people who hear voices the opportunity to discuss them freely, and to help them learn and grow from their experiences in whatever way seems most helpful. (In practice, this often involves finding ways of coping while avoiding conventional psychiatric treatment.)

Romme's discovery that many people have psychotic symptoms without requiring treatment has been supported by later evidence from large-scale population surveys. For example, in the Epidemiological Catchment Area study, the proportion of the US population with a lifetime history of hallucinations was estimated to be between 11 and 13 per cent.[46] In a similar study of more than 7,000 randomly selected Dutch citizens, researchers at the University of Maastricht found that 1.7 per cent had experienced 'true' hallucinations but that a further 6.2 per cent had experienced hallucinations that were judged not to be of clinical significance because they were not causing distress.[47] The same study reported that 3.3 per cent of the population had 'true' delusions but a further 8.7 per cent had delusions that were clinically irrelevant because they were not distressing. In a series of epidemiological studies conducted by psychiatrist Jules Angst at the University of Zurich, it was estimated that hypomanic episodes were experienced

* Discussing this work, Romme once memorably told me that voice-hearers were like 'homosexuals in the 1950s, in need of liberation, not cure'.

by about 5 per cent of the population and that more than 10 per cent experience less severe 'subdiagnostic' hypomanic symptoms.[48]

The results from these and other studies[49] suggest that there is no clear dividing line between severe mental illness and normal functioning. Rather, there seems to be a continuum running from ordinary personality traits, through eccentricity, to full-blown psychosis. Interestingly, people who show psychotic traits without being disabled are often highly creative, sometimes reaching high levels of achievement in the sciences and especially the arts.[50]

One further insight that can be extracted from the epidemiological data forms an addendum to our earlier examination of the way that symptoms correlate with each other. In 1946 a statistician called Joseph Berkson pointed out that, if different symptoms independently provoked people into seeking help, the apparent correlations observed between symptoms in patients receiving treatment will be inflated compared to the true correlations observed in the population at large.[51] This phenomenon is now known as the Berkson selection bias, and works as follows.

Imagine, for example, that a symptom X causes enough distress to drive a proportion of sufferers to seek treatment, and that another symptom, Y, has a similar effect. Individuals who, perhaps by chance, experience both symptoms will be especially distressed and hence will be more likely to seek treatment than individuals suffering from either symptom on its own. The clinician, watching patients arrive at the clinic under these circumstances, will notice that the combination of symptoms X and Y appears to be quite common, and may falsely conclude that they are related.

The effect of the bias can be investigated by comparing the co-occurrence of symptoms in patients attending hospital and in the population at large, and this has been done by the researchers at the University of Maastricht, using data from their survey of Dutch citizens. In one study, it was found that the positive and negative schizophrenia symptoms occurred together much less often in the general population than in individuals who were receiving psychiatric treatment.[52] In a second study, they found that the same was true of mania and depression.[53] This last finding is consistent with other studies which suggest that mania can sometimes occur in the absence of a history of depression[54] so that the two types of extreme mood are not as closely related as has often been assumed.

Are schizophrenia and bipolar disorder scientific delusions?

All this inevitably provokes the question: are schizophrenia and bipolar disorder real conditions or are they (to borrow a metaphor suggested by the British psychologist Mary Boyle[55]) scientific delusions? Of course, by asking this question I am not casting doubt on the fact that people are often distressed by symptoms such as voices or bizarre beliefs, or that those experiencing these problems need help. What is at issue is how these experiences should be described and classified.

I first argued against the usefulness of the schizophrenia concept almost exactly twenty years ago (a confession that makes me feel rather old).[56] Since that time, and certainly not entirely as a consequence of my own efforts, it has become increasingly common for psychiatrists and psychologists to question the validity and utility of the diagnosis. Recently, calls for it to be abandoned became so vociferous that, as I was writing the final draft of this chapter, the editors of the *British Medical Journal* decided to publish an editorial defending it.[57] It was perhaps inevitable that the authors of the editorial were American: Jeffrey Lieberman, a psychiatrist who is well known for his research on psychiatric drugs, and his colleague Michael First, who was the author of the SCID-IV, the structured clinical interview schedule, designed to enable psychiatrists to make *DSM* diagnoses.[58]

In their editorial, Lieberman and First claim that 'Many studies have shown that these diagnostic criteria [for schizophrenia] can be applied reliably and accurately', but, as we have seen, this is not the case. They go on to argue that a diagnosis of schizophrenia is useful in guiding treatment but this claim also seems empty in the light of the evidence we have just considered. Finally, they argue that 'Schizophrenia is not caused by disturbed psychological development or bad parenting', and that 'abnormalities in brain structure and function seen in neuroimaging and electrophysiological tests', together with indisputable 'evidence that vulnerability to schizophrenia is at least partly genetic', establish the reality of the illness as a biological disorder. These last claims are challenged in the next two chapters; suffice it to say for the present that neither the genetic nor the neuroscience evidence, when examined carefully, supports the concept of schizophrenia as it is usually understood.

It is less common to hear arguments raised against the concept of bipolar disorder, perhaps because the diagnosis is often viewed as less stigmatizing than schizophrenia, and hence less problematic for patients. However, we have seen that a substantial number of patients seem to have a mixture of bipolar and schizophrenia symptoms, raising as many questions about the boundaries of the former diagnosis as the latter. To confuse matters further, recent studies have questioned the distinction between bipolar disorder and unipolar depression. For example, it has been suggested that a substantial proportion of agitated unipolar patients experience brief episodes of hypomania.[59] In the grip of the idea that patients must be assigned to categories, some psychiatrists have tried to accommodate these findings by arguing for an increasing fractionation of the bipolar spectrum into bipolar 3 disorder, bipolar 4 disorder and so on, for example to encompass people with mild hypomanic episodes which do not meet the current criteria for either bipolar 1 or bipolar 2 disorder.[60] This looks like an increasingly desperate strategy to preserve categories in the face of evidence that they simply do not work. My own view is that most psychiatric diagnoses are about as scientifically meaningful as star signs, a diagnostic system which is similarly employed to describe people and predict what will happen to them, and which enjoys a wide following despite compelling evidence that it is useless.

American psychiatrists have not always been as wedded to their diagnostic concepts as they are today. During the middle years of the twentieth century many briefly abandoned their preoccupation with labelling patients, and instead tried to treat each patient as an individual. The most prominent exponent of this approach was Adolf Meyer, who famously remarked, 'We should not classify people as plants.'[61] This was perhaps a mocking reference to Kraepelin, who had drawn inspiration from the work of his older brother Karl, a distinguished botanist well known for his research on the classification of plant species.

Andrew

From the point of view of patients, the limitations of current approaches to psychiatric classification become all too obvious when they find themselves confused by multiple diagnoses given by different doctors, or when they find that their complex difficulties are being explained away with a single, stigmatizing label.

Shortly after Andrew visited me, his grandmother died. At her funeral, he became very upset. Fearing that he might be suffering a relapse one of his brothers (with whom he had a very bad relationship) decided to alert his doctor, who in turn called out the psychiatric team. Knowing that he was prone to anger, the social worker and community psychiatric nurse chose to turn up at Andrew's home accompanied by six policemen. Andrew was told that he had no option but to accompany the policemen to a local psychiatric ward, where he would be subjected to a psychiatric examination.

Many ordinary people confronted in this way would be furious. However, to Andrew's credit, he realized that any attempt to resist the policemen would only lead to more trouble. A few days later, just before the Christmas holiday, I went to visit him on the bleak psychiatric ward where he had been detained against his will. He was sitting quietly, wearing a suit, and reading a novel. (I later learned from the clinical notes that the fact he was well dressed was seen as evidence that he was 'grandiose'.) Although affronted by what had happened to him, he seemed completely rational. The junior doctor who was on duty could not give me a credible explanation why he had been sectioned, but explained that he would remain under observation in the hospital over the Christmas period.

As I left the ward, I asked one of the psychiatric nurses how Andrew had settled in, hoping to glean some evidence – any evidence – of the kind of psychotic and irrational behaviour that might justify what was being done to him.

'He's excessively polite,' the nurse explained darkly.

I raised an eyebrow. 'Can you be excessively polite?' I asked.

She sensed that this might be a trick question. 'Who exactly are you?' she enquired and I explained that I was Andrew's clinical psychologist.

'Well,' she said, 'we're trying to work out whether his politeness is part of his normal personality or his illness.'

David Rosenhan is now retired and disabled, after suffering a series of strokes. I like to think that, should he ever get the opportunity to read this story, it will elicit from him a wry smile.

6

The Fundamental Error of Psychiatry: The Myth that Psychiatric Disorders are Genetic Diseases

> Some day a child is going to sue its parents for being born. They will say, My life is so awful with these terrible genetic defects.
>
> James D. Watson[1]

The letter from Hannah's psychiatrist said that she had been suffering from auditory hallucinations for more than a decade. As her voices had not been touched by medication, he wondered whether she might benefit from psychotherapy.

Patients arriving for their first appointment with a clinical psychologist are often nervous and hesitant, not knowing what to expect from a stranger with whom they will shortly be sharing their most troubling experiences. Those with long-standing psychotic problems are often poorly dressed, a consequence of their impoverished circumstances, or unkempt, having long ago given up the struggle to maintain their appearance. Some who have had lengthy and difficult entanglements with psychiatric services are sullen and defensive. It was therefore with a sense of mild surprise that I found myself greeting a large, colourfully dressed black woman in her mid-fifties, who smelt of expensive perfume, and who rewarded me with an enormous smile as I shook her hand and introduced myself.

Leading her to the interview room, I offered her a seat and waited for her to make herself comfortable. I then began to explain the purpose of our meeting in my usual way, pointing out that I was not a medical doctor, and that I worked most of the time in the University but spent one day every week in the clinic.

'I often find that it is better if we just put your psychiatrist's letter to one side,' I went on, waving aside the referral letter for emphasis, 'and if you just tell me what's been troubling you in your own words. That way, we get to focus on the problems that are most important for you.'

'Well, I don't really know,' Hannah said, as if surprised to be asked the question.

'What is that upsets you most?'

'Nothing really.'

'So there's nothing troubling you? No particular problem you'd like my help with.'

'Not really. No.'

I was only a few minutes into the first session, and already feeling stuck. 'Well, I'm guessing that there must be some reason why your doctor has asked me to see you.'

She smiled sweetly, as if finding this idea mildly entertaining.

'Did Dr Brown tell you what he thinks you're suffering from?' I asked, departing from my usual script in the hope of eliciting some useful information.

'Oh yes,' she replied, beaming even more broadly. 'Schizophrenia!' She spoke 'the S word', the subject of such dread to so many patients and their relatives, as if she was referring to an eccentricity that made her more colourful and interesting than most other people.

'And why do you think he says you're suffering from schizophrenia?'

'Because I hear a voice,' she answered. 'It's the voice of Mr Pinkerton.'

'And this voice? Do you hear it when Mr Pinkerton isn't there?'

'I hear it all the time. Or at least nearly all the time.'

'Maybe that's why your doctor has asked me to see you. I think he hopes that I might be able to help you get rid of this voice.'

Hannah looked visibly shaken by this suggestion.

'Would you like to get rid of it?' I asked.

'Oh goodness, no,' she protested. 'Mr Pinkerton loves me. I wouldn't want to be without Mr Pinkerton.'

'And do you know who Mr Pinkerton is?' I asked.

'Oh yes,' she said. 'He's my psychologist.'

When faced with a person who has a diagnosis of schizophrenia or something similar, but who is not troubled by their experiences and does not want help, the obvious thing to do is to wish the person well and call the interview to a close. After all, there are always other patients on the waiting list and, in any case, the work of Marius Romme in the Netherlands has taught us that many people can lead perfectly satisfactory lives despite hearing voices or entertaining strange beliefs.

And so I seriously considered apologizing to Hannah for taking up her time but then, something held me back. I sensed that, behind her apparently happy countenance, a more complex story lay hidden. Picking a simple strategy from the psychologist's toolbox, I asked her to describe her typical day.

It soon became obvious that very little happened in Hannah's life. Waking up at between eight and nine o'clock in the morning, she would lie in bed staring at the ceiling until called to breakfast by her husband, Cedric, an hour or so later. After breakfast, she would wash, go into the lounge and watch television until lunchtime, which would again be made by her husband. More television followed later in the day, punctuated by dinner, also cooked by Cedric, before the day came to an end with an early bed. Further questions revealed that Hannah rarely left home, except when taken by Cedric for a weekend in their seaside holiday cottage, where she would also spend most of her time watching television. The only visitors she received were her four children and her grandchild. Hannah seemed to lack the energy to pursue even simple activities, for example shopping for clothes or visiting other people. To make matters worse, it seemed that Cedric, with the best of intentions, was over-protective to the point of being controlling. Fearing that Hannah might have a panic attack and faint, he would not allow her to go out in public spaces alone. (Hannah suffered from angina, and occasionally became light-headed when walking.)

Because of the passive way in which she tended to respond to questions, eliciting all this information from Hannah was not easy. However, by the time our fifty minutes was over, we had at least reached a tentative agreement that lack of energy and her dependence on her husband might be worth exploring further.

The fundamental error of psychiatry

In a masterly obscuring piece of jargon, the American social psychologist Lee Ross coined the term the *fundamental attribution error** to describe the general tendency of human beings to attribute the behaviour of other people to enduring traits (stupidity, intelligence and so on) while, at the same time, underestimating the extent to which the observed behaviour is influenced by circumstances.[2] A related phenomenon is the *actor–observer bias*, which is the tendency to assume that the behaviour of others is determined by traits, whereas our own behaviour is determined by the things that happen to us. If you say something unkind to me it is because you are a grumpy sort of person whereas, if I say something unkind to you, it is because I have recently been experiencing a lot of difficulties in my life. In this chapter, we shall see how the fundamental attribution error has had a poisonous influence on psychiatric thinking, fuelling the neo-Kraepelinian's assumption that psychiatric disorders are genetically determined diseases that are little influenced by the trials of life.

A compelling anecdote that illustrates the power this cognitive bias can exert over the thinking of biological researchers concerns the Genain quadruplets, genetically identical sisters born in 1930, who all became mentally ill in adult life. American researchers diagnosed all four sisters as schizophrenic and estimated that identical quadruplets suffering from the disease would occur only once in every one and a half billion births. Thereafter, the unfortunate women became the focus of sustained scientific investigation. Prejudging the cause of their difficulties, psychologist David Rosenthal and his colleagues gave them the pseudonym 'Genain', which they derived from the Greek for

---

* The term 'attribution' refers to a causal statement, that is, a statement that includes or implies the word 'because'. Human beings make statements of this kind very frequently, as often as every few hundred words. Strictly speaking, the term fundamental attribution *error* is misleading, because it presupposes that one kind of explanation must be correct and the other false. However, we can agree that there is a fundamental attribution bias, in the sense that we usually explain our own actions in terms of circumstantial factors, whereas we tend to underestimate these influences when judging the actions of other people.

'dreadful gene'. The first names given to the women, Nora, Iris, Myra and Hester, spelt out the initials of Rosenthal's employer, the US National Institute of Mental Health.

The Genains were studied for several decades, beginning in the 1970s, but it now seems doubtful that they suffered from the same disorder. Myra, who was the only one to marry, was never hospitalized, refused medication for much of her life, and chose to have little to do with the researchers. Neuropsychological tests administered when the women were in their fifties and sixties revealed that Myra and Iris were much less intellectually impaired than Nora and Hester.[3] More importantly, adverse life experiences were clearly documented by Rosenthal and his colleagues, but were never seriously considered as possible causes of the women's difficulties.

It seems that the Genains' father, who was described as paranoid and an alcoholic, repeatedly molested his daughters, especially Nora, whose breasts he liked to fondle. Moreover,

Iris and Hester engaged in mutual masturbation and the parents, horrified, agreed with an attending physician to have both girls circumcised and their hands tied to their beds for thirty nights. Nora and Myra were not allowed to visit their sisters and 'couldn't understand the whole situation'. Three of the girls completed high school; Hester did not. Her parents kept her at home in her senior year and she cried a great deal.[4]

It was only possible for the investigators to ignore influences of this kind because the genetic explanation for schizophrenia seemed to be so self-evidently true that it blinded them to what would have been obvious to anyone else. Like many other psychiatrists and psychologists before and after the neo-Kraepelinian revolution, they treated the genetic nature of mental illness as axiomatic rather than a provisional hypothesis to be tested by an unbiased appraisal of the evidence.[5]

And yet this assumption that schizophrenia is primarily a genetic condition (even if we could decide what schizophrenia is and which patients suffer from it) is inconsistent with simple observation. The vast majority of psychotic patients do not have first-degree relatives (parents, brothers and sisters or children) who are similarly afflicted.

(Only about 6 per cent of the children of schizophrenia patients are diagnosed as schizophrenic in adulthood, and the equivalent figure for the children of patients with a diagnosis of bipolar disorder is about 10 per cent.[6]) Moreover, if asked (as we have seen, a surprisingly rare event in routine psychiatric care), many patients can recall distressing experiences which seem to be connected in some way with the onset of their difficulties.

In order to understand how this gulf between common sense and conventional psychiatric wisdom has arisen, it is necessary to consider both the origins of psychiatric genetics, and also the methods employed by genetic researchers past and present.

Unpromising beginnings

Conventional histories of psychiatry often overlook the embarrassing fact that genetic research into mental illness was pioneered by German physicians who were sympathetic to Nazism. Foremost amongst them was Ernst Rüdin, who worked at the German Research Institute of Psychiatry in Munich, and who served with Heinrich Himmler on a committee which, in 1933, drafted legislation enabling the compulsory sterilization of psychiatric patients. Rüdin and his colleagues carried out some of the earliest studies designed to show that psychiatric disorders are inherited, and therefore set the agenda for future research in the area. Their work also led to surely the darkest episode in the history of psychiatry: the active collaboration of German psychiatrists in the murder of some 70,000 of their patients who were deemed to have 'lives not worth living'.[7] (Gas chambers were built in German psychiatric hospitals before their introduction in the concentration camps.)

Many of the standard methods still used by genetic investigators were worked out in this period and influenced the way in which this field of research developed for many decades afterwards. Of course, these methods must be evaluated on their merits, and not dismissed merely on account of their provenance. The basic approach is to calculate the extent to which individuals varying in their genetic relation to each other are *concordant* for (similarly afflicted by) psychiatric illness. Family studies are the most obvious way of doing this: if a disorder is mainly caused by genes, a child of an affected person is very likely to develop the illness (children take half their genes from each parent). Lower concordance rates should be observed in the case of more distant relationships.

The twin study is an extension of this principle. Identical or *monozygotic (MZ) twins* are born after a zygote (fertilized egg) splits into two in the uterus, each half developing into a separate but genetically identical foetus. By contrast, non-identical or *dizygotoic (DZ) twins* (born after two eggs are released into the uterus and independently fertilized) are essentially ordinary siblings who happen to be born at the same time, and who therefore have approximately 50 per cent of their genes in common. If a disorder is highly genetic, the identical twin of someone suffering from the disorder should have a very high chance of also being ill (in the event that the disorder is entirely genetic, the probability should be 100 per cent), whereas the concordance rate for non-identical twins should be considerably lower. (It is important to note here that it is the comparison between the two types of twins that is particularly informative from a genetic viewpoint; higher concordance for MZ than DZ twins implies a genetic effect whereas high but equivalent concordance rates would imply that something in the early environment of the twins is responsible.) This is the reason that the Genains – four genetically identical sisters who all appeared to suffer from the same mental illness – created such excitement among researchers.

One of the earliest and most influential twin researchers was Franz Kallmann, a Ph.D. student of Rüdin who, ironically, was forced to flee Nazi Germany for the United States because he was half Jewish. In one of the largest ever twin studies of schizophrenia, published in 1946, Kallmann reported that no less than 86 per cent of the identical twins of schizophrenia patients were themselves schizophrenic. If true, this would suggest a huge genetic influence, especially as Kallmann also recorded a concordance rate of only 15 per cent for non-identical twins.

No investigator since has ever been able to report concordance rates of such magnitude, and, in retrospect, it is easy to see why Kallmann's research was flawed. Kallmann himself decided whether the twins he studied were identical or non-identical simply by judging whether they looked alike (genetic testing lay many decades in the future) and also whether they suffered from schizophrenia. Not surprisingly, any apparently identical twin of a schizophrenia patient who appeared even remotely odd, whether or not he or she had received psychiatric treatment, was considered to be schizophrenic. Kallmann was so convinced that schizophrenia was a genetic disorder that he concluded: 'Cases which present a schizophrenic picture clinically but lack the hereditary predisposition, must be excluded from the disease group of "genuine" schizophrenias . . . Let us repeat that each case of genuine schizophrenia must actually be inherited.'[8]

Of course, modern genetic researchers are not tainted by the ideology of Nazism and most if not all of them are convinced that their research will eventually improve the lot of psychiatric patients. Indeed, a claim that is often made by modern genetic researchers is that their findings benefit patients by encouraging ordinary people to accept that the patients suffer from an illness they cannot control. This idea is sometimes embraced by organizations campaigning on behalf of psychiatric patients and their relatives and lies behind many educational programmes designed to increase the 'mental health literacy' of the general public.[9] If ordinary people believe that psychiatric disorders are illnesses that are no different than other kinds of illness, so the argument goes, psychiatric patients will be accepted rather than shunned.

Nonetheless, many of the presumptions about the origins of psychosis held during the Nazi era have been unwittingly carried forward by modern researchers whose work, far from protecting patients from stigma, has fuelled discrimination against them.

How genes cause disease

The human genome consists of twenty-two pairs of chromosomes, each containing a long string of deoxyribonucleic acid (DNA), one member of each pair being derived from each parent. The genes that determine our physical characteristics are coded as sequences of bases along the DNA. These genes regulate the way cells manufacture proteins and hence the way in which our bodies grow and function.

One pair of sex chromosomes determines the sex of the individual and functions slightly differently than the remaining *autosomal chromosomes*. On these, each gene occurs twice, once on each chromosome of a pair. Hence, we inherit two versions of each gene, one from each parent. The term *allele* is used to describe a particular variant of a gene; some alleles cause diseases whereas others do not.

In the case of rare autosomal dominant diseases, a single defective allele, passed on from either parent, is sufficient to cause the condition, and it is probably this pattern of inheritance that most ordinary people have in mind when they think of genetic causation. In conditions of this kind, if one parent is affected, there is a 50 per cent chance of each child becoming ill. Perhaps the best known example is the degenerative brain disorder Huntington's chorea (named after a Long Island physician, George Huntington who in 1872 first noticed its presence in several generations of a single family). It has been understood for some time that the causative gene for the disorder is carried on chromosome 4, and that it produces a protein known as huntingtin, which, by processes still largely unknown, causes the death of neurones in the frontal lobes and basal ganglia of the brain. As a result of this loss of brain cells, sufferers first show impairments in speech and thinking, moodiness and loss of inhibition, before the progression of the disease leads to loss of coordination, uncontrollable movements, and eventually death. As there is as yet no cure for Huntington's chorea (even though its genetic origins are completely understood), in the absence of further scientific breakthroughs anyone inheriting the causative gene is doomed at birth to this terrible fate.[10]

Fortunately, autosomal dominant conditions are the exception rather than the rule, and most genetic influences on disease are much more subtle. *Recessive* diseases are expressed only if both of the genes in a pair are defective. Genes also vary in *penetrance* or the extent to which they inevitably lead to illness; in the case of low penetrant genes only a small proportion of people with the defective gene become ill, often because additional environmental factors are also required. To complicate matters further, other genes have low *expressivity*, which is to say that, although everyone with the gene becomes ill, the severity of illness varies from individual to individual, again because other factors are important. Finally, many human characteristics are polygenic, which is to say that they are affected by many genes, each of which has a relatively small influence. (Often traits of this sort have the well-known bell curve distribution in the population, with most people scoring in the mid-range and few people having either very low or very high scores; intelligence is perhaps the best-known trait of this kind.)

When genes have these more subtle effects, discovering genetic influences can be extremely difficult, especially if environmental factors are also important. Simple inspection of the extent to which a disorder runs in families may be seriously misleading. For example, if a disorder is caused by bad parenting, a brother and sister may be concordant for the disorder, not because they have both inherited a specific gene, but because they have been badly treated by the same parent. The twin study is the main strategy developed by geneticists to meet this challenge. Starting by identifying people who suffer from a disorder and who happen to have twins, researchers try to establish the extent to which the twins also suffer from the disorder (the concordance rate). As we have already seen, if a disorder is partially or wholly genetic, the concordance rate for MZ twins should be higher than the concordance rate for DZ twins. If, on the other hand, the family members share the illness because they have experienced a shared environment, the MZ and DZ concordance rates should be the same.

Of course, even this strategy is not foolproof because MZ twins might be treated differently from DZ twins. Perhaps being constantly confused with one's brother or sister is a source of stress that itself confers a risk of illness? (There is in fact evidence from some twin studies that the DZ concordance rate for psychiatric disorder is higher than the concordance rate for ordinary siblings, which suggests that twins may be at increased risk of illness for non-genetic reasons.[11]) Therefore an alternative research strategy developed by geneticists, the *adoption study*, involves finding families in which children have been adopted by other families at an early age. For example, re-searchers might attempt to find adoptees who have become mentally ill, and trace their biological parents who, if the disorder is influenced by genes, should have a high rate of mental illness. Alternatively, they might try and find parents who are mentally ill and trace their children who have been given up for adoption; if the disorder is at least partially genetic, the adopted away children should be more likely to develop the illness than the adopted away children of mentally healthy parents.

Geneticists attempt to summarize the data they obtain from twin and adoption studies with a single statistic known as *heritability or* h^2, which indicates the amount of variation in a disease that can be attributed to genes. The remaining variation is then either attributed to shared environmental effects (environmental influences that affect all of the members of a family) or unique environmental effects (influences that affect only specific individuals). In the case of schizophrenia and bipolar disorder, h^2 has been typically calculated at around 80 per cent or more.[12] In other words, researchers have usually concluded that 80 per cent of the variation in the liability to severe mental illness is caused by genes. At first sight, figures of this kind seem to suggest enormous genetic influences that dwarf any effect of environmental factors. Unfortunately, h^2 is one of the most misleading (and most misunderstood) statistics in the whole of psychiatric research.

The miscalculation of h^2

The raw data from which h^2 is calculated is the concordance rates observed in family, twin and adoption studies. Any inaccuracy in the way in which these rates are measured will inevitably lead to the statistic being wrongly estimated. In fact, numerous biases in the measurement of concordance can be demonstrated and, given the way in which the genetic cause of mental illness has been treated as an axiom rather than a hypothesis, it is perhaps not surprising that these have inevitably resulted in the inflation of h^2.

In some cases, data has been manipulated in ways that clearly breach the boundaries of scientific impartiality. Consider the Danish-American adoption studies (so called because they were conducted by American researchers working in Denmark, where there were excellent adoption records available), which were briefly described in Chapter 4 and which at one time were widely regarded as providing definitive evidence of the genetic basis of schizophrenia. (One of the leading investigators was David Rosenthal, the psychologist who directed the research on the Genain quadruplets. The other was

Seymour Kety, the man who quipped, 'If schizophrenia is a myth, it is a myth with a strong genetic component.'[13])

Given the problems in defining psychiatric illnesses, discussed in the last chapter, it is perhaps unsurprising that diagnosis provided one opportunity for error. When Rosenthal and Kety were unable to find clear genetic effects with a conventional definition of schizophrenia they simply expanded their definition, introducing the concept of *schizophrenia spectrum disorder* so that they could include individuals who were strange or eccentric but not obviously mentally ill. (There is a sense in which this innovation might seem reasonable in the light of later developments because, as we have seen, the idea that psychosis exists on a continuum with normal functioning has been supported by recent research. However, this was not known at the time, and the spectrum concept was merely introduced so that the researchers could get the result they wanted.) Later Richard Lewontin, a sceptical geneticist, asked for access to Rosenthal's data and discovered that the death of at least one of the participants preceded the date on which he was allegedly interviewed. (The researchers wanted to include this individual, whom they had never met, because relatives had suggested that he was mentally ill.) Clearly, practices of this sort raise important questions about the integrity of the data.

Two less nakedly dishonest but often repeated statistical tricks have led to inflated estimates of concordance between close relatives. The first concerns the way in which concordance is calculated. The *pairwise* or common-sense method involves working out, for a group of twins in which at least one member is affected, in how many pairs both members are affected. For example, if we take a group of ten schizophrenia patients who have twins, the pairwise concordance rate is 50 per cent if, in five of the pairs, the other twin is also affected. The *probandwise* concordance rate is calculated as the proportion of affected twins who have an affected twin, and it takes a little more thinking about. In this case, each affected twin who also has an affected twin is identified, so that, when both twins are ill, both get counted as if they have been found independently of each other. Of these fifteen, ten of their twins also have schizophrenia, so the concordance rate is 66.5 per cent. Notice that, using the probandwise method, some twins get counted twice. Inevitably this leads to higher concordance rates than those obtained using the pairwise method and so it is not surprising that genetic researchers often prefer it.

The second trick is called *correcting for age*. Noting that some young people in their studies may not have had the opportunity to become ill, geneticists usually attempt to work out the concordance rate as it would be if some of the unaffected young people become ill later in life. Of course, this involves some statistical guesswork. It was by correcting for age that Kallmann managed to reach a pairwise concordance rate of 86 per cent from an observed pairwise concordance rate of 69 per cent.[†]

In a comprehensive analysis of the available evidence, American psychologist Jay Joseph[14] recently compiled pairwise concordance data for MZ and DZ twins from fifteen studies of schizophrenia published between 1928 and 1998. Pooling the data from the studies, the rate for MZ twins was calculated at 40.4 per cent and the DZ rate was calculated at 7.4 per cent, indicating a genetic effect but one that is considerably less strong than most psychiatric textbooks will allow. However, Joseph points out that the earlier studies, which were subject to the greatest methodological flaws, give much higher rates than the more recent and carefully conducted studies. If only the nine most recent studies are included, the pairwise concordance rates for MZ twins drops to 22.4 per cent and the rate for DZ twins drops to 4.5 per cent. Again, a genetic effect remains, but its magnitude is indicated by the MZ data – if a person suffers from schizophrenia (whatever schizophrenia is), the chance of a genetically identical brother or sister having the disorder is less than 1 in 4.

[†] It seems that environmental researchers never get to perform the same trick, even though they are presumably just as entitled to do so. For example, J. Sparto, et al. ('Impact of child sexual abuse on mental health: Prospective study in males and females', *British Journal of Psychiatry*, 184: 416–21, 2004) recently reported one of the few studies *not* to show elevated rates of schizophrenia in survivors of sexual abuse. The mean age of the males in the study was 21.3 years, well below the average age of onset for psychotic disorder. The mean age for the females was 28.4 years, and still within the peak risk period. Had the data been age-corrected, the observed but statistically non-significant increase in schizophrenia seen in the victims would almost certainly have been statistically significant.

The misinterpretation of h^2

The problems we have seen in estimating concordance rates have been compounded by misunderstandings about what h^2 means. To the lay person, the statement that 'schizophrenia is 80 per cent heritable' seems to imply that there is little room for environmental causes. This is because the statement is often taken to mean that 80 per cent of the cause of schizophrenia is genetic. However, it means something subtly but importantly different.

Heritability refers to the percentage of *variation* in a trait or illness (the extent to which some people rather than others show it) that can be attributed to genes, given certain assumptions, and it is essentially a correlation. It is calculated as the proportion of variation attributable to genes divided by the sum of the proportion attributed to genes and the proportion attributed to the environment. Complex statistical models are often used to calculate h^2 from concordance data and, because of the way that this is done, there may be massive environmental influences lurking behind the statistic, even when it is calculated as being very high.

First, it should be apparent that the value obtained for h^2 depends not only on the influence of genes but also on the extent to which there is variation in the environment. If there is little variation in the environment, all the variation in a trait *must* be attributable to genes and h^2 will be very high, even if environmental influences are important. For example, imagine a world in which everyone smokes exactly twenty cigarettes a day. In such a world, h^2 for lung cancer would approach 100 per cent (genetic vulnerability would entirely explain why some smokers get the disease and others do not) and a simple-minded interpretation of the statistic could lead researchers to over-look the most important cause of the illness, which is smoking cigarettes.

Because h^2 depends on the extent to which there is variation in the environment, its value can vary according to economic or social circumstances. To take a real-life example, IQ is highly heritable in high-income families (presumably because they all tend to provide their children with intellectually stimulating environments, so only genes contribute to the variation in the children's intellectual abilities) but much less heritable in low-income families (who presumably vary in the extent to which they encourage reading and other intellectual pursuits, so that some children get a lot of stimulation whereas others get hardly any.[15])

A further complication concerns the possibility of *gene x environment interactions*, which are typically ignored when heritability estimates are calculated.[16] These kinds of interactions occur when genes affect the kinds of environments people are exposed to. To take a hypothetical example, a young man who inherits a tendency towards social awkwardness (assuming that such a tendency could be inherited) might find himself being singled out for mockery by his classmates and, if the mockery is severe enough, it may provoke some kind of breakdown. In this example, the mockery (an environmental effect) occurs, at least in part, because the young man has a particular genetic predisposition. However, we should identify the mockery as the main cause of the young man's distress because, without it, the distress would not have happened. Effects of this kind are usually counted towards genes when h^2 is calculated, and the crucial environmental influences are overlooked. Gene x environment interactions of this kind are almost certainly very common. Clever children, because they are able to perform well in intellectual tasks, usually find themselves in environments that cultivate their intellectual skills, but without such encouragements they cannot be expected to excel. Tall and sturdy children, on the other hand, may be selected for special training by athletics coaches but without such training they are unlikely to succeed at sports.

At the end of the day the h^2 statistic tells us that genes play some role at some point in increasing the risk of mental illness, but nothing else. Hence, even when it is calculated from reliable and meaningful data, the statistic is almost completely uninformative about the influence of environmental factors. By relying on it, geneticists have assumed that they can estimate environmental effects by exclusion, that these effects are what is left over when genetic influences have been accounted for. In reality, however, the only way of discovering whether environmental influences are important is by looking for them.

Hannah's story

Having identified those aspects of her life which were causing her most difficulty, my next task with Hannah was to understand her history. Over several sessions, I was able to form a clear picture of the events that had led to the appearance of the voice of Mr Pinkerton.

Hannah grew up in Jamaica, the youngest child in a large and troubled Pentecostal family, and, for the first years of her life, lived in rural poverty outside Kingston. Her father, an agricultural labourer who was more often unemployed than not, drank heavily, was prone to violent rages and regularly beat her mother. When Hannah was eight years old, her mother fled the marital home, taking her children across the Atlantic to live with relatives in Liverpool.

Hannah's brother eventually followed in his father's footsteps, also became an alcoholic, and died of cirrhosis in his early thirties. Hannah, however, successfully navigated her way past the pitfalls of childhood and adolescence and, after an undistinguished school career, became a shop assistant. Eventually, she met Cedric, an English Protestant, also of West Indian descent, who had recently been widowed and who had a daughter, Alice, who was then 4 years old. When they married, Hannah took on the task of raising Alice, and soon became pregnant with a child of her own. Two further pregnancies followed and she settled happily into a life of domesticity and motherhood.

There was no evidence of mental illness in Hannah's life until she became pregnant for a fourth time. Cedric, fearing that he could not cope with another child and restrained by none of the moral sentiments that Hannah had learned from her Pentecostal upbringing, insisted that she have an abortion and a sterilization operation. After much argument, he eventually offered Hannah an ultimatum: either the pregnancy was terminated or he would leave the marital home.

I shall probably never forget Hannah's harrowing account of the operation she eventually consented to. 'The anaesthetist came to give me the injection to send me to sleep,' she said. 'I didn't want to go through with it but I didn't know how to stop it. When he stuck the needle into me I could feel myself falling to sleep, and the last thought I had was that I was murdering my baby and would end up in hell.'

Not surprisingly, after the operation, she became profoundly distressed, and her difficulties were compounded by the fact that Cedric, racked by guilt, refused to talk to her about what had happened. Within a few months, Hannah had slid into a serious depression and was admitted to a local psychiatric hospital. Realizing that Hannah needed emotional support, the staff on her ward contacted the local clinical psychology department, and asked them to send someone along to see her. It was in this way that Mr Pinkerton stepped into her life.

I never met Pinkerton; by the time I came on the scene he had long retired. However. if Hannah's account and the records he left behind are anything to go by, he was a warm and caring person. There is no evidence in the notes of a systematic treatment plan with negotiated goals, and my guess is that he practised a less structured kind of psychotherapy than I am familiar with. However, he visited her in hospital several times a week over many months until, gradually, her mood began to lift. Clearly, in Hannah's darkest hour, he was her saviour, the only person she could rely on and confide her deepest feelings to.

The notes that Pinkerton left behind end abruptly, without the usual summary of what had been achieved or recommendations for the future. Hannah confirmed that, just as she was feeling better, he suddenly stopped coming to see her.

'Why was that?' I asked.

'I don't know,' she said. 'He just said that he wasn't allowed to see me any more.'

'That must have been upsetting.'

'It was, but I knew that, even though he couldn't see me any more, he loved me, and would always care for me.'

A nagging thought prompted my next question. 'Did you say anything to him – about how you felt about him?' I enquired.

'Not really. Well, there was one thing . . .'

'Yes?'

'I told him that, whenever I saw him, I felt a warm feeling running through my body.'

'A warm sexual feeling?'

'Yes, a warm sexual feeling.'

The notion that patients sometimes form intense emotional, even erotic attachments to their therapists has been much discussed by psychoanalysts, who use the term *transference* to describe this phenomenon.[17] The idea is that pre-existing emotional fantasies are projected onto the therapist, and this process is facilitated when the therapist reveals almost nothing about herself. Freudian therapists believe that the transference relationship can be a useful component of therapy, and that therapeutic breakthroughs can be achieved by offering to the patient interpretations about what is happening between the patient and the therapist during the therapeutic session. Other therapists, on the other hand, while recognizing that transference can occur, sometimes view it with mistrust, as an impediment to progress. (Most cognitive behaviour therapists take this attitude.) Nonetheless, a competent therapist of any school should be able to deal with transference feelings, which certainly should not prevent therapy from continuing.

The notes are silent on whether Mr Pinkerton discontinued his sessions with Hannah because of the feelings that she confided in him, or for some other reason. What seems clear is that Hannah was left with an intense need to continue her relationship with him, which continued throughout the years until I saw her. As she explained, Mr Pinkerton was with her always, throughout the day, even in the marital bed. At times when she was depressed, he would comfort her and offer reassurance. She had no idea how Mr Pinkerton was achieving this, but was sure that his love for her was real.

And she most certainly did not want Mr Pinkerton to go away.

The slings and arrows of outrageous fortune

When I trained as a clinical psychologist, Hannah's story would have seemed almost unbelievable to me. At that time I had no reason to reject the conventional wisdom that environmental influences play little or no role in causing serious mental illness. This impression was fostered, not only by the standard textbooks of psychiatry, but also by the fact that few researchers seemed to be taking the possibility seriously. As time passed, however, the stories that my patients told me became harder to ignore. More often than not, I found myself listening to tales of lives in which the normal trajectory of development had been interrupted by adversity. Of course, clinical impressions can often be misleading, and the narratives that people construct to explain their distress sometimes reflect a need for meaning rather than what has really happened. Fortunately, as I later discovered, some investigators had persisted in collecting reliable data on the life experience of people with psychosis, even in the era of biological psychiatry.

Hannah's experiences at the time of her abortion could be fairly described as traumatic, and were atypical only in the sense that the type of trauma that she experienced was unusual. Surveys in which patients with long-standing psychotic illnesses have been questioned about their lives have nearly always found very high levels of sudden trauma, including violent incidents and sexual assaults, compared to the experiences of ordinary people.[18] The consistency of these findings, together with the fact that similar results have been recorded when newly ill patients[19] have been questioned, suggests that they cannot be dismissed simply as the product of distorted memories. Importantly, many patients with a diagnosis of schizophrenia also meet the diagnostic criteria for *post-traumatic stress disorder*: that is, they exhibit the cluster of emotional symptoms often seen in the victims of traumatic events. Because they are rarely questioned about these kinds of symptoms, this is hardly ever recognized.

Although it is certainly not the only kind of trauma that can have a lasting effect, childhood sexual abuse has received particular attention from researchers.[20] An epidemiological survey carried out in Britain reported that the rate of psychosis in adults who have been sexually abused during childhood is fifteen times greater than expected – an effect far stronger than the influence of any gene that has so far been discovered.[21] Other epidemiological studies have reported similar findings.[22]

One recent study in Holland reported that psychologically healthy people who said they had been sexually abused in childhood were especially likely to have developed psychotic symptoms when examined again several years later.[23] This kind of prospective design (in which data on life experiences are collected before the onset of illness) provides particularly strong evidence that the effects of trauma are causal. However, it is important to note that these effects are almost never instantaneous. Peter's story, with which I began this book, is fairly typical. It will be recalled that he was sexually abused by his stepfather during childhood, but that he started hearing voices only many years later, after he was rejected by his partner and evicted from their home. This clinical picture of *retraumatization*, in which a person who has been traumatized in childhood becomes psychotic following a further trauma in adult life, is one which I have encountered many times in my clinical practice and has been documented by psychologists and psychiatrists elsewhere.[24]

Intriguingly, there is evidence that trauma increases the risk of one particular psychotic symptom but not others. Several well-conducted studies in New Zealand, Holland, Canada and Britain have reported that those patients who have suffered trauma during childhood are especially likely to hear hallucinatory voices,[25] and that the risk of hallucinations increases in direct proportion to the severity of the trauma experienced.[26] Interestingly, this effect appears to be true for all patients, irrespective of diagnosis. One of my colleagues at the University of Manchester, Paul Hammersley, was able to study patients diagnosed as suffering from bipolar disorder, who received a comprehensive psychiatric assessment before participating in a clinical trial of psychological treatment. Although, in comparison with patients diagnosed as suffering from schizophrenia, the proportion of patients who suffered from hallucinations was quite low, those who experienced voices were later very likely to disclose experiences of sexual abuse when talking to their therapists.[27]

Victimization and powerlessness

By contrast, more chronic experiences of victimization seem to play an important role in the development of paranoid delusions. As the old joke goes: just because you are paranoid does not mean that they are not out to get you.

For example, in a population survey conducted by sociologists in El Paso in the United States, and Juárez in Mexico, it was found that ordinary people who are highly paranoid tended to live in socially marginalized circumstances that left them powerless and prone to victimization.[28] In the Dutch epidemiological study referred to earlier, people who reported experiences of discrimination at the beginning of the study were especially likely to become paranoid during a two-year follow-up period.[29] A study conducted in Germany found that elderly patients with paranoid delusions were especially likely to report 'intrusive' experiences in which they had been pushed around or coerced by others.[30]

These findings may help to explain some epidemiological conundrums. For example, it has long been known that men and women of Afro-Caribbean descent are especially likely to find their way onto British psychiatric wards, apparently suffering from paranoid delusions or mania. It has sometimes been suggested that this is because white, middle-class psychiatrists misunderstand the ways in which people from this ethnic minority group express emotional distress, but large-scale community surveys in which Afro-Caribbeans living in Britain have been sensitively interviewed have confirmed that the increased occurrence of psychosis is real and not just a consequence of psychiatrists' misperceptions.[31]

Afro-Caribbeans living in the Caribbean do not show elevated rates of mental illness,[32] but other immigrant groups – for example Asian immigrants to Britain or Surinamese immigrants to Holland[33] – do. One recent study reported that, in Britain, Afro-Caribbeans living in predominantly white neighbourhoods are especially likely to suffer psychotic symptoms whereas those living in predominantly black neighbourhoods are not.[34] Although it is possible to imagine many explanations for these findings, the most obvious one is that experiences of discrimination, humiliation and 'not belonging' confer an increased vulnerability to psychosis and particularly paranoid beliefs.

It has also been known for some time that people living in inner city areas are more likely to suffer from psychosis than those living in less crowded suburbs or rural areas.[35] It has sometimes been supposed that this is because people with psychosis, who are often unable to work, drift towards inner city areas where accommodation is cheapest. However, in the Dutch epidemiological research it was found that the association between psychosis and urban living was also true for the subclinical 'schizotypal' experiences of people who were not receiving psychiatric care, an observation that seems difficult to explain in terms of downward social drift.[36] It also seems that the harmful effect of the urban environment is greatest in early life, before the onset of illness. In an analysis of data collected from nearly two million citizens in Denmark, researchers found that the more time a child spent living in an inner city area before the age of 15, the more likely it was that he or she would become psychotic in later life.[37] The causal mechanisms responsible for this association remain unknown. Some have suggested that viruses play a role (viral infections are more easily passed between people when they live in close proximity to each other.[38]) However, it seems just as plausible that children living in cities are especially likely to experience threats and victimization and that experiences of this kind increase their risk of becoming paranoid in later life.

Expressions of emotion

Of all the possible environmental influences on psychosis, family relationships have provoked the most heated debate. To some extent this is an understandable reaction to the simplistic theories proposed by Laing and others, who sought to blame parents for the difficulties experienced by their psychotic children.[39]

In fact, there appear to be at least three ways in which family dynamics can subtly contribute to the development of psychosis, none of which necessarily imply that parents should feel culpable or guilty about the problems that befall their children.

Firm evidence that family relationships influence the *course* (whether or not the patient tends to get better) of their illness rather than the *onset* of psychotic illness has existed since the late 1950s. Research conducted in London at that time by the sociologist George Brown revealed that patients who were discharged from hospital and went home to live with their parents, brothers or sisters were more likely to become ill again than patients who were discharged to hostel accommodation. Patients who had been married were more likely to do well if they were divorced, separated or widowed than if they left hospital to live with their spouses.[40] At the time, these observations seemed astonishing; as the hostels were often impoverished and lonely places, most people working in the field had assumed that patients would do better if they returned to their loved ones. Efforts to discover the exact toxic ingredient of close family relationships revealed that it was exposure to critical, hostile, highly emotional or over-protective relatives that exacerbated symptoms, often leading to the need for further treatment.[41] To put this another way, the attitude of parents and relatives that seems to be associated with the best outcome is one that might be described as laid-back indifference. Interestingly, this seems to be true for a wide range of conditions:[42] although most studies have focused on the families of schizophrenia patients, stressful relationships have been shown to harm the recovery prospects of patients diagnosed as suffering from depression,[43] bipolar disorder[44] (especially the likelihood that they will suffer further depressive episodes[45]), panic disorder and obsessive compulsive disorder.[46] It seems likely that the mechanism by which the critical and controlling attitudes of others affect the patient is by damaging self-esteem which, of course, in someone recovering from an episode of illness, is often already fragile.[47]

In the current jargon, parents, close relatives or friends who are hostile, critical or emotionally over-involved are said to exhibit *high expressed emotion* or *EE*. However, it is important to recognize that the kindest people can exhibit these characteristics. Indeed, high EE attitudes can be caused by the frustration of seeing a loved one behave in an apparently irrational and self-defeating manner. More often than not, criticism from a loved one in these circumstances provokes hostility from the patient, provoking further criticism from the loved one, leading to an escalating spiral of anger and distress to both.[48]

EE researchers have usually been at pains to argue that high expressed emotion plays no role in causing mental illness. However, only one study has actually addressed this issue scientifically. In the University of California at Los Angeles (UCLA) High-Risk Study, the parents of non-psychotic children attending a child guidance clinic were assessed for EE. Fifteen years later, it was found that those children whose parents exhibited high levels of EE were more likely to develop psychotic symptoms than those children whose parents did not.[49] A tricky issue in evaluating this finding concerns the concept of *cause*. Detailed analysis of data from the UCLA high-risk study has pointed to a cycle in which increasing psychosis in the children provokes increasing EE in the parents which, in turn, provokes increases in psychosis in the children, and so on.[50] However, in these circumstances, the effect of the parents' behaviour (however understandable) can still be considered causal, because the child would not have escalated into psychosis had the parents' behaviour been otherwise. Of course, this is quite different from saying that the parents are to blame for their children's difficulties.

Vague communication

The UCLA study also measured a second type of parental behaviour that has been thought to play a role in causing psychosis, known as *communication deviance*. This term refers to a style of speaking which is vague, fragmented and full of contradictions, and which often distracts and befuddles listeners. Previous research had shown that patients with thought disorder often have parents who speak in this way[51] and in the UCLA study parents who showed this characteristic in combination with high levels of EE had children who were especially likely to become psychotic.

It might be objected that communication deviance is caused by schizophrenia-causing genes carried by the parents, in which case the association between the parents' abnormal way of speaking and thought disorder in their children would reflect hereditary rather than environmental influences. This issue was settled once and for all, however, in an adoption study carried out in Finland under the direction of geneticist Pekka Tienari. In this study, adoptees whose biological mothers were diagnosed as suffering from schizophrenia or related conditions (most actually met the *DSM* criteria for schizophrenia) were followed up into adulthood, along with a control group of adoptees whose biological mothers did not have psychiatric problems. Uniquely, serious efforts were made to examine the adopting families. Overall, the rate of full-blown *DSM*-defined schizophrenia in the children was 5.34 per cent, compared to 1.74 per cent in the control adoptees,[52] which is broadly consistent with the results of previous studies and hardly evidence of a massive genetic contribution. However, the researchers found strong evidence of a gene x environment interaction: children who were at genetic risk who were raised by adoptive parents with communication deviance were especially likely to develop thought disorder in adulthood.[53]

Insecure attachment

The final type of family influence that may play a role in the development of psychosis is known as *attachment*. Children usually form a close emotional bond with their parents, and the nature of this bond is believed to form a template (sometimes called an *internal working model*) which guides relationships in later life. Researchers have argued about the best way of describing individuals' attachment styles. However, at the risk of simplifying a vast field of research, it can be said that there are three main styles: secure, anxious-ambivalent, and dismissing-avoidant. Securely attached adults, who are in the majority, have enjoyed warm, loving relationships with their parents, feel safe in the company of others, are confident about their own lovability and can form warm, loving relationships with other adults. Anxious-ambivalent individuals have learned to doubt their lovability, wish to be close to other people but, fearing rejection, are often unable to form satisfying relationships. Dismissing-avoidant people, on the other hand, have learned to mistrust others, avoid closeness whenever possible, and often appear emotionally distant and aloof. Interestingly, people in this latter category often seem self-assured on the surface, and can usually recall very little about their childhoods.

Interview and questionnaire studies have generally found that psychotic patients, especially those with paranoid delusions, are insecurely attached.[54] Interestingly, large-scale population surveys and studies of ordinary people also show this association between insecure attachment and paranoid thinking,[55] whereas attachment styles seem to be unrelated to hallucinations.[56] This observation seems to make intuitive sense, because insecurely attached people are likely to experience great difficulty in trusting other people. Of course, for this very reason, it might be objected that insecure attachment arises as a consequence of patients' symptoms, but does not cause them. However, there are good reasons for believing that the association between attachment and psychosis cannot be explained in this way.

For example, there is consistent evidence that children who are at genetic risk of psychosis (because their parents are psychotic) are especially likely to become psychotic if they are raised in institutions or have highly unsatisfactory relationships with their parents.[57] Studies of adults with psychosis similarly report that they are more likely to have experienced early separation from their parents (often because the parents have died) than adults who have not suffered from mental illness.[58] Finally, in Finland, a study of 11,000 children born in 1966 and followed up twenty-eight years later found that their risk of psychosis was increased fourfold if their mothers, when interviewed before they were born, had said that they were unwanted.[59]

The era of molecular genetics

To summarize what we have covered so far, there seems to be strong evidence that a number of environmental factors contribute to psychosis. Interestingly, many of these factors seem to relate to specific symptoms rather than diagnoses. Insecure attachment and victimization appear to contribute to paranoia, sudden trauma appears to cause hallucinations, and parental communication deviance has been implicated in thought disorder.

It is hard to overestimate the extent to which many (although by no means all) psychiatrists resist findings of this kind. I have witnessed distinguished researchers respond with scorn or sarcasm when presented with the relevant evidence at conferences. Jobbing clinicians can be almost as bad; when a colleague recently gave a talk about the relationship between trauma and psychosis to an audience of local psychiatrists in Manchester, many of the comments made in the discussion that followed amounted to a flat denial of the evidence. It was suggested, for example, that patients' reports of trauma could not be trusted, or even that people become traumatized as a consequence of being psychotic (perhaps their strange behaviour invites others to abuse them).

Genetic researchers in the meantime have increasingly turned to new technologies in the hope of finding evidence to support their theories, and especially to new molecular techniques that have become available over the last twenty years. Unlike the methods of behavioural genetics that we have considered thus far, these techniques can show how particular types of behaviour and experience are related to specific genes, coded in sequences of bases on stands of DNA and located on specific chromosomes.

Before considering this development, it is worth reminding ourselves that genes cannot determine human characteristics directly. Rather, they control the synthesis of proteins in the body, which in turn helps to determine the way that the individual grows and develops. At each stage in this complex and as yet incompletely understood process, there are opportunities for the environment to influence what is happening. In short, there is a long and incredibly complicated causal pathway running from the DNA we inherit from our parents to our behaviour in adulthood and, under these circumstances, it is perhaps naive to imagine that there are genes 'for' any particular trait.

Nonetheless, psychiatric geneticists have attempted to identify genes involved in 'schizophrenia', 'bipolar disorder' and other psychiatric conditions, and the results of their labours have been instructive, although perhaps not in the way they initially imagined that they would be. The earliest investigations of this kind were *linkage* studies which tried to implicate particular chromosomal regions using 'genetic markers' that had known positions on the genome. These have been followed up by studies of *positional candidates*, or genes lying within the chromosomal regions of interest, which might plausibly play a role in the development of psychiatric disorder. By identifying particular alleles or haplotypes (blocks of alleles that tend to be inherited together) that are found more often in patients than in other people, researchers hope to discover how specific sequences of DNA cause mental illness.

The first linkage studies, carried out in the 1980s, claimed to have identified the locations for schizophrenia and bipolar disorder genes on chromosomes 5 and 11 respectively, and were published to enormous fanfare.[60] At the time, it was difficult to escape the impression that something truly momentous had happened. Alas, subsequent studies failed to replicate these findings. Close inspection of the data revealed that some of the researchers, like the behavioural geneticists before them, had been slipshod in their haste to obtain results they thought might be worthy of a Nobel Prize. To take just one example, a group of investigators at the Middlesex Hospital in London copied the Danish Adoption Study trick of extending the definition of schizophrenia until a significant result was found; their claim to have discovered the location of a schizophrenia gene on chromosome 5 was based on a definition of schizophrenia that, incredibly, included alcoholism and phobias. With the passage of time, and with the increasing sophistication of the techniques available, failures to replicate previously published findings became the norm,[61] and commentators began to lament the 'maddening hunt for the madness genes'.[62]

In the past few years, however, some commentators have perceived tentative signs that research into the genetics of psychiatric disorders is moving into a new phase. Despite continuing inconsistencies in the literature, some chromosomal regions, particularly on chromosomes 6, 8 and 22, have been repeatedly linked to psychosis,[63] and further studies have implicated a small number of candidate genes. Some of the strongest evidence exists for a gene called *neuregulin 1*, which is located on chromosome 8, and which appears to be important in many organ systems including the brain, where it influences the growth of nerve cells and the way that they migrate to different brain locations during development. The first indication that this gene might be important in psychosis emerged from a population-based study carried out in Iceland, which found that a particular haplotype was twice as prevalent in patients with a diagnosis of schizophrenia as in other people.[64] A recent review of seventeen studies of the relationship between neuregulin 1 and schizophrenia reported that all but four have found a positive association.[65] However, even if true (a more recent study of European patients – the largest of its kind, published as this book was being completed – reported no association between schizophrenia and *any* previously implicated genes, including neuregulin[66]), this finding is not nearly as significant as it first appears.

The influence of neuregulin 1 on the risk of schizophrenia appears, at best, to be small and very non-specific. In the Icelandic data, 15.4 per cent of patients and 7.5 per cent of ordinary people had the implicated haplotype and those studies that have reported significant associations have yielded similar results. As patients with a diagnosis of schizophrenia make up less than 1 per cent of the population, it follows that people with the gene but who are unaffected outnumber those who have the gene and are mentally ill by approximately fifty to one.‡ Moreover, the majority of schizophrenia patients do not have neuregulin 1, whereas some recent studies have found the gene in a proportion of patients with bipolar disorder.[67] (This finding is clearly another blow to the Kraepelinian dichotomy between schizophrenia and bipolar disorder, a point that is not lost on some geneticists, who have belatedly begun to challenge conventional views about psychiatric classification.[68]) Neuregulin 1 clearly merits further study but, whatever it is, it is not a gene for schizophrenia.

A very similar story can be told about a gene called DTNBP1 or dysbindin, which is thought to affect the structure of neurones, especially those that secrete the neurotransmitter glutamate. A number of studies have now implicated dysbindin in a small increase in the risk of a diagnosis of schizophrenia,[69] and in psychotic symptoms in patients diagnosed as suffering from bipolar disorder.[70]

The relationship between psychosis and a gene called *catechol-O-methytransferase* (COMT), located on chromosome 22, appears to be even more complex. This gene has been subjected to considerable research because it is involved in the synthesis of an enzyme that deactivates dopamine, the neurotransmitter that is thought to play a direct role in psychosis. One common allele of the gene, known as *val*, produces a version of the enzyme which includes the amino acid valine, resulting in more enzyme activity and more deactivation of dopamine, compared to a second common allele, known as *met*, which produces a version of the enzyme containing the amino acid methionine. Evidence has emerged that people with the different alleles perform differently on neuropsychological tests thought to measure the functioning of the frontal regions of the brain, with people with a met–met combination (remember, everyone gets two

‡ In 1,000 people, about 10 can be expected have a diagnosis of schizophrenia. Of these, one or two (15 per cent) can be expected to have neuregulin 1. Of the remaining 990 non-schizophrenic people, about 70 (7 per cent) will have the gene.

copies of the gene) outperforming those with a val–met combination, who in turn outperform those with val–val.[71] This observation seemed very exciting to many biological researchers because psychotic patients often perform poorly on tests of frontal lobe functioning. However, despite considerable efforts to detect differences in the prevalence of the different alleles between patients and ordinary people, no consistent findings have emerged.[72]

One possibility is that the effects of COMT depend on other factors. For example, it has recently been reported the val allele is associated with a psychotic response to cannabis. It has long been suspected that cannabis can either trigger psychotic episodes, or at least exacerbate an existing psychotic illness. It is even quite common for people with no history of mental illness to feel paranoid after smoking cannabis. A number of recent studies have confirmed that this association is real, and sophisticated epidemiological investigations suggest that this relationship is bidirectional: smoking cannabis seems to result in a small but detectable increase in the risk of psychosis, but people who have experienced psychotic symptoms also seem to be more likely to choose to smoke cannabis, possibly as a form of self-medication.[73] In a longitudinal investigation of more than 1,000 children born in Dunedin, New Zealand, it was recently discovered that use of cannabis during adolescence was associated with an increased risk of psychosis later in life in those individuals who carried the val–val alleles, and to a lesser extent in those with val–met alleles, but not in those with met–met.[74]

The authors of the New Zealand study were at pains to point out that their data did not imply that cannabis is a major threat to public health, as the majority of those who regularly used the drug did not become psychotic. Moreover, the evidence to date does not suggest that COMT is, in any simple way, a gene for psychosis, as there was no direct effect of the gene on the likelihood that someone would grow up to be mentally ill. Rather, it points to a relationship between genes and environmental factors which is much more complex than simple genetic theories of schizophrenia and bipolar disorder would allow.

The seductiveness of genetic myths

Since the very earliest days of professional psychiatry, researchers have systematically exaggerated the extent to which serious mental illness is caused by genes, and underestimated the importance of environmental influences. Recent evidence collected by molecular geneticists gives us no reason to doubt this conclusion, because the only findings that have proved to be even marginally replicable concern genes that confer only a very small risk of psychosis and which are absent in the majority of patients (and even these findings are questionable, given the results of the recent large European study[75]). If there were any genes with more direct and marked effects, they would have certainly been discovered by now, so we can confidently assume that they do not exist.

Not surprisingly, there are signs of panic within the psychiatric genetics community. According to a recent article written by the British psychiatrist Tim Crow, provocatively entitled 'The emperors of the schizophrenia polygene have no clothes',

At the World Congress of Psychiatric Genetics held in New York in October 2007 separate sessions addressed the state of genome-wide association studies in relation to bipolar disorder and schizophrenia. Full publications are not yet available but it was apparent that no strong findings had emerged, and that such weak associations as were observed were neither in relation to the candidate genes, nor in agreement between different studies.

The discussion was sombre. In the morning Francis Collins, Head of the Human Genome Project, had predicted sure future progress with these technical advances. In the afternoon it was seen that just such a strategy had failed to yield decisive findings.[76]

However, this mood within the research community has not stopped some people from reviving the dream of using genetic knowledge to eradicate psychosis from society. A prominent advocate of using genetic screening for this purpose is James D. Watson, the co-discoverer of the structure of DNA. Watson has a son who has been diagnosed as suffering from schizophrenia and, in response to a question about what he would have done had a genetic test for the disorder been available, was recently quoted as saying, 'I think I would be a monster to want someone to suffer the way he has . . . so, yes, I would have aborted him.'[77]

In addition to fuelling eugenic fantasies, the fundamental error of psychiatry has had a number of other important consequences for patients and mental health professionals. First, by blinding doctors to factors in their patients' histories that would be obvious to anyone without a psychiatric education, it has prevented the medical profession from addressing patients' psychological and social needs. This was most obvious during the period of asylum psychiatry, when drastic interventions to alter patients' brains were preferred to attempts to change the circumstances of their lives, but it continues today, in the form of psychiatric services that are focused on the delivery of medication and which fail to take patients' stories seriously.

Second, as we saw earlier, educational campaigns designed to address the stigma experienced by psychiatric patients have often encouraged the belief that serious mental illnesses are genetically determined. It is assumed that the public will be more tolerant towards the mentally ill if they know that psychiatric patients are not to blame for their misfortunes. However, research conducted in many countries has consistently shown that these efforts are counterproductive.[78] Ordinary people find a psychological account of mental illness more plausible than an exclusively biological account, and those individuals who embrace a biological account are most likely to find people with mental illness frightening. Educating ordinary people that mental illness is caused by genes actually *increases* the extent to which they want to keep psychiatric patients at a distance.[79] It is not hard to see why: an account that attributes strange behaviour to biology implies that it is likely to persist. Most people would much prefer to live close to a person whose unpredictable actions are a consequence of stress and trauma, than next door to someone whose dangerous behaviour is a consequence of an enduring disorder of the brain.

Finally, substantial resources have been spent, and continue to be spent, in the attempt to discover the genetic origins of mental illness, whereas its social origins continue to be neglected. I should perhaps make it clear at this point that I am not opposed to research on the way that genes influence behaviour, but it seems to me that resources should be allocated in proportion to the likely benefits that will be obtained by individuals and society.

In this context, it is important to note that no patient, not a single one, has ever benefited from genetic research into mental illness, although many have been indirectly harmed by it (because it has discouraged the development of adequate services for patients and, during one shameful period, was used to justify their slaughter). No effective treatments have so far been devised on the basis of genetic information and, given what we now know, it seems very unlikely that further research into the genetics of psychosis will lead to important therapeutic advances in the future.¶ Indeed, from the point of view of patients, there can be few other areas of medical research that have yielded such a dismal return for effort expended.

Living with Mr Pinkerton

Hannah told me that she had never discussed her feelings about the abortion with Cedric and I decided that it would be unwise to bring up the topic during our sessions together. Surprisingly, despite (or perhaps because of) his role in the events that triggered Hannah's psychosis, Cedric proved to be an important and eager ally. When I presented the idea that a caring spouse, through being over-protective, could actually exacerbate his mentally ill partner's symptoms, he embraced it enthusiastically. A warm and essentially kind man, he had long ago accepted Mr Pinkerton as an invisible member of the household.

¶ A possibility that seems inconsistent with this negative appraisal has recently been drawn to my attention. It has been suggested that genetic research will help identify patients who have liver enzymes that break down psychiatric drugs before they can reach the brain, rendering them ineffective or even increasing the extent to which they cause side effects. Hence genetic tests might be used to decide which patients should not receive drugs (see, for a discussion, J. Bray and C. Clarke (in press), 'Should we be "pushing meds"? The implications of pharmacogenomics', *Journal of Psychiatric and Mental Health Nursing*). I discuss this development in Chapter 9. However, it is worth noting here that the relevant research concerns the genetics of *liver function* and not the genetics of mental illness.

'It's true,' he said. 'I'm very controlling. I know I am. I should stop but somehow I can't.' I sensed that the abortion had been almost as traumatic for him as it had been for Hannah.

An important point of contention between the two of them turned out to be Hannah's occasional use of alcohol. She was not a heavy drinker, but sometimes liked to down a can or two of lager in the afternoon. Cedric was convinced that even moderate drinking could precipitate a relapse. Every so often he would find an empty can at the bottom of a rubbish bin or secreted elsewhere in the house, evidence that she had been drinking behind his back, and the result was inevitably an almighty row. It seemed to me that the best strategy for dealing with this was to try and negotiate some kind of compromise.

Over the course of a number of sessions the three of us worked together to address other aspects of their relationship. We began to identify activities that Hannah used to enjoy but had not done for some years, such as going to the theatre or cinema. Trips out were planned, first as decided by Cedric, but then planned by an increasingly confident Hannah. Together they took steps to revive their long-dormant social life, and made visits to restaurants with friends. It was not rocket science or sophisticated psychology, but it seemed to be working.

On one memorable occasion, Cedric paused in the middle of speaking, raised his eyebrows and gave me a knowing look.

'What is it?' I asked.

'He's here. Mr Pinkerton.'

I turned to Hannah. 'Is it true?' I asked.

'Oh yes.'

'What is he saying?'

'He's telling me to tell you not to listen to anything *he* says,' she answered, pointing accusingly in the direction of Cedric.

During another session I asked Hannah to describe Mr Pinkerton's personality, and then to describe Cedric.

'Notice something?' I asked Cedric, when she had finished.

'We're opposites,' he said ruefully.

'Which means?'

'I know. I know. I've got to try and be more like Mr Pinkerton!' And we all laughed at the thought of this.

It was never a goal of therapy for Hannah to lose Mr Pinkerton and, after several months of regular meetings, she and Cedric told me that things were very much better in the home, and that they no longer felt they needed my help. At my last session with Hannah, with Cedric absent, she told me that, during the preceding week, Cedric had confessed his guilt about the abortion.

I was curious to know whether Hannah's beliefs about Mr Pinkerton had changed during our time together. By way of an answer she told me a story.

'Yesterday I was walking through the town when I saw your face in front of me,' she said. 'It seemed as real as you are now. Then I thought to myself, no it's just my imagination. Sometimes I think that Mr Pinkerton is like that.'

She paused and then added, 'But I know that he's real.'

7

Brains, Minds and Psychosis: The Myth that Mental Illnesses are Brain Diseases

Brain: an apparatus with which we think we think.
Ambrose Bierce, *The Devil's Dictionary*

Short of imprisoning Paul, or following him around for twenty-four hours a day, there was little we could do to prevent him from killing himself. Afterwards, all of us involved in his care – the psychiatrist, the clinical psychologist, the community psychiatric nurse and the social worker – gathered in a dingy office for the formal review of what had happened. Mulling over our notes, we expressed our collective feelings of impotence. With the benefit of hindsight, his death seemed as inevitable as a collision between a rudderless supertanker and distant rocks.

I had first met Paul in the winter of 1998. A grey-haired, overweight but neatly dressed middle-aged man, he had already been known to psychiatric services for many years. During this time he had received various diagnoses. After an admission to hospital a couple of years before I saw him, his psychiatrist had decided that he was suffering from 'paranoid schizophrenia'. Apparently, his main problem was that he suffered from *delusions*, irrational beliefs that were resistant to evidence or reason.

Paul was quiet and had difficulty articulating his feelings, so it was a struggle to get him to talk about his problems. However, it was apparent from his cowed demeanour that he felt depressed and very threatened. He spent most of our first session together staring at the floor, only occasionally daring to glance upwards to catch my eye. Although he had once believed that there was an organized conspiracy of freemasons who were attempting to have him assassinated, after his hospital treatment this belief had faded to the mere suspicion that others – almost everyone he encountered on the street – bore him ill will. No longer fearing for his life, his main worry seemed to be that his wife was being unfaithful to him and would shortly leave the marital home. This conviction seemed to be based on no evidence that he could explain, and was resistant to the most obvious lines of attack, for example by asking him to draw up a list of the evidence that supported it (his wife sometimes failed to answer her mobile phone when she was supposed to be at work) or which appeared to refute it (they continued to have a reasonably good sex life).

There is a psychiatric literature on delusional jealousy that stretches back for at least a century. My own reading of this literature suggested that it can be difficult to distinguish between jealousy that is pathological and jealousy that is more reality-based. Confusingly, although the American Psychiatric Association's diagnostic manual describes delusions as false personal beliefs, 'based on incorrect inference about external reality and firmly sustained in spite of what almost everyone else believes and in spite of what usually constitutes incontrovertible and obvious proof or evidence to the contrary',[1] experts had suggested that delusional jealousy is unique in that it can be both irrational and true.[2] This is because the jealous patient's behaviour is sometimes so damaging to the marital relationship that the spouse elects to leave into the arms of another. More helpfully, the evidence suggested that this kind of problem typically arises in the context of chronic feelings of low self-esteem or, for reasons that remain unknown, alcoholism. Consistent with these insights, Paul's self-esteem was obviously as low as it could get and, although not strictly an alcoholic, he was prone to heavy drinking while his wife was out working and he remained at home alone.

Exploring Paul's history, I discovered that his mother had died when he was young and that he had been raised by a father who was domineering and had always made him feel inadequate. It seemed that his psychiatric troubles had begun about a decade before our first meeting, when he had been working as a taxi driver in Liverpool. After a series of terrifying encounters with drunken men in the early hours of the morning, he had gradually become too frightened to work. Feeling wretched, he had cowered at home, and his wife – the more outgoing and less neurotic of the two – had become the breadwinner in the family. Eventually, he had succumbed to severe depression and, while his wife was out shopping with their two young children one Saturday afternoon, had decided to kill himself. It was his 7-year-old son who was the first through the door, and who had found him hanging from a rope tied to the banister. Paul's wife had managed to cut him down just in time to save his life, and in this way began his decade-long involvement with the psychiatric services.

Deciding that Paul's low self-esteem was probably the root of his difficulties, I decided to focus on how he felt about himself. Over the following few months, I saw Paul once a week, and worked with him to build up a more positive self-image. We identified areas of his life that he could be proud of, and found ways of testing his fears about what other people thought of him. More importantly, perhaps, we explored things that he could do to regain the feelings of pleasure and mastery that had for so long deserted him. Beginning with country walks and visits to the local pub, Paul began to enjoy simple pleasures in the company of his wife. Although his guilt about the shock he had caused his son was a constant impediment to progress, his mood gradually lifted and he began to feel more optimistic. He cut down on his drinking and, by the time I had finished seeing him, he was looking for a job as a commercial van driver. I congratulated myself on a job well done.

It was nearly two years later that Paul's community psychiatric nurse contacted me again, to tell me that he was in crisis. It seemed that his wife really had abandoned him for another man. To make matters worse, he had been unsuccessful in searching for a job, and now found himself facing a future of loneliness, poverty and, possibly, homelessness. It was just before the Christmas of 2004. Naturally I offered him an appointment as urgently as possible, but it was obvious that this time my task would be much more difficult.

Paul never actually said, 'I told you so,' but his attitude suggested a certain defiance and anger at being disbelieved earlier. When questioned about the future he seemed completely without hope and, to make matters worse, he responded to my enquiries about suicide with clear plans about how he might do it. The only thing holding him back, apparently, was his wish not to further hurt his children, who were now young adults. He was also drinking heavily again, and each binge seemed to leave him more depressed. As soon as he left my office, I urgently wrote a note to his psychiatrist saying that I thought that Paul was now seriously at risk.

In the following weeks everyone in the clinical team fought hard to support Paul. The psychiatrist saw him regularly and increased his antidepressant medication. I saw him several times a week to help him make positive plans for the future, although the haste with which his wife wanted to sell the marital home made this difficult. The nurse, a wonderfully kind and dedicated woman, with whom I talked about Paul frequently, began visiting him almost on a daily basis. To our relief, Paul seemed to realize that his drinking was only making matters worse and promised to lay off the booze. As Christmas approached the team, by email and telephone, debated whether he should be 'sectioned' (compulsorily admitted to hospital) but Paul was adamant that this would only make him feel worse. Compulsory hospitalization is always a difficult step, which can damage the relationship between a patient and the team. We decided to hold our breath and continue to monitor him closely.

After the event, the circumstance that brought about Paul's death seemed so predictable that I was horrified by my failure to anticipate it. By now Paul was living with his son and daughter in his home of more than twenty years, from which he was shortly to be evicted as it went up for sale. His wife had long since moved in with her new lover. A few days before Christmas, she arrived to take the children to a family party to which Paul was not invited. Remaining behind, he found a crate of beer cans hidden in his son's bedroom. I imagine him wondering whether he should take a drink, or follow the psychiatric team's advice. 'What the hell,' he probably thought. 'How can things get any worse?' And one drink no doubt led to another. From the post-mortem report it was apparent that he must have been heavily intoxicated when he secured the noose to the banister and jumped from the upstairs landing. History repeated itself in the most horrible way, and Paul's body was found by his son when he returned from the party.

The meeting in which we reviewed Paul's case was one of the saddest in my professional life. Towards the end, the nurse, who had worked so tirelessly to save him, remarked that Paul had described my work with him as 'Brilliant' and 'Really helpful'.

'Obviously not helpful enough,' I answered grimly.

The significance of biology

Throughout the history of psychiatry, almost totemic significance has been attributed to the question of whether the brains of psychiatric patients are abnormal. Emil Kraepelin assumed that the answer to the question was 'yes', but was unable to provide definitive evidence to support his conviction that dementia praecox, now schizophrenia, was a neurodegenerative disease. Almost half a century after Kraepelin's death, Thomas Szasz retorted that the answer was 'no', and made this assumption the foundation stone of his objections to conventional psychiatry. Once the influence of the antipsychiatry movement had waned, medically orientated psychiatrists drew renewed inspiration from studies that pointed to chemical and ana-tomical peculiarities in the brains of their patients and then, in recent years, have retreated to this evidence as a last line of defence against modern criticisms of the neo-Kraepelinian system. Almost everyone, it seems, has assumed that a great deal hangs on this issue.

In this chapter we shall see that this question is nowhere near as straightforward as has often been supposed, and that attempts to answer it have led more often to confusion than to clarity. It is not simply that the brain is difficult to study; following recent technologi-cal advances, demonstrating that the brains of patients are different from the brains of ordinary people has become almost ridiculously easy. Rather, the problem is working out what these differences mean.

This difficulty has arisen partly because many biological researchers have neglected to consider how the brain abnormalities they have observed might cause the actual problems experienced by patients. It is as if the mere demonstration of differences is sufficient. However, any link between abnormal biology and mental illness will remain obscure in the absence of some understanding of the functions of the relevant circuits in the brain, and of how these functions influence patients' per-ceptions and thinking to cause hallucinations, delusions and other unusual mental phenomena. To compound this oversight, biological investigators have almost universally failed to consider the possibility that their findings might reflect the tribulations of life, rather than some lesion or genetic scar carried by the victim from birth. The picture of severe mental illness that emerges once these factors have been taken into account is at once more complex and more human than the conventional way of thinking about psychiatric disorder.

Brain structure and psychosis

In an earlier chapter, we saw how researchers at Northwick Park Hospital, near London, carried out the earliest modern neuroimaging study of patients with psychosis, which was published in 1976.[3] This paper was the first of many to report that lateral ventricles (fluid-filled cavities in the brain) are enlarged in patients with a diagnosis of schizophrenia, suggesting that there must have been some kind of atrophy of the surrounding neural tissue. For many biological psychiatrists, this has been taken as incontestable evidence of a disease process at work.

The Northwick Park study used computerized axial tomography (CT) to create cross-sectional 'slices' of the brains of patients. CT is an advanced form of X-ray technique, and is therefore poor at visualizing soft tissue. More recently, it has been superseded by a new technology, known as *magnetic resonance imaging* (MRI), in which the body is subjected to a powerful magnetic field and then probed with radio waves, causing it to radiate radio waves itself that are then decoded to provide a more detailed, three-dimensional picture of the internal organs. In a variant of this technique known as *functional magnetic resonance imaging* (fMRI) it is possible to measure not only brain structure but to identify which brain regions demand most oxygenated blood as an individual performs various tasks. This *blood oxygenated-haemoglobin level dependent (BOLD) response* is recorded in the form of a map showing which areas of the brain are most active as the individual performs one task as opposed to another. Careful use of this technique is allowing psychologists to understand how different brain regions work together to sustain our thoughts, feelings and actions.

The rapid proliferation of MRI machines (whereas they were available only to the best resourced hospitals in the early 1990s, quite a few university departments of psychology now have their own) has led to an industry of psychiatric imaging research. For example, in one review of no fewer than 193 structural MRI studies of schizophrenia patients published between 1988 and 2000,[4] the earlier observation of enlarged lateral ventricles was confirmed but abnormalities were also observed in many other brain regions, for example in the medial temporal lobes (especially the amygdala, hippocampus and para-hippocampal gyrus, thought to be involved in memory and the regulation of emotion) and the frontal lobes (which are thought to be involved in higher-level intellectual activities and, in the case of the left frontal lobes, speech production). Similar reviews of the less extensive data available from structural scans of depressed and bipolar patients have also reported differences between patients and ordinary people, especially decreased volume of the hippocampus in the case of depressed patients[5] and enlarged right lateral ventricles in the case of bipolar patients.[6]

Although it is hard not to be impressed by these findings, the results of different studies have often varied, partly because many factors other than illness can affect the shape of the human brain. For example, sex, age, head size, educational achievement, social class, ethnicity, alcohol and medication consumption, water retention and even pregnancy are known to influence what appears on a structural MRI scan.[7] Unless all of these factors are taken into account, which is virtually impossible unless very large numbers of patients and healthy controls are examined, the results obtained can be misleading. There is good evidence, for example, that early CT scan studies exaggerated the extent of ventricular enlargement in schizophrenia patients because the healthy participants used as controls were not representative of the population at large.[8]

Correcting for these sources of bias is only the first of many difficulties faced by the researcher attempting to understand neuroimaging data. In order to appreciate some of these difficulties, it will be useful to consider a particular study, a well-conducted structural MRI comparison between schizophrenia patients, bipolar patients, the patients' relatives and healthy controls, published by researchers at the Institute of Psychiatry in London.[9] I have chosen this study because, unlike many similar investigations (which sometimes have as few as ten people in each group), large numbers of participants (243) were examined, and the patients were carefully diagnosed using detailed psychiatric interviews. The statistical analyses of the data conducted by the researchers attempted to take into account the effects of sex, age, height, whether or not the participants were left- or right-handed, and whether or not they had abused alcohol or drugs. The inclusion of patients' relatives was a further strength and, in order to try and determine whether any brain abnormalities might be inherited, the researchers divided the schizophrenia patients into those they suspected suffered from an inherited disorder (these *familial schizophrenia* patients had a first- or second-degree relative who also had a diagnosis of schizophrenia) and those with a non-inherited disorder (*non-familial schizophrenia*). Another reason for selecting this study is that, in contrast to many others that have reported similarities between schizophrenia and bipolar patients, this study reported important differences. In the case of the schizophrenia patients, the lateral ventricles were enlarged and the volume of the hippocampus was reduced, but the brains of the bipolar patients were not similarly affected. The relatives of patients with familial schizophrenia had enlarged lateral ventricles but the ventricles of the relatives of bipolar patients were normal. (In a separate study, the same investigators reported that both schizophrenia and bipolar patients had low volumes of white matter – the tracts connecting different parts of the brain – but that the schizophrenia patients, uniquely, also had reduced volumes of neuronal grey matter.[10]) As the authors of the study conclude, if these findings are accepted at face value they are powerful evidence that schizophrenia and bipolar disorder are separate diseases.

It is first worth noting that, despite the average differences between patients with different diagnoses, careful inspection of the data reveals enormous variability within each of the groups, especially with respect to ventricular volume. Five of the schizophrenia patients appeared to have particularly large ventricles, whereas those of the remaining thirty-seven do not look obviously outside the normal range. Furthermore, the extent to which the findings might have been influenced by the medication taken by the patients is unclear. The patients diagnosed with schizophrenia were receiving, on average, about twice as much antipsychotic medication as the patients diagnosed as suffering from bipolar disorder, and both animal and human studies[11] have shown that treatment with some antipsychotic drugs can cause a reduction of grey-matter volume.[12] To complicate matters further, there is also evidence that the volume of some brain regions, particularly the mid-brain structures that are rich in dopamine neurones, may increase following drug treatment.[13] Not surprisingly, other researchers have attempted to overcome this problem by conducting MRI studies on first-episode patients who have not yet received medication; however, the results of these studies have generally been less consistent than the results obtained from patients who have been ill and receiving treatment for some time.[14]

Of course, the relatives of the schizophrenia patients studied by the Institute of Psychiatry researchers were not receiving medication, and it was concluded that the increase in ventricular volume observed in this group was evidence that it is probably inherited by patients with familial schizophrenia. However, if this observation is correct it could well mean that ventricular enlargement is only distantly related to psychotic symptoms as, of course, none of the relatives were actually ill.

A more important limitation of this study is that we do not know how patients diagnosed as suffering from schizoaffective disorder would have appeared had they been included. It is possible that the results obtained from these patients would have fallen somewhere between those of the schizophrenia and bipolar patients, in which case the findings, far from supporting Kraepelin's distinction between two major types of psychiatric disorder, would be evidence that they are related. This *fallacy of the excluded middle* was identified as a serious flaw in many biological studies of psychosis more than a decade ago by the British psychiatrist Tim Crow.[15]

We also do not know whether the observed brain abnormalities were related to any particular symptoms. Current diagnostic rules ensure that patients with negative symptoms are almost invariably diagnosed as suffering from schizophrenia rather than bipolar disorder, and there is evidence from other studies that symptoms of this kind may be specifically related to ventricular enlargement.[16] Again, if this is the explanation for the differences observed between the groups it would undermine the researchers' conclusion that schizophrenia and bipolar disorder are meaningful diagnoses, reflecting distinct disease processes.

A final and perhaps crucial limitation of this and every other psychiatric neuroimaging study that has so far been conducted is that no account was taken of the patients' life experiences. The Institute of Psychiatry researchers do not tell us how many of the patients in the two diagnostic groups (or, for that matter, their relatives and the controls) had been traumatized, victimized, or separated from their parents at an early age, because they simply assumed that this kind of information was irrelevant. However, far from being irrelevant it is crucial, not only because many psychotic patients have suffered difficult life experiences, but also because there is compelling evidence that these kinds of experiences can alter the structure of the brain.[17] For example, the brains of people who have survived sexual abuse in childhood, compared to the brains of other people, show reduced volume in the hippocampus[18] and corpus callosum,[19] altered symmetry in the frontal lobes, and reduced neuronal density in the anterior cingulate[20] – all regions that have been implicated in psychosis at one time or another.

Some years ago, John Read, a British psychologist living in New Zealand[21] pointed out that it is entirely possible that the structural abnormalities seen in the brains of psychotic patients are the consequence of environmental stress. So far, no evidence has emerged to challenge this hypothesis, which has been almost completely overlooked by biological researchers studying psychosis. An obvious way of addressing this possibility would be to compare the brains of psychotic patients who have experienced trauma and those who have not, with those of non-psychotic people who have been traumatized. Studies of this kind have yet to be conducted, presumably because it has never occurred to neuroimaging researchers that they might be informative.

The neurochemistry of psychosis

A parallel set of issues affects the interpretation of neurochemical evidence collected from psychotic patients. It will be recalled that the *dopamine theory* of schizophrenia, which states that the disorder is caused by some kind of over-activity in the mid-brain neural circuits that use dopamine as a neurotransmitter, appears to be supported by two lines of evidence. First, all antipsychotic drugs are known to block a particular type of dopamine receptor (the D_2 receptor). Second, drugs that stimulate the synthesis of dopamine in the brain, for example amphetamine and 1-dopa (used to treat Parkinson's disease) can provoke psychotic episodes in ordinary people. Hence psychosis seems to be associated with oversensitivity of the dopamine system, whereas reducing its sensitivity seems to lead to an improvement in patients' symptoms.

However, attempts to demonstrate that the dopamine system is dysfunctional in patients have been fraught with difficulty. Researchers first attempted to measure the major metabolites of dopamine (the chemicals that are created as dopamine is broken down in the body) such as homovanillic acid (HVA) in cerebrospinal fluid (the clear fluid that occupies the cerebral ventricles and the subarachnoid space between the brain and the inside of the skull). However, these studies generally failed to find any evidence that these metabolites were more abundant in patients, suggesting that levels of dopamine were not elevated in their brains.

This failure suggested a second possibility, which was that the number of D_2 receptors was increased in schizophrenia patients. Initial excitement at post-mortem studies that appeared to demonstrate this was the case was muted by the discovery, from animal studies, that prolonged treatment with antipsychotics causes the brain to proliferate D_2 receptors.[22] Researchers therefore tried to exploit the new neuroimaging technologies to try and measure the density of D_2 receptors in the brains of living patients who had yet to receive antipsychotic drugs. The method exploited for this purpose was *positron emission tomography* (PET), a technique which predated MRI and is better suited to detecting particular chemical processes in the brain, but which is much more expensive and difficult to use. Patients examined by PET are injected with radioactive tracers which can be tracked through the body by cameras that detect the emission of subatomic particles called positrons. In what was once billed as the most important experiment in the history of psychiatry,[23] researchers at Johns Hopkins University in the United States injected radiolabelled haloperidol (an antipsychotic drug) into seven drug-naive patients and, by observing the extent to which it binded to receptors in the mid-brain, appeared to find evidence that these patients had more D_2 receptors than healthy controls.[24]

Unfortunately, some later studies failed to find evidence of increased numbers of D_2 receptors in the brains of untreated schizophrenia patients,[25] others have reported different kinds of receptor abnormalities (e.g. reductions in the density of D_2 receptors in the anterior cingulate, and in the density of D_1 receptors in the frontal cortex) and at least one has reported increased D_2 receptor density in non-psychotic bipolar patients.[26] Although some of these inconsistencies no doubt reflect the considerable technical difficulties involved in this kind of work, with different researchers choosing to use different radioactive tracers,[27] the overall picture provides little support for the idea that dopamine receptor abnormalities cause psychosis.

The most recent evidence available from PET studies suggests that the mid-brain dopamine system is abnormal only in the midst of a psychotic crisis and not before or afterwards. When given amphetamine (which is converted into dopamine in the brain), patients suffering from florid delusions and hallucinations but not those whose symptoms are in remission, show a greater surge in the synthesis of dopamine than ordinary people. Hence, it has been suggested that abnormal dopamine functioning is 'the wind in the psychotic fire',[28] which is, in turn, a consequence of a more complex network of chemical processes elsewhere in the brain.[29]

In order to understand how an abnormality of this sort might be connected to symptoms, it is obviously important to know what the dopamine neurones in the mid-brain do. Over the past twenty years evidence has accumulated to show that they play an important role in learning and specifically in the anticipation of rewards ('wanting' rather than 'liking', in the terminology of one account[30]). It seems that, in both classical and operant conditioning, dopamine neurones signal a 'reward prediction error' whenever there is a discrepancy between an expected reward and the actual reward that is experienced.[31] This reward prediction error, in turn, allows the animal to adjust its behaviour so that it becomes better able to predict and obtain rewarding stimuli in the future. This mechanism may help to explain why antipsychotic drugs are so effective in the treatment of mania, which is sometimes triggered by goal attainment experiences that are highly rewarding (for example, getting a new job; obtaining a qualification).[32]

The role of dopamine neurones in the anticipation of negative events has been neglected until recently, partly because there is little evidence that they fire in response to the mere presentation of unpleasant stimuli.[33] However, as we saw in Chapter 3, it has been known since the very beginning of modern psychopharmacology that all the effective antipsychotic drugs prevent animals from *avoiding* such stimuli. This suggests, of course, that dopamine neurones play a role in the prediction of aversive events that parallels their role in the prediction of rewards. Recent fMRI studies have confirmed this by showing that the mid-brain regions that are rich in dopamine neurones become highly activated as people learn to anticipate not only positive events but also negative events.[34] Adapting the terms that have been used to describe dopamine's role in reward learning, it might be said that it is involved in not-wanting, but not in disliking.

A little later we shall see how a disruption of this process might be specifically related to paranoid beliefs. However, for the moment we may note that there is compelling evidence that the dopamine system, like the gross anatomy of the brain, can be affected by lifetime experiences of unpleasant events. Animal researchers have been able to engineer experiences of victimization in rodents by placing them in cages in which other rodents are already living. In these circumstances, the resident animal usually attacks the intruding animal, provoking submissive behaviour. It has been found that animals that are socially defeated in this way show increased sensitization of the dopamine system (as evidenced, for example, by their increased sensitivity to dopamine-stimulating drugs), especially if they are isolated from other animals immediately afterwards, or if the process is repeated a number of times.[35]

This finding makes sense in the light of the evidence that dopamine neurones are involved in anticipating threats.[36] Indeed, from this perspective it seems hardly surprising that the nervous system of an animal living a life of repeated victimization will become highly attuned to the detection of further threatening events. The perceptive reader may already see the glimmerings of an account of paranoia that brings together the psychological and biological evidence but, before chasing this idea further, we must look at one more way in which researchers have attempted to show that psychosis is a consequence of brain disease.

Cognitive functioning and psychosis

Psychologists have their own methods of studying how well the brain is functioning, and have developed various *neurocognitive tests* for this purpose. The most general kind is the intelligence test, which most people are familiar with. Many IQ tests, such as the Wechsler Adult Intelligence Scale, in fact measure a wide range of verbal and non-verbal thinking skills, and these subtests can either be examined independently, or a summary score can be calculated on the assumption that each skill relies, to a large degree, on a single underlying trait of general intelligence (sometimes referred to simply as 'g'). Other tests measure specific cognitive abilities such as attention, memory, or higher order 'executive functions' responsible for planning and abstract thought. Still others are neuropsychological tests, designed to detect damage to particular regions of the brain. (Perhaps the best known of these is the Wisconsin Card Sort Task, a kind of game in which the person being tested has to try and work out a rule which changes without warning. People suffering from damage to the frontal lobes of the brain find this task particularly difficult.)

All these tests have been employed by psychologists at one time or another, in the hope of discovering the neurological difficulties presumed to be underlying schizophrenia, bipolar disorder and major depression. The patients participating in these studies have consistently been shown to perform poorly compared to 'healthy controls', but close scrutiny of the findings reveals that they provide only limited evidence in support of the idea that brain damage plays an important role in psychosis.

One problem in making sense of the findings is that the performance of patients is affected by their motivation. Beginning in the 1930s, the American psychologist David Shakow (who played an important role in establishing the profession of clinical psychology in the

United States) found that patients diagnosed as suffering from schizophrenia performed, on average, less well than other people on a wide range of tests, but also that their performance improved markedly if they were offered the right encouragement and incentives.[37] This problem of the effect of motivation on test performance, identified by Shakow, continues to dog modern studies; for example, poor performance on the Wisconsin Card Sort Task has often been interpreted as evidence that schizophrenia patients fail to use the frontal lobes of their brain effectively – sometimes called the *hypofrontality hypothesis* – but this claim is undermined by studies showing that patients perform much better if paid to do well.[38]

This problem also applies to functional neuroimaging studies. A recent attempt to synthesize the findings from 155 fMRI studies with schizophrenia patients used a statistical technique known as *meta-analysis* to combine the data from all the studies and obtain an overall result from 4,043 patients and 3,977 healthy controls.[39] Strong evidence that patients fail to switch on or engage the frontal lobes when attempting the Wisconsin Card Sort or similar tasks was reported, which looks like clear evidence in support of the hypofrontality hypothesis. However, an MRI scan requires the patient to lie in a narrow aperture and to ignore the very loud noises emitted by the machine, so motivational factors are even more likely to be an issue in this kind of environment.

In the 1990s research on the relationship between neurocognitive performance and psychosis was given new impetus by the discovery that intellectual deficits appeared to be present before people became ill. This finding emerged from large 'cohort' studies of people who have been administered IQ tests or related measures early in life, and who have been followed up for many years afterwards. For example, in a series of studies in which thousands of British infants were followed into adulthood in order to investigate how their health needs changed with age, it was found that those who were later diagnosed as suffering from schizophrenia were slower to reach early developmental milestones such as walking or speaking their first words, and performed poorly on measures of verbal skills administered while at school.[40] In another study, carried out in Israel, it was found that people who were diagnosed as schizophrenic in adulthood performed poorly in intelligence tests administered in adolescence during that country's screening process for military service.[41]

At first sight, this seems to be impressive evidence that brain damage predates the onset of severe mental illness. However, as usual it is important to read the fine print. The first question to ask is whether it is possible to be 'schizophrenic' and have a very high IQ, and it seems that the answer to this question is a definitive 'yes'. John Forbes Nash, winner of the 1994 Nobel Prize for economics, who has spent many years of his life diagnosed as suffering from paranoid schizophrenia, is perhaps the best known example of genius wracked by psychosis, thanks to a celebrated biography[42] which was later turned into a feature film. However, there are so many others that some researchers have been moved to investigate whether psychotic tendencies are associated with abnormal levels of creativity (a proposition for which there is considerable evidence[43]).

Because high IQ does not seem to preclude severe mental illness, some researchers have tried to find out whether psychosis in highly intelligent people differs from psychosis in patients with obvious cognitive difficulties. A recent study comparing schizophrenia patients who had graduated from university with those who had been less successful academically found that the former were more likely to be depressed but were less likely to suffer from negative symptoms.[44] Hence, emotional disturbance seemed to be more prominent when cognitive impairment was absent. However, no other differences were observed.

A further complication concerns the non-specificity of the cognitive evidence. Whenever adult patients diagnosed as suffering from schizophrenia, bipolar disorder and major depression are compared, similarities are more evident than differences.[45] Like patients diagnosed as suffering from schizophrenia, children who are later on diagnosed as suffering from bipolar disorder or major depression perform relatively poorly on cognitive tests, well before the onset of their illnesses.[46]

Schizophrenia patients' performance on most intellectual and neuropsychological tests does not seem to be related to the severity of their hallucinations and delusions[47] (although some very specific cognitive skills may play a role in some symptoms). Indeed, in a recent US study of almost 1,500 schizophrenia patients, the correlation between cognitive ability and positive symptoms was essentially zero.[48] In contrast, many studies have shown that positive symptoms are closely related to feelings of depression and anxiety.[49] For example, in a series of studies conducted by psychologist Inez Myin-Germeys in Holland, in which patients kept detailed diaries, it was found that even patients with prominent negative symptoms were extremely sensitive to minor negative events experienced in their everyday lives[50] and that this kind of sensitivity was unrelated to their performance on a range of cognitive tests.[51] (Of course, this observation is entirely consistent with the pharmacological evidence we looked at earlier, which highlights the role of the dopamine neurones in the processing of emotionally salient stimuli.* However, it is hard to square with Kraepelin's assumption that schizophrenia is a neurodegenerative disease or with most modern biological accounts of psychosis.)

Inevitably, some psychologists have begun to rethink the role of cognitive impairment in psychosis. For example, Michael Foster Green[52] at the University of California in Los Angeles has noted that performance in general cognitive tests is closely related to social functioning. Patients who perform poorly in these tests also have difficulty maintaining friendships, in negotiating other kinds of interactions with other people, in holding down jobs and so on. As the most complex and difficult kind of stimulus we encounter in everyday life is another person, it is perhaps unsurprising that handicaps in thinking and reasoning should result in difficulties in these areas.

Green still believes that cognitive dysfunction is a central feature of psychosis but, to my mind, this discovery seems to point to a very different conclusion. Perhaps people who lack mental agility, who are socially isolated and who suddenly experience voices or paranoid thoughts are typically overwhelmed and terrified by these experiences. Under these circumstances they will very likely end up receiving psychiatric treatment. Those who are able to take a step back and think

---

* In recent years there has been an increasing tendency to use the term *non-affective psychosis* instead of schizophrenia (by contrast, patients who would typically be diagnosed as suffering from bipolar disorder or major depression with psychotic features are sometimes lumped together under the term *affective psychosis*). It should be absolutely clear from the evidence I have outlined in this chapter that there is no such thing as a non-affective psychosis.

carefully about their symptoms, on the other hand, will be more likely to find ways of coping without psychiatric help, especially if they already have good social networks, careers and long-term goals.

The crucial test of this hypothesis is how well functioning people with psychosis perform in cognitive tests. We must remember that for every patient who receives treatment, there are about ten psychotic non-patients who have not sought psychiatric help. If cognitive impairment plays a central role in psychosis these people should still be impaired. If, on the other hand, cognitive functioning affects the ability to cope outside the psychiatric system, these people should perform as well as or perhaps even better than ordinary people.

The only study I know of which has attempted to address this question is as yet unpublished and was recently conducted by Caroline Brett, a Ph.D. student at the Institute of Psychiatry in London. She found that the performance of healthy psychotic people on most tests was slightly better than average, or at least as good as that of people who have never experienced symptoms.[53]

How to explain psychosis

The critique of the biological evidence that I have outlined in this and the two preceding chapters implies that conventional psychiatry, which reached its zenith with the neo-Kraepelinian movement, has not only failed to deliver tangible benefits for patients (antipsychotics, it will be recalled, were an accidental discovery) but has also failed to deliver a credible explanation of psychosis. It is not that there is a lack of biological evidence; rather, the evidence has been misinterpreted and shoehorned into a biomedical framework that fits it poorly. A radical new approach to understanding severe mental illness, which brings together the evidence on the social, psychological and biological causes of psychosis, is urgently required.

In my previous book, *Madness Explained*, I attempted to describe in detail an emerging alternative to the neo-Kraepelinian system[54] and, in the remaining part of this chapter, I give a brief flavour of this new approach. The key to it is to recognize that, whereas we may not be able to agree about who has 'schizophrenia' and who has 'bipolar disorder', we can agree about who experiences auditory hallucinations, who experiences paranoid delusions, who is hypomanic and so on. Indeed, unless educated to do so by well-intentioned mental health professionals, patients arriving at the psychiatric clinic never complain of 'schizophrenia' or 'bipolar disorder', but of various types of behaviours and experiences which doctors call 'symptoms' but which might be better called 'complaints'. When trying to understand the mechanisms underlying complaints, we need not worry about whether the person who, say, hears a voice is diagnosed as suffering from 'schizophrenia' or 'bipolar disorder' and the problem of psychiatric classification can therefore be safely ignored altogether. Once the complaints have been explained, there will be no 'schizophrenia' and 'bipolar disorder' left behind to explain afterwards.

To convincingly demonstrate how this approach can lead to a complete account of psychosis, it would be necessary to describe the substantial research that has been conducted on the full range of psychotic symptoms, but the limited space available here precludes this (the interested reader is referred to *Madness Explained*). However, I can illustrate the approach by describing first, in some detail, how recent research has led to an understanding of the processes that lead to paranoid delusions (the symptom I have studied most intensively) and then, in less detail, the considerable advances that have also been made in understanding the causes of auditory hallucinations.

The engine of paranoia

Bizarre or delusional beliefs are perhaps the most obvious expression of psychosis, but they tend to be limited to a small number of themes. In some patients they involve ideas of *grandiosity* (for example, that the patient is a historically important figure, has enormous wealth or possesses superhuman abilities). In other patients they involve feelings of *guilt* (the patient believes he has committed a terrible crime), *jealousy* (in the absence of any evidence, a partner is believed to be unfaithful) or *love* (the patient irrationally believes that she is adored by someone important, for example a pop star or famous politician). However, worldwide, by far the most common type of delusion is

Instinctive Behaviour _
Survival - kill or be killed
power

Dramatic change in
behavior

166

paranoid or persecutory, in which the patient believes that he or she is the focus of some kind of malevolent plot or conspiracy.[55] In one of my own studies, of 255 psychotic patients admitted to hospital for the first time, about 90 per cent had this kind of belief.[56]

Sometimes patients are convinced that they are being persecuted by people living nearby. Peter, whom we met at the very beginning of this book, thought that former friends who he had lost touch with were planning to attack and perhaps even murder him. Others, like Paul whom I described at the beginning of this chapter, suspect that they are the victims of organized conspiracies conducted by government agencies or secret organizations such as the freemasons or the CIA. In the last chapter, we saw that these kinds of beliefs tend to arise following experiences of victimization, especially when individuals already have difficulty in forming close, trusting relationships with other people. The task of psychology is to explain the mechanisms that lead from these kinds of experiences to the kinds of beliefs observed in the clinic.

In the grip of the disease model of psychosis, psychiatrists have sometimes insisted that delusions are 'empty speech acts, whose informational content refers to neither world nor self'.[57] However, the fact that the most frequently observed delusional beliefs reflect almost universal worries about our position in the social universe suggests that they must be closely related to commonplace existential concerns. Not surprisingly, distinguishing between delusional and non-delusional beliefs can sometimes be a tricky business. In Chapter 5, I described the case of Andrew, the ex-soldier whose psychiatrists insisted that he suffered from paranoid schizophrenia. If his behaviour was considered in isolation it was easy to see why his doctors thought he was delusional. On the other hand, once his history was known, his beliefs seemed more understandable, and his escalating feelings of paranoia appeared to be a predictable reaction to what was being done to him. Difficulties of this sort become less perplexing when we recognize that most people at times experience mild fears of persecution or disapproval, and that paranoia therefore exists on a continuum of severity.[58] It is worth noting that the distribution of paranoid tendencies in the population does not fit the normal 'bell-curve'. In this respect, paranoia is unlike IQ or height, traits for which most people exhibit values in the middle range with few individuals showing either very low or very high scores. Rather, the majority of people show very low levels of paranoia, and highly paranoid people are fairly rare. This difference is potentially informative because normally distributed traits like height or IQ tend to be caused by many independent but additive factors, whereas the kind of distribution exhibited by paranoid beliefs usually indicates that some of the causal factors are required to interact (occur together).[59]

Nonetheless, some differences can be observed within the paranoid continuum. Two British psychologists, Peter Trower and Paul Chadwick,[60] have argued that some patients, whom they describe as suffering from *poor-me paranoia*, feel that their persecution is undeserved, whereas other *bad-me* patients believe that they deserve to be persecuted, perhaps because they possess some loathsome characteristic, or because of some kind of terrible crime that they have committed. Bad-me paranoia tends to be associated with much lower self-esteem and higher levels of depression than the poor-me variety, although even in poor-me patients self-esteem tends to be lower than in ordinary people.[61]

Of our two paranoid patients discussed earlier, Peter was clearly poor-me whereas Paul was bad-me. In clinical practice, poor-me delusions are much more common than bad-me beliefs.[62] However, patients often oscillate from one type of paranoia to the other so that, although they are poor-me most of the time, they become bad-me for short periods.[63] Highly paranoid people who are not psychotic, on the other hand, nearly always have consistently bad-me beliefs and think that others hate them for good reason.[64] Piecing all of this information together, it seems likely that, for most paranoid patients, the perception that persecution is deserved evolves from bad-me to poor-me during the progression from non-psychotic paranoia into a full-blown psychotic episode, but then fluctuates afterwards (see Fig. 1).

These observations suggest that problems of self-esteem may be the engine that drives paranoid thinking. This is not a particularly original hypothesis. For example, the early psychoanalysts suggested that fears of persecution are caused by dysfunctional defences against unacceptable feelings about the self. Although different analysts proposed

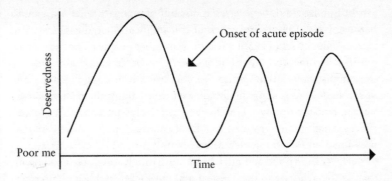

Figure 1. The possible evolution of paranoid beliefs.

different versions of this theory (Freud himself argued that paranoia is a consequence of attempts to deny latent homosexual feelings[65]), the general idea is that, by attributing misfortunes to the malevolence of other people, the paranoid person protects himself from assuming responsibility for them.[66] This account has seemed so compelling to some psychologists that they have proposed that paranoia should be regarded as a form of 'camouflaged depression'.[67]

The paranoid mind

Of course a good psychological account of paranoia will have to be supported by experimental evidence; it is not enough, as the psychoanalysts have done, to rely on clinical judgement. During the last twenty years, I have tried to make progress in this area by studying how paranoid patients explain their life experiences.

To understand why this approach is likely to be fruitful, it will help to think about how we use explanations in our daily lives. Most people think about the causes of their experiences all the time; it has been estimated that we produce a sentence that either includes or implies the word 'because' in about every one hundred words of speech.[68] Psychologists have long suspected that the way we construct statements of this kind – sometimes called *causal attributions* – has profound implications for our mental health. For example, a causal attribution is said to be *internal* if it is self-blaming ('I failed the exam because I am stupid') and *external* if it implicates circumstances ('It was an unlucky set of exam questions') or other people ('The examiner tried to trip me up'). Attributions can also be classified as *stable* if they imply causes that cannot be changed ('I lack intelligence') or *unstable* if there is something that we can do about them ('I was too busy to revise properly'). Finally, they can be classified as either *global* if they affect many areas of our life ('I don't cope very well under pressure') or *specific* if they affect us only in certain circumstances ('I've never been good at maths'). Not surprisingly, research has shown that people who are in the habit of making global, stable and internal explanations for negative events ('I failed the exam because I'm stupid') are especially likely to become depressed.[69] In the face of adversity, they think badly of themselves, their self-esteem plummets and they crumble. By contrast, mentally healthy people tend to make internal, stable and global attributions for positive events ('If it goes right it's because I am a hard worker') and external, unstable and specific attributions ('It was bad luck on the day') when things go wrong. Although hardly fair-minded, this style of thinking acts as a buffer against the slings and arrows of outrageous fortune, allowing us to bounce back after setbacks.

In some of my earliest studies, I found that patients with paranoid delusions, even when compared to ordinary people, tend to make excessively external explanations for negative events,[70] and especially explanations that implicated the actions of others.[71] It was as if they were masters at attributing blame to other people when things went wrong. Like the early psychoanalysts, I assumed that this was a dysfunctional mechanism for avoiding feelings of low self-esteem, which produced paranoia as a by-product. According to this idea, when avoiding negative beliefs about the self by attributing their misfortunes to external causes, paranoid patients inevitably blame other people, thereby feeding their persecutory beliefs.

This theory was interesting enough to prompt other researchers to study causal reasoning in patients with delusions. The results of these efforts were not always consistent. Disappointingly, although many investigators replicated our findings[72] some did not.[73] However, these inconsistencies can be resolved by looking more closely at the patients selected for these studies. Recently, researchers in the United States, Australia and Holland have independently reported that external, defensive attributions for negative events are made only by acutely ill patients (who are nearly always poor-me), and not by ordinary people who score highly on measures of paranoia (who, we have seen, tend to have bad-me beliefs).[74] Another group at the Institute of Psychiatry has recently reported that only those patients who are both grandiose and paranoid (presumably poor-me) make defensive attributions, whereas less grandiose paranoid patients do not.[75] At the same time, careful examination of data collected from patients as they switched from poor-me to bad-me beliefs has revealed that it is only during the poor-me phase that patients respond abnormally on our attribution measures.[76] Hence, it seems that the attributional defence is present only in acutely ill poor-me patients, and then only intermittently.

This observation has led me to take a closer look at self-esteem in paranoid patients. One limitation of most previous studies is that patients were examined only once, allowing researchers to get a mere snapshot of their mental processes. However, people are more like movies than still photographs – our mental processes are changing all the time as we solve the problems we encounter in our lives. Psychologist Inez Myin-Germeys and her colleagues in Maastricht, Holland, have developed a technique known as the *experience sampling method*, which can be used to examine these kinds of shifts in thinking and emotion. Patients in these studies wear electronic watches that bleep at random intervals several times a day. They are asked to fill in a short diary recording what they are doing and what they are thinking and feeling, every time they hear a bleep.

Viviane Thewissen, one of Inez's Ph.D. students, asked a group of patients with (mostly poor-me) paranoid delusions, a group of healthy people who scored highly on a questionnaire measure of paranoia, and a group of non-paranoid people to record their self-esteem using this method. She found that paranoia was associated with self-esteem that was, on average, quite low, but which was extremely unstable, as reflected by dramatic fluctuations from one bleep to the next.[77] In a further as yet unpublished analysis of the data from this study, Viviane, Inez and I have recently found that periods in which the patients felt intensely paranoid were typically preceded by a sudden drop in self-esteem and an increase in anger. From these data, it looks as if paranoid patients are locked into a constant struggle to maintain their self-esteem, very often failing.

Although these findings make the attributional model of paranoia appear quite plausible, it is not completely satisfactory as it stands because it does not seem to explain some of the more bizarre conspiracy theories developed by patients when they are acutely ill. Paul had at one time believed that he was about to be harmed by freemasons. Other patients attribute their persecution to a variety of supernatural (the Devil, Satanists, malevolent spiritual forces), technological (aliens from another world, a secret cabal of scientists) or political forces (the Home Office, the South African secret service), or to imaginary conspiracies comprising people they have met (everyone in the neighbourhood, led by the young man who lives down the road). It is as if something stops them from questioning their bizarrest fantasies about what is happening to them. This brings us to the two other mechanisms that other researchers have suggested might play an important role in paranoid thinking.

Some years ago, Philippa Garety, a psychologist at the Institute of Psychiatry in London, discovered that patients with delusions make very hasty decisions when trying to make sense of sequentially presented and inconsistent information, a situation we often encounter in ordinary life.[78] Imagine, for example, working for an employer who sometimes issues praise for the slightest achievement and at other times is scathing and critical. Under these circumstances, it might be difficult to form a clear impression about what the employer really thinks. The more we wait and collect the evidence before rushing to a judgement, the more likely we are to form an accurate impression.

The Institute of Psychiatry researchers used a deceptively simple test to measure the tendency to jump to conclusions in these kinds of circumstances. They showed people two jars filled with beads, one with mostly white beads and a few that were coloured red, and one with mostly red beads and a few that were coloured white. The jars were then hidden away and the participants were shown a single bead and told that they could *either* guess which jar it had been taken from *or* ask to see another bead from the same jar. Most people taking this test wait until they have seen a few beads before reaching a decision. Studies by the team at the Institute, which were subsequently replicated by researchers elsewhere, showed that patients with psychotic disorders, and especially those with delusions, tend to guess prematurely.[79] In fact, many guess after seeing just one bead.

The third mechanism that has been implicated in paranoia was first identified by psychologists Rhiannon Corcoran and Chris Frith, at University College London. They suggested that paranoid patients might have difficulty understanding what other people are thinking.[80] In ordinary life, we constantly try and imagine what other people are thinking and anticipate what they are likely to do. This skill, sometimes misleadingly described as having a 'theory of mind'† (ToM) is, so far as we know, unique to human beings, and is necessary to maintain the kinds of rich and complex social networks that most people typically enjoy. The skill can be tested by, for example, asking people to interpret hints ('I'm late for work and my shirt isn't ironed, darling'), or to solve problems that involve working out whether other people have false beliefs or are using deception. Autistic children have very serious difficulties with problems of this kind and it has therefore been argued that their inability to understand other people is responsible for the enormous social and language problems they experience as they grow up.[81] Rhiannon Corcoran and Chris Frith's idea was that paranoid patients might suffer from a more subtle theory of mind impairment that prevents them from correctly understanding the intentions of others. This idea has some intuitive plausibility, as misreading the attitudes of other people might, in some circumstances, lead to the perception of threatening intentions when none exist. In fact, although research has consistently shown that currently ill but not recovered psychotic patients perform poorly on theory of mind tests, the idea that this difficulty is specifically related to paranoia has not always been supported.[82] However, one possibility is that the influence of theory of mind deficits on paranoid thinking is indirect. For example, in one of my own studies I found that poor ToM skills in ordinary people tended to be associated with a tendency to make

† The term was first used by American animal behaviourists David Premack and Gary Woodruff, who, in a much-celebrated paper, asked 'Does the chimpanzee have a theory of mind?' (*Behavioural and Brain Sciences*, 4: 515–26, 1978).

other-blaming attributions for negative events – it appears that, if we have a bad experience with another person (for example, if a friend ignores us) we tend to assume that this reflects some enduring trait in the person (that he is evil) unless we can see the world from her point of view (we can imagine that the friend is not feeling well or is suffering from stress).[83]

Recently, I had the opportunity to investigate all three of the mechanisms I have just described – problems of self-esteem, jumping to conclusions and theory of mind problems – in the same sample of patients, making it possible for the first time to assess the relative importance of each mechanism. The study was funded by the Wellcome Trust, a UK medical research charity, and was carried out by a team that, in addition to myself, included Rhiannon Corcoran (now at the University of Nottingham), Peter Kinderman (University of Liverpool), Georgina Rowse (University of Sheffield) and Robert Howard and Nigel Blackwood (University of London Institute of Psychiatry).[84] One of our aims was to compare paranoid patients diagnosed as suffering from schizophrenia with paranoid patients whose primary diagnosis was depression. We wanted to ensure that the psychological processes that we were studying were specifically related to persecutory beliefs rather than to a particular diagnosis. Another aim was to compare patients who were currently paranoid with those who had recovered from their delusions. We looked for schizophrenia patients with persecutory delusions and some who no longer had them,‡ depressed patients with paranoid beliefs and depressed patients who had never been paranoid. We also found a group of psychotic patients who had developed paranoid beliefs late in life (after turning 65) because, according to some psychiatrists, this type of late-onset illness might be different from the more common types of psychosis which begin in early adulthood. To provide appropriate comparisons, we also recruited people, both young and old, who had never been mentally ill. In total, we gave about three hours of psychiatric and psychological tests to more than 230 people (to

‡ We also attempted to find schizophrenia patients who had never been paranoid. However, this proved extraordinary difficult, presumably because the diagnostic rules make it very unlikely that anyone could be diagnosed as schizophrenic without experiencing paranoia at some point in time.

avoid exhaustion, the tests were administered over several days). Although the findings were complex, the main conclusion we reached was a simple one: all three mechanisms seemed to be important in paranoid delusions.

The reader may by now be wondering how these findings connect to the research I discussed in the last chapter, which implicates insecure attachment and victimization in paranoid beliefs. The answer is that these kinds of experiences provide exactly the circumstances in which individuals are most likely to develop low self-esteem and a highly defensive attributional style. Indeed, this is what we often observe clinically: Paul's self-esteem problems seemed to be the consequence of the early loss of his mother and his difficult relationship with his father, and his paranoid beliefs developed following repeated experiences of being threatened while driving his taxi.

We are therefore led to a fairly simple but plausible account of the pathway leading from adversity to paranoid thinking, shown in Fig. 2. Note that, in this theoretical model, excessive anticipation of threat is the final step in the pathway. This is consistent with the results of studies which I have not had the space to describe here, which show that a tendency to overestimate threats correlates so highly with clinical measures of paranoia that it can almost be regarded as definitional of paranoid thinking.[85] Importantly, these studies show that paranoid patients tend to overestimate the likelihood of all kinds of unpleasant social interactions (for example, snubs and criticism by friends), and not just threats specifically related to their delusional beliefs.

The model raises the prospect of an account of paranoia that draws together both psychological and biological data because, as we saw earlier, the dopamine system in the mid-brain is responsible for anticipating future threats and initiating avoidance behaviour. Consistent with this idea, drugs that affect the dopamine system, for example amphetamine, sometimes provoke paranoid reactions in ordinary people, presumably because they produce a heightened estimation of threat. This does not mean that the delusions seen in patients are *caused* by an abnormality of the dopamine system. It seems more likely that, in patients, the dopamine system becomes sensitized as a consequence of adverse experiences that predate the onset of illness. Indeed, up to a certain point, this sensitization can be regarded as

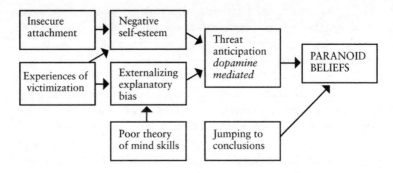

Figure 2. A model of paranoia.

adaptive – in an environment in which threats are frequently encountered, it makes sense for the brain to develop a sensitivity to the likelihood of further adverse experiences.

An intriguing possibility is that the brain's mid-brain dopamine machinery is involved not only in the anticipation of threats from other people, but also the poor-me patient's anticipation of threats from the self. After all, the abnormal attributions made by acutely ill patients with poor-me paranoia can be thought of as a kind of avoidance response, which is executed in order to reduce the threat of negative thoughts about the self.[86] If this intuition is correct – and we are a long way from proving that it is – it would explain why, during an acute psychotic crisis in which the brain produces abnormal levels of dopamine, patients switch from bad-me to poor-me and begin to make highly external attributions for negative events. This admittedly speculative hypothesis raises a further intriguing possibility – that, by further studying the role of the dopamine system in regulating thinking, we may begin to catch glimpses of the biological machinery that underlies the kinds of psychological defences which, until now, have been the province of the psychoanalyst.

Hearing voices

Auditory hallucinations are not quite as common as paranoid delusions but, nonetheless, they are a frequent source of distress for people attending psychiatric clinics. (In our sample of 255 first-episode patients – most of whom met the *DSM* diagnostic criteria for schizophrenia – 69 per cent reported them[87] and it has been estimated that voices are also heard by about 10–15 per cent of patients with a diagnosis of bipolar disorder[88].) Sometimes patients' voices appear to be external to themselves, but for many patients they appear to be coming from somewhere inside their own heads, although they nonetheless seem alien. (Not surprisingly, it is fairly common for patients to reach the conclusion that they have been implanted with some kind of radio receiver.)

When I took up my first clinical post in the mid-1980s and found myself talking to patients who were hearing voices, nothing in my training had seemed to prepare me for these encounters. And yet, as I listened to what the patients told me, it quickly became apparent that the voices were far from random spasms of damaged nervous systems. One patient heard a voice accusing him of being a homosexual, an experience that caused him so much distress that he attacked a passer-by whom he thought might be responsible. Another heard a voice he attributed to the devil, and yet another heard a group of voices taunting her and encouraging her to commit suicide. Later, I would come across patients like Hannah, described in the last chapter, who experienced pleasant and soothing voices. In each case, the voices seemed to have recognizable identities, and the patients appeared to form complicated but meaningful relationships with them. In my attempts to understand what the patients were telling me, I found myself reaching back to an apparently unrelated field of psychological research that I had learned about as an undergraduate psychology student.

In the 1920s the celebrated Swiss psychologist Jean Piaget entered into a debate with a Russian counterpart, Lev Vygotsky, at that time little known in the West but later to be recognized as one of the most important researchers in the field of developmental psychology. Both had observed that children between about 2 and 4 years of age spend a lot of time talking to themselves. According to Piaget,[89] this was because, at this age, children are egocentric and do not understand that nobody is listening. Vygotsky's view,[90] which eventually prevailed, was that, on the contrary, the child was communicating perfectly well with the one person who really mattered: herself. Vygotsky went on to map out the process by which children acquire the capacity for verbal thought. He argued that, at first, the child's thinking processes are like those of non-verbal animals. However, towards the end of the first year of life, the child begins to acquire the ability to use words, at which point thought and language remain separate processes. Soon, however, the child learns that she can use language not only to pass and receive instructions from caregivers, but to pass and receive instructions to and from herself. At this point, Vygotsky says, thought and language fuse. As the child grows older still, she eventually learns to use language silently, at which point social speech and 'inner speech' become once more separate, the latter becoming highly abbreviated and telegraphic.

Inner speech is such a ubiquitous aspect of our mental life that, unless it is drawn to our attention, we rarely reflect on it. If you close your eyes and allow your mind to wander, you will discover an almost ceaseless inner chatter swirling within you. Using this inner voice, we comment to ourselves about what is happening to us, silently express our pleasure or dismay, plan what to do next, and censure ourselves whenever we make mistakes. As I discovered soon after I began working with psychotic patients, the idea this mechanism has somehow gone awry in people who hear voices had been proposed many years before I had even begun to dream of a career in clinical psychology.

In adulthood, when we use words to think silently, there remains a neuromuscular echo of the time in childhood when we could only think out aloud. If electrodes are placed over the lips and larynx, microcurrents can be recorded in the underlying speech muscles as we engage in verbal thought, a phenomenon known as *subvocalization*.[91] (Of course, this does not mean that we need our speech muscles in order to think – if you lose them in some kind of dreadful accident, your intelligence will be unaffected.) It was an American psychiatrist, Louis Gould, working in Connecticut in the 1940s, who first thought to take electrical recordings from the speech muscles of patients as they heard voices. In a series of remarkable studies,[92] he reported that voices were associated with an increase in subvocalization, a finding which has since been replicated many times.[93] In one study, Gould was even able to record actual hallucinated speech from a subvocalizing patient (the patient was whispering) using a very sensitive microphone.[94]

These findings have been recently supported by neuroimaging studies, using new technologies such as fMRI, which have investigated which brain regions are activated as patients hear voices. Not surprisingly, these studies have shown that auditory hallucinations are associated with activations in the language-related centres in the left frontal and temporal lobes of the brain.[95] The obvious implication is that the person hearing voices is actually misattributing his or her own inner speech to an external agent. In other words, hallucinations arise, not from perceptual difficulties, but from an error in deciding the *source* of perceptions.

It has been possible to test this theory by measuring, in patients and ordinary people, the ability to distinguish between self-generated thoughts and externally presented stimuli, a skill known as *source monitoring*. For example, in a series of studies I conducted more than twenty years ago[96] and replicated by others since,[97] I asked hallucinating and non-hallucinating patients to listen to brief bursts of white noise (the kind of sound that comes from a badly tuned radio) with a voice that was present only half the time. After each burst, the participants were asked whether they thought the voice was present or not. By using a mathematical technique known as *signal detection analysis* to assess their judgements, it was possible to derive two measures: *perceptual sensitivity* (roughly, how sensitive their hearing was) and *perceptual bias* (roughly, their tendency to assume that a voice was present in conditions of uncertainty). As expected, the hallucinating patients did not differ from the controls on the measure of sensitivity, but they showed a much greater bias towards assuming that a voice was present. In conditions of uncertainty, it was almost as if their default option was to assume that a voice was present whereas ordinary people tended to assume the opposite.

Other methods of measuring the source monitoring skills of

hallucinating patients have yielded similar results. For example, at the Institute of Psychiatry in London, psychologist Louise Johns[98] has carried out a series of experiments in which patients and control participants were asked to read out aloud and listen to their own speech after it had been distorted electronically and played back through headphones. At various points in the experiment, the voice of the participant was replaced by someone else's voice – also distorted – and the participant was asked to say when they thought this had happened. Johns found that, in these circumstances, patients suffering from hallucinations often mistakenly assume that their own distorted voice belongs to someone else.

Other researchers have studied the physiological processes underlying source monitoring. In an important series of electrophysiological investigations conducted by Judith Ford[99] at the University of San Diego, it was found that, when ordinary people talk or think in words, the auditory perception areas in the temporal lobes of the brain become less sensitive to sounds because they are 'switched off' by messages from the speech generation areas in the left frontal cortex. This mechanism apparently reduces the risk that self-generated speech will be mistaken for an external voice. It is as if the brain is saying to itself: 'Don't listen, that's you doing the talking.' Ford found that this mechanism was absent in hallucinating patients.

The suggestion that hallucinations arise as a consequence of source monitoring failures helps to explain why they tend to be experienced at particular times, and often only under certain circumstances. Patients are most likely to hear voices during periods of relative silence, or when exposed to unpatterned stimulation, for example when there is a washing machine or poorly tuned radio in the background.[100] Presumably this is because, under these circumstances, it is especially difficult to tell the difference between what we are thinking and what we are hearing. Conversely, reading or listening intently to something interesting seems to suppress auditory hallucinations, presumably because these activities occupy the speech and hearing processes in the brain.

The theory also helps to explain the apparent link between hallucinations and trauma, noted in the last chapter. It is known that traumatic experiences often provoke a continuous flood of intrusive, vivid and distressing thoughts.[101] Non-psychotic people who have experienced life-threatening events, for example as a consequence of accidents or warfare, often complain of flashbacks, vivid dreams or thoughts that are unbidden and disturbing (typical symptoms of post-traumatic stress disorder). Experimental studies show that these kinds of low cognitive effort thoughts (they happen without intention or an act of will) are particularly difficult to recognize as self-generated, a problem that is often exacerbated by the individual's emotional reaction to them. Studies conducted by my former colleague Tony Morrison at Manchester University show that hallucinating patients, terrified that their minds are going out of control, sometimes engage in extreme attempts to suppress unwanted thoughts.[102] However (as you will discover if you try NOT to think of a white bear), suppressing unwanted thoughts is often counter-productive, often leading to a rebound of the very experiences that are suppressed.[103]

As we found in the case of paranoia, we can piece together these findings to make a relatively simple model of the processes leading to auditory hallucinations, which is shown in Fig. 3.

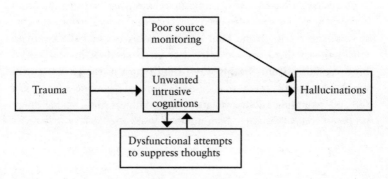

Figure 3. A model of auditory hallucinations.

Psychiatric disorders are not simply brain diseases

In this chapter I have attempted to illustrate the complaints-orientated approach to psychopathology by describing our current understanding of the mechanisms responsible for paranoid delusions and hallucinations. There have been similar advances in studies of thought disorder[104] and mania,[105] and more limited progress in understanding the processes that cause negative symptoms such as apathy and social withdrawal. Although I do not have the space to describe these developments here, I hope I have made it obvious how the new approach differs from the Kraepelinian paradigm that preceded it. By focusing on symptoms rather than diagnoses, we can see how the experiences of patients arise understandably from their misfortunes. Far from assuming that abnormal cerebral functioning is the primary cause of illness, complaints-orientated research shows that the troubled brain cannot be considered in isolation from the social universe. Clinically, it leads us to recognize that the stories patients tell us are important, and that there is a very thin dividing line between the 'them' who are ill and the 'us' who are sane.

Of course, if we have to rethink the relationship between the brain and psychosis, we shall also need to reconsider the value of treatments that aim to fix it. In the final section of this book, I shall explain why modern therapies are often less effective than mental health professionals assume. In this way I shall return to the paradox with which I began this book: that despite claims of dramatic advances in the understanding and treatment of mental illness, patients are doing no better today than they did a hundred years ago.

PART THREE

MEDICINE FOR MADNESS

8

Science, Profit and Politics in the Conduct of Clinical Trials

> Many a small thing has been made large by the right kind of advertising.
>
> Mark Twain, *A Connecticut Yankee at King Arthur's Court*

Freud once remarked that an important aim of psychological treatment is to transform 'hysterical misery into common unhappiness'.[1] He was conceding that therapy is powerless to alter the realities of existence; the best we can hope for is that it helps us cope with the inevitable disappointments and misfortunes we encounter in our lives.

Graham, a patient I saw more than a decade ago, keeps in touch by ringing once or twice a year to tell me how things are going for him. For quite some time now he has been working happily as a teacher, a remarkable achievement considering how hopeless and lost he seemed when I first met him. His marriage continues to lurch between periods of stability and moments of crises – the last time we spoke he was enduring a temporary separation from his wife – but he seems to survive these difficulties with alacrity. He is devoutly religious, is very active in his local church, and has many good friendships with like-minded people. He also excels at sports, and plays for his local cricket team.

When I first saw him, he had just been discharged from hospital following an acute psychotic episode. As he told me his story, I discovered that he had been admitted to hospital at least once a year over the previous five years. It was easy to see a pattern to these admissions. A graduate in history who came from a successful family (his father was an internationally respected scientist and his brother and sister had excelled in medicine and law), he would make determined efforts to find employment as soon as he felt well enough. Exploiting connections through his family and the church, he was often successful. However, soon after beginning work, he would begin to develop suspicions about the intentions of the people he was working with. Very quickly, these suspicions would spiral into full-blown paranoid delusions, prompting angry outbursts at those he imagined were plotting against him. This pattern was repeated almost immediately after I began to see him. Within a few days of falling out with the managers of a religious charity he had been working for, he was back in hospital. When I went to see him, he was boiling with hostility, and made it very clear that my incompetence and lack of understanding had made a major contribution to this latest development. Unable to think of anything else to do, I listened passively as he ranted at me for the best part of an hour. Later, he told me that my willingness to hear him out had made a powerful impression on him.

One factor that seemed to be important in Graham's difficulties was the way he thought about his relationships with other people, so we worked together to devise some simple exercises that might help him develop a more realistic attitude. Whenever he began to feel frightened or suspicious, he would write his thoughts down in a diary. First in our sessions, and later on his own, he would examine his initial interpretations of unsettling events and then try to think of alternative explanations for what had happened. Very quickly, he became skilful at noticing incipient paranoid ideas, before cross-examining them and reasoning them away. A breakthrough moment occurred when, during a cricket match, he found himself ruminating about a more aggressive member of his own team, who he imagined was planning to humiliate him and have him ejected from the club. Suddenly realizing that the other player was an awkward sort who seemed to have irritated almost everyone on the team, Graham found himself chuckling at his own foolishness.

Another factor that seemed to be exacerbating Graham's difficulties was his recent marriage to a charming but fiery Brazilian, whom he had swiftly romanced after running into her while on holiday in South America. Somehow, he had neglected to inform her about his long-standing mental health difficulties. Perhaps this oversight would have angered any woman but, to make matters worse, it turned out that Maria had her own problems, the consequences of a very difficult childhood. It took very little to provoke Graham and Maria into an escalating spiral of argument and recrimination, creating exactly the kind of highly charged environment which, according to research, is most likely to precipitate a psychotic relapse. I tried seeing Graham and Maria together but, in the end, they both agreed that Maria had issues she could only address by seeing me alone. Gradually, the couple became more settled. Months passed without any recurrence of Graham's symptoms and we decided that it was time to bring our meetings to an end. Before saying goodbye, we spent some time discussing strategies for avoiding the kind of stress that might lead to further bouts of illness in the future. I asked Graham to keep in touch; hence his regular telephone calls.

Was the therapy helpful? I like to think so, and so does Graham, but it is almost impossible to be certain in the individual case. Although it is encouraging that a man who was regularly falling ill has now been out of hospital for the best part of a decade, perhaps he has been the beneficiary of some spontaneous, random and mysterious process of recovery and, in the overall spreadsheet of our clinical achievements, his improvement must be balanced against our treatment failures, such as Paul, whose tragic story I told in the last chapter. Maybe after tinkering around with different doses and combinations of medication, Graham's psychiatrist had finally hit on a cocktail that worked. Graham's friends and family have continued to be supportive, whatever has happened. And finally, although I am sceptical about the existence of a personal God, it seems to me that Graham's very strong faith has furnished him with the inner strength needed for him to grapple the many obstacles that he has encountered over the passing years.

We all need to understand randomized
controlled trials

Despite the difficulties we encounter when trying to judge whether a treatment has been decisive in the individual case, a principled method of deciding which treatments are generally effective is obviously required; otherwise how would doctors know which therapies to offer their patients? The demand for accurate information about treatment effectiveness has become especially pressing in recent decades, as increased spending on health has consistently failed to match escalating demands for medical resources.[2] This has happened because we now expect clinicians to deal with a wide range of difficulties (infertility, cosmetic challenges, moderate depression, for example) which were simply tolerated as bad luck a few decades ago, because new medical technologies (for example MRI and genetic screening) are increasingly expensive, and because people are now living longer.[3]

During the 1970s, two books written by British researchers led to a great debate about the impact of medicine on society and highlighted the senselessness of spending money on ineffective treatments, or therapies which are so expensive that other services have to be compromised to pay for them. *The Role of Medicine: Dream, Mirage or Nemesis?*,[4] written by Birmingham University professor Thomas McKeown and published in 1979, argued that many of the health gains achieved during the nineteenth and early twentieth centuries were the consequence, not of advances in medical science, but of improvements in nutrition and sanitation. According to McKeown, both professionals and lay people had therefore acquired unrealistic expectations about what medicine could do. Later commentators would challenge McKeown's analysis, claiming that, although public health measures have been decisive in reducing infant mortality, the improvements in health after the Second World War were largely attributable to advances in the treatment of the diseases of later life, such as heart disease, cancer and stroke.[5]

Effectiveness and Efficiency: Random Reflections on Health Services,[6] published a few years earlier by the University of Cardiff-based epidemiologist Archie Cochrane (memorably described by McKeown as 'An itinerant preacher who emerges at intervals from his Welsh retreat to admonish the faithful for failure to submit all aspects of their lives and works to scientific appraisal'), similarly observed that medical interventions were often costly and ineffective, but attributed the apparent impotence of clinical services to poor scientific methods, and particularly the failure to rigorously evaluate new treatments.

These challenges stimulated a global movement towards *evidence based medicine*, which has been defined as 'the conscientious, explicit and judicious use of current best evidence in making decisions about the care of individual patients'.[7] This movement has been embraced by governments worldwide hoping to limit expenditure on health care. It has also been embraced by doctors and other health care professionals anxious to provide the best treatments for their patients. It has led to the establishment of new research centres in universities in many countries, where clinicians and statisticians comb the available evidence to try and reach general conclusions about which treatments are effective and affordable. In this chapter, I argue that this movement has *not* so far led to conspicuous improvements in the treatment of psychiatric disorders, partly because the way that evidence has been interpreted has been affected by psychiatrists' adherence to an outdated way of thinking about the problems of their patients, but also because powerful financial forces have ensured that medical remedies for human misery have been promoted even in the face of evidence that they do not work.

Taking Cochrane's lead, advocates of evidence based medicine assume that a hierarchy of research can be drawn on to inform choices about the treatments offered to patients.[8] At the top of the hierarchy is a type of medical experiment known as a *randomized controlled trial* (RCT), which is believed to provide gold-standard evidence about the *efficacy* of treatments (the extent to which they work in precisely defined conditions), their *effectiveness* (the extent to which they work in the real world of routine clinical practice) and their *cost effectiveness* (whether they can be considered value for money when compared to alternative therapies). Other kinds of research, for example observational studies of patients receiving different kinds of treatment during routine care and investigations of single cases, are considered to be of less value.

It is therefore hard to overestimate the impact of RCTs on modern health care. On the basis of data obtained from clinical trials, regulatory authorities such as the US Food and Drugs Administration and health care providers such as the British NHS decide which treatments should be available for use by doctors. RCTs might just save your life one day, because the evidence obtained from them will probably determine what your doctor will do to you in a life-threatening emergency. They might also affect your tax bill, if a new but expensive treatment is found to be sufficiently effective to require funding from the public purse. They could also make you a lot of money if you happen to own shares in a pharmaceutical company that has manufactured a new blockbuster drug, or cost you your shirt if you have invested in a company that has spent many years developing a therapy that turns out to be useless. Hence, the way that RCTs are conducted not only has implications for the advancement of medical science, but also has huge political and economic implications.

For all of these reasons, everyone needs to know something about how RCTs are conducted, and whether or not the evidence that is obtained from them can be trusted. By dealing with this last question, I shall address once more the apparent paradox with which I began this book, namely that, despite the many new remedies that have become available to psychiatrists over recent decades, there is little evidence that psychiatric services have had a positive impact on human welfare.

What is a randomized controlled trial?

The prize for the first person to carry out a RCT is usually handed to James Lind (1716–94), a Scottish surgeon serving in the Royal Navy.[9] At the time, the vulnerability of sailors to disease, especially on long voyages, was a major impediment to the navy's ability to project British power across the globe. Suspecting (correctly) that one of the worst of these diseases, scurvy, was caused by a lack of citrus fruit, Lind conducted a simple experiment:

On the 20th of May 1747, I took twelve patients in the scurvy, on board the *Salisbury* at sea. Their cases were as similar as I could have them. They all in general had putrid gums, the spots and lassitude, with weakness of the knees. They lay together in one place, being a proper apartment for the sick in the fore-hold; and had one diet common to all, *viz.* water-gruel sweetened with sugar in the morning; fresh mutton-broth often times for dinner; at other times puddings, boiled biscuit with sugar; and for supper barley with raisins, rice and currants, sago and wine or the like. Two of these were ordered each a quarter of cider a-day. Two others took twenty five gutts of elixir vitriol three time a-day, upon an empty stomach; using a gargle strongly acidulated with it for their mouths. Two others took two spoonfuls of vinegar three times a-day, upon an empty stomach; having their gruels and their other foods acidulated with it, and also the gargle for their mouth. Two of the worst patients with the tendons in the ham rigid, (a symptom none of the rest had), were put under a course of sea water. Of this they drank half a pint every day, and sometimes more or less as it operated, by way of gentle physic. Two others had each two oranges and one lemon given them every day. These they eat with greediness, at different times, upon an empty stomach. They continued for six days under this course, having consumed the quantity that could be spared. The two remaining patients took the bigness of a nutmeg, three times a-day ... The consequence was, that the most sudden and good effects were perceived from the use of the oranges and lemons.

This experiment had one crucial feature of modern trials, namely that patients were randomly assigned to the different treatments. Without random assignment, it was possible that the different outcomes merely reflected differences between the patients (perhaps those given the citrus fruits were younger and stronger than the rest).

Despite this early example, the introduction of the RCT into modern medicine is usually dated to the late 1940s, when a team of researchers from the UK Medical Research Council, led by the statistician Austin Bradford Hill, carried out a small study in which tuberculosis patients were randomly chosen to receive either the antibiotic streptomycin or conventional treatment without antibiotics. In the short term, the survival rate of those in the experimental group was found to exceed by far that of the patients receiving the conventional 'control' treatment.[10] Since that time, there has been a spectacular

9. James Lind (1716–1794, *left*) and Sir Austin Bradford Hill (1897–1991)

growth in this kind of research; by the late 1980s approximately 5,000 trials were being published each year and by the end of the twentieth century the annual number of published RCTs had passed 12,000.[11]

Of course, modern RCTs often involve very large numbers of patients, so that the process of randomization usually leads to groups that are well balanced (similar in age, intelligence, education, severity of illness, and so on). They also involve much more elaborate strategies for avoiding and controlling bias than either James Lind or Austin Bradford Hill could have imagined.

One major source of bias is patients' and clinicians' expectations. Patients treated with a sugar pill or other pharmacologically inert substance (a *placebo*) often show dramatic improvements. Although the exact mechanisms responsible for the *placebo effect* continue to be debated by doctors and psychologists, it is clear that patients' optimistic expectations play an important role. Patients will get better just because they think they are being given an effective remedy. To compound this problem, clinicians' expectations can affect their perceptions of the way their patients respond to treatment. When examining patients they believe to have received an effective treatment, doctors, nurses and psychologists will tend to see improvements even when none have in fact occurred. Both of these effects appear to depend upon complex social-psychological processes affecting the perceived potency of the intervention so that, for example, a sham injection is likely to seem more beneficial than a sham pill.[12] The placebo effect appears to be a factor in many kinds of therapies so, for example, there is evidence that sham ECT (in which patients are anaesthetized, have electrodes placed on their heads, but do not receive a shock) is considerably more effective than not being exposed to any kind of ECT procedure at all.[13] However, some kinds of conditions seem to be more amenable to the placebo effect than others. For example, hyperglycemia (raised blood sugar) seems to be very little affected by placebo treatments whereas psychiatric conditions appear to be very much affected.[14]

To control for these sources of bias, since the 1960s it has been common practice for both the patients taking part in trials and the clinicians assessing them to be kept ignorant about which patients have received which treatment. In the simplest type of *double-blind* RCT, this is achieved by randomly assigning patients to the drug of interest or to some kind of control treatment (for example, a placebo) which is made to look as similar as to the active treatment as possible. In the case of a drug trial, the tablets given to the patient may be labelled with the patient's case number but with no information to suggest which kind of medicine – active treatment or placebo – they contain. *Open trials* (in which everyone – patients and clinicians – knows who has received which treatment) almost invariably report more positive results than properly blinded studies[15] and, hence can give a seriously misleading impression of what a treatment can do, except when the outcome being measured (e.g. survival versus death) is beyond ambiguity.*

---

* A complication here is that patients taking part in RCTs sometimes correctly guess that they are receiving an active treatment because they are experiencing side effects. Occasionally, researchers try to prevent this from happening by using an active placebo, a non-therapeutic chemical that causes side effects that are similar to those of the drug that is being evaluated. In the case of antidepressant drugs, for example, a

Because it is important to establish whether treatments have lasting effects, well-designed trials will usually involve the patients being followed up for a considerable period (at least a year) beyond the point at which treatment is completed. Many trials of psychiatric drugs have been almost worthless because the investigators have simply failed to study the participating patients for more than a few weeks, and the same criticism can be made of studies of other types of medical treatment for mental illness, such as ECT. Those conducting the trial must also take great care in choosing the way that they measure the results of treatment. In psychiatric trials, patients' symptoms are usually measured but, from the patients' point of view, an overall measure of quality of life may be more informative (some treatments may improve symptoms without affecting quality of life whereas others may have the opposite effect). It is also important that the measures employed have been shown to be sensitive (that they are able to measure change) and reliable (that they give consistent results no matter who administers them). A recent review of drug and psychological treatment trials conducted on schizophrenia patients found that studies using previously unpublished measures were more likely to yield positive results than studies using measures that had previously been shown to be sensitive and reliable.[16]

It is only at the end of a double-blind study that a list recording which patients have been assigned to which treatments (until then kept under lock and key) is used to *unblind* the data and reveal which treatment was most effective. At this stage, a further opportunity for bias arises as the trialists face a choice between several different methods of analysing the data. If a number of different outcome measures have been administered, some may give a positive result whereas others may not, so different impressions will be created according to which measures are reported. To make matters worse, different statistical techniques can be applied to the data, to provide a summary of the findings and also to give some indication of the

small number of trials of this kind have been carried out. In general, these studies, like more conventional trials that we will consider shortly, have shown at best very weak evidence in favour of the antidepressants (see J. Moncrieff, S. Wessely and R. Hardy (1998), 'Meta-analysis of trials comparing antidepressants with active placebos', *British Journal of Psychiatry*, 172:227–31).

researcher's confidence in the findings (often expressed as a estimate of the probability that the findings could have occurred by chance). Although these usually lead to a similar conclusion, they will occasionally give differing indications of the degree of improvement experienced by patients.

One problem is that at the point of analysis there may be a strong temptation to report only the measures and methods of analysis that give the best impression of what a treatment can do. In order to prevent this from happening, researchers are usually expected to use a method that was planned before the data was collected. (Leading medical journals often refuse to publish the results of a trial unless the design, including the method of analysis, has been published in a 'trials register' before the study commences.[17] This has the additional advantage of allowing trials to be tracked so that independent investigators can find out what happened to them – an important development as researchers are sometimes reluctant to publish negative results.)

When analysing data, one of the main choices that must be made by researchers is between a *per protocol analysis* and an *intention-to-treat analysis*. In the case of a per protocol analysis, patients are considered only if they complete the treatment. For example, in the trial of an antidepressant, patients who fail to take their medication for the prescribed number of weeks are not considered. This may seem a sensible approach if we want to find out the efficacy of a treatment, but it is not the approach generally favoured by health economists and policy makers, who usually want to know what will happen (and how much it will cost) if a particular treatment is given to, say, a thousand typical patients, some of whom will refuse or discontinue the treatment for a variety of reasons (perhaps they have no faith in it, or are upset by its side effects). In an intention-to-treat analysis, which has become the preferred approach, all patients are included, even if they refuse their treatment immediately after it has been offered. Assiduous attempts are made to follow up those who refuse or drop out and, if they cannot be found, various statistical techniques are used to estimate their outcomes, usually on the conservative assumption that they will not have got better. Not surprisingly, it is much harder for an intention-to-treat analysis to show a positive result than a per protocol analysis.

In practice, the point at which trial data is unblinded and analysed can be a difficult moment in the life of a trialist. (I was once a member of a team conducting a trial of a psychological treatment for patients with a diagnosis of bipolar disorder. Based on what the therapists told me about the progress made by their patients, I was confident that the treatment had been effective. However, after more than five years of work, the awful truth about what we had all achieved was revealed in an email from the statistician on the team, which ominously began, 'The results are disappointing but definitive . . .'[18])

Of course, many drugs have adverse effects – side effects – as well as the positive therapeutic effects that clinicians hope for. It is therefore important that these effects are systematically recorded and reported at the end of the study. In the past, the failure to consider possible harmful effects has occasionally led to tragedy, perhaps most famously in the case of thalidomide, an effective tranquillizer which caused severe birth defects to the children of pregnant women who took it.[19] The under-reporting of side effects continues to be a problem in some clinical trials.

Many RCTs are more complex than the simple two-arm design I have just described. More than two arms are sometimes employed, for example when comparing the effectiveness of different doses of a treatment. In some circumstances, it may be unethical to give patients a placebo, especially if they are suffering from a life-threatening condition. (Early placebo controlled trials of AZT, the first antiviral drug used to prevent HIV patients from developing AIDS, had to be discontinued when preliminary analyses of the data revealed that patients receiving the placebo were dying much more quickly than those receiving the active treatment.) If an effective treatment is already known, trials are usually designed to compare a new treatment with the established therapy. Sometimes, if the treatments being considered are ameliorative (that is, they do not cure a condition but do keep the symptoms under control), a *cross-over design* will be employed in which some patients are randomized to treatment A, others receive treatment B, and then, after a period of time, the two treatments are switched.

It should be apparent by now that most trials are difficult and complex experiments. Conducting them can be a very costly business.

Most of the RCTs I have helped to carry out have been funded at the taxpayers' expense by grants, typically exceeding £1 million, given by the UK Medical Research Council. However, government organizations like the MRC in Britain and the National Institutes of Health in the United States have limited budgets, and an increasing majority of drug trials are being funded by manufacturers hoping to get their products licensed.[20] Clearly, this creates a very serious conflict of interest for the drug companies, which can turn a profit only if their drugs are shown to be effective. This conflict of interest has been responsible for many patients receiving treatments that are either ineffective, or which have unexpected harmful effects.

There's gold in them thar pills[21]

When considering the role of the pharmaceutical industry in psychiatric research, it is important to recognize that the industry's main purpose is to make money for its shareholders. Drug companies are no more driven by the desire to do good than the manufacturers of automobiles, canned soup or other household products. Of course, they hope that consumers will buy their products because they are effective and (like the manufacturers of cars and fast food) they also hope to avoid being sued for selling products that are dangerous to the consumer. However, within these limitations, they are willing to use any and every method to promote their products to the citizens of the industrialized nations, who have learned (or been taught) to look to the medical profession for solutions to a wide range of physical, social and existential ills.

That they have been successful is evident from the fact that the pharmaceutical industry is the most profitable in the world. According to an exposé by Marcia Angell,[22] former editor of the prestigious *New England Journal of Medicine*, in 2001, spending on prescription drugs by the public in the United States alone exceeded $200 billion per year, a figure which excludes the cost of medicines administered in hospitals, nursing homes and doctors' offices. Worldwide sales in the same year were several times this amount. Following the introduction of industry-friendly legislation in the 1980s, which increased the patent life of new medications (the period during which they can be sold only by the patent-holder, and hence when there can be no competition from other companies manufacturing the same drug), the profits from making medicines soared so that, by the beginning of the twenty-first century, the top ten companies were making an 18.5 per cent return on sales, compared to an average return for other industries of 3.3 per cent. Even commercial banking could not equal this level of profit, making a return of 13.5 per cent. By 2002, the combined profits for the ten drug companies in the Fortune 500 (a list of 500 American public corporations with the highest gross revenues) had grown to exceed the profits of all the other 490 companies put together.[23]

Industry leaders often try to justify these vast profits by pointing to the high costs involved in developing their products, and the substantial risks involved in investing in research which, depending on how the trials finally work out, may prove to be a dead end. However, as Angell points out, this argument is unpersuasive for three reasons. First, by far the majority of the research conducted by the industry is not targeted at the discovery of novel medications, but on the development of 'me-too' drugs which are as similar as possible to the existing products of rival companies, but sufficiently different to allow fresh patents to be issued. For example, when, in the mid-1990s the American pharmaceutical company Eli Lilly marketed Prozac, a new type of antidepressant known as a *selective serotonin re-uptake inhibitor* (SSRI) it quickly become obvious that it was a blockbuster, accounting for sales within the United States of more than $2 billion per annum. Not surprisingly, very similar drugs marketed by other companies appeared very soon afterwards (for example, Seroxat, manufactured by GlaxoSmithKline, which entered the market in 1997, and Zoloft, manufactured by Pfizer, which became available in 1999). Second, much of the research that leads to the development of truly innovative treatments is funded by public bodies such as the MRC in Britain and the National Institutes of Health in the United States. (This was true, for example, in the case of AZT.) Finally, and most importantly, according to Angell's estimates, only about 11 per cent of pharmaceutical industry revenues are spent on research, whereas an almost staggering 36 per cent is spent on marketing.

This marketing takes a variety of forms, some of which are more obvious than others. Many medical journals would be financially unviable without payments received for glossy drug company advertisements, which are scattered between the pages of scholarly articles, and which actively promote a chemical imbalance model of mental illness.[24] At first sight, these seem to have many of the characteristics of advertisements for ordinary household products, but with the addition of scientific information in detailed footnotes, apparently supporting the claims made for the advertised drug's effectiveness. American psychologist Timothy Scott[25] recently described his efforts to examine the evidence claims in a typical advertisement of this kind, a multi-page plug for the antidepressant Effexor (venlafaxine), manufactured by Wyeth. The advertisement showed an attractive but obviously unhappy woman on one page followed by, on another, the same woman laughing and surrounded by friends as she arm-wrestled with an attractive man. Printed alongside these pictures were claims such as 'proven to achieve remission of symptoms in 32 double-blind comparative trials with over 7,000 patients', 'proven to resolve emotional and physical symptoms' and 'proven tolerability with once-daily dose'. Without carefully examining the footnotes accompanying these captions, it would be easy to assume that they referred to trial data published in reputable medical journals. However, Scott found that the footnotes to the first of these claims referred to 'data on file' with the company, and to a presentation, by a psychiatrist who was a paid consultant for the company, at a conference in the Czech Republic which was also sponsored by the company. When Scott contacted Wyeth, asking whether he could examine the data on file, he received a letter from a company lawyer informing him that the information he sought was confidential. Short of breaking into the company's offices, there seemed to be no way of verifying the company's claims.

The pharmaceutical industry also promotes its wares by sending representatives to hospitals and clinics, where they often fund academic meetings in exchange for the opportunity to say a few words about their products. For example, a free lunch may be provided for a journal club (a meeting of clinicians to discuss recently published journal articles) or a grand round (a talk by a speaker invited from elsewhere, whose travel expenses and accommodation costs may also be paid). At the end of these meetings, the representatives (often attractively dressed young men and women) will usually present a few slides extolling the virtue of their particular medicine in comparison with a similar drug sold by another company. Sometimes the representative will distribute free trinkets such as cups or pens bearing company logos. (Many, perhaps even most of NHS clinicians drink their morning coffee out of cups adorned with the names of widely used drugs, and write their reports with pens bearing drug company logos.)

Trinkets are also prominent at large psychiatric conferences. The following is a description of a typical encounter with the pharmaceutical industry at a recent meeting of the World Congress of Biological Psychiatry in Berlin,[26] written by American psychiatrist Fuller Torrey:

I counted 15 major displays on the way to the lunch area, including an artificial garden (Janssen-Cilag), a brook running over stones (Lundbeck), and a 40-foot rotating tower (Novartis). Almost all offered free food and drink, T-shirts, or other inducements designed to get psychiatrists to pause so that an army of smiling sales representatives could give their sales pitch. Eli Lilly's display included two large, walk-through tunnels set up like funhouses ... My favorite display, by the Dutch firm Organon, advertised Remeron, an antidepressant. It featured a small, multihued tent with purple doors and the painted head of a genie. Inside, a red-robed young woman with sprinkles in her hair was taking Polaroid pictures, one by one, of psychiatrists who had waited patiently in line for 20 minutes or more. This was no ordinary picture but rather a snapshot of one's aura, taken, as the Organon brochure noted, 'with advanced biofeedback equipment.' The equipment consisted of two small machines, on which I placed my hands. The result was a picture of my head peering out of a red, orange, and yellow cloud. According to the brochure, 'The aura colours give you information about your appearance, character, talents, and future energy.' After taking my picture, the red-robed young woman escorted me to a yellow-robed young woman with even more sprinkles in her hair. 'Hi! My name is Amber,' she said, and proceeded to interpret the picture of my aura as indicating intelligence and good judgment, although with some hints of scepticism.

However, free lunches and trinkets pale into insignificance compared to the largesse available to some doctors. After flying economy class to give a talk at an American Psychiatric Association meeting in Chicago several years ago, I was bemused to find that some of my psychiatrist friends (most of whom were not even presenting papers) had been flown out business class by a leading drug company and were being accommodated, free of charge, in a magnificent hotel. The floor that they occupied had a free bar, so that they would have a convivial environment in which to discuss the latest pharmacological research. When my friends invited me to join their party for the evening, I found myself being wined and dined at the top of the Sears Tower, before being taken on a pub crawl, accompanied by a drug company representative, who bought all the drinks. Sometimes entire conferences are paid for in this way. Pharmaceutical companies are being neither irrational nor altruistic when sponsoring these kinds of events – studies have shown that doctors often change their prescribing habits after attending industry-sponsored meetings.[27]

Physicians in the United States sometimes receive substantial bonus payments from drug companies when they prescribe certain medications. In the United States and in Britain they may also be able to inflate their incomes by acting as paid consultants to the pharmaceutical industry. The kind of work undertaken may vary, from attending 'educational meetings' (I once declined £1,000 for merely attending an informal dinner at which I was expected to offer my opinions about the treatment of bipolar patients), to presenting talks in favour of particular medications at industry-sponsored conferences, to providing advice and assistance in the conduct of pharmaceutical trials. It is not uncommon for US psychiatrists to earn hundreds of thousands of dollars each year for these kinds of activities, and an ongoing investigation by Senator Chuck Grassley of Iowa has exposed a number of prominent academic psychiatrists who have failed to properly disclose earnings running into millions of dollars.[28] Although such sums are not earned by British academic psychiatrists, I was recently told by an industry insider that a small number earn more than £100,000 per year on top of their university salaries.

Aside from direct payments from drug companies, some US doctors have found that they can make fortunes by setting up private contract research organizations, which carry out clinical trials for the industry. It is not uncommon for these organizations to receive fees of up to $10,000 for each patient they successfully recruit into a trial. With such huge sums to be made, malpractice is perhaps inevitable. For example, the American investigative journalist Robert Whitaker,[29] who has become a crusader against psychiatric bad practice, has reported the example of a psychiatrist at the Medical College of Georgia, Dr Richard Borison, who ran a company which conducted early trials of Zyprexa (olanzapine), a novel antipsychotic, during the 1990s. By using attractive but unqualified assistants to cajole and bribe patients to take part, Borison and his pharmacologist colleague Bruce Diamond earned $4 million from these studies alone. It is difficult to have confidence in the data obtained, even though it was used in support of Lilly's Zyprexa licensing application to the Food and Drugs Administration. Ironically, Borison and Diamond are currently serving long prison sentences, not because of the way in which they conducted these trials, but for defrauding the University of Georgia of the profits they made while remaining on the university payroll.

Not surprisingly, some psychiatrists have begun to protest about the way in which their profession has been corrupted by the pharmaceutical industry. In a preface to a pamphlet entitled *Is Psychiatry for Sale?*, authored by British psychiatrist Joanna Moncrieff,[30] Fuller Torrey (whose description of the Berlin Congress I quoted earlier) remarked:

Dr Moncrieff's question has already been answered in the United States, where it is clear that psychiatry has already been sold. The buyer was Big Pharma. The sale price has not been disclosed, but rumour has it that the pharmaceutical industry got a bargain ... But do not blame Big Pharma – they are just doing what companies are expected to do in a free enterprise society. They are selling their goods any way they can. Instead, blame our psychiatric colleagues who are colluding with this process and should know better.

These sentiments were echoed in 2005 by the then president of the American Psychiatric Association Stephen Sharfstein,[31] who lamented,

'As a profession, we have allowed the biopsychosocial model [of mental illness] to become the bio-bio-bio model.' He went on to observe that 'Drug company representatives bearing gifts are frequent visitors to psychiatrists' offices and consulting rooms', and then added, 'We should have the wisdom and distance to call these gifts what they are – kickbacks and bribes.'

RCT wars

Not surprisingly, given the huge sums involved, drug companies have not been slow to exploit loopholes in RCT methodology in order to portray their medicines as more effective than they really are. In recent decades this has led to a kind of war of attrition between the industry and independent scientists and regulators, who have sought to find ways of ensuring that RCTs lead to objective and reliable data.

One tool employed by the independent scientists and regulators is a set of internationally recognized standards for reporting the results of trials. Originally proposed in 1996 by a multinational working group of trial investigators and later revised in 2001,[32] and then adapted for non-pharmacological studies in 2008,[33] the Consolidated Standards for Reporting Trials (CONSORT) statement[34] includes a checklist of good practice, covering everything from the titles of scientific papers describing the results to the way that statistical analyses of the data are reported. One of the most important recommendations is that all reports should include a CONSORT diagram that shows at a glance the flow of patients through the study (how many were assessed, how many were assigned to each treatment, how many refused and so on). The CONSORT statement has been adopted as a standard by most medical journals and a good few psychology journals.

A second major tool is the *systematic review*, in which evidence from a large number of trials is compiled to reach an overall conclusion about the effects of a particular treatment. Often, these reviews employ a statistical technique known as *meta-analysis*, which allows the findings from many studies to be added together as if they are from a single experiment, perhaps with thousands of patients. The

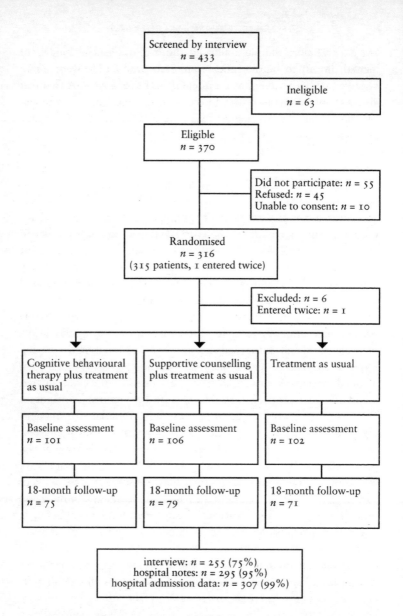

Figure 4. CONSORT diagram of an eighteen-month follow-up of a randomized controlled trial of cognitive behaviour therapy on first episode and early schizophrenia.

origins of this technique can be traced back to the earliest years of the twentieth century, but the modern era of meta-analysis began with the work of Gene V. Glass, a statistician at the University of Colorado. In the 1970s Glass developed a method of calculating a standard measure of outcome for each trial, known as an *effect size*.† Individual effect sizes could then be used to calculate an overall effect size for a large number of studies. Glass's first use of this method, published with his colleague Mary Lee Smith,[35] considered the effectiveness of psychotherapy, and sparked a debate about the relative effectiveness of different types of therapy that continues to this day (this study is discussed in detail in Chapter 10).

Effect sizes can be interpreted in a number of different ways.[36] Perhaps the simplest way to understand them is to see them as an indication of the proportion of people in the control group (those who receive a placebo in a placebo-controlled trial) who do worse than the average outcome achieved by the experimental group (those receiving the active treatment). It has become convention to regard an effect size of 0.20 or less as indicating a small effect, whereas effect sizes greater than 0.80 are considered large.[37]

Before conducting a meta-analysis, researchers trawl through the scientific literature to make sure no studies are overlooked, and then exclude any studies that seem to be fatally flawed (for example, because they were not double-blind). Sometimes the trials that are eventually included are weighted so that those that were most rigorously conducted are most influential in determining the overall outcome. Alternatively, some design characteristics of the trials might be built into the analysis to find out, for example, whether trials which are sponsored by drug companies give results different from those sponsored by government agencies, or whether those that are single-blind give more positive results than those that are double-blind. Some meta-analyses also include *file drawer calculations*, which estimate how many negative results would have to be languishing unpublished (hidden away in file drawers) to negate an apparently positive result.

† For the statistically minded, the effect size g is defined as standardized difference between the mean outcomes of the different treatments. In a two-arm trial:

$$g = \frac{\text{(mean for treated group} - \text{mean for the control group)}}{\text{standard deviation of the data from both groups}}$$

Table 1. A crude guide to the interpretation of effect sizes

Effect size	Magnitude	Controls doing worse than the mean for the experimental group (%)	Success rate of untreated persons (%)	Success rate of treated persons (%)
0.2	small	58	45	55
0.5	medium	69	38	62
0.8	large	79	31	70
1.0		84	28	72

Adapted from B. E. Wampold (2001), *The Great Psychotherapy Debate: Models, Methods and Findings*. Mahwah, NJ: Laurence Erlbaum Associates

Critics of meta-analyses point out that they are sometimes used as an excuse not to think. Indeed, although health service planners have come to rely on them, they are far from infallible. Sometimes, there is simply not enough evidence to carry one out. (A spoof paper published in the *British Medical Journal* in 2003 famously reported an attempt to evaluate the effectiveness of the parachute in the prevention of injury from 'gravitational challenge' and, finding no randomized controlled trials to include in a meta-analysis, concluded that there was no evidence that parachutes worked.[38]) At other times, competing meta-analyses of the same evidence reach different conclusions, usually because the researchers have made different decisions about which studies to include and how they should be weighted. Inevitably, this had led to systematic reviews of meta-analyses, which I suppose might be called meta-meta-analyses. (An anonymous wag writing shortly after the invention of meta-analysis looked forward to meta-meta-meta analyses in which, it was claimed, the raw data would be photographs of the covers of the journals in which the original trials had been published.[39])

Anticipating their importance, in 1993 the UK National Health

Service established a network of research centres to carry out systematic reviews. The network was named the Cochrane Collaboration, after Archie Cochrane. The main purpose of the network is to publish up-to-date summaries of the evidence on treatment effectiveness for all of the medical specialities, which are made publicly available on an easily accessible website.[40] Since its inception, the Collaboration has grown so that there are now Cochrane centres scattered in universities throughout the world.

Unfortunately, despite these developments, there is evidence that the war with the pharmaceutical industry is slowly being lost. Comparisons of industry-funded and independently sponsored trials have consistently shown that the former are much more likely to report positive results.[41] For example, a recent survey of five leading American psychiatric journals identified 397 trials published between 2001 and 2003.[42] Of these, 239 (60 per cent) were at least partly funded by a pharmaceutical company and, in the case of 187 (47 per cent of the total), at least one of the authors declared a financial conflict of interest (for example, ownership of shares in the company manufacturing the drug being investigated). Those studies which were sponsored by industry and in which a conflict of interest had been declared were 4.9 times more likely to report a positive result in comparison studies that were independently funded.

This kind of bias is especially evident in head-to-head comparisons between almost identical drugs, conducted by companies in order to 'prove' that their medicines are better than those of their rivals. As a consequence, these kinds of trial (which are often touted by company representatives giving brief talks at the end of sponsored journal club meetings) are virtually worthless. A recent review of psychiatric drug studies of this kind reported that the product of the sponsoring company was found to be superior in 90 per cent of comparisons.[43] Hence, whenever there is one trial that shows that drug A is better than drug B, there is nearly always another which shows the exact opposite.

The case of the SSRIs

Specific examples of naked data manipulation by drug companies can be found across the full range of medical specialities. However, in what follows I focus mainly on the serotonin re-uptake inhibitors (SSRIs) which, as we have seen, first became available in the late 1980s. These drugs were developed on the theory that depression is associated with a reduction in the availability of serotonin in the brain. When the re-uptake of the neurotransmitter is inhibited, the amount of serotonin at the receptor is increased and therefore, so the theory goes, the chemical imbalance is corrected and the patient's depressive symptoms will disappear.

Beginning with Prozac, the SSRIs were marketed with enormous hype, even by the already extravagant standards of the industry, with dramatic claims about their superior efficacy compared to the older tricyclic antidepressants. That these efforts were successful is evident from the number of antidepressant prescriptions written by family doctors. Between 1991 and 2001, these rose by 173 per cent in Britain.[44] In the United States, the total number of antidepressant prescriptions tripled between 1995 and 2004.[45]

The hype extended beyond the medical profession to the general public. Indeed, Prozac achieved almost iconic status, as reflected by the titles of popular books such as Elizabeth Wurtzel's *Prozac Nation* (1994) and Lauren Slater's *Prozac Diary* (1998). A best-selling 1993 book, *Listening to Prozac*, written by American psychiatrist Peter Kramer, included the observation that many patients felt 'better than well' after taking SSRIs.[46] Although Kramer also advocated psycho-therapy for depression, he looked forward to a world in which 'cos-metic psychopharmacology' might be used to bring about subtle but desirable changes in the personalities of mentally well people.

Fortunately or unfortunately, depending on one's perspective, when the actual evidence in support of the new drugs is carefully examined, it becomes clear that this almost terrifying impression of their effec-tiveness is completely unjustified. As early as 1993 (the year Kramer's book was published and in which the Cochrane Collaboration was founded) a systematic review could find no evidence that the new drugs were better than the older ones.[47] Indeed, subsequent meta-analyses have reported that nearly all of the therapeutic response to both the old and new antidepressants can be attributed to the placebo effect.[48] Defenders of antidepressants, although not disputing this finding, have argued that it is inconsistent with everyday clinical experience and have suggested that the poor showing of the SSRIs may be the consequence of testing them on the wrong patients, particularly those with less severe forms of depression.[49] A more likely explanation for the apparent effectiveness of these drugs in everyday practice, however, is that ordinary clinicians underestimate their power as placebos.

Given the contested evidence on the SSRIs, some readers might wonder how they ever got licensed. This was possible because the main requirement of the US Food and Drug Administration when approving a drug is not that it is better than existing alternatives, but that the new compound has been shown to be safe and more effective than placebo in two 'pivotal' trials. However, what counts as a 'pivotal' trial has never been clearly defined. As Paul Leber, one-time head of the FDA, once acknowledged: 'That could just mean, in a sense, that the sponsor could just do studies until the cows come home until he gets two of them that are statistically significant by chance alone, walks them out and says he has met the criteria.'[50]

In fact, many of the studies that were submitted to the FDA in support of SSRI licensing applications had negative results,[51] and most suffered from serious methodological flaws. When American psychologist Irving Kirsch[52] used the US Freedom of Information Act to obtain data from 47 trials of the six most popular new antidepressants, he found that the most rigorous of the studies had examined the patients for a mere eight weeks without any attempt to find out what happened to them afterwards, and that drop-out rates were so high that only 4 out of the 47 were able to report what happened to more than 70 per cent of the patients. In many of the studies, patients had been administered a sedative in addition to the antidepressant (one reason for this will become apparent later) so that it was not obvious to which of the drugs a therapeutic effect could be attributed. In some, patients were removed and replaced by new patients if they failed to show an early response to the antidepressant, a violation of the intention-to-treat principle so egregious as to render those studies more fraudulent than worthless. A meta-analysis of the data found that, although patients receiving antidepressants showed a substantial improvement in their depression (an average of 10 points on the widely used Hamilton Rating Scale for Depression) so did placebo-treated patients (an average of 8 points), a difference that was clinically trivial.

The poor quality of this evidence may not have been obvious to clinicians because drug companies often make the final decision about whether and in what form their data becomes publicly available. This exacerbates a problem that pervades the scientific literature from all disciplines, known as *publication bias*, the tendency for studies with positive results to find their way into journals while negative findings remain hidden away in drawers. Even if the data from a trial is released for publication by a drug company, industry employees or a medical writing agency employed by the company may ghost-write a scientific article, which is then published in a high-profile journal under the name of an apparently independent psychiatrist who is in fact a consultant to the company. (Many papers on the therapeutic effects of the SSRIs seem to have found their way into print this way.[53]) As a consequence, what appears in scientific journals may bear very little relation to the truth – even the list of authors at the beginning of the paper may be misleading.

Of 42 SSRI trials submitted to the Swedish regulators, exactly half showed a significant advantage of the drug over placebo. Nineteen of the 21 positive studies eventually appeared as medical journal articles, compared to only 6 of the negative trials.[54] A similar analysis of trial data submitted to the American FDA recently found almost identical results, but with the additional twist that the data from some trials deemed negative by the regulator were spun so that they eventually appeared in print as supporting the effectiveness of the drug.[55]

This kind of misrepresentation, however, seems almost trivial when compared with efforts made by some companies to hide the harmful side effects of their products. In the case of the SSRIs, public debate about these effects was dramatically provoked when on 14 September 1989 Joseph Wesbecker, a printworker of Louisville, Kentucky, walked into his workplace and shot twenty people with an automatic rifle, killing eight before turning the gun on himself. Wesbecker had been prescribed Prozac only a month before the incident, even though he had become highly agitated after first trying the drug a year earlier.[56]

The Wesbecker case was not the only homicide in which Prozac was possibly implicated but it was the first to reach court. The plaintiffs in the case were the relatives of the deceased, who claimed that the drug, by making Wesbecker agitated, had contributed to his actions. Without any sense of irony, lawyers representing Eli Lilly, the manufacturer, argued that Wesbecker's behaviour was not caused by his brain chemistry but was a consequence of a series of adverse events, such as his divorce and his almost brutal working conditions. Expert witnesses for the plaintiffs, on the other hand, pointed out that Lilly's practice of administering a sedative in combination with Prozac would obscure any agitation felt by the patients during their clinical trials. This was why Lilly could claim that no evidence of aggressive behaviour had emerged during their research on the drug.

During the trial, the plaintiffs sought permission to inform the jury that Lilly had previously failed to report to the FDA deaths associated with its anti-inflammatory drug Oraflex. (Lilly pleaded guilty to this in a 1985 case filed against the company by the US Department of Justice.) Judge John Potter initially refused this request on the grounds that the evidence concerned another drug but then changed his mind following Lilly's lawyers' repeated assertion that the company had a good track record of reporting adverse effects. As the trial progressed, the plaintiffs failed to present the Oraflex evidence to the jury, however, which found in favour of the company, allowing it to insist that Prozac was safe. A troubled Potter conducted a post-trial investigation which revealed that Lilly's lawyers had entered into a secret agreement with the plaintiffs for an undisclosed sum. Potter's decision to replace the not-guilty verdict with a verdict of 'dismissed with prejudice as settled' was challenged by Lilly in the Kentucky Supreme Court which ruled in the judge's favour, concluding that 'There may have been deception, bad faith conduct, abuse of the judicial process or perhaps even fraud'.[57]

There is a footnote to this story, which concerns David Healy, an Irish psychiatrist and psychopharmacologist who was asked to testify in the Wesbecker trial. Healy was initially sceptical about the claim that SSRIs could cause impulsive behaviour but, after examining evidence obtained from the FDA, became convinced that a small number of homicides and suicides were provoked by the drugs. As a consequence of his willingness to express this opinion publicly, he has been treated as a pariah by many of his medical colleagues. In August 2000 Healy was offered a chair in the Department of Psychiatry at the University of Toronto, only to have the offer withdrawn after the department (which receives substantial pharmaceutical industry funding) learned of his views.[58] A subsequent legal action against the university, initiated on Healy's behalf by the Canadian Association of University Teachers, was settled for an undisclosed sum.

Following Healy's claim that SSRIs could provoke suicide attempts in vulnerable people, there have been several recent attempts to re-examine the randomized control trial data. While one large systematic review found that rates of suicide are higher in those taking SSRIs than in those treated with a placebo,[59] others have reported no evidence of an increased suicide risk, while concluding that more research on this issue is needed.[60] What is perhaps most remarkable about this debate is that no one is arguing that the new antidepressants prevent suicides, which is what they might have been have expected to do.

Can psychiatric trial data be trusted?

In this chapter I have suggested one explanation for the paradoxical ineffectiveness of psychiatric services. Some of the psychiatric treatments in wide use today are not nearly as effective as is commonly supposed; their potency has been systematically exaggerated by the pharmaceutical industry's ruthless manipulation of the clinical trial data. Antidepressants, in particular, do not seem to be particularly antidepressant at all. However, they undoubtedly provoke a powerful placebo response and it might therefore be argued that they should continue to be used. Of course, this raises a number of ethical concerns, particularly about doctors' duty to be honest to their patients, which I leave the reader to contemplate.

Ironically, critics of the pharmaceutical industry have included advocates of ECT, who have complained, 'The opportunity for inde-

SCIENCE, PROFIT AND POLITICS

pendent assessment and open dialogue about the efficacy and safety of psychoactive drugs, and especially comparisons with other treatments such as electroshock has been virtually eliminated.'[61] And yet this kind of argument can cut both ways. Many ECT researchers have financial links to companies manufacturing electroshock machines, and their studies suffer from the same shortcomings that have distorted industry-sponsored drug trials. In particular, those studies which have reported that ECT is effective have nearly always been of very short duration, observing outcomes over a period of just a few weeks.[62] When ECT patients have been followed up for longer, relapse rates have sometimes exceeded 80 per cent and have remained high even after the addition of drug treatment, an observation that must surely call into question its value as a psychiatric treatment.[63] (Aware of this problem, some ECT researchers have suggested that patients should continue to receive shocks at regular intervals for six months or more; even with this kind of extreme intervention, however, relapse rates remain very high.[64])

A cynic might therefore conclude that very little of the evidence on medical treatments for mental illness can be trusted, but this would be going too far. A more reasonable conclusion is that an accurate assessment can only be reached after examining the evidence in detail and with a sceptical eye. In the next two chapters I take this approach when examining the effectiveness of modern treatments for psychosis.

9

Less is Probably Better: The Benefits and Costs of Antipsychotics

No longer do we seek to understand whole persons in their social contexts – rather we are there to realign our patients' neurotransmitters. The problem is that it is very difficult to have a relationship with a neurotransmitter – whatever its configuration.

Loren Mosher, resignation letter to the American Psychiatric Association, 1998

Following Laborit's discovery of chlorpromazine, antipsychotic drugs became widely accepted as the treatment of choice for people with psychosis. They are now used almost everywhere in the world, even (I discovered during a trip to Uganda) in rural Africa, where they are often distributed by health workers who have no formal qualifications in medicine or nursing. Psychiatric services have become so dependent on these medications that, in Europe and North America, researchers wanting to study drug-naive patients usually have great difficulty finding any. When I embarked on such a project in the mid-1990s I soon gave up.

At about that time, a new doctrine was being embraced in the United States, Britain and elsewhere, according to which treatment with antipsychotics should be introduced as early as possible. This idea was enthusiastically promoted by the American psychiatrist Richard Wyatt.[1] Drawing together evidence collected from patients as they became ill for the first time, he concluded that the longer the duration between the onset of symptoms and the start of treatment (now known as the duration of untreated psychosis, or DUP) the more likely patients were to suffer long-term disability. Untreated psychosis, Wyatt concluded, is toxic to the brain, damaging it beyond repair.

Following further studies, which have seemed to support Wyatt's observation,[2] this relationship between DUP and prognosis is now widely accepted as a fact, and has been used to justify the development of specialized early intervention services. In Britain, for example, the Department of Health has established early intervention teams throughout the country during the last few years, and similar services have been established in some parts of the United States, in Canada, Austalia, New Zealand and a number of European countries. However, as in all matters psychiatric, the arguments made for this kind of approach require careful scrutiny. To begin with, it is worth noting that long DUPs are fairly uncommon. For example, in a recent British study, the median DUP was just twelve weeks (that is, half of patients had DUPs that were shorter than this) and the much higher average DUP of thirty-eight weeks was the consequence of a small number of patients who had gone for a very long time without treatment (16 out of the 248 patients had been ill between two and twelve years before finding their way to services).[3] Moreover, as British psychiatrist Richard Warner[4] has pointed out, much of the evidence used by Wyatt and others to justify early intervention is probably misleading, because patients whose hallucinations and delusions appear suddenly (and who often find their way in to services quickly), tend to have a good prognosis (some even recovering without treatment), and often respond well to medication. On the other hand, patients whose symptoms appear insidiously, and who therefore take some time to find their way into treatment, often have a poor outcome.[5] According to Warner, the apparent advantages of treating patients early may therefore be illusory; patients who find their way quickly to psychiatrists would probably do relatively well whatever was done to them.

A randomized controlled trial (RCT) would be the only sure way of establishing whether Warner's interpretation of the DUP data is correct. Some patients would have to be assigned to early treatment and others would have to have their treatment delayed for a number of weeks. However, this would require treatment to be temporarily withheld in the case of the control patients, which, according to early intervention enthusiasts, would be unethical (of course, this assumes that early treatment is beneficial, which is precisely what the trial would attempt to determine).

The nearest thing to a study of this kind that has actually been carried out is the Scandinavian Early Treatment and Intervention in Psychosis Study (known as TIPS for short). The study, designed by a team of Norwegian and American psychiatrists, began in early January 1997, when an early intervention service was established in some parts of Norway. New patients attending the early intervention service in Rogaland County were compared with similar patients attending conventional services in Oslo County in Norway and Roskilde County in Denmark. The TIPS service was successful at reducing DUP to an average of five weeks compared to sixteen weeks in the control areas,[6] mainly because a substantial public information campaign alerted the public to the importance and availability of early treatment (when the campaign was suspended, DUP returned to its previous level[7]). However, during their first two years of treatment, the TIPS patients did not differ from the control patients in positive symptoms, social functioning, quality of life or their likelihood of relapse, which would seem to support Warner's analysis.[8] Unexpectedly, the only apparent benefit for TIPS patients was for *negative symptoms*. This was unlikely to be the consequence of the early provision of drugs because, as we shall see, negative symptoms are unresponsive to this kind of treatment. It was more likely the consequence of the high quality of emotional support provided by an enthusiastic team introducing a new service. Consistent with this hypothesis, Australian researchers found that patients attending their early intervention services were less likely to commit suicide than those attending conventional services, but that this effect did not persist when, after three years, patients were passed on to conventional psychiatric teams.[9]

Nonetheless, the enthusiasm for early intervention has proved so infectious that some researchers are now arguing for the next logical step: providing treatment before patients become psychotic. This may be a realistic proposition because it has recently been discovered that, in some very specific circumstances, it is possible to predict who will become ill.

It has been known for some time that first episodes are often pre-ceded by a period in which patients experience subtle disturbances of mood and thinking. At the University of Melbourne during the late 1990s, psychiatrists Alison Yung and Patrick McGorry developed a method of identifying people with *late prodromal symptoms*, who are likely to become psychotic within a few months. These people are usually already experiencing transient hallucinations and delusional beliefs (they might be said to be suffering from *hypopsychosis*) which are not sufficiently severe to meet the *DSM* criteria for schizophrenia. However, to be identified as being at ultra-high risk according to the Melbourne criteria, potential patients must also show evidence of a loss of everyday functioning (for example, a reduction in their ability to work or maintain relationships) and, in practice, this means that most are already very unhappy and seeking help. In a one-year fol-low-up of a small group of people identified in this way, Yung, McGorry and their colleagues found that an astonishing 40 per cent became clinically psychotic, usually within a few months of being assessed.[10]

At the same time, researchers in Cologne in Germany tried to identify more subtle *early prodromal symptoms* (in their terminology, *basic symptoms*), which appear long before the onset of psychosis. Based on previous research, they assumed that these include subjective disturbances of thought and language, peculiar bodily sensations, an impaired ability to cope with stress, emotional disturbances and problems in relating to other people. In a study of patients who were referred to a specialist psychiatric service because of non-psychotic but difficult-to-diagnose problems, and who were followed up for an average of 9.6 years, it was found that those with basic symptoms were much more likely (70 per cent) to receive a *DSM* diagnosis of schizophrenia compared to those who did not (1.6 per cent).[11] Of the symptoms the researchers examined, subtle disturbances of thought and language were the best predictors of future illness.

These findings look spectacular, but are perhaps not quite as impressive as they at first appear. Remember that both the Melbourne and Cologne research groups started by studying people who were already distressed (most were quite severely anxious or depressed), effectively excluding everyone who became psychotic without seeking help for earlier difficulties. Indeed, the Melbourne researchers have reported that the majority of first-episode psychotic patients are not detected in advance by their criteria.[12] Nor is it certain how many individuals identified by each method eventually become ill. More than two-thirds of those with basic symptoms at the beginning of the Cologne study were not available for follow-up later (they were either untraceable or refused); if we assume that the majority did not become psychotic, the actual proportion of patients who became ill drops to around a quarter. A more recent study in Melbourne reported lower transition rates than those reported in earlier studies, about 10 per cent within six months,[13] although another recent study in North America reported a conversion rate of 35 per cent over two and a half years.*[14] Given the evidence on the limitations of psychiatric classification which we looked at in Chapter 5, it is also interesting that high-risk individuals who do become psychotic end up with a variety of diagnoses, including schizoaffective disorder, bipolar disorder and major depression, and not just schizophrenia.[15]

Nonetheless, the ability to even hazard a guess about who will become seriously mentally ill creates opportunities for research. For example, researchers using the Melbourne criteria have reported that ultra-high-risk patients who later become psychotic, compared to those who do not, perform poorly on neurocognitive tests,[16] and have a reduced volume of grey matter in some areas of the brain (the right cerebral hemisphere[17]) but not in others (the hippocampus[18]). When patients who became ill were given further brain scans later, they had apparently lost more grey matter during the transition to psychosis, especially in the cingulate cortex and temporal lobes.[19] Of course, for reasons that were explained in Chapter 7, it is difficult to interpret these findings without knowing something about the social environ-

---

* The researchers also reported that they were able to identify combinations of criteria (e.g. genetic risk, plus recent loss of function, plus paranoia) that identified individuals with a much higher risk of conversion, up to 68–80 per cent. However, their use of statistical techniques to search through possible predictors to find the best combination carries a high risk of spurious results, and it will therefore be necessary to replicate the findings in an independent sample. A further problem is that, the higher the positive predictive power, the narrower the group identified, and the greater the likelihood of false negatives (future psychotic patients who are wrongly judged as not being at risk).

ment in which the patients' symptoms worsened. For example, the changes in the brain might have been caused by stress. Consistent with this idea, one study found that volume of the pituitary gland predicted transition to psychosis in high-risk patients (the pituitary plays a role in regulating stress hormones).[20]

For clinicians, the ability to predict the onset of psychosis has suddenly created the possibility of developing therapeutic strategies to prevent symptoms before they occur. This idea is being enthusiastically pursued in some parts of the world, but presents some important ethical challenges. There is a danger that individuals at high risk will be harmed by being informed of their at-risk status, by being stigmatized as a result of being unnecessarily embroiled with psychiatric services, or by being coerced into receiving treatments that cause more harm than good. These risks must be taken very seriously because many people identified as being at high risk (according to most studies, over half if the Melbourne criteria are used) will not actually become psychotic.[21] Any decision about the wisdom of prescribing antipsychotic medication to high-risk patients must be informed by a careful analysis of the benefits and costs of this type of treatment, which we shall now consider.

The short-term therapeutic effects of antipsychotic medication

The first effective antipsychotic, chlorpromazine, was discovered by French researchers in the early 1950s. Chlorpromazine was quickly followed by other similar medicines introduced by pharmaceutical companies eager to get a share in the new market for treatments for severe mental illness. These drugs are sometimes known as *first-generation* or *typical antipsychotics*, to contrast them with *second-generation* or *atypical antipsychotics* which have been introduced over the past decade. For convenience, the chemical names of the most widely used drugs of both types are listed in Table 2, together with their US and UK trade names.

Table 2. Commonly used antipsychotics

Drug name	UK trade name	US trade name
First-generation antipsychotics:		
chlorpromazine	Largactil	Thorazine
flupenthixol	Fluanxol/Depixol	
zuclopenthixol	Clopixol	
perphenazine	Fentazin	Trilafon
trifluoperazine	Stelazine	Stelazine
pericyazine	Neulactil	Neulactil
promazine	Sparine	
loxapine	Loxitan/Loxapac	Loxitane
sulpiride	Sulpitil/Dolmatil/Sulparex	
haloperidol	Serenace/Haldol/Dozic	Haldol
tetrabenazine	Xenazine	
molindone		Moban/Lidone
Second-generation antipsychotics:		
clozapine	Clozaril	Clozaril
risperidone	Risperdal	Risperdal
olanzapine	Zyprexa	Zyprexa
quetiapine	Seroquel	Seroquel
ziprasidone		Geodon
amisulpride	Solian	
aripiprazole	Abilify	Abilify
zotepine	Zoleptil	

Adapted from D. Healy (2005), *Psychiatric Drugs Explained*, 4th edition.
London: Elsevier.

It is important to note first that, in contrast to the antidepressants (which, we saw in the last chapter, are marginally if at all more effective than placebos) no doubts exist about the short-term benefits of antipsychotic treatment. After taking either a first- or second-generation drug for the first time, many patients very quickly experience relief from their hallucinations and delusions. Indeed, anyone working with patients or who watches as a loved one responds to antipsychotic treatment would find it hard not to be impressed by this effect. Clinical lore used to state that treatment must be continued for several weeks before an improvement will be noticed. As the blockade of D_2 receptors (the putative therapeutic mechanism) is achieved within an hour or so of taking the medication, this was once thought to pose a problem for the dopamine theory of psychosis, which would seem to predict that any therapeutic effects will be almost immediate. However, it is now recognized that beneficial effects are seen much more rapidly than was once thought. Indeed, considerable improvement is usually seen within a few days and continues before typically levelling out after about a month.[22]

It is worth noting in passing that some of the earliest trials of antipsychotics were independently funded and hence were fairly rigorous when compared to more recent drug trials conducted by the pharmaceutical industry. For example, in a series of studies funded by the US National Institute of Mental Health, antipsychotics were compared with barbiturates that were selected because they had an equally sedating effect, and it was shown that positive symptoms responded to the antipsychotics and not the barbiturates.[23] Therefore, although antipsychotics have sometimes been described as 'chemical straitjackets', it is wrong to assume that they simply knock patients out and stop them from complaining (although they will have this effect if, as is all too often the case, they are administered at a high enough dose).

However, it may also be wrong to assume that the drugs have a direct effect on the frequency and severity of symptoms. In a recent study, first-episode patients were asked, in advance of receiving medication, whether they expected antipsychotic treatment to remove their symptoms or to make the symptoms more tolerable. Although most anticipated that their symptoms would go away, when questioned eight weeks later they reported a much greater effect on the extent to which they were bothered by their symptoms.[24] Of course, from the patient's point of view, this kind of effect may be almost as beneficial as eliminating their hallucinations and delusions altogether.

Dose, side effects and the development of second-generation drugs

The real problem with the antipsychotics is not their effectiveness, but the way that they are used. Despite the benefits experienced by many patients, others experience no relief from their symptoms whatsoever. With one possible exception, to be discussed later, there is good evidence that patients who fail to respond to one antipsychotic will almost certainly not respond to any other.[25] The proportion of patients who are antipsychotic non-responders is difficult to estimate but is probably somewhere between a quarter and a third of those who receive the drugs.[26] None of these patients should be receiving them.

Sometimes enzymes in the liver metabolize the drugs before they can find their way to the brain.[27] This has led to the speculation that it might be possible to use genetic tests to identify patients who have high levels of the relevant enzymes, so that they are not given antipsychotics unnecessarily.[28] However, liver metabolism cannot be the whole story because neuroimaging studies show that the blockade of dopamine neurones in the mid-brain is often as extensive in non-responders as in responders.[29] In some patients, it seems, and for reasons that are not yet fully understood, the drugs get to the brain but have no therapeutic impact.

Nonetheless, in psychiatric services in Britain and the United States, where medication is very often the first and sometimes the only kind of treatment offered to patients, psychiatrists usually persist in the face of initial failure by trying a series of different drugs, sometimes in combination, and often at escalating doses. Often patients mistreated in this way continue to experience severe hallucinations and delusions which, instead of being taken as evidence that the drugs are ineffective, are interpreted as evidence that ever higher doses are required. This practice would not be worrying if antipsychotics were safe and easily tolerated. However, *all* antipsychotics have alarming side effects and in the long term these can be threatening to health and sometimes the cause of premature death.

When I first walked onto a psychiatric ward in the North Wales Hospital, Denbigh, in the late 1970s, I was struck by the fact that many of the patients I met there seemed to move in an odd, stilted way, that many of them were shaking, and that some grimaced, opening their mouths, sticking out their tongues and rolling their jaws dramatically. My naive assumption was that these patients were suffering from some kind of brain disease. In fact, this intuition was correct, but what I did not realize at the time was that their neurological symptoms were caused by the treatment they were receiving from their psychiatrists.

The patients were showing classic *extrapyramidal side effects* (EPS), so called because they involve disruption of the extrapyramidal system, a network of neurones that is involved in coordination and movement. These side effects are caused by all of the first-generation antipsychotics and, to a lesser extent, by some of the second-generation drugs. They include *Parkinsonism* (stiffness and tremor), *dystonias* (involuntary muscle movements), *akathisia* (an extremely distressing kind of restlessness, leading to obvious fidgeting) and *tardive dyskinesia* (involuntary movements, usually of the jaw and tongue).[30] The first three of these side effects are reversible, either by discontinuing treatment or by using additional anticholinergic drugs such as Kemadrine (procycladine) (which, of course, have their own side effects, such as constipation, dry mouth and impaired short-term memory). However, tardive dyskinesia is much more difficult to reverse, and may persist for many years after the last dose of antipsychotic has been taken.

Astonishingly, although these side effects were well recognized from the start of the modern era of psychopharmacology, the first studies that systematically investigated the relationship between antipsychotic dose and their costs and benefits were not published until the early 1990s,[31] approximately forty years after the drugs were first introduced. Before this time most psychiatrists believed that the therapeutic effect of the antipsychotics correlated with their effect on the extrapyramidal system.[32] Hence, patients were deliberately given doses that provoked Parkinsonism, in the belief that this would maximize the impact on their illness.

The results of the studies appearing in the early 1990s were therefore surprising to many psychiatrists, because they showed that low doses are as effective as high doses, and that the only consequence of increasing the medication beyond a dose equivalent to approximately 350 milligrams a day of chlorpromazine is an escalating risk of side effects.[33] Despite advice to the contrary from professional organizations such as the Royal College of Psychiatrists[34] and the US National Institute of Mental Health,[35] surveys show that psychiatrists nonetheless continue to treat many of their patients with irrationally high doses. For example, in a recent study of more than 200 patients receiving treatment in the north-west of England, about half the patients were receiving the equivalent of 600 milligrams a day of chlorpromazine or more, and about a quarter were receiving the equivalent of more than a gram of chlorpromazine a day (about three times the optimum dose).[36] Many of the patients on the highest doses were probably antipsychotic non-responders who would have been much better off with no medication at all.

Around the time that the relationship between antipsychotic dose and treatment response became known, concern about the extrapyramidal effects led to the increasing use of the second-generation drugs, which were thought to minimize the unwanted consequences of therapy. The first of these was clozapine,[37] which was synthesized by German researchers in the 1960s and which seemed to have a much less severe side-effect profile than the already established antipsychotics. However, clozapine almost immediately fell out of favour, for two reasons. First, at that time many psychiatrists believed that the therapeutic response to antipsychotics was closely related to their effect on the extrapyramidal system, and most had difficulty believing that clozapine could be effective. Second, shortly after clozapine was licensed for use in Finland, nine patients died of secondary infections after developing agranulocytosis, a reduction in the ability of their bone marrow to manufacture white blood cells. (In fact, although agranulocytosis was reported in patients receiving clozapine elsewhere, this was never to the same extent as in Finland, and the relatively large number of cases observed there has never been properly explained.) Hence, it quickly came to be believed that clozapine was a drug that was only marginally effective and potentially lethal to the patients who received it. Not surprisingly, no one felt very enthusiastic about its use.

Clozapine was rehabilitated in the 1980s after psychiatrists in the

United States became worried about the increasing number of patients who were suffering from tardive dyskinesia. Realizing that clozapine was the one drug that might be given to such patients without making matters worse, tentative studies were conducted to establish whether it could be given safely. It was soon discovered that the risk of agranularcytosis could be reduced to within acceptable limits if patients were given regular blood tests (initially at weekly intervals but later less frequently) and if treatment was discontinued immediately after an abnormal white cell count.

These developments eventually led to a large-scale randomized controlled trial comparing clozapine to chlorpromazine in patients who had previously been unresponsive to first-generation drugs, which was published in 1988. The trial was funded by the manufacturer of clozapine, Sandoz, and was conducted by American psychiatrists John Kane and Herbert Meltzer.[38] To many psychiatrists, the results, when they were reported, seemed nothing short of miraculous: the patients treated with clozapine not only experienced fewer side effects, but also showed a greater improvement in their symptoms. Given that a substantial proportion of psychotic patients responded poorly to the first-generation drugs, and given that no antipsychotic had ever before been shown to beat chlorpromazine, this discovery seemed to mark an important advance in the treatment of severe mental illness.

Clozapine was described as atypical because pharmacological studies revealed that it differed in important ways from the first-generation antipsychotics. Unlike these drugs, it had a relatively low affinity for the D_2 receptor. Some researchers thought this finding undermined the dopamine theory of psychosis. However, defenders of the theory argued that clozapine's D_2 affinity, although less than that of the other antipsychotics, was not low enough to require the theory to be abandoned.[39] Nonetheless, they recognized that clozapine was a much less specific drug than the other antipsychotics because it also blocked adrenergic, cholinergic, histaminergic and serotonergic receptors.

Not surprisingly, rival drug companies were soon working hard to develop their own atypicals. As there was no accepted definition of atypicality, some tried synthesizing compounds with a similar structure to clozapine (Lilly's olanzapine), while others searched for compounds which, although chemically dissimilar, affected a wide range of receptor systems (Janssen's respirodone).† As psychopharmacologist and historian of psychiatry David Healy has remarked: 'The emergence and survival of concepts in both the business and academic marketplaces is often determined by the "slogan" value of the concept . . . The notion of atypicality was the ultimate marketing dream. If it was not possible to make another atypical, the next best thing was to label your compound an atypical. Sales would follow.'[40]

The hype that surrounded the new drugs included not only the usual glossy advertisements in psychiatric journals and sponsored colloquia at medical conferences, but also efforts to influence the wider community of mental health professionals, patients and their families. In the late 1990s it was almost impossible for anyone working in the field to have a conversation about the treatment of psychosis without discussing the impact that the new drugs were having (or were promised to have). Even clinical psychologists were caught up in the moment. In 1997 I attended an international conference on cognitive behaviour therapy in Venice, and found myself sitting in on a symposium on the implications of the new medications for psychological treatments.

A couple of years later I was asked to represent the British Psychological Society at a London meeting to launch the 'Psychopharmacology of Schizophrenia Initiative', which turned out to be a front for a consortium of drug companies. The meeting began with a tearful presentation from a patient who told the attendees that olanzapine had saved his life. Clearly, the organizers hoped to provoke a groundswell of opinion, which would lead the National Health Service to embrace the new drugs, despite their high cost. In fact, the attempt was so crude that it provoked a backlash from many in the audience, who had not realized that they had been invited to a drug company marketing event.

Despite occasional setbacks of this kind, there can be no doubt that, from the point of view of the pharmaceutical industry, their efforts

† In fact, the distinction between typical and atypical antipsychotics remains unclear. For example, if the relative absence of EPS is considered to be the defining feature of the atypicals, sulpiride qualifies despite the fact that it is usually considered to be a first-generation drug and is a relatively pure D_2 agonist.

were very successful. Throughout the 1990s and into the new century, prescriptions of the second-generation drugs rose dramatically. This success reflected official guidelines, drawn up by leaders in psychiatry, which were issued in 1998 by the US National Institute for Mental Health Schizophrenia Patient Outcome Research Team,[41] and in 2002 by the National Institute of Clinical Excellence in Britain.[42] In both reports, the authors extolled the new drugs over the old ones, and recommended that they be made available as first-line treatments, even for patients who were experiencing their first episode of psychosis and who had never been given a first-generation drug. As the new drugs are considerably more expensive than the old, this change in practice has led to a troubling increase in the funds that services have to find to pay for the drugs they are giving their patients,[43] a development that is no doubt satisfying to the pharmaceutical companies and their shareholders.

There are more side effects than stiffness and shakes

In the furore that surrounded the arrival of the atypicals, it was easy to forget that the extrapyramidal side effects, although highly visible, are often less troubling to the patient, and less threatening to health, than other less obvious adverse reactions caused by both generations of drugs.

For example, most antipsychotics produce an increase in the hormone prolactin, leading to lactation in women and swelling of the breasts in men. Loss of sexual function is also very common, affecting about 50 per cent of patients taking either typical or atypical medications. Some patients suffer from skin rashes (chlorpromazine, in particular, can cause severe sensitivity to sunlight, resulting in burning on even mild days). Rapid weight gain is also very common. Although most of the first- and second-generation drugs can have this last effect, the atypical olanzapine (Zyprexa) is notorious for it. Although prescribers often regard these kinds of effects as relatively unimportant,[44] they can sometimes cause as much distress to patients as the symptoms that the drugs are used to treat.[45] For many patients, they are also stigmatizing (imagine, for example, being a young man whose life, at the age of 17, has been interrupted by a psychotic breakdown, who is forced to watch as his friends leave home, find partners and set out on their careers, and whose medication then makes him impotent and fat).

The weight gain caused by antipsychotic treatment increases the risk of high blood pressure, heart disease, and stroke, and some patients undoubtedly go to an early grave as a consequence.[46] Some antipsychotics also cause a high risk of diabetes (olanzapine appears to be particularly problematic in this respect[47]). Aside from this hidden morbidity, there are a number of fortunately rare but well-documented side effects that can be immediately threatening to life. These include epileptic convulsions, cardiac failure (antipsychotics cause a small but quantifiable increase in the risk of sudden death from heart attack),[48] agranularcytosis (as we have seen, a particular problem with clozapine), and the *neuroleptic malignant syndrome*, a condition which at first seems like fever and stiffness and which is sometimes mistaken for a viral infection, but which can be fatal unless treated promptly. These problems are compounded by the fact that psychotic patients often have lifestyles (heavy smoking, lack of regular exercise) which already confer a high risk of some of these ailments.[49]

Not surprisingly, perhaps, there is evidence that life expectancy is reduced in patients who receive more than one antipsychotic.[50] A further indication of their toxicity comes from studies that have examined their effects on patients who are not psychotic. For example, they are often used to reduce agitation in patients suffering from dementia or other degenerative neurological conditions of later life (patients, who, incidentally, are usually in no position to complain about their treatment). Elderly patients who receive antipsychotics suffer a reduced life expectancy as a consequence.[51]

It is not only their physical effects that make these drugs a mixed blessing. Often it is their subjective effects that cause the most distress to patients. During the first few hours of treatment with the first-generation drugs, many patients experience a deep depression, which is sometimes described as *neuroleptic dysphoria*.[52] As this feeling is often coupled with akathisia, the patient finds herself in the unenviable position of being unable to initiate actions or make decisions, while at the same time feeling extremely agitated and restless. A more long-term problem, caused by both the first- and second-generation drugs, is mental clouding and sedation coupled to a profound loss of motivation which can persist for as long as the treatment continues. The detrimental effect on motivation is easy to understand physiologically because, as we saw earlier, the dopamine pathways in the brain which are blocked by antipsychotics are known to play an important role in anticipating and hence striving for rewards.[53] In one clinical trial in which treatment with a typical antipsychotic was compared with a placebo, the researchers took the unusual step of assessing patients' achievements as well as their symptoms. It was found that the patients receiving antipsychotics not only experienced a reduced risk of relapse but also achieved less than the patients treated with placebo.[54] Unfortunately, these effects are often mistaken for negative symptoms, and hence seen as part of a patient's illness rather than a consequence of treatment.[55] Even those doctors who are prepared to acknowledge that these symptoms are side effects may underestimate their impact and may be reluctant to discuss them with patients.[56] Sometimes this seems to reflect a fear that, if patients really understand what the medication is doing to them, they will discontinue taking it.

The evidence I have just described can be summarized as follows: despite their obvious benefits for some, perhaps even the majority of patients, antipsychotics come with a very high personal cost. It is fair to say that this cost has been historically underestimated, or even neglected altogether, by most psychiatrists. Of course, side effects have special implications for the treatment of high-risk patients, many of whom will never become psychotic if left to their own devices. To most ordinary people the idea of exposing large numbers of mentally well individuals to treatments that have hazardous consequences for health seems morally repugnant. Alas, this view is not shared by a small minority of psychiatrists and psychologists, who insist that the failure to prescribe psychiatric drugs to high-risk patients is as wicked as refusing to give insulin to people with diabetes.‡[57] The results

‡ An amazing example of this kind of reasoning came in the form of the remarks made by an anonymous referee who was asked to comment on one of my grant applications, which proposed a trial of psychological treatments for high-risk patients (the trial was eventually funded). Because we did not plan to give our patients antipsychotic drugs, the referee likened our study to experiments conducted by American doctors in

of the only two trials to evaluate the effects of antipsychotics with prodromal patients are instructive. In Melbourne, a small study in which high-risk patients were offered a combination of respirone and psychotherapy found a short-term effect at six months' follow-up, but no reduction in risk of psychosis after one year.[58] A study carried out at Yale University in the United States[59] which tried to randomize prodromal patients to either olanzapine or placebo found that patients with prodromal symptoms were reluctant to take part.[60] By the end of the study, about two-thirds of the participants had dropped out, many because they had found olanzapine to be intolerable. No significant differences were observed in the numbers of patients making the transition to psychosis, although an observed trend in the expected direction was interpreted as evidence that drug treatment delayed the onset of illness. However, a very dramatic effect was observed on the patients' weight – those receiving olanzapine had put on an average of 20 pounds (9 kilos).

Not surprisingly, no one has managed to make money by selling antipsychotics on street corners. Formal surveys of psychotic patients have found that their attitudes towards this kind of treatment vary enormously. Some undoubtedly regard the drugs as life-saving, or decide that the benefits outweigh the costs, but others are eager to stop using them as quickly as possible.[61] Although a patient's reasons for wanting to discontinue treatment may be perfectly rational (the drugs may be ineffective or the side effects intolerable), refusing medication is often regarded by the prescribing psychiatrist as evidence that the patient lacks insight, and hence is an indication that more aggressive treatment is required.[62] Aware of this risk, many patients are reluctant to discuss their worries about their treatment with their

---

Tuskegee in the 1940s, in which black men were deliberately refused antibiotic treatment for syphilis so that the long-term course of the disease could be studied. I suspect that the ethical differences between these two studies are obvious to anyone without an ideological axe to grind but I will spell them out anyway: (i) my study did not involve selecting patients on racial grounds (white men in Tuskegee were given treatment); (ii) it was known that all of the untreated black men in Tuskegee would become seriously ill as a consequence of their treatment being withheld whereas it is known that only a minority of high-risk patients become psychotic; (iii) antibiotics have few side effects whereas antipsychotics have many; (iv) there was (and still is) no evidence that antipsychotics can be used to prevent psychosis.

doctors. Sometimes, as we saw in the case of Peter (described at the beginning of this book), they abruptly cease taking their medication without telling anyone. Psychiatrists and psychologists, observing a high risk of relapse when this happens, usually assume that the patient's illness has resurfaced because the suppressing effect of the medication has been removed. However, as we shall see, many of the relapses that occur under these circumstances almost certainly have a very different explanation.

Do antipsychotics help in the long term?

Despite the persistent and unpleasant side effects experienced by many patients, most people suffering from psychosis are told that they should continue to take their drugs indefinitely. Conventional psychiatric wisdom is apparently supported by many studies that have looked at the effects of antipsychotic treatment over the long term, nearly always concluding that continued use is beneficial. Some studies have compared *maintenance treatment*, in which patients take their drugs even after they have completely recovered from an episode of illness, with *intermittent therapy*, in which antipsychotics are given only when patients feel stressed or unwell. The results have shown, apparently decisively, that relapse is much more likely with intermittent treatment.[63]

The usual inference drawn from these findings is that, in order to obtain maximum benefit from antipsychotics, patients must keep taking them even when they feel well. Apart from the distress caused by the discovery that they must continue to tolerate their side effects for years or even decades, this advice creates many practical difficulties. Patients have to remember to take their drugs at the correct time, and to develop a routine that allows them to use the drugs as prescribed. This can be more difficult than it sounds: I know from personal experience that it is very hard to adhere to even a benign treatment for a very long time (like many middle-aged men I take a daily tablet to control my blood pressure). Even patients who are trying to follow their doctors' instructions will forget to take their medication on occasions, and some develop their own idiosyncratic patterns of drug-taking. For example, most patients are told not to combine their drugs with alcohol but, as a visit to the pub may be one of their few pleasures in life, may be reluctant to abstain from drinking altogether. In one of my own studies, some patients tried to cope with this problem by taking more than the prescribed dose after a visit to the pub, whereas others abstained from medication when drinking.[64]

Doctors sometimes try to get round these difficulties by prescribing long-lasting depot medications that are slowly released from an oily vehicle that is injected into the buttocks every few weeks. It is sometimes thought that this is a good method for treating poorly adherent patients in particular. However, attending a depot clinic to receive a painful injection is not a particularly pleasant experience so, not surprisingly, many patients avoid the treatment by the simple expedient of being elsewhere at the time of the appointment.

Such strategies are based on the assumption that continuous treatment is always preferable. In fact, a number of factors cloud this assumption. First, as we have already seen, a sizeable minority of psychotic patients – perhaps as many as one in three – obtain little or no benefit from antipsychotics. Despite extensive research, there is no known way of predicting who will respond and who will not, but what is certain, as we saw earlier, is that diagnosis does not predict who will do well.[65] Indeed, both first- and second-generation drugs are now widely used to treat patients diagnosed as suffering from bipolar disorder, leading some researchers to wonder belatedly whether there might be common pathological processes in the two diagnostic groups.[66] Obviously, insisting that non-responsive patients receive antipsychotics continuously can only cause more harm than good.

Contrary to the conventional wisdom that antipsychotic therapy should be administered as early as possible, there is some evidence that first-episode and prodromal patients benefit less from this kind of treatment than patients who have been ill for some time. By far the majority of antipsychotic RCTs have been carried out with long-term patients, sometimes withdrawing them from medication in order to put them on placebo, so surprisingly little data exists on patients who are experiencing symptoms for the first time. John Bola,[67] an American social worker based at the University of Southern California, has recently attempted to combine evidence from all trials in which the majority of patients were suffering their first episode, in which some patients were unmedicated and in which the follow-up period was at least one year.¶ After an extensive search of the scientific literature, he could find only six studies, including a total of 632 patients, which met all of these criteria. These included Loren Mosher's Soteria study,[68] the Swiss replication of Soteria[69] and the long-term follow-up of the patients in the Camarillo State Hospital study (see Chapter 4) comparing psychodynamic therapy to biological treatments (which showed much less advantage for drug treatment at long-term follow-up[70]). Bola's meta-analysis of the data from these studies found no evidence that the medicated first-episode patients did better than the patients who did not receive medication. Perhaps this finding helps to explain why the Scandinavian TIPS project found no advantage (in terms of positive symptoms) in providing drug treatment early during a first episode, and why the Melbourne and Yale trials failed to demonstrate a clear advantage to giving medication to prodromal patients.

At first sight, the evidence that antipsychotics have few lasting benefits for patients in the earliest stages of psychosis seems to be hard to square with the results of trials comparing maintenance therapy to intermittent therapy. However, only two studies have specifically compared these treatment methods in first-episode patients, and the results from these studies have been inconsistent. In one of the studies, no advantage for maintenance treatment[71] was observed whereas in the other, patients receiving maintenance therapy did considerably better.[72] These findings are difficult to interpret because neither study included a group of patients who received no antipsychotic drugs at

¶ Bola's paper was turned down by many psychiatric journals. Most of the journals it was submitted to criticized it, not because of its methodology, but because there were only six studies that could be included in the meta-analysis. (As Bola told me, 'That's the point!') Of course, the fact that his findings contradicted conventional wisdom may also have been a factor. To ensure its publication in the journal *Schizophrenia Bulletin*, Bola rewrote the paper so that it appeared to be addressing the question of whether it is ethical to withhold medication from first-episode patients for research purposes (the answer being yes, because withholding antipsychotics appears to cause no harm).

all. Hence, at the time of writing, the balance of the available evidence seems to suggest that many first-episode patients may do well with only a brief period of antipsychotic treatment, or without any drug therapy at all.

Could antipsychotics make patients more vulnerable to future episodes?

Some readers will probably be wondering why, if antipsychotics have such a limited effect on the well-being of first-episode patients, they seem to prevent relapse in patients who have been ill for some time. It will be apparent by now that the bulk of the evidence for this effect comes from studies of patients who become ill after withdrawing from their medication, either by their own decision, or as part of a placebo-controlled study. However, the emergence of symptoms under these circumstances may reflect long-term changes to the brain caused by the medication, rather than a return of illness. This seems to be a general phenomenon observed following prolonged treatment with most kinds of psychiatric medication, and is the consequence of the way that the brain adapts to assaults on its neurotransmitter systems.

In the case of antipsychotics, both animal and human studies[73] show that one consequence of long-term treatment is a proliferation of the number of D_2 receptors in the brain. The brain responds to having its dopamine receptors blocked by making more of them. If, as the dopamine hypothesis proposes, psychosis is associated with excessive sensitivity of the dopamine system, we should expect that the withdrawal of long-term antipsychotic treatment will lead to relapse, not because the original illness is no longer suppressed, but because the brain has been made super-sensitive to stress by drug treatment.

It is difficult to devise scientific tests of the *dopamine super-sensitivity hypothesis*. However, the theory predicts that patients who rapidly discontinue their drugs will be more likely to relapse than patients who discontinue gradually, and whose brains have had the chance to adjust to the removal of the dopamine blockade. In fact, those studies which have compared patients who (like Peter in Chapter

1) withdraw quickly with patients who withdraw slowly have generally found a greater risk of relapse in the former group.[74] Furthermore, when patients discontinue their medication under any circumstances, the greatest risk of relapse occurs within the first few months. Although by no means definitive, these findings suggest that the prolonged use of antipsychotics may have precisely the opposite effect to that intended. They also imply that any patient withdrawing from medication, either with or without a psychiatrist's consent, would be well advised to do so in small steps.

On the basis of this evidence, the American investigative journalist Robert Whitaker has claimed that the widespread use of antipsychotics has been responsible for the increase in the number of people suffering from psychiatric disability that has been observed over the last fifty years.[75] I think this claim is probably overstated, or at least as yet remains unproven. However, once we take into account the very severe side effects of antipsychotic drugs, the fact that many first-episode patients seem to do well without them, the failure of some patients to show any kind of clinical response, no matter how much medication they are given, and the possibility that some patients are made more sensitive to stress as a consequence of being treated in this way, the faith placed by modern psychiatric services in antipsychotics seems hard to justify.

Fooled again?

Many psychiatrists would concede the limitations of the first-generation antipsychotics, but would argue that the second-generation drugs are different. As we have seen, the main selling point of these compounds is that they apparently produce fewer extrapyramidal effects but, especially when they first became available, pharmaceutical companies marketed them with extravagant claims about their superior efficacy compared to first-generation compounds.

At about the same time as I attended the ill-fated inaugural meeting of the Psychopharmacology of Schizophrenia Initiative, a group of psychiatrists in the North of England invited me to take part in a debate about the virtues of clozapine. I was a bit taken back by this invitation because, lacking a medical degree, I felt poorly qualified to address the issue (apparently, it was felt that I could be relied on to take a sceptical position). In preparation for the debate, I began to gather together the relevant scientific literature. The obvious place to start, it seemed to me, was the Kane and Meltzer[76] trial which had shown that clozapine was more effective and better tolerated than chlorpromazine in the treatment of patients who had failed to respond to first-generation drugs. This trial had by then become one of the most widely cited studies in psychiatry, and was even mentioned in some introductory textbooks for undergraduate psychology students. It was by studying it very closely that I first learned the importance of taking a forensic approach to pharmaceutical-industry sponsored research.

The first thing I noticed was that the trial had a very short follow-up period: patients were studied for only six weeks. The 268 patients had been selected because they had failed to respond to high doses of the first-generation drugs on at least three occasions over the previous five years. Half were randomly assigned to clozapine and the remaining half received up to 1.8 grams of chlorpromazine a day – a huge dose by any standards. At the end of six weeks, the clozapine-treated patients had experienced a greater reduction in their symptoms, and also had fewer side effects – or so it seemed.

Given that the control group was receiving up to six times the optimum dose of chlorpromazine, any failure to find differences in the side effects experienced by the two groups would have been incredible. Amazingly, of the two measures of side effects that were employed only one, a measure of extrapyramidal symptoms, showed a difference between the two groups. The second scale, which measured a wider range of adverse reactions, did not favour clozapine, even when hyper-salivation (a very common side effect of clozapine) was removed from the scale. It is possible that the inappropriate comparison dose of chlorpromazine also led to a distorted view of the relative efficacy of the two treatments. At least one study has reported that patients who have failed to respond to mega-doses of first generation drugs (the very group of patients selected for the trial) often do better if their medication is reduced.[77]

Inappropriately high comparison doses of first-generation antipsychotics were a regular feature of subsequent studies of the second-generation drugs. It is hard to imagine that pharmaceutical companies were unaware that this would lead to a distorted picture of the merits of their products and, indeed, this practice seems to have been a deliberate strategy designed to fool mental health professionals, patients and regulators. As was the case with the selective serotonin re-uptake inhibitors, most studies have also been of short duration (4–6 weeks) and with high drop-out rates, making firm conclusions all but impossible. In a meta-analysis published in 2000,[78] trials were divided into those which used comparison doses equivalent to less than 12 mg per day of haloperidol (still quite a high dose – haloperidol is a high-potency first-generation drug and the optimum dose is probably about 5 mg per day) and those which used higher comparison doses. There was no evidence that the second-generation drugs were more efficacious and, with the exception of extrapyramidal effects, there was no difference in the severity of side effects in those studies which used a low dose of comparison drug. Not surprisingly, in those studies in which the comparison dose was irrationally high, the new drugs looked much better.

This lack of difference between the two types of drugs has been confirmed in two recent trials which were designed to assess their relative efficacy in real-life clinical conditions, and which have provoked much soul-searching in the mental health community.[79] In a British study,[80] known as the CUtLASS (Cost Utility of the Latest Antipsychotic drugs in Schizophrenia Study) trial, more than 200 patients who had previously failed to respond to antipsychotic therapy were randomly assigned either to first- or to second-generation drugs (the actual choice of drugs within each category was left to the prescribing psychiatrists, with the exception that clozapine was not used). After a year of treatment, there was no evidence that the second-generation drugs led to improved quality of life; indeed there was a trend towards greater quality of life and symptom improvement in those who continued to receive first-generation drugs. Moreover, when all the costs incurred in treating the patients were calculated, the old drugs turned out to be more cost-effective.[81]

In the larger CATIE (Clinical Antipsychotic Trials of Intervention Effectiveness) study,[82] funded by the US National Institute of Mental

Health, approximately 1,400 American patients were randomly assigned to one of four second-generation drugs: olanzapine, respirodone, ziprasadone or quetiapine, or to the first-generation drug perphenazine. The main aim of the study was to determine whether the new drugs were better tolerated than the older typical compounds. However, after eighteen months of treatment, an astonishing 74 per cent of all the patients had discontinued their drugs, mainly because they were perceived to be ineffective, or because the side effects were too unpleasant, a sure indication that many patients did not find that the benefits of antipsychotic treatment outweighed the costs. Although patients less readily gave up olanzapine (64 per cent) than respirodone (74 per cent) or quetiapine (82 per cent) the difference between olanzapine and perphenazine (74 per cent) was not statistically significant (that is, the researchers could not be confident that a difference this small was not due to chance). A subsequent examination of the side effects experienced by the patients in the trial found no evidence that those receiving the second-generation drugs experienced less extrapyramidal side effects.[83] Moreover, although it was hoped the new drugs would lead to greater improvements on cognitive tests than the old drugs, this proved not to be the case.[84] Commenting on this study, an editorial in the *New York Times*[85] observed that, 'the system for approving and promoting drugs is badly out of whack' and that billions of dollars had been wasted on the marketing of the second-generation drugs which, because they are about ten times more expensive than the older but equally effective typicals, have been of greater benefit to drug company shareholders than to patients.

The results of the CUtLASS and CATIE trials leave open the question of whether clozapine is uniquely beneficial, because it was not used in these studies. Today, even those psychiatrists who are sceptical about the claims made for the second-generation drugs tend to argue that clozapine might still be exceptional. This widespread view that this drug is special may be partly a lingering effect of the impression created by the original flawed Kane and Meltzer trial. Whether it is justified by more recent evidence remains debatable.

Noting that more recent RCTs have often failed to replicate the extraordinary advantages reported for clozapine in early studies, British psychiatrist Joanna Moncrieff[86] carried out a meta-analysis to identify factors that distinguished between those trials in which clozapine did well and those which in which it did not. She found that clozapine looked superior only in those studies with short follow-up periods, which were sponsored by the manufacturer, and in which patients were severely ill at the outset. This analysis suggests that, while clozapine may be especially helpful to seriously ill patients, many of its apparent advantages can be attributed to the kind of methodological flaws which have plagued research into other drug treatments over the past few decades.

More recently, the CUtLASS and CATIE research groups have carried out small studies in which they have randomly assigned patients to either clozapine or other second-generation drugs. The British researchers reported modest advantages for clozapine in terms of symptoms, but no advantages for side effects or quality of life.[87] In the American study, patients persisted with clozapine for longer than the other antipsychotics but, again, no differences in symptoms were observed.[88] Although these findings suggest that clozapine may be a unique type of treatment, both studies were single- rather than double-blind (patients and prescribers both knew which treatment was being received but treatment allocation was hidden from the psychiatrists conducting the follow-up assessments) and so a placebo boost for clozapine cannot be completely ruled out.

Defenders of clozapine sometimes argue that it may be uniquely effective in preventing psychotic patients from committing suicide. However, the evidence on this is not entirely consistent and the largest study that has reported this effect to date has been carried out by the Kane–Metzler team, again with industry sponsorship.‖[89] Furthermore, it has been estimated that, even if the drug does reduce the risk of suicide, this effect on mortality is entirely balanced by the increased

---

‖ In the study, 5 out of 490 clozapine-treated patients committed suicide during the two-year follow-up period, compared with 3 out of 490 olanzapine-treated patients. On first glance, this is not compelling evidence of the superiority of clozapine. However, the number of suicides overall was less than expected, and the authors note that participation in the trial – and the increased attention that patients received as a consequence – may well have had a positive effect on suicide risk. On all other measures – attempted suicides, hospitalizations to prevent suicide, patients reporting suicidal ideas – clozapine did better than olanzapine.

health risks associated with clozapine compared to other antipsychotics.[90] The only realistic conclusion that can be reached about clozapine is that the jury is still out; whatever the truth about its effectiveness, it is certainly not the breakthrough in psychiatric treatment that it was once trumpeted to be.

First do no harm

The Hippocratic Oath, which has been regarded as a foundation stone of medical ethics since ancient Greek times, tells doctors that they should first do no harm (*primum non nocere*) and this principle has been embraced in modern codes of medical ethics.[91] Although it is inconceivable, for example, that oncologists would debate the wisdom of continuing to use cytotoxic drugs on patients who do not respond to them, psychiatrists have been much more reluctant to take into account the impact that side effects have on their patients. Despite the constant assertion that 'psychiatric disease is just like any other kind of disease', it seems that, in this respect at least, psychiatric patients continue to be treated differently from the patients treated by other branches of medicine.

Indeed, far from striving to restrict the use of antipsychotics to patients who clearly receive some benefit from them, psychiatrists, with encouragement from the pharmaceutical industry, are using these drugs to treat an ever-widening range of problems. Not only are high-risk patients being targeted, but some psychiatrists are prescribing antipsychotics to children, a practice that seems to be widely accepted in the United States[92] but which is becoming increasingly common in Britain.[93] Sometimes this happens when it is suspected that a child is showing the earliest signs of psychosis, but more often the drugs are used as a method of behavioural control in children diagnosed as suffering from autism, intellectual handicap, attention deficit disorder or 'disruptive behaviour disorders'.[94] My impression is that they are often prescribed without any serious attempt to understand or remedy the awful social circumstances in which psychologically disturbed children often live. Given our understanding that these drugs have a profound effect on the reward systems in the brain, no doubt the children who receive them find themselves living in a world that is even more stripped of joy than it was beforehand. The long-term impact that the drugs might have on the developing brain – as yet largely unknown – seems not to trouble the doctors who prescribe them. As American psychologist Abraham Maslow once remarked, 'It is tempting, if the only tool you have is a hammer, to treat everything as if it were a nail.'[95]

This does not mean that antipsychotics have no place in the treatment of adult patients suffering from psychosis. For many who experience terrifying voices and delusional fears, or who are dangerously lost in the excitement of acute mania, they are undoubtedly a useful therapy, at least in the short term. But they are flawed tools and certainly not the panacea for madness they have often been assumed to be. Some patients are more harmed than helped by them and they should therefore be used cautiously. Despite these serious limitations their use has become almost synonymous with psychiatric treatment. Weaning services from this dangerous addiction will necessitate completely rethinking the values and goals of psychiatric care.

IO

The Virtue of Kindness: Is Psychotherapy Effective for Severe Mental Illness?

> The experience of every clinic would bear out the viewpoint that a full knowledge of psychiatric and psychological information, with a brilliant intellect capable of applying this knowledge, is of itself no guarantee of therapeutic skill.
>
> Carl Rogers, *The Clinical Treatment of the Problem Child*

I do not really want to know how much of my working life is spent in front of computers but it is obviously too much. I spend many hours writing applications for grants to fund my research, many more hours engrossed in the pleasurable but slightly autistic task of analysing the data that is accrued as my projects are completed, and still more hours writing up my findings for publication as papers in scientific journals. The research students and assistants who are in daily contact with the people we study pass through my office, telling me about the problems they encounter and asking my advice. When I respond to their enquiries I often seem able to muster a confidence that surprises me. Sometimes, I feel as if I have climbed so far up my ivory tower that I can scarcely see the ground. Of course, there is a reason why I live this life. Step by step, over a period of years, and without understanding where my decisions would lead me, I chose it. Sometimes I feel more comfortable with theories, observations and statistical tests than with other people.

I temper this tendency to retreat into the realm of ideas by engaging in regular clinical work and this has rewarded me in many ways. It has been a privilege to hear patients tell me about their struggles with their symptoms, and what they have told me has inspired much of my research. However, the amount of time I can devote to working with patients is almost trivial compared to what my National Health Service colleagues are able to achieve. I tell myself that this is because I have many other commitments, which of course is true. But it is also because I find psychotherapy extremely difficult. Perhaps because of something in my background or upbringing, intensive and prolonged contact with distressed people has always been hard for me. It requires an ability to put one's own sensitivities completely to one side in a way that I have never completely mastered. The psychotherapeutic relationship is therefore quite different from other relationships, for example friendships, which it superficially resembles, in which the needs of both parties are balanced and equitably addressed.

When I first qualified as a clinical psychologist in the early 1980s, I was more optimistic about my ability to help individual patients. I very much wanted to be a good therapist and was drawn to those suffering from severe mental illness, partly because I was curious about what their extraordinary experiences might tell me about the human mind, but also because their troubles seemed very different from my own. At the time most mental health professionals believed that psychological treatments were completely ineffective with patients suffering from psychosis, but I nursed the hope that I might be able to discover some technique – a therapeutic trick – that would allow me to cure patients of the voices or their apparently bizarre beliefs. It was only slowly that I discovered that there is no simple shortcut to helping people.

The case of Osheroff v. Chestnut Lodge Hospital came to its conclusion at about this time. Fortunately for me, it had little immediate impact in Britain, and the psychiatrists at the forensic unit where I worked were surprisingly supportive of my efforts. However, as we saw in Chapter 4, in the United States it was a different matter. In his commentary on the case, Gerald Klerman,[1] reflecting the movement towards evidence-based medicine, asserted that randomized controlled trials (RCTs) provide the best evidence on the effectiveness of different treatments. According to Klerman, antidepressants and antipsychotics had proved their worth in numerous studies of this kind. Although he did not question the value of more recently developed forms of psychological treatment (for example, cognitive behaviour therapy) for non-psychotic disorders such as anxiety and depression, he noted that clinical trials had failed to show any benefit to psychotic patients receiving psychotherapy.

Perhaps because of the impact of the Osheroff case in the United States, further developments in the psychological treatment of psychosis had to occur elsewhere. Recent studies, conducted mainly in Britain, have painted a more optimistic picture of what can be achieved. However, before considering these developments we must examine Klerman's assumption, shared by many psychiatrists and psychologists, that RCTs are the best method of investigating what can be achieved by talking to patients.

How can we find out if psychotherapy works?

Faced with a bewildering number of psychotherapy schools (at the time of writing, the online encyclopedia Wikipedia listed 144 different varieties although, of course, these fall into a small number of major groups such as psychodynamic, person-centred, behavioural, and cognitive behavioural), it is tempting to think that the field is even more confused and unsatisfactory than drug therapy. Certainly, there is less consensus about the best way of practising psychotherapy, and the various schools sometimes look more like cults than scientific enterprises.

In response, researchers have turned to randomized controlled trials in the hope of finding out which methods of psychological treatment are the most effective. An enormous amount of evidence has been accumulated in this way, allowing some fairly definite conclusions to be reached. Before discussing these conclusions, however, it is important to consider whether psychological therapies really can be evaluated using the placebo-controlled double-blind methods which have become the gold standard when measuring the effectiveness of drugs.

The American clinical psychologist Martin Seligman[2] once famously advised that, 'Whenever you hear someone demanding the double-blind study of psychotherapy, hold on to your wallet.' Seligman was alluding to the fact that the effects of psychotherapy cannot be evaluated using the double-blind method because, obviously, both psychotherapists and patients inevitably know what kind of treatment is being delivered. The best that can be achieved, therefore, is a single-blind design in which only the researchers carrying out the outcome assessments, and not the therapists or patients, remain ignorant of the treatment that each patient receives. (This, of course, means that patients have to be told not to let the cat out of the bag when talking to the researchers, an injunction that they may have difficulty adhering to, for example because they are feeling distressed or enthusiastic about the treatment.)

However, this is only the most obvious way in which drug and psychotherapy trials must inevitably differ. Warmth, kindness and the instilling of hope, which usually occur in the context of a positive relationship between the clinician and the patient, are intrinsic elements of psychotherapy but not of drug treatments. Hence, in drug trials, these are considered to be complications that must be controlled for and removed from the equation in order to determine whether the chemicals are having the desired effect. In studies of psychological treatments, by contrast, warmth, kindness and the instilling of hope are essential ingredients without which nothing can be expected to happen. Hence the concept of a placebo has much less meaning in psychotherapy research than in psychopharmacology. Indeed, it is almost impossible to imagine what a plausible but non-therapeutic placebo psychotherapy would look like. (In recent years there has been a tendency to use Rogers' person-centred therapy as a control treatment in trials of more elaborate therapies[3] but, of course, person-centred therapy was originally designed to be an effective form of treatment.)

Because the relationship between the therapist and the patient is the vehicle through which psychological treatment is delivered, psychotherapy researchers have recognized the importance of measuring the quality of this relationship, whereas in drug trials it is almost always overlooked. Studies of the therapeutic relationship began with Freud and the early psychoanalysts, who believed that transference (the patient's creation of emotional fantasies about the therapist) is a critical mechanism that can be exploited during treatment. However, it was Carl Rogers who pioneered empirical research into the way that the therapeutic relationship influences the patient's progress.

Although Rogers emphasized the importance of the therapist's empathetic understanding, unconditional positive regard for the patient, and congruence – his so-called necessary and sufficient conditions[4] – the bulk of subsequent research has focused on the *therapeutic alliance* (sometimes called the working alliance). This is usually defined in terms of the affectional bond between the patient and the therapist and their ability to work together towards mutually agreed goals.[5] In recent years, researchers have developed various questionnaire measures of the alliance that can be completed by patients, therapists or by independent observers listening to tape recordings of therapeutic sessions.[6]

When designing RCTs, psychotherapy researchers usually take steps to take into account not only the therapeutic alliance but also other characteristics of the therapists that might plausibly influence the outcome, for example their personality and professional training. One way of attempting this is the so-called cross-over design in which each therapist delivers all of the treatments (the therapists cross over from one treatment to the other). For example, in a comparison of person-centred therapy and cognitive behaviour therapy, each therapist might be trained to deliver both types of treatments to different patients. The assumption behind this design is that the personal characteristics of the therapists will equally influence each treatment. However, the problem with this approach is that therapists may have an allegiance towards one type of therapy or the other, and this may affect the enthusiasm with which the treatments are delivered. Indeed, there is good evidence that therapists are most effective when carrying out a type of treatment that they are committed to. A further difficulty of the cross-over design is the danger that the therapists will somehow confuse the treatments, so that patients in both groups receive a mixture of the two.[7] An alternative approach is the so-called nested design in which expert therapists deliver the kind of treatment they are most familiar with. However, the problem with this approach is that it is difficult to ensure that the therapists assigned to the different treatment conditions are equally skilled.

It is doubtful whether the confounding effects of the therapists' skills and experience can ever be completely eliminated, so that 'pure' psychotherapy effects can be measured in the same way that trialists can estimate the true effect of drugs. However, in order to minimize these influences, the techniques that the therapists are allowed to employ during a trial are usually written down in treatment manuals and costly fidelity checks are often carried out (usually by having independent researchers listen to tapes of the sessions). Unfortunately, these constraints sometimes lead to a style of therapy that does not reflect best practice, in which flexibility, innovation and on-the-spot problem solving are essential components.

Nonetheless, and despite occasional ill-informed complaints to the contrary from pharmaceutical researchers,[8] once these constraints have been acknowledged, the quality of psychotherapy trials has often been very good, with longer follow-up periods and lower drop-out rates than has been typical in many drug trials. Perhaps this should be unsurprising given that the financial incentives which have led to the corruption of much of the data published by the pharmaceutical industry have been largely absent in psychotherapy research (which is typically funded by grants from government agencies). Furthermore, psychotherapy researchers have developed increasingly sophisticated forms of meta-analysis that have allowed them to at least partially disaggregate patient, therapist and treatment effects from data collected in large numbers of trials.[9] Of course, one of the most important goals of this kind of research has been to determine which kinds of therapy are most effective with which kinds of problems. In outlining the major findings from these efforts, I shall confine myself, in the first instance, to studies that have focused mainly on the less severe and more common non-psychotic psychiatric disorders, because the results of these studies have important implications for the way in which we interpret the less extensive body of research on patients with psychosis.

With several important caveats that I shall come to shortly, the question of whether psychotherapy is helpful has been definitively answered. When Mary Smith and Gene Glass[10] reported their first meta-analysis in 1977, they discovered that it is remarkably effective, and this finding has been repeated in numerous meta-analyses since.[11] The observed effect sizes average out at about 0.80 compared to no psychotherapy which, according to the criteria discussed in Chapter 8, amounts to a fairly large effect. Expressing this finding in another way, about 80 per cent of patients who do not receive psychotherapy fare worse than the average patient who receives it.

However, Smith and Glass reached a further, more startling conclusion. They could find no evidence that any one type of psychotherapy is more effective than any other. The hypothesis that all psychotherapies are equally effective has since been known as the Dodo bird conjecture (after a character in Lewis Carroll's *Alice's Adventures in Wonderland*, who organizes a chaotic race, with no clear start or finish, and then, in response to Alice's query about the outcome, announces, 'Everybody has won and all must have prizes'). *
In a subsequent, larger meta-analysis, Smith and Glass were also able to investigate therapist allegiance effects, finding that these were potent predictors of outcome.[12] Hence, when one type of therapy seemed to be more effective than another, this was often because it was the type of therapy that the trialists believed in from the outset.

The Dodo bird conjecture has taunted psychotherapy researchers in the three decades following Smith and Glass's groundbreaking reports, and continues to be vigorously debated today.[13] Official guidance from the UK National Institute of Clinical Excellence tends to recommend cognitive behaviour therapy for most conditions – for example, as the preferred treatment for moderate to severe depression – but critics argue that, although it is undoubtedly an effective treatment, CBT's relative effectiveness compared to other therapies reflects the fact that most of the available trials have been conducted by committed cognitive behaviour therapists.[14]

Extreme sceptics have sometimes suggested that the evidence supporting the Dodo bird conjecture should lead us to question whether there really is anything of value in any of the wide range of therapies that are offered to patients today[15] but this is obviously going too far (after all, we must not forget the good news that psychotherapy actually works). Others have argued for a contextual model, in which

* In fact, this conjecture, and the term used to describe it, was first introduced much earlier by the American psychoanalyst Stanley Rosensweig ('Some implicit common factors in diverse methods of psychotherapy: "At last the Dodo bird said, 'Everybody has won and all must have prizes' " ', *American Journal of Orthopsychiatry*, 6: 412–15, 1936). However, the conjecture was ignored by most psychotherapy researchers until the publication of Smith and Glass's meta-analysis.

it is assumed that the critical requirement for success is the patient's and therapist's shared enthusiasm for a particular approach (according to this account, it does not really matter if the theory underlying a method of treatment is little better than myth).[16] Still others have argued that the findings in support of the conjecture point to the necessity of improving our understanding of factors that might be common to all kinds of psychotherapy, such as the therapeutic alliance.

The importance of these factors is now beyond dispute. Studies which have used complex statistical techniques to investigate whether some therapists consistently perform better than others have shown that they do. It seems likely that the differences in effectiveness between therapists carrying out the same type of psychotherapy often exceed the differences observed between different psychotherapies.[17] Why this should be the case is not completely understood, but the ability to form a strong therapeutic alliance is undoubtedly a skill that is likely to affect the outcome of any kind of treatment. Indeed, meta-analyses of trials in which the therapeutic alliance has been measured have consistently reported that it is a powerful predictor of outcome, with some evidence that the patient's estimate of the quality of the alliance is a better predictor than the therapist's (presumably because therapists nearly always prefer to think that they form good relationships with their patients). We will see that this finding has important implications when we attempt to understand whether psychological treatment is helpful to people with more severe forms of psychiatric disorder.[18]

Is psychotherapy helpful to people with psychosis?

At the time that Klerman was writing his commentary on the Osheroff case, psychoanalysis was the only type of psychological treatment that had been carefully evaluated with patients suffering from severe mental illness. As we have seen, Freud, the creator of this kind of treatment, believed that it did not help patients with psychotic symptoms.[19] Psychoanalysis usually requires the patient to meet with a therapist several times a week over a period that sometimes extends for several years, so it is also very expensive. During the treatment sessions, the patient is encouraged to free-associate, or talk about anything that enters his mind, and the therapist focuses her attention on the patient's fantasy life, and on the emotionally charged aspects of his relationships with other people, rather than on symptoms or real-life problems. The treatment can be described as 'exploratory' rather than 'directive', because the therapist avoids offering direct advice; indeed, aside from making the occasional interpretation of what the patient says the therapist for the most part remains silent. Klerman was unimpressed by the evidence of psychoanalysis's effectiveness; one of the trials to which he drew his readers's attention suggested that it was no more helpful than a control treatment described as 'reality-adaptive supportive (RAS) therapy', which was poorly specified but which seemed to involve encouraging patients by discussing the routine difficulties they encountered in their daily lives.[20] Some later commentators even argued that the results of this study proved that psychoanalytic therapy was harmful to some patients.[21]

However, psychotherapy research has moved on substantially since Klerman's time (he died in 1992) and recent investigations of the effects of therapy on psychosis have differed from previous studies in several important ways. First, despite the challenges listed earlier, most recent RCTs have been methodologically rigorous, and compare very well with trials of selective serotonin re-uptake inhibitors and the atypical antipsychotics. For example, researchers have usually followed up patients for at least six months after the end of treatment and often for much longer (compared to typical follow-up periods of four to six weeks in drug trials) and drop-out rates have usually been very low. Taking their lead from pharmacological investigators, psychotherapy researchers now almost always analyse their data using the conservative intention-to-treat approach (which includes patients who refuse or drop out of treatment). Finally, the therapies that have been evaluated have usually been very different from psychoanalysis, and two types of treatment have been particularly carefully scrutinized.

Behavioural family therapy is a type of treatment developed in the 1980s, mainly by psychologists and psychiatrists working at the

Institute of Psychiatry in London.[22] As its name suggests, its theoretical roots lie in behaviour therapy, with its emphasis on using practical techniques to reduce undesirable behaviours.

The rationale of behavioural family therapy is based on the observation that criticism, hostility and/or over-protectiveness by loved ones can increase the likelihood that a patient will relapse. (It is important to remember that parents and spouses who behave in this way should not be considered as somehow culpable for a patient's difficulties – often they are reacting to feelings of anger or guilt which have been provoked by the patient's bizarre and distressing behaviour.) The aim of behavioural family therapy is to reduce this kind of 'high expressed emotion' behaviour by teaching the mentally well members of the family better ways of dealing with stress. In practice, the treatment can be carried out with the patient either present or absent, and includes a number of components. The family is usually taught a stress-vulnerability model of psychosis, which allows them to see that the patient has limited control over his difficulties (thereby reducing anger) and that they are not responsible for what has happened (thereby reducing guilt). Simple problem-solving skills are also taught, so that the family can avoid the kind of heated arguments that are toxic to the patient. Treatment usually extends over a period of about a year, during which time the family will meet the therapist about once every two weeks. For understandable reasons, families are often apprehensive when they first begin the treatment, but they usually report considerable satisfaction afterwards, valuing the opportunity to discuss the difficulties they have experienced and a closer link with psychiatric services.[23]

A number of trials have examined the effects of behavioural family therapy. The general finding is that it can bring about a long-term reduction in the likelihood of patients relapsing and being readmitted to hospital.[24] However, there are a couple of important drawbacks to this kind of treatment. First, it is time-consuming and appropriate only for patients living with carers who are prepared to take part; many patients either live alone or with carers who are not prepared to make this kind of commitment. Second, it has proved quite hard to roll out the treatment so that it is used routinely. In Britain, where training programmes have been established to teach this approach to National Health Service psychologists and psychiatric nurses, a common difficulty is that the trained therapists find the work difficult to fit in with their other commitments.[25]

A more recent therapeutic approach that does not suffer from these difficulties, at least to the same degree, is cognitive behaviour therapy (CBT). This type of therapy, which also grew out of behaviour therapy, was first established as a treatment for depression by American psychiatrist and one-time psychoanalyst Aron T. Beck,[26] and involves helping patients to question and evaluate their own beliefs. In Beck's original approach, it is assumed that the immediate trigger for a depressed mood is a negative thought about the self, the world or the future. Depressed patients are prone to such thoughts because of their pessimistic reasoning style, their dysfunctional assumptions about the world, and their tendency to recall negative rather than positive events. Patients being treated for depression are therefore taught to recognize the pessimistic thoughts behind their feelings, and to consider alternative interpretations about what is happening to them. The idea is that, once the patient learns to interpret events less catastrophically, his mood will improve.

In contrast to psychoanalysis, CBT often involves the patient being asked to carry out specific tasks, and each session usually ends with a homework assignment. For example, the patient may be asked to keep a diary of his thoughts, or may be asked to carry out simple risk-taking exercises or 'behavioural experiments' to test out his pessimistic predictions. However, it is a mistake to imagine that the treatment involves the therapist hectoring the patient to 'think properly'. For CBT to be effective, it has to be conducted in a spirit of collaborative empiricism, in which the patient and therapist agree to work together to discover the most helpful interpretations of events without any preconceptions. Sometimes very bad things happen and, under these circumstances, the therapist will not deny the reality of the situation, but will try hard to empathize with the patient's distress. Working with patients in this way can be quite stressful and demanding.

CBT has been adapted to treat a wide range of conditions and, as we have already seen, has been more intensively researched than any other kind of psychotherapy. In contrast to psychoanalysis it is usually time-limited; a course of treatment for depression or anxiety will typically last about six months during which time the patient and therapist will meet about once a week. RCTs generally show that it compares very well with pharmacological treatments for depression and anxiety and that, unlike drug therapies, it affords patients with some protection against further episodes of illness in the future.[27] However, as we have seen, whether or not it is more effective than other kinds of therapy remains a matter of debate. Nonetheless, a recent review by the economist (Lord) Richard Layard suggested that making CBT more available would probably have a positive impact on the British economy as it would allow patients with mood disorders to more rapidly return to work.[28] Largely as a consequence of this report, the then Secretary of State for Health, Patricia Hewitt, announced a UK government-funded Increasing Access to Psychological Therapies initiative, which will involve the creation of a national network of centres providing CBT to people with depression and anxiety.[29] Although no such scheme exists in the United States, American health insurance schemes often cover time-limited CBT treatments.

Attempts to adapt CBT for the treatment of psychotic patients began during the 1990s, when a number of clinical psychologists and psychiatrists, mainly in Britain, began to report detailed studies of individual patients. Most of this work focused on developing methods to help patients who had delusional beliefs or who experienced hallucinations. In the case of delusions, many of the strategies that had previously been developed for working with depressed patients proved to be applicable, although it was discovered that great care had to be taken when challenging patients' most tenaciously held beliefs, and that a collaborative, warm relationship was essential for this purpose. Paradoxically, it seems important that the therapist who attempts this kind of treatment makes every effort to treat the patient's beliefs, no matter how implausible, as if they might just be true. Not surprisingly (given the evidence we looked at in Chapter 6), during treatment it often becomes obvious that there is a nugget of truth in even the most paranoid belief system.

In the case of hallucinations, CBT often involves trying to address the patient's fears about his voices. Patients often believe that their voices are omnipotent and that their source is omniscient.[30] These beliefs often lead to high levels of distress. The therapist will there-fore usually encourage a less catastrophizing attitude towards the voices, with the hope that the patient will become emotionally detached from them.

A very important element of CBT for psychosis, which helps to reduce patients' catastrophic reactions to their unusual experiences, is sometimes described as *normalization*.[31] The patient is encouraged to see himself, not as someone in danger of descending into madness, but as a person who is not so very different from other people. This is sometimes achieved by educating the patient about how common psychotic symptoms really are (some therapists even give their patients relevant scientific papers to read) but also by asking the patient to consider similarities between their symptoms and more mundane experiences (for example, paranoia can be compared to the feeling of discomfort commonly experienced when walking into a room full of strangers).

Reasonably sized trials of CBT for psychosis began to appear at the beginning of the present decade. Most have involved patients who had failed to respond to many years of treatment with antipsychotic drugs.[32] However, two studies that I helped design and carry out have involved patients experiencing their first episode of psychosis[33] (the CONSORT diagram for this trial appeared as Fig. 3 in Chapter 8) and patients suffering from prodromal symptoms as defined according to the Melbourne criteria discussed in the last chapter.[34] In the former study of more than 300 patients, known as the SoCRATES (Study of Cognitive Re-Alignment Therapy for Early Schizophrenia) trial, those treated with just five weeks of CBT had fewer positive symptoms at the end of an eighteen-month follow-up period than patients receiving conventional treatment, although the differences observed were not very large. In the latter study of just fifty-eight patients, those offered CBT were less likely to develop a psychotic illness during a twelve-month follow-up in comparison with patients who were closely moni-tored over the same period.

A recent meta-analysis was able to identify thirty-four RCTs of CBT for psychosis in total, which have varied considerably in quality and the number of patients treated.[35] The main finding was a modest effect size for positive symptoms of 0.40 when CBT was compared to treatment as usual, and this reduced to an even more modest 0.22 when only the most rigorous studies were considered. There was also evidence that CBT helped to reduce negative symptoms and to improve patients' mood.

Parallel to these developments, a smaller number of trials of CBT for patients with a diagnosis of bipolar disorder have also begun to appear, most[36] but not all (sadly, my own[37]) reporting positive results. A recent meta-analysis of eight studies with bipolar patients reported an overall reduction in the rate of relapses of about 40 per cent.[38]

Not surprisingly, results of this kind have sparked a resurgence of enthusiasm for psychotherapy for patients with severe mental illness. For example, the UK National Institute for Clinical Excellence now recommends that CBT should be made available, alongside conventional medical treatments, for people diagnosed as suffering from schizophrenia.[39] Inevitably, this has led to a backlash from some biologically orientated psychiatrists, who have remained sceptical about the benefits of psychotherapy for patients suffering from severe mental illness.

The new insulin coma therapy?

Perhaps the most strident critic of CBT has been British psychiatrist Peter McKenna, a neuroimaging researcher at the University of Glasgow, who, in a letter published in the *British Journal of Psychiatry* in 2001, argued that CBT would meet 'the fate of an earlier treatment for schizophrenia where advocacy preceded rigorous evaluation – insulin coma'.[40] This analogy between CBT and insulin coma is obviously perverse, not least because people sometimes died as a consequence of receiving insulin therapy (the worst that a clinical psychologist can be accused of is being useless; we do not usually poison our patients). However, putting this objection to one side, it is obviously important not to dismiss McKenna's arguments before considering them carefully.

One thrust in his argument is to identify numerous, often relatively minor methodological limitations in some of the larger clinical trials (in the process suggesting that CBT researchers should strive to carry out double-blind, placebo-controlled studies which, as we have seen, is impossible). For example, he criticizes a study carried out by researchers at the Institute of Psychiatry in London[41] because they chose to conduct an open trial, believing that patients would inevitably reveal to the assessors what treatment they had received (as discussed earlier, it can be difficult to stop patients from doing this). This approach allows McKenna to dismiss some of the trial data on CBT out of hand but it is a dangerous strategy because, as we have seen, many of the psychological treatment trials have been more rigorous than the trials carried out to evaluate the drug treatments he supports.

A second and more important thrust of McKenna's argument is that, in many studies, CBT did not turn out to be superior to the less specific psychological treatments used as a comparison. When making this point, he sometimes interprets the evidence in the most sceptical way possible. For example, he notes that, in a trial conducted in Newcastle and London,[42] CBT was not superior to befriending (the control treatment) at the end of the treatment period, forgetting to mention that the patients who received befriending tended to worsen after treatment ended whereas the improvements made by the CBT patients were generally maintained.

Of course this argument, even if it is correct, does not establish that psychological treatment is ineffective; rather it shows that CBT is not appreciably superior to other psychological treatments that probably require less skill. In other words, it seems to support the Dodo bird conjecture. In fact, one of the most surprising findings from the CBT literature is that patients receiving control therapies such as person-centred therapy and befriending do appear to fare better than patients who receive treatment as usual (that is, drugs without any kind of therapy). This was true, for example, in the SoCRATES trial, which was briefly described a few paragraphs back. Of course, this observation can be interpreted as reflecting very badly on conventional treatment, as there is no good reason why, say, befriending should not be a routine component of normal psychiatric care.

A more telling point made by McKenna is that CBT, even if it affects symptoms such as hallucinations and delusions, does not affect relapse rates. This objection seems to have more merit, and points to an important contrast with behavioural family therapy, which appears to affect relapse rates but not symptoms.[43] The truth is that the results of most CBT trials have been very poor when patients' likelihood of being readmitted to hospital has been considered but, as always in clinical research, this disappointing finding demands further scrutiny.

First, it is important to recognize that not all cognitive behavioural therapists have attempted to influence relapse rates or even symptoms. Indeed, some CBT researchers, notably Max Birchwood, a psychologist at the University of Birmingham, have argued that it is foolish to expect CBT to have the same effects as antipsychotic medication.[44] In a recent trial, Birchwood and his colleagues instead tried to reduce the extent to which patients hearing hallucinatory commands complied with the demands of their voices, reporting considerable success.[45] Other studies conducted by Gill Haddock and Christine Barrowclough at the University of Manchester suggest that CBT can be used to help psychotic patients stop taking street drugs that might exacerbate their symptoms[46] or to help patients with a history of violence to control their anger.[47] Even if CBT does not reduce the risk of relapse, these kinds of benefits surely make it worthwhile.

Second, two CBT trials have investigated novel methods specifically designed to affect relapse rates, apparently with success. One, conducted by Andrew Gumley, a clinical psychologist at the University of Glasgow, involved a system in which patients received psychological treatment when they most needed it.[48] In an initial period of five sessions with the therapist, the patients were questioned about previous relapses and an attempt was made to draw up a series of warning signs that might indicate that another relapse was imminent. Nurses monitored the progress of the patients over a twelve-month period. If they detected signs that the patient was in danger of relapse (for example, high levels of depression and anxiety) they notified the therapist, who then saw the patient for a small number of further sessions, and who used a variety of cognitive behavioural strategies to reduce the patient's catastrophic thoughts, to enhance his coping skills, to improve his tolerance of criticism, and to discourage self-defeating behaviours such as excessive drinking or the use of street drugs. At the end of twelve months, 18 per cent of the CBT patients had relapsed compared to 34 per cent of patients who received treatment as usual.

The second study that managed to affect relapse rates was carried out by Patricia Bach and Steven Hayes of the University of Nevada, and is one of the few cognitive behaviour therapy trials conducted with psychotic patients living in the United States.[49] The study involved a new variant of CBT developed by Hayes[50] known by the horribly Californian-sounding name of Acceptance and Commitment Therapy, or ACT for short. The assumption behind this approach is that patients often become disturbed and distressed as a consequence of their self-defeating efforts to avoid unpleasant thoughts and feelings. Hence, unlike traditional CBT therapists, who encourage their patients to question their negative thoughts, ACT therapists encourage patients to treat their negative thoughts with indifference. A rich repertoire of metaphors is used to reinforce this attitude (for example, patients are encouraged to think of their minds as huge chessboards on which infinite numbers of white and black pieces fight never-ending duels), and meditation techniques are used to help patients to focus their attention on the world rather than on their own mental processes. A number of simple exercises are also carried out; for example, in the 'taking the mind for a walk' exercise the patient goes for a walk and tries to ignore the therapist who simulates the patient's negative thoughts by whispering in his ear. Finally, once the patient has learned to develop an accepting but distant relationship with his negative thoughts and feelings, he is encouraged to commit himself to pursuing those goals that he most values (hence the name of the therapy).

Hayes' research team has reported some remarkable results from small-scale trials with patients suffering from a range of conditions, but critics have argued that the methodological limitations of these studies preclude a definitive judgement about whether his approach is more effective than conventional CBT.[51] In their psychosis study, acutely ill psychotic patients who received just four sessions of ACT, compared with those who received none, were about half as likely to be readmitted to hospital during the four months following treatment, a difference that borders on the amazing. Of course, neither Gumley's study nor the trial conducted by Bach and Hayes is without flaws, and both require replication. However, these studies show how researchers are developing increasingly innovative CBT strategies in their efforts to address the particular needs of patients with severe mental illness.

A universal therapeutic good?

In this chapter I have offered a realistic account of developments in psychological treatments for people with psychosis. When comparing what has been achieved so far in this field with what has been achieved in psychopharmacology, it is very important to remember that this work remains in its infancy (excluding the early studies of psychoanalysis, tens of trials conducted over the last decade, compared with thousands of trials of antipsychotic medication conducted over more than half a century). Clearly it is important at this early stage that enthusiasts for psychotherapy, among whom I count myself, do not make inflated claims about what can be achieved with specific psychological techniques. After all, the effects of therapy, although real, seem modest, and we have seen that the Dodo bird conjecture cannot be rejected, at least as yet. Nonetheless, it would be equally rash to believe that the evidence available at the present time constitutes the last word on what psychological treatments can do for people with severe mental illness. Just as psychopharmacologists continue to innovate, so too must psychological therapists.

The evidence supporting the Dodo bird conjecture suggests that non-specific factors, and specifically the quality of the relationship between the patients and the therapist, have a significant influence on outcomes. My own eyes have been opened to the importance of these factors by further scrutiny of the data from the SoCRATES trial in which, it will be recalled, more than 300 patients experiencing their first or second episode of psychosis, received, in addition to their drugs, cognitive behaviour therapy, Rogerian psychotherapy or no psychotherapy at all. When conducting the study, we asked therapists and patients to rate the therapeutic alliance after the third and ninth session of treatment.

Using conventional statistical techniques we found, as expected, that the quality of the alliance as rated by the patients predicted improvements in both positive and mood symptoms, eighteen months after the start of treatment. However, on its own, this observation does not establish that the therapeutic alliance is causal – it was always possible that those patients who found it easier to form good alliances would have done better anyway. Fortunately, new statistical methods developed by Graham Dunn, a statistician at the University of Manchester, allowed us to eliminate this possibility. Remarkably, using these methods, we found that the differences between the treatment groups, and indeed the differences in the extent to which the therapies worked in the three centres, could be entirely accounted for by the therapeutic alliance rated by the patients at the end of the third session of treatment. The extent to which the therapists could relate effectively with the patients, rather than specific psychotherapeutic techniques, seemed to completely explain the positive effects of treatment.[52]

This finding is consistent with other studies that have shown that the quality of the therapeutic alliance can have a profound impact on the well-being of patients with severe mental illness, affecting responses to a wide range of treatments. For example, in a study I carried out with pharmacist Jenny Day when we worked together at the University of Liverpool in the late 1990s, we found that the quality of the relationship between patients and their doctors strongly predicted the patients' attitudes towards their medication (the more they felt they had a good relationship with the psychiatrist, the more they were prepared to persist with their drug treatment),[53] an observation that has also been reported by other investigators.[54]

Indeed, as psychiatrist Stephan Priebe and psychologist Rose McCabe at University College London have recently demonstrated in a detailed review of a growing body of research,[55] there is now evidence that the quality of the alliance predicts, not only symptoms and attitudes towards treatment, but also a wide range of outcomes, including the patient's quality of life, how much time is spent in hospital, the patient's ability to function socially and his willingness to engage with psychiatric services. Conversely, there is also some evidence that bad relationships predict poor outcomes; patients living in hostels or on wards with high expressed emotion staff (that is, where the staff are critical and over-controlling) do worse than patients living in more benign environments.[56]

Good relationships, it seems, are a universal therapeutic good, and may yet turn out to be the single most important ingredient of effective psychiatric care. Efforts to improve therapeutic relationships are therefore likely to result in substantial benefits for everyone concerned.

At the tail-end of the neo-Kraepelinian era, after decades in which clinicians have neglected the personal dimensions of treatment and placed their faith in biomedical remedies for the miseries of life, this idea seems almost revolutionary.

II

What Kind of Psychiatry Do You Want?

> If I were St Peter, admitting to heaven on the basis of achievement
> on earth, I would accept on proof of identity the accident sur-
> geons, the dentists and, with a few doubts, the obstetricians; all,
> it should be noted in passing, dealing mainly with healthy people.
> The rest I would refer to some celestial equivalent of Ellis Island,
> for close and prolonged inspection of their credentials.
>
> Thomas McKeown, *The Role of Medicine: Dream,*
> *Mirage or Nemesis?*

It was late in the afternoon and I was in my office at the University of
Manchester. I had spent most of the day tying up loose ends in
preparation for starting my new job in Wales. Time had moved slowly
as I had sorted a seemingly endless series of files into their packing
boxes, each one eliciting a memory, culminatively provoking a heavy
feeling of melancholy. I wanted to catch the next train back home to
my family, but I knew I had cut things fine. Hastily shutting down my
computer and grabbing my bag, I switched off the office light behind
me and sprinted for the exit. Outside, on the Oxford Road, a fine
drizzle was painting the streets grey. Other commuters scuttled along
the pavement in front of me, huddled inside their raincoats, their faces
turned disconsolately towards the ground as they struggled along their
way. At the bus stop, a long queue of people stood in glum silence,
slowly getting wet. Looking back along the road, I could see that,
unusually, there was not a bus in sight.

Suddenly, I spotted a cab and, waving frantically, managed to flag
it down.

'Where to, mate?' the driver asked as I jumped in. Catching a glance of his face as he looked back towards me, I could see a middle-aged man with broad features, bright eyes and an impressive smile. Pinned to his dashboard was a black-and-white photograph of a scantily clad young woman, perhaps culled from a tabloid newspaper. Somehow, I just knew he was going to be the chatty sort.

'Oxford Road Station, please.'

'Late for the train, are we?' he asked, as he edged the cab into a slowly moving stream of traffic. Ordinarily, the journey would take no more than five minutes but today it looked as if it might take much longer.

'Yes.'

'What time does it leave?'

'Five forty.'

'You should just make it.'

After lapsing into silence for no more than thirty seconds, he then asked, 'Work in the University then?'

'Yep.'

'Which department?'

I hesitated. Admitting to being a clinical psychologist can lead to a wide variety of responses, not always positive. Often, it is interpreted as an invitation to tell a particularly convoluted life story and I was not in the mood. Finally, reflecting on the short time for which I would be in the driver's company, I relented.

'Ah, clinical psychology!' he said knowingly. 'That's mental illness and things.'

'Yes.'

'So you treat psychiatric patients?'

'I mainly do research.'

'What do you research into then?'

'Schizophrenia . . . bipolar disorder . . .' This wasn't the time to get into my doubts about diagnostic labels.

He digested this information for a second, and then said, 'I had a schizophrenic in the cab the other day.'

'Really? How did you know?'

'He told me. A young chap. He jumped in the back, just like you did and then told me he was a schizophrenic.'

'Amazing!' I expected that I would soon have to correct some widely held prejudices about the mentally ill, but my interest was piqued. 'So what did you say to him?'

'I asked him what it was like. He said he saw huge rabbits following him around everywhere.'

'Huge rabbits? That's not typical.'

'I asked him if they were pink.'

'What did he say?'

'He said, "No, stupid. Everyone knows that rabbits are grey!"' We both laughed.

'Mind you,' the cabby continued, 'mental illness is no laughing matter.'

I agreed.

'I was mentally ill once.'

Here comes the convoluted life story, I thought. 'When was that?' I asked.

'It was . . . oh, more than twenty years ago now. My wife died. Cancer. I was left with two young kids, a boy and a girl. I was really struggling to cope. It was really grim. I had to take antidepressants.'

'Did they help?'

'Maybe. Dunno.'

Two visions of psychiatry

In this book I have argued that, by any reasonable standard, the dominant paradigm in psychiatry, which assumes that mental illnesses are genetically influenced brain diseases, has been a spectacular failure. Despite enormous expense, its benefits for those suffering from the most severe forms of mental disorder have been slight. It has failed to make a measurable contribution to the well-being of society as a whole.

It could be argued that psychiatry is in good company amongst the medical professions. Following Thomas McKeown's demonstration[1] that increases in life expectancy during the first half of the twentieth century were largely attributable to improved nutrition and cleanliness, many health professionals have reluctantly conceded that the impact of medical science on society is often less dramatic than commonly perceived. Nonetheless, there can be hardly any doubt that since the Second World War there have been tangible advances in the treatment of illnesses such as cancer and heart disease. Psychiatry seems different. Its failures have been the consequence of tenaciously held but erroneous assumptions about the nature of mental illness. They reflect a kind of intellectual myopia, which has blinded professionals to the fact that distress in human beings is usually caused by unsatisfactory relationships with other human beings. They are the consequence of ignoring what has been obvious to most ordinary people, that warmth and kindness are necessary to promote psychological healing.

I am committed to the scientific world-view, and expect that intelligence and hard work will eventually make the mysteries of mental illness tractable. I also remain hopeful that research will eventually lead to new and genuinely effective methods of treatment. However, I think it is unlikely that technical advances alone will remedy the problems that beset psychiatric services today. What is needed is a more compassionate approach that places the therapeutic relationship at the centre of clinical practice. In recent years the broad outlines of such an approach have begun to emerge, inspired by researchers such as American psychologist Courtenay Harding and psychiatrist John Strauss,[2] who have shown that the outcomes of severe mental illness are often much better than supposed by clinicians working within the Kraepelinian tradition.

Importantly, this research has shown that recovery is a multifaceted phenomenon.[3] For example, some patients are liberated from their symptoms by their drug treatment but continue to struggle with severe social disabilities, whereas others function perfectly well despite the persistence of voices and unusual beliefs. It is therefore difficult to devise a universally acceptable definition of recovery, but defining it merely in terms of symptoms – still meeting the diagnostic criteria according to the *DSM* or the *ICD* – seems hopelessly narrow.[4] Patients more often highlight the importance of improved quality of life,[5] the sense of being empowered to rebuild their relationships and careers, improved self-esteem and hope for the future.[6]

Recovery must therefore be seen as an evolving and unavoidably subjective process. William Anthony,[7] a psychologist specializing in the rehabilitation of chronically disabled patients, has described it as 'A deeply personal, unique process of changing one's attitudes, values, feelings, goals, skills, and/or roles. It is a way of living a satisfying, hopeful, and contributing life, even with limitations caused by the illness. Recovery involves the development of new meaning and purpose in one's life as one grows beyond the catastrophic effects of mental illness.' Anthony has argued that the evidence-based medicine movement, with its emphasis on randomized controlled trials in which the outcome measured is usually symptoms, has had little impact in psychiatry precisely because it has failed to seek evidence that is meaningful to patients. Instead of conventional trials, he suggests[8] that researchers should focus on those domains of functioning that patients think are most important (for example, quality of life), using methods (for example, interviews) that allow subjective outcomes to be measured, administered as far as possible in real-life settings. He also argues that researchers should make more effort to study the impact of the therapeutic relationship.

In recent years some services in Europe and North America have explicitly adopted a *recovery approach*. Although what this means is not always clear, these services typically encourage optimistic expectations in their patients, and try to help them define their own treatment goals. Services of this kind prioritize the fostering of close, collaborative relationships between clinicians and service users. Care is supportive and based on a detailed assessment of patients' needs, rather than intrusive and driven by diagnosis. There is an emphasis on providing patients with choices between a range of treatment options whenever possible. Following a 2003 report, *Achieving the Promise: Transforming Mental Health Care in America*,[9] published by the President's New Freedom Commission on Mental Health (established by George W. Bush), this approach has become official doctrine in some parts of the United States.*

* Some of the Commission's recommendations proved controversial, however. In response to lobbying by the pharmaceutical industry, they advocated the use of newer, more expensive medicines and mass screening for psychiatric difficulties (J. Lenzer (2004), 'Bush plans to screen whole US population for mental illness', *British Medical Journal*, 328: 1458). Responding to this last suggestion, the doctor and comedian

It is fair to say that developments such as these are provoking some anxiety amongst more traditionally minded psychiatrists, who can see their prestige and claim for a place at the high table of medicine slipping from their grasp. In the summer of 2008, an article which described itself as a 'wake-up call' for the profession appeared in the *British Journal of Psychiatry*.[10] The authors, nearly all researchers in psychiatric genetics, neuroscience or epidemiology, griped that

British psychiatry faces an identity crisis. A major contributory factor has been the recent trend to downgrade the importance of the core aspects of medical care. In many instances, this has resulted in services that are better suited to delivering nonspecific, psychosocial support rather than a process of thorough, broad-based diagnostic assessment with formulation of aetiology, diagnosis and prognosis followed by specific treatments aimed at recovery with maintenance of functioning.

Many of the authors' complaints are difficult to take seriously. For example, they objected that the 'lack of a thorough diagnostic assessment, including physical examination and investigations, may result in inappropriate, suboptimal or ineffective management between episodes and a failure of relapse prevention'. (Psychiatric diagnoses have almost no scientific or prognostic value. Moreover, I have never witnessed a psychiatrist give a patient a physical examination and doubt that most are competent to do so.) Absurdly, they fretted that, 'Use of the term "mental health" to describe services for those with mental illness risks undermining the real importance and impact of these conditions on patients.' (By the same logic, they would presumably like to see the National Health Service re-christened the National *Illness* Service.) They looked fondly back to a time when services were directed by medical practitioners who, they argued, alone understood all of the treatment options available, and who could therefore be relied on to choose the best remedies for specific

---

Patch Adams – who became famous after he was portrayed by Robin Williams in a feature film – volunteered to screen President Bush on the grounds that, 'He needs a lot of help. I'll see him for free.'

conditions, forgetting that those were the days in which patients were given prefrontal leucotomies and insulin coma treatments. They offered no evidence that a medically led approach works better than services that delivered 'nonspecific psychosocial support' because, as we have seen, there is not any. Rhetorically, they suggested the following thought experiment: 'If a member of your family were a patient, is a distributed responsibility model [in which the doctor is not automatically in charge] the one for which you would opt?' The possibility that many, perhaps the majority of patients and carers might answer in the affirmative does not seem to have crossed their minds.

Comparing the claims made by traditionalists, for example the authors of the 'wake-up call', with those who advocate the recovery approach, it is possible to see the outlines of two contrasting visions of the future of psychiatry. In Table 3 I list what I think are the main differences between these two visions. Of course, many mental health professionals would perhaps place themselves between the two poles indicated by this table, but this does not mean that the distinctions drawn here are not real and important. Although the poles could be given a variety of labels, I called them 'paternalistic-medical' and 'autonomy-promoting', reflecting the fact the most important difference between advocates of the recovery approach and those mental health professionals who favour more traditional services concerns their willingness to trust the judgements of the people they claim to help.

Table 3. Two visions of the future of psychiatric care

	Paternalistic-medical	Autonomy-promoting
Principle advocates	Biological psychiatrists; researchers studying the neuroscience and genetics of psychiatric disorders	Clinical psychologists, many psychiatric nurses, CBT therapists, some psychiatrists, advocates of the recovery approach

	Paternalistic-medical	*Autonomy-promoting*
Beliefs about mental illness	Severe mental illness is a genetically determined brain disease. Environmental factors are only responsible for triggering episodes in people who are already biologically compromised	Severe mental illness is an understandable reaction to the tribulations of life; genes may make some people more vulnerable but play a relatively minor role
Attitude towards diagnosis	Diagnosis is the essential first step before treatment can be carried out	Conventional psychiatric diagnoses are usually unhelpful, and can be stigmatizing and harmful; it is more important to have a clear understanding (a 'formulation') of the events that caused the patient to become ill, and circumstances that make recovery difficult
Goals of treatment	Management of mental illness by symptom reduction	Whatever the patient thinks is most important, but especially improvement in self-esteem, self-efficacy, relationships with others and quality of life
Attitude towards patients' judgements	Patients' preferences about treatment are not to be trusted because they are often cognitively impaired and lack insight	Patients should be actively involved in deciding what kind of treatment is appropriate; service user input into the design and management of services is essential

	Paternalistic-medical	*Autonomy-promoting*
Attitude towards treatment	Drugs are essential in order to correct neurotransmitter imbalances; psychological therapies are sometimes useful for providing patients with support	Psychological therapies are very important, but not more important than dealing with social and occupational difficulties; drugs are useful for some patients but not others
Attitude towards the therapeutic alliance	Psychiatrists should try and get on with their patients in order to persuade them to take their medication	The therapeutic alliance is an essential element of care, without which other elements will fail
Attitude towards risk and coercion	Psychotic patients are often dangerous unless properly controlled; coercion is a necessary element of psychiatric care	The risk to others associated with psychosis is small and best managed by creating services that patients want to use; coercion is to be used only as a last resort
Attitude towards medical skills	The doctor is the only professional who has skills in all therapies; doctors should lead psychiatric teams	Most doctors are valued members of psychiatric teams, but have few unique skills (for example, other mental health professionals can learn to prescribe drugs); it would be nice if more psychiatrists developed skills in psychological therapies and relied less on medication

Do *as you are told*

If patients are to be helped to navigate their own pathways to recovery, it follows that their opinions about treatment must be respected. In practice, traditional services are often paternalistic, assuming that the clinician (especially the psychiatrist) knows what is in the patient's best interests.

Services working with patients living at home, in sheltered accommodation or on hospital wards, often see their main task as ensuring adherence with the recommended treatment. Some ominously characterize themselves as *assertive treatment services*, and focus their efforts on closely supervising patients living in the community. Although patients with severe mental illness usually have a strong desire to be consulted about their treatment[11] this rarely happens,[12] and many are poorly informed about the drugs they are given or the side effects they can expect to experience. Research shows that coercion is common-place in traditional services. It is not only that psychiatrists have become more willing to use their powers of involuntary detention[13] (although substantial regional differences exist in the use of such measures†[14]), but that informal methods of leverage are often used to persuade patients to do as directed.[15] In these circumstances, the psychiatric interview is often reduced to a polite meeting in which the patient's adherence to the prescribed regimen is the one item on the agenda, and which finishes when the patient agrees to conform.[16] Patients may be told that their access to benefits or housing, or even their right to raise their own children, will be rescinded unless they follow instructions.[17] This increasing resort to intimidation (let us call a spade a spade) has culminated in many countries with the introduction of community treatment orders (CTOs), which require patients to continue their treatment (invariably medication) after discharge from hospital on the threat of some kind of sanction (usually a return to the locked ward). Not surprisingly, patients often object to

† For example, the risk of being compulsorily detained in Finland is about 20 times the risk in Italy. There are also within-nation regional differences – the risk of compulsory detention in London is about twice that elsewhere in England.

being managed in this way, and sometimes complain that paternalistic methods of care undermine their efforts to lead a normal life:

When those of us with psychiatric disabilities come to believe that all of our efforts are futile; when we experience that we have no control over our environment; when nothing we do seems to matter or to make the situation better; when we follow the treatment team's instructions and achieve their treatment goals for us and still no placement opens up in the community for us; when we try one medication after another after another and none of them seem to be of any help; when we find that staff do not listen to us and they make all of the major decisions for us; when staff decide where we will live, with whom we will live; under what rules we will live, how we will spend our money, if we will be allowed to spend our money, when we will have to leave the group home, and at what time we will be allowed back into it, etc. etc., then a deep sense of hopelessness, of despair begins to settle over the human heart.[18]

Nevertheless, coercion has become so universally accepted amongst mental health professionals that many no longer see it as ethically troubling. For example, at a recent conference, I heard a distinguished professor of psychiatry from one of Britain's most prestigious medical schools remark, in front of an audience of hundreds, that he could see no problem with using threats and leverage to make patients do as they are told. This attitude flies in the face of one of the most important principles of medical ethics, known as respect for *autonomy*, where autonomy can be (roughly) defined as 'The capacity to think, decide, and act on the basis of such thought and decision freely and independently and without . . . let or hindrance.'[19]

Modern concerns about respect for autonomy grew out of the Nuremberg trials at the end of the Second World War, which documented the terrible crimes committed by Nazi doctors against concentration camp inmates and prisoners of war. The principle has since been enshrined in international conventions and codes of practice governing clinical practice and medical research (for example, the World Medical Association's 1964 Declaration of Helsinki on the ethics of research involving human subjects,[20] the World Medical Association's 1981 Declaration on the Rights of Patients,[21] and the Council of Europe's 1996 Convention on Human Rights and

Biomedicine[22]). Professional philosophers usually justify the principle by referring to one of the two main traditions in Western moral philosophy.[23] Those who follow the deontological tradition (which seeks to discover universal moral laws) argue that people should always be treated as ends in themselves, rather than as means to ends. Hence, on this view, there is a moral imperative to respect individuals' goals and wishes. Utilitarians, by contrast, argue that we should seek to increase the happiness and well-being of as many people as possible, and see respect for autonomy as an essential condition for achieving this end. Although countless tomes have been penned on the relative virtues of these two approaches, both are concordant with the everyday experience that life is better (richer, pleasanter, full of hope) when we are allowed to decide what is in our own interests and to set our own course in the world.

It is sometimes objected that the principle of autonomy runs into difficulties when subjected to close scrutiny.[24] One problem is that different philosophers have defined autonomy differently, so that it is difficult to devise a test of whether a patient's choices are truly autonomous. Another is that some conceptions of autonomy look like appeals to free will, and are difficult to square with naturalistic (scientific) accounts of human behaviour. (If all our decisions are caused by deterministic processes, it is difficult to see why some – those that are made 'freely' – should be respected and others should not.) However, these problems can be circumvented if we take as a very broad definition of autonomy the absence of coercion. There are at least four compelling (but surprisingly rarely articulated) reasons why coercion should be avoided in psychiatric care.

First, almost by definition, paternalism and coercion could be justified only if doctors and other mental health professionals reliably knew what was in their patient's best interests. However, their track record is appalling (think not only of insulin coma and the prefrontal leucotomy but also of the large numbers of patients who continue to be treated with excessive doses of antipsychotics). Just as importantly, as this book should adequately testify, there is very little consensus amongst mental health professionals about how psychiatric disorders are best described, let alone what causes them. If we clinicians cannot agree among ourselves about such fundamental issues, it is difficult to see why our patients, who will suffer the consequences of our decisions, should be asked to put aside their own opinions.

A second and related objection is that compelling patients to undergo treatment is obviously wrong if the treatment is ineffective. The evidence reviewed in this book raises serious questions about the therapeutic value of some of the most widely used psychiatric remedies, for example antidepressant drugs, ECT and the antipsychotics. Indeed, it is almost a certainty that many compulsory treatment orders will result in patients who are unresponsive to medication being coerced into receiving drugs at high doses, causing serious side effects but providing benefit to no one.

Third, coercion is intrinsically damaging to mental health. It is not just unpleasant to be told what we should do with our lives; coercion diminishes the sense of self-efficacy and self-empowerment, which is essential for healthy psychological functioning. Indeed, the use of threats and leverage replicates the very conditions – the loss of power and the experience of victimization – that contribute to the development of symptoms such as depression[25] and paranoia[26] in the first place.

Finally, coercion is usually damaging to the therapeutic relationship. We have seen that the quality of this relationship impacts, not only on symptoms and attitudes towards treatment, but also the patient's quality of life, how much time is spent in hospital, the patient's ability to function socially and his willingness to engage with services.[27] In moments of crisis, the clinician who is seen as controlling is avoided rather than consulted. The patient who is distressed by side effects may covertly discontinue his medication, suddenly and with disastrous consequences, rather than by seeking advice about how to withdraw from drugs safely. Attempts to cajole the patient into following psychiatric instruction may provoke reactance (active opposition), and a determination to do something different.[28] In an atmosphere of coercion, the dark cloud of suspicion may obscure the judgement of both patients and therapists.

These arguments are not mere philosophical posturing: they are utilitarian and practical.‡ Not surprisingly, controlled trials of CTOs

‡ My approach is therefore somewhat different from that of Thomas Szasz, whose objections to coercion seem to be based on a deontological conception of human rights.

have revealed little or no impact on hospital admissions, the number of days spent in hospital, compliance with medication or contacts with out-patient services.[29] There is better evidence to support the assertive treatment approach (which of course includes some elements that are favourable to therapeutic relationships, such as a high ratio of staff to patients) but even in the case of these kinds of services the main benefit obtained, a reduction in the amount of time that patients spend in hospital, is seen only in those areas which make heavy use of in-patient treatment.[30] In short, there is no reason to think that coercive methods are effective in achieving even the short-term goals of psychiatric services, and every reason for believing that they are counter-productive in the long term.

Nonetheless, coercive practices persist, partly because they are sustained by powerful financial and political forces. The pharmaceutical industry has spent enormous sums on persuading mental health professionals, lay people and politicians that patients suffering from chemical imbalances in the brain can only be cured by medication. At the same time, services have developed an increasing aversion to risk, fuelled by unrealistic perceptions (perpetuated by the mass media) of the dangerousness of patients suffering from psychosis, and an unrealistic expectation that psychiatrists should be able to protect the public from random acts of violence. Any psychiatrist who arrives at work in the morning to discover that one of her patients has committed a violent assault overnight is likely to find herself the focus of a painful formal inquiry and may even be vilified in the local and national press. Since the end of the Cold War, meanwhile, politicians throughout the developed world have increasingly exploited our anxieties about public order, promising to protect us from danger whereas, in the past, they had promised us a better life.[31] There are few votes to be won from making psychiatric services better but plenty to be won from appearing to defend ordinary people from dangerous madmen.

Psychosis and violence

Although policymakers sometimes attempt to justify coercion in mental health care on the grounds that psychiatric patients are dangerous, academic research has not demonstrated a close relationship between psychosis and violence. This gulf between perception and reality is largely the creation of the mass media. For example, one survey of British newspapers found that 46 per cent of press reports about mental illness concerned crimes of violence.[32] As the human brain calculates risk according to the ease with which information about specific threats can be brought to mind,[33] it is not surprising that the repeated suggestion of an association between violence and mental illness has led to inflated estimates of the hazards presented to the public by psychotic patients.

Only a small proportion of homicides are committed by people suffering from severe mental illness. (In Britain, about 5 per cent of murderers have, at some point in their lives, been diagnosed as suffering from schizophrenia.[34]) Furthermore, given that a diagnosis of psychosis is often associated with other crime-related factors, for example poverty, a history of victimization and the use of illicit drugs, it is not clear that the small increased risk of violence associated with mental illness is always attributable to the patient's condition.[35] Some studies have suggested that symptoms that provoke an exaggerated feeling of threat, particularly paranoid delusions, do occasionally lead to violent acts[36] but others have cast doubt on even this association.[37] In simple statistical terms, the risk of being killed randomly by a person with psychosis is exceedingly small – about 1 in 10 million, approximately the same as the risk of being killed by lightning.[38]

Although a violent act committed by a psychotic patient invariably provokes much soul-searching amongst the responsible clinicians, often fuelled by twenty-twenty hindsight, it is unrealistic to expect that a greater use of coercive measures will produce a significant decrease in risk to the general public, at least not without an unacceptable impact on civil liberties. The factors that predict dangerous behaviour in patients are those that predict violence in ordinary people (particularly a past history of violence). Although psychiatrists and psychologists can sometimes use their clinical judgement to guess which patients will present a danger to others at better than chance level, the most accurate methods of prediction use detailed checklists of actuarial data (data from the patient's life history that can be codified and summed using empirically derived rules which, in principle, can be executed by a computer program).[39] Given that violence is a rare event, even these methods, if widely employed, would lead to the compulsory detention of many more non-violent than violent patients. For example, it has been estimated that, in a group of 100 patients of whom 20 are prone to aggression, the best methods available would lead to 14 (70 per cent) of the violent patients being detained at the cost of detaining 24 (30 per cent) of the non-violent patients. For very serious acts of violence, perhaps committed by 1 per cent of patients, the test would be wrong about 97 times out of a 100.[40] More vigorous efforts to control unappreciative psychiatric patients might make us feel safer, but it seems very unlikely that they would actually make the world a safer place.

Insight and psychosis

The argument for compulsorily treating patients on the grounds of their apparently diminished capacity to reason is no more compelling. This argument is often invoked by those who object to recovery-orientated, autonomy-enhancing services. For example, some psychiatrists have suggested that it makes no sense to speak of patient empowerment when psychosis can subvert a patient's thinking processes 'to the point that the self is taken over by disease'.[41] Others, for example psychologist and former psychiatric patient Fred Frese,[42] have suggested that the recovery approach may be appropriate for moderately impaired patients, but not for those patients who are most severely ill. Responding to this argument, Debbie Fisher and Laura Ahern, two former psychiatric patients, have objected that

When people are in the greatest distress, they experience despair, isolation, hopelessness, and a lack of control. It is at those trying times that they need hope, social connection, and a belief that they can regain control of their life, which are the principles of the evidence-based recovery model. Use of approaches based on the recovery model is crucial at the beginning of the recovery process and throughout it. We know – we recovered from schizophrenia. We were able to begin recovery only when we felt we could connect and borrow someone else's hope until ours returned.[43]

Although psychotic patients often perform relatively poorly on neurocognitive tests, only a tiny minority are impaired enough to be described as intellectually disabled.[44] Lack of reasoning capacity in patients is therefore usually attributed to psychotic processes, which prevent the patient from realizing he is ill. In these circumstances, it is usually decreed that the patient lacks insight, where insight is defined as 'the correct attitude to morbid change in oneself, and moreover, the realisation that the illness is mental'.[45] Note that, according to this idea, the belief that one is not mentally ill is seen as a symptom of mental illness. In practice, this way of thinking often leads to a kind of catch-22, in which the patient's objection to treatment is seen by the clinician as evidence that more aggressive treatment is required.

On close examination, patients' theories about their difficulties are complex and difficult to segregate into those that are insightful and those that are not. Sometimes service users embrace a conventional medical account of mental illness but, more often, they see their problems arising from their life experiences. Patients who accept that they have a genetically determined brain disorder may nonetheless object that the drugs they are given are unpleasant and ineffective, whereas those who see themselves as victims of a stressful environment may ask for drugs to tide them over a difficult patch. Not surprisingly, the relationship between formal measures of insight and outcome are complex. There is little evidence that measures of insight predict a willingness to take medication,[46] the persistence of psychotic symptoms or social functioning, but recently ill patients who are classified as having poor insight nonetheless seem to be at an increased risk of relapse (defined in terms of rehospitalization).[47] A plausible interpretation of these findings is that psychiatric teams often admit patients to hospital *because* they appear to lack insight (which is what happened to Andrew, described in Chapter 5).

Of course, we all struggle to make sense of our experiences, and it seems unlikely that psychiatric patients are different from anyone else in this respect. Patients may have different theories from those of their psychiatrists for a variety of reasons, and it seems naive to expect that there will be just one explanation for this kind of disagreement. Even the most deluded patients are able to think rationally about matters unrelated to their delusional beliefs.[48] There is little evidence that neurocognitive impairment is related to formal ratings of insight[49] which usually assume that a traditional model of mental illness is correct. (One widely used scale, for example, scores patients as lacking in insight if they disagree with such statements as: 'My doctor is right in prescribing medication for me' and 'My stay in hospital is necessary'[50]). Resistance to this model is understandable when its prognostic implications are spelled out. Given the standard assumption that schizophrenia is a genetically determined brain disease, and that patients will need to take their medication indefinitely, it is unsurprising that some patients grasp at an alternative theory – *any* theory – to account for their difficulties. This kind of preference for an account of oneself that has positive implications, far from being a symptom of a diseased mind, is perfectly healthy and, when seen in ordinary people, has long been recognized as an adaptive coping strategy that allows the individual to remain optimistic in the face of adversity.[51] On this view, embracing a medical model of mental illness might be expected to be harmful and, indeed, numerous studies have shown that, when recovering patients gain 'insight' (that is, when they finally accept that they are suffering from a genetically determined brain disease) they often become seriously depressed.[52] Patients who feel that their diagnosis is stigmatizing are especially likely to feel hopeless and inferior to others once they have reluctantly accepted it.[53]

In the clinic, the failure to respect patients' efforts to understand the events that have led to a breakdown can be the source of unnecessary conflict and confusion. I once saw a young man whose psychiatrist thought he lacked insight because he refused to believe that he had 'schizophrenia'. The unfortunate patient, who had become floridly paranoid following the collapse of an ambitious business venture, had no doubt that he had been experiencing delusions, and believed that his brain had been affected by the extreme stress he had been experiencing. Although he was adamant that the psychiatrist had made the wrong diagnosis, he was hopeful that his doctor would be able to offer him medication to help him overcome his difficulties. They were at loggerheads for no good reason.

I am not attempting to deny that violence or a diminished capacity to think clearly are problems that are sometimes encountered in psychiatric practice, but they are much rarer and less often an impediment to treatment than is usually supposed. Given the arguments against coercion considered earlier, stringent criteria should be met before deciding that dangerous behaviour or cognitive impairment necessitate a controlling response. Within an autonomy-enhancing framework, these problems can be often tackled without resort to intimidation. When faced with behaviour that is risky and threatening to others, psychiatric teams should first try to establish a strong therapeutic alliance, and then attempt to provide a service that the patient finds useful. The task for the clinician faced with the patient who lacks 'insight' is not to dispute the patient's explanations for his symptoms, but to understand these explanations, to explore their origins, and to respect them as genuine attempts to account for experiences that are puzzling and frightening. By a process of empathetic understanding and skilful negotiation it is usually possible to find a way forward that allows the patient to work towards his life goals without causing harm to others.

The place of drugs in psychiatry

A move towards a less coercive, more autonomy-enhancing approach to mental health care will require the reappraisal of all kinds of treatment, but especially psychiatric drugs. Their escalating use over the last twenty years testifies to the fact that, for many psychiatrists, they seem to be the only tool available. As traditional psychiatrists hammer away with them, too many patients find themselves on doses that are unnecessarily high, or on combinations of drugs that cannot be justified by evidence from clinical trials. It is not uncommon to find patients who have been prescribed two or three different kinds of antipsychotics, or an antipsychotic in combination with an antidepressant and a benzodiazapine, surely evidence of a clinician who is destitute of ideas.

Of course, drugs do have a place in modern mental health care, but the way that they are used needs to change radically. First, those who prescribe them should liberate themselves from the delusion that they are specific treatments for diseases such as 'schizophrenia' and 'bipolar disorder'. Instead, as British psychiatrist Joanna Moncrieff has argued,[54] we should try to understand the specific psychological effects of drugs, so that they are employed only when there is good reason to think that these effects will be useful.

Moncrieff has tried to classify drugs on the basis of their subjective effects, arguing, for example, that both antipsychotics and antidepressants cause reduced mental activity, emotional indifference, restlessness and, in some cases, sedation. This approach is not entirely convincing, because subjective appraisals of drug effects are imprecise and heavily affected by context. (In a celebrated experiment carried out in the early 1960s, American psychologists Stanley Schachter and Jerome Singer showed that students injected with adrenalin responded differently – either feeling elated or fearful – according to the behaviour of a stooge they were asked to sit with.[55]) A better approach would be to classify drugs according to their effects on cognitive and emotional functioning as measured in carefully controlled laboratory conditions. For example, on the basis of the evidence described in earlier chapters, antipsychotics might be classified as *reward responsivity and avoidance inhibitors* (which I admit is quite a mouthful).

As we learn more about the psychological processes underlying symptoms such as hallucinations and delusions, and as the science of psychopharmacology makes progress in understanding how changes in brain biochemistry affect mental functioning, we should be able to look towards a time when drugs are used more rationally than at present. In the meantime, like it or not, drugs can only be prescribed on a suck-it-and-see basis, and it is far better to admit this than to persist with the myth that they are specific treatments for specific conditions. Given the evidence that delaying the introduction of drug treatment is not harmful, alternatives to drug treatment should be considered from the outset. When drugs are introduced, there should be an explicit agreement with the patient that they will be discontinued if, after a trial period, they turn out to be ineffective or intolerable. This approach will require psychiatrists to monitor more carefully the progress of their patients than is common practice at the moment. The development of easily administered measures of symptoms and drug side effects would undoubtedly help. (I have made a small contribution by developing a questionnaire measure of antipsychotic side effects,[56] but much more could be done.)

For both ethical and practical reasons, patients need to be given accurate information about the likely effects of the drugs they are taking. As American psychiatrist Grace Jackson has pointed out, the widespread dissemination of misinformation about these effects is a serious threat to patients' ability to give informed consent to treatment. (Recent books by Jackson, David Healy and Joanna Moncrieff[57] are valuable attempts to provide consumers with the necessary information. The psychiatric pharmacist, whose potential contribution often goes unrecognized, can also play an important role in making sure that patients have a realistic understanding of what drugs might do to them.) Patients' decisions to discontinue medication should be respected as far as possible. It is difficult to know how many psychotic patients would be better off without taking drugs, but my guess is that the number might be as high as 50 per cent.

A realistic appreciation of the limitations of psychiatric drugs will have implications that stretch far beyond the psychiatric clinic. The medical profession and the regulators have so far proved impotent in their efforts to ensure that patients receive only the safest and most cost-effective treatments. Some observers, for example medical journalist Jacky Law,[58] have suggested that, in a world in which medical information is increasingly available through the internet, consumers must expect to play an increasingly active role in deciding which kind of treatment is most appropriate. Anticipating this development, the pharmaceutical industry is becoming adept at manipulating consumer choice to meet its own ends. In the United States, when drug companies were permitted to advertise directly to the general public (for some time they have been lobbying for the same right in the European Union) sales of the advertised medications skyrocketed.[59] Moreover, many consumer advocacy groups are extensively funded by the industry (in the United States, the National Alliance for the Mentally Ill received $12 million from drug companies between 1996 and 1999), and some are little more than industry lobbying organizations.[60] In bleak moments I find it difficult to see anything but disaster on the horizon. If the industry is to maintain its high level of profits, we may have to live in a society in which we all have our brain biochemistry tinkered with between the cradle and the grave. If we are able to resist this kind of madness, the industry will have to expect a more realistic return from its efforts in line with other industries; I am not an economist, but I imagine this kind of adjustment is likely to have painful consequences.

Psychotherapy for the masses?

If drugs are not the answer, do we need more psychotherapy? Certainly, in the case of the less severe psychiatric disorders, even if we accept the Dodo bird conjecture, the case for therapy looks strong.

Psychotherapy is already becoming increasingly available in Britain where the National Institute of Clinical Excellence has recommended that cognitive behaviour therapy (CBT) should be offered to most patients with psychosis,[61] and where the government has announced the release of substantial funds to increase depressed and anxious patients' access to psychological treatments.[62] However, this trend is not without hazards. The first and most obvious difficulty is the problem of recruiting and training psychological therapists. In the case of services for patients with severe mental illness, these therapists must be taught to use not only individual treatments such as CBT, but other evidence-based approaches such as behavioural family therapy. Moreover, training must be supported by the opportunity to use these skills in routine care. In the case of family interventions in particular, clinicians too often return to their services after a period of training only to discover that high case loads and other institutional barriers prevent them from putting their skills into practice.[63] The same is sometimes true of practitioners trained in CBT.[64]

In a recent editorial in the *Journal of Psychopharmacology*, psychiatrists David Nutt and Michael Sharpe expressed deep anxieties about the consequences of making psychotherapy more widely available.[65] Given where the editorial appeared, it is perhaps unsurprising that it gives a very unbalanced account of the risks associated with psychological treatment. Many of the issues raised by Nutt and Sharpe are spurious – they chastise psychotherapy researchers for not carrying out double-blind trials (no doubt causing Martin Seligman to check his wallet), bizarrely suggest that large numbers of therapists sexually abuse their patients (forgetting, of course, that malpractice is not unknown amongst medical practitioners), and claim that many others discourage patients from taking medication (citing the thirty-year-old Osheroff case as the only evidence in support of this claim). Nonetheless they raise some important questions about the quality control of psychological treatments. For example, their suggestion that there is need for a system for recording adverse reactions to psychotherapy is hard to disagree with (although I suspect that working out an effective method might be difficult). I would go further and argue that it is important to find ways of identifying those therapists who are most effective (whatever their professional background) and those whose talents lie elsewhere. The best way of doing this would be to collect and routinely analyse a common set of outcome measures that are administered to all patients. In the British National Health Service, there are already moves to use such measures with patients receiving psychotherapy for less severe disorders.[66]

Although the evidence for CBT and behavioural family therapy is stronger than the evidence for other kinds of psychotherapy in the treatment of severe mental illness, it is important to remember that, at the moment, they are at best only modestly effective when used to treat the symptoms of psychosis. Moreover, it is unlikely that one size of therapy will fit all patients. Recently, positive results have been reported from small-scale trials of more exotic kinds of therapy, for example body psychotherapy[67] (which incorporates various physical exercises) and music therapy.[68] (Each of these studies was a small pilot investigation, with a follow-up period of just a few months, but the findings obviously provide further support for the Dodo bird conjecture.)

However effective any therapy might be, and however widely available it becomes, it is likely that some patients will not want to make use of this kind of assistance. For a variety of reasons, some will not benefit from therapy and other, less glamorous interventions will be much more helpful. For example, the role of employment in facilitating recovery from severe mental illness is insufficiently recognized by many services. Surveys show that the majority of severely ill patients who have been unemployed (sometimes for decades) want to return to work and feel that their exclusion from the labour market is an impediment to recovery.[69] Evidence from follow-up studies of patients who have begun to work suggest that these opinions are realistic; those patients who gain competitive employment show improvements, not only in their social functioning but also in their symptoms.[70] This is presumably why recovery from psychosis is more likely during periods of economic boom (when work is easier to find) than in periods of recession.[71]

However, making this step is often fraught with difficulty. There is good evidence that supported-employment schemes (in which patients are helped to find jobs that suit their abilities and preferences, and in which there is continuing support for the patient and liaison between the employer and the mental health services) can be effective in returning some (but not all) patients to work,[72] but (in Britain, at least) these schemes seem to have low priority. The benefit systems in European countries often present a further hurdle; patients face the risk of losing income when they return to work. Emerging evidence from the United States (where there has been much more research on the effects of therapeutic employment than in Britain) has begun to point to ways in which these schemes can be enhanced by employing psychological interventions specifically designed to help the patient cope with the stresses of the workplace.[73]

Mental health tribalism

During the early 1970s British social psychologist Henri Tajfel and his colleagues conducted a remarkable series of experiments.[74] They assigned volunteers to different groups on the basis of trivial or arbitrary criteria, for example their preference for different kinds of art or on the toss of a coin, and then asked them to distribute some valuable resource (money, or points on an evaluative scale) to the groups (the volunteers were not allowed to interact with each other, or to distribute resources to themselves). Despite the arbitrary nature of these *minimal groups*, the participants typically contrived to reward members of the out-group less then members of the in-group, even in circumstances in which doing so resulted in less reward for both. The mechanisms behind this kind of irrational prejudice are not entirely understood, but it is thought that labelling oneself as belonging to a particular group and then favouring it helps to maintain one's sense of potency and self-esteem.[75] It has been suggested that religious fundamentalism is fuelled by this process, which becomes more pernicious when individuals feel that their identities are under threat.[76] This process may also help to explain the behaviour of different groups of mental health professionals towards each other.

At various points in this book I have described the professional rivalry between psychiatry and clinical psychology. Because I am a human being, and subject to the same psychological laws as everyone else, it is possible that I have failed to characterize this conflict completely fairly. I am sure that a few of my colleagues in clinical psychology, propelled by the same forces, eagerly hope that, as services become increasingly psychological in orientation, psychologists will acquire an automatic right of leadership, supplanting the current position held by medicine. Energy expended on debating who is in charge, however, is energy that could be better devoted to helping patients. The solution to the problem of psychiatric unaccountability is not to place some other kind of mental health professional in an equally unaccountable position, but to recognize that the tribal boundaries that have imposed their structure on mental health services are destructive and no longer relevant.

We live in an age in which professions have skill monopolies only by default; anyone of good will who is smart enough can be trained to do almost anything within the clinical domain. There are psychiatrists and psychiatric nurses who are as proficient at psychotherapy as the best clinical psychologist and, in some parts of the world, clinical psychologists and nurses who have been trained to prescribe psychiatric drugs. We need to learn how to exploit all of these talents and abilities and organize our teams so that no one profession has the absolute power to dictate the way that services are delivered. Perhaps the most important lesson of the past century for mental health professionals of all kinds is that we must set aside our hubris and be humble in the face of madness.

A recovery-orientated, autonomy-enhancing approach requires us to relinquish whatever power we have, and to find ways of giving more authority to the consumer. It is difficult to believe that many of the horrors that were perpetrated against patients in the past would have been possible if they had been allowed a voice in the way that services were run. Even in modern services, patients are too often intimidated into silence when faced with treatments that are distressing and unhelpful. Perhaps the greatest force for good in modern mental health care is therefore the rise of an organized and increasingly vocal consumer movement.[77] Organizations such as the Hearing Voices Network[78] empower patients to pursue avenues of recovery chosen by themselves, and are increasingly acting as a bulwark against mental health professionals who fail to address their members' needs.

This is a fast-changing front on the battlefield of psychiatric care. I am aware of some services that have begun to employ ex-patients in their psychiatric teams, and it is becoming increasingly common for psychiatric researchers to have to demonstrate that they have consulted consumers before seeking funding for investigations. But we can go much further. There is no reason why consumers should not have a decisive presence on committees appointing psychiatrists, psychologists and nurses. In many universities, lecturers are now required to collect formal feedback from their students, and bad feedback can blight their chances of promotion. Would it not be wonderful if the same were true for mental health professionals? Perhaps then we really would see services that people in distress would want to make use of.

Journey's end

My taxi journey was coming to an end. I could see the station ahead. 'So what happened after your breakdown?' I asked the driver.

'It was hard, really hard. But I got through it. You get through these things. You think you won't survive, but you do.'

There was very little time left but I was curious to know how he was now.

'I'm fine,' he said, in answer to my question.

'And what about the kids?'

'Smashing. The oldest, the boy, he's a lawyer. Doing really well. And the girl, she has a really successful modelling career.' He tapped the photo on his dashboard as the cab drew to a halt and, for the first time, I noticed that the model's smile bore a resemblance to the cabby's.

'Good luck with your research, mate,' he said as I paid him.

Sometimes ordinary stories of triumph over adversity are inspiring. They remind us that hope is the fire that will guide us through darkness. Psychiatry's greatest sin has been to crush hope in those it has claimed to care for. Without hope the struggle for survival seems pointless. With hope, almost anything seems possible.

Notes

Preface

1. T. L. Beauchamp and J. F. Childress (2001), *Principles of Biomedical Ethics*, 5th edition. Oxford: Oxford University Press.

2. T. S. Szasz (1960), 'The myth of mental illness', *American Psychologist*, 15: 564–80.

3. R. D. Laing (1960), *The Divided Self*. London: Tavistock Press.

   R. D. Laing (1967), *The Politics of Experience and the Bird of Paradise*. London: Penguin Press.

   R. D. Laing and A. Esterson (1964), *Sanity, Madness and the Family: Families of Schizophrenics*. London: Tavistock.

4. R. Whitaker (2002), *Mad in America: Bad Science, Bad Medicine and the Enduring Mistreatment of the Mentally Ill*. New York: Perseus Books.

5. M. H. Stone (1997), *Healing the Mind: A History of Psychiatry from Antiquity to the Present*. New York: Norton.

6. E. Shorter (1997), *A History of Psychiatry*. New York: Wiley.

7. N. Lester (2003), review of *Madness Explained: Psychosis and Human Nature* by Richard Bentall. *British Medical Journal*, 327: 1055.

Chapter 1

1. This work has evolved rapidly over the past ten years. For some of my own publications describing cognitive behaviour therapy at different stages in its development, see for example: R. P. Bentall, G. Haddock and P. D. Slade (1994), 'Cognitive behaviour therapy for persistent auditory hallucinations: From theory to therapy', *Behavior Therapy*, 25: 51–66; P. Kinderman and R. P. Bentall (1997), 'Attributional therapy for paranoid delusions: A case study', *Behavioural and Cognitive Psychotherapy*, 25: 269–80; N. Tarrier et al. (2004), '18-month follow-up of a randomized controlled

trial of cognitive-behaviour therapy in first episode and early schizophrenia', *British Journal of Psychiatry*, 184: 231–9; A. P. Morrison et al. (2004), 'A randomized controlled trial of cognitive therapy for the prevention of psychosis in people at ultra-high risk', *British Journal of Psychiatry*, 185: 281–7; A. P. Morrison et al. (2003), *Cognitive Therapy for Psychosis: A Formulation-based Approach*. Hove: Brunner-Routledge.

2. P. Chadwick and M. Birchwood (1994), 'The omnipotence of voices: A cognitive approach to auditory hallucinations', *British Journal of Psychiatry*, 164: 190–201.

3. Z. V. Segal, J. M. G. Williams and J. D. Teasdale (2002), *Mindfulness-based Cognitive Therapy for Depression*. London: Guilford.

4. J. J. McGrath (2005), 'Myths and plain truths about schizophrenia epidemiology', *Acta Psychiatrica Scandinavica*, 111: 4–11.

5. T. Lloyd et al. (2005), 'Incidence of bipolar affective disorder in three UK cities: Results from the AeSOP study', *British Journal of Psychiatry*, 186: 126–31.

6. A. Jablensky (1995), 'Schizophrenia: The epidemiological horizon', in S. R. Hirsch and D. R. Weinberger (eds.), *Schizophrenia*. Oxford: Blackwell, pp. 206–52.

7. F. K. Goodwin and K. R. Jamison (1990), *Manic-depressive Illness*. Oxford: Oxford University Press.

8. J. Perala et al. (2007), 'Lifetime prevalence of psychotic and bipolar I disorders in a general population', *Archives of General Psychiatry*, 64: 19–28.

9. B. A. Palmer, V. S. Pankratz and J. M. Bostwick (2005), 'The lifetime risk of suicide in schizophrenia: A reexamination', *Archives of General Psychiatry*, 62: 247–53.

10. G. S. Leverich et al. (2003), 'Factors associated with suicide attempts in 648 patients with bipolar disorder in the Stanley Foundation Bipolar Network', *Journal of Clinical Psychiatry*, 64: 506–15; L. B. Marangell et al. (2006), 'Prospective predictors of suicide and suicide attempts in 1,556 patients with bipolar disorders followed for up to 2 years', *Bipolar Disorders*, 8: 566–75.

11. D. Wiersma et al. (2000), 'Social disability in schizophrenia: Its development and prediction over 15 years in incidence cohorts in six European centres', *Psychological Medicine*, 30: 1155–67.

12. R. F. Prien and W. Z. Potter (1990), 'NIMH workshop report on treatment of bipolar disorder', *Psychopharmacology Bulletin*, 26: 409–27.

13. I. Leudar and P. Thomas (2000), *Voices of Reason, Voices of Insanity: Studies of Verbal Hallucinations*. London: Routledge.

14. Department of Health (1998), *In-patients Formally Detained in Hospitals under the Mental Health Act 1983 and Other Legislation: NHS Trusts, High*

Security Hospital and Private Facilities: 1996–97. London: The Stationery Office; J. Bindman et al. (2005), 'Perceived coercion at admission to psychiatric hospital and engagement with follow-up', *Social Psychiatry and Psychiatric Epidemiology*, 40: 160–66; H. Dressing and H. J. Salize (2004), 'Compulsory admission of mentally ill patients in European Union Member States', *Social Psychiatry and Psychiatric Epidemiology*, 39: 797–803; M. Hotopf et al. (2000), 'Changing patterns in the use of the Mental Health Act 1983 in England, 1984–1996', *British Journal of Psychiatry*, 176: 479–84. C. W. Lidz et al. (2000), 'Sources of coercive behaviours in psychiatric admissions', *Acta Psychiatrica Scandinavica*, 101: 73–9.

15. E. Q. Wu et al. (2005), 'The economic burden of schizophrenia in the United States in 2002', *Journal of Clinical Psychiatry*, 66: 1122–9.

16. P. McCrone et al. (2008), *Paying the Price: The Cost of Mental Health Care in England to 2026.* London: The King's Fund.

17. C. Dowrick (2004), *Beyond Depression: A New Approach to Understanding and Management.* Oxford: Oxford University Press.

18. Any attempt to characterize the everyday realities of psychiatric care must inevitably be impressionistic, and important exceptions exist to the picture I am painting here (for example, within the NHS there are a few units that prioritize social and psychological approaches to helping people with psychosis). Nonetheless, I think this description of psychiatric care for people with severe mental illness gives a reasonably fair account of what is typical. For a more detailed critical account of everyday psychiatric practice in Britain, see J. Laurence (2003), *Pure Madness: How Fear Drives the Mental Health System.* London: Routledge. For a critical account of psychiatric practice in the United States, see R. Muller (2007), *Doing Psychiatry Wrong: A Critical and Prescriptive Look at a Faltering Profession.* New York: Analytic Press.

19. National Institute for Clinical Excellence (2002), *Schizophrenia: Core Interventions in the Treatment and Management of Schizophrenia in Primary and Secondary Care.* London: National Institute for Clinical Excellence.

20. A. F. Lehman et al. (2004), 'The Schizophrenia Patient Outcomes Research Team (PORT): Updated treatment recommendations 2003', *Schizophrenia Bulletin*, 30: 193–217.

21. S. Lewis and J. A. Lieberman (2008), 'CATIE and CUtLASS: Can we handle the truth?', *British Journal of Psychiatry*, 192: 161–3.

22. J. Moncrieff (2008), *The Myth of the Chemical Cure: A Critique of Psychiatric Drug Treatment.* London: Palgrave.

23. J. A. Kaye, B. D. Bradbury and H. Jick (2003), 'Changes in antipsychotic drug prescribing by general practitioners in the United Kingdom from 1991 to 2000: A population-based observational study', *British Journal of Clinical Pharmacology*, 56: 569–75.

24. Moncrieff (2008), op. cit. See also Chapter 9 of this book.

25. R. J. Wyatt (1995), 'Early intervention in schizophrenia: Can the course of illness be altered?', *Biological Psychiatry*, 38: 1–3; R. J. Wyatt, M. F. Green and A. H. Tuma (1997), 'Long-term morbidity associated with delayed treatment of first-admission schizophrenic patients', *Psychological Medicine*, 27: 261–8. The scientific evidence relating to this change in practice is discussed in detail in Chapter 9.

26. T. Miller and T. McGlashan (2003), 'The risks of not intervening in pre-onset psychotic illness', *Journal of Mental Health*, 12: 345–9.

27. See for example: C. D. Frith and E. C. Johnstone (2003), *Schizophrenia: A Very Short Introduction*. Oxford: Oxford University Press; M. F. Green (2001), *Schizophrenia Revealed: From Neurones to Social Interactions*. New York: Norton; P. Williamson (2006), *Mind, Brain and Schizophrenia*. Oxford: Oxford University Press. Each of these books, written for the intelligent lay reader, starts from the assumption that schizophrenia is a meaningful diagnosis, and is caused by brain disease. None gives substantial space to the role of social factors in causing psychosis.

28. J. Read (2008), 'Schizophrenia, drug companies and the internet', *Social Science and Medicine*, 66: 98–109.

29. Quoted from the website of the National Alliance for the Mentally Ill, www.nami.org, accessed 30 October 2007.

30. R. McCabe et al. (2004), 'Engagement of patients with psychosis in the consultation: Conversation analytic study', *British Medical Journal*, 325: 1148–51.

31. A. Lewis (1934), 'The psychopathology of insight', *British Journal of Medical Psychology*, 14: 332–48.

32. A. S. David (1990), 'Insight and psychosis', *British Journal of Psychiatry*, 156: 798–808.

33. J. Le Fanu (1999), *The Rise and Fall of Modern Medicine*. London: Little, Brown and Co.

34. E. M. Brown (2000), 'Why Wagner-Jauregg won the Nobel Prize for discovering malarial therapy for general paresis of the insane', *History of Psychiatry*, 11: 371–82.

35. J. Rowland et al. (2004), 'Cancer survivorship – United States, 1971–2001', *Morbidity and Mortality Weekly Report*, 53: 526–9.

36. M. P. Coleman et al. (1999), 'Cancer survival trends in England and Wales, 1971–1995: Deprivation and NHS region', *Studies in Medical and Population Subjects*, no 61. London: The Stationery Office.

37. J. A. Volminik et al. (1998), 'Coronary heart event and case fatality rates in an English population: Results from the Oxford myocardial infarction incidence study', *Heart*, 80: 40–44; H. Tunstall-Pedoe et al. (1999), 'Contribution of trends in survival and coronary-event rates in coronary heart disease mortality: 10-year results from 37 MONICA Project populations', *Lancet*, 353: 1547–57.

38. R. Warner (1985). *Recovery from Schizophrenia: Psychiatry and Political Economy*. New York: Routledge & Kegan Paul.

39. Hegarty et al. (1994), 'One hundred years of schizophrenia: A meta-analysis of the outcome literature', *American Journal of Psychiatry*, 151: 409–16.

40. R. Whitaker (2005), 'Anatomy of an epidemic: Psychiatric drugs and the astonishing rise of mental illness in America', *Ethical Human Psychology and Psychiatry*, 7: 23–35.

41. D. Healy et al. (2005), 'Service utilization in 1896 and 1996: Morbidity and mortality data from North Wales', *History of Psychiatry*, 16: 27–41; D. Healy et al. (2006), 'Lifetime suicide rates in treated schizophrenia: 1875–1924 and 1994–1998 cohorts compared', *British Journal of Psychiatry*, 188: 223–8.

42. E. F. Torrey (2001), *The Invisible Plague: The Rise of Mental Illness from 1750 to the Present*. New Brunswick, NJ: Rutgers University Press.

43. D. M. Parkin et al. (2005), 'Global cancer statistics, 2002', *CA: A Cancer Journal for Clinicians*, 55: 74–108. The proportion of patients in the developed world suffering from stomach cancer expected to survive for five years was estimated to be 35 per cent in the case of males and 31 per cent in the case of females, but the comparable rates in the developing world were 21 per cent for males and 20 per cent for females. The respective figures for cancer of the colon, to take another example, were 56 per cent for males and 54 per cent for females in the industrialized nations and 39 per cent for both sexes in the developing world.

44. World Health Organization (1973), *International Pilot Study of Schizophrenia*. Geneva: World Health Organization.

45. W. Reich (1984), 'Psychiatric diagnosis as an ethical problem', in S. Bloch and P. Chodoff (eds.), *Psychiatric Ethics*. Oxford: Oxford University Press, pp. 61–88. See also R. P. Bentall (2003), *Madness Explained: Psychosis and Human Nature*. London: Penguin, Ch. 3.

46. World Health Organization (1979), *Schizophrenia: An International Follow-up Study*. New York: Wiley.

47. A. Jablensky et al. (1992), 'Schizophrenia: Manifestations, incidence and course in different cultures', *Psychological Medicine*, supp. 20: 1–97. The participating sites were Aarhus in Denmark, Agra and Chandigarh in India, Cali in Colombia, Dublin in Ireland, Honolulu and Rochester in the USA, Ibadan in Nigeria, Moscow in Russia, Nagasaki in Japan, Nottingham in the UK and Prague in the former Czechoslovakia.

48. D. Bhugra (2006), 'Severe mental illness across cultures', *Acta Psychiatrica Scandinavica*, 113, suppl. 429: 17–23.

49. C. J. L. Murray and A. Lopez (1996), *Global Health Statistics: A Compendium of Evidence. Prevalence and Mortality Estimates for over 2000 Conditions*. Cambridge, Mass. Harvard School of Public Health.

50. For publications that make this argument in detail, see: D. Pilgrim and R. P. Bentall (1999), 'The medicalisation of misery: A critical realist analysis of the concept of depression', *Journal of Mental Health* 8: 261–74; A. V. Horwitz and J. C. Wakefield (2007), *The Loss of Sadness: How Psychiatry Transformed Normal Sorrow into Depressive Illness*. New York: Oxford University Press; D. Summerfield (2006), 'Depression: Epidemic or pseudo-epidemic?', *Journal of the Royal Society of Medicine*, 99: 161–2.

51. T. B. Ustrun et al. (2004), 'Global burden of depressive disorders in the year 2000', *British Journal of Psychiatry*, 184: 386–92.

52. The letter can be seen in full at www.moshersoteria.com (accessed 1 December 2007).

53. This account of Mosher's life is largely based on a magazine article that drew on an interview with Mosher: J. De Wyze (2003) 'Still crazy after all these years', *San Diego Weekly Reader*, 32 (9 January). The article can be found at www.moshersoteria.com (accessed 1 December 2007).

54. See, for example, R. D. Laing (1967), *The Politics of Experience and the Bird of Paradise*. London: Penguin Press.

55. J. Bola and L. Mosher (2003), 'Treatment of acute psychosis without neuroleptics: Two-year outcomes from the Soteria project', *Journal of Nervous and Mental Disease*, 191: 219–29; L. R. Mosher (1999), 'Soteria and other alternatives to acute psychiatric hospitalization', *Journal of Nervous and Mental Disease*, 187: 142–9; L. R. Mosher (2004), 'Non-hospital, non-drug intervention with first episode psychosis', in J. Read, L. R. Mosher and R. P. Bentall (eds.), *Models of Madness: Psychological, Social and Biological Approaches to Schizophrenia*. London: Routledge, pp. 349–64; L. R. Mosher and A. Z. Menn (1978), 'Community residential treatment for schizophrenia: Two-year follow-up', *Hospital and Community Psychiatry*, 29: 715–23. L. R. Mosher, R. Vallone and A. Menn (1995), 'The treatment of acute psychosis without neuroleptics: Six-week psychopathology outcome data from the Soteria project', *International Journal of Social Psychiatry*, 41: 157–73.

56. L. Ciompi, H. P. Dauwalder and C. Maier (1992), 'The pilot project "Soteria Berne". Clinical experiences and results', *British Journal of Psychiatry*, 161: 145–53; L. Ciompi and H. Hoffmann (2004), 'Soteria Berne: An innovative milieu therapeutic approach to acute schizophrenia based on the concept of affect-logic', *World Psychiatry*, 3: 140–46. For a comprehen-

sive review of the literature on Soteria and related projects, see T. Calton et al. (2008), 'A systematic review of the Soteria paradigm for the treatment of people diagnosed with schizophrenia', *Schizophrenia Bulletin*, 34: 181–92.

Chapter 2

1. E. Shorter (1997), *A History of Psychiatry*. New York: Wiley.

2. A. Meyer (1898/2003), 'Remarks on Hecker's address', *History of Psychiatry*, 14: 493–6.

3. C. A. Logan (1999), 'The altered rationale for the choice of a standard animal in experimental psychology: Henry H. Donaldson, Adolf Meyer, and "the" albino rat', *History of Psychology*, 2: 3–24.

4. O. Marx (1993), 'Conversation piece: Adolf Meyer and psychiatric training at the Phipps Clinic: An interview with Theodore Lidz', *History of Psychiatry*, 4: 245–69.

5. E. J. Engstrom and M. Weber (2007), 'Making Kraepelin history: A great instauration?', *History of Psychiatry*, 18: 267–73.

6. E. Kraepelin (1904/1974), 'Comparative psychiatry', in S. R. Hirsch and M. Shepherd (eds.), *Themes and Variations in European Psychiatry*. Bristol: Wright, pp. 3–6.

7. E. Kraepelin (1887/2005), 'The directions of psychiatric research', *History of Psychiatry*, 16: 350–64. See also: E. J. Engstrom and M. Weber (2005), 'The *Directions of Psychiatric Research* by Emil Kraepelin', *History of Psychiatry*, 16: 345–9; A. Jablensky (2007), 'Living in a Kraepelinian world: Kraepelin's impact on modern psychiatry', *History of Psychiatry*, 18: 381–8.

8. E. J. Engstrom (1991), 'Emil Kraepelin: Psychiatry and public affairs in Wilhelmine Germany', *History of Psychiatry*, 2: 111–32.

9. E. Bleuler (1911/1950), *Dementia praecox or the Group of Schizophrenias*, trans. E. Zinkin. New York: International Universities Press.

10. R. Noll (2007), 'Kraepelin's "lost biological psychiatry"? Autointoxication, organotherapy and surgery for dementia praecox', *History of Psychiatry*, 18: 301–20.

11. R. E. Kendell (1975), *The Role of Diagnosis in Psychiatry*. Oxford: Blackwell.

12. R. M. Ion and M. D. Beer (2002), 'The British reaction to dementia praecox 1893–1913', part 1, *History of Psychiatry*, 13: 285–304; part 2, *History of Psychiatry*, 13: 419–31.

13. R. Noll (2004), 'The American reaction to dementia praecox, 1900', *History of Psychiatry*, 15: 127–8.

14. These case studies can be found in E. Kraepelin (1904), *Lectures in*

Clinical Psychiatry, revised 2nd edition. London: Bailliere, Tindal and Cox.

15. For an account of Dix's influence in the USA and also the UK (where she travelled in 1854), see M. H. Stone (1997), *Healing the Mind: A History of Psychiatry from Antiquity to the Present.* New York: Norton. The quotation from her *Memorial* to the Legislature of the State of Massachusetts is taken from Wikipedia (http://en.wikipedia.org/wiki/DorotheaDix, retrieved 4 November 2007).

16. R. Porter (2002), *Madness: A Brief History.* Oxford: Oxford University Press.

17. A. W. Beveridge (1998), 'Life in the asylum: Patients' letters from Morningside, 1873–1908', *History of Psychiatry*, 9: 431–69.

18. I visited Pilgrim State Psychiatric Hospital in the early 1990s, when it still had about 3,000 patients. The historical information given here was obtained from a number of websites, including that of the New York Office of Mental Health (www.omh.state.ny.us, retrieved 4 November 2007) and the Opacity website, which is dedicated to striking photographs of abandoned psychiatric hospital buildings (www.opacity.us/site23pilgrimstatehospital.htm, retrieved 4 November 2007).

19. A. Scull (2005). *Madhouse: A Tragic Tale of Megalomania and Modern Medicine.* London: Yale University Press. See also H. Freeman (2005), 'Infectious lunacy', *Times Literary Supplement* (11 September).

20. My account of the development of ECT is based on the following sources: U. Cerletti (1956), 'Electroshock therapy', in A. M. Sackler et al. (eds.), *The Great Physiodynamic Therapies in Psychiatry: An Historical Reappraisal.* New York: Hoeber-Harper, pp. 91–120; M. Fink (1999), *Electroshock: Healing Mental Illness.* Oxford: Oxford University Press; Shorter (1997), op. cit.; E. Shorter and D. Healy (2007), *Shock Therapy: A History of Electroconvulsive Treatment in Mental Illness.* New Brunswick, NJ: Rutgers University Press; Stone (1997), op. cit.

21. Cerletti (1956), op. cit.

22. This account of the prefrontal leuctomy operation is taken from various sources, principally: R. Whitaker (2002), *Mad in America: Bad Science, Bad Medicine and the Enduring Mistreatment of the Mentally Ill.* New York: Perseus Books; J. El-Hai (2005), *The Lobotomist: A Maverick Medical Genius and his Tragic Quest to Rid the World of Mental Illness.* New York: Wiley.

23. Howard Dully's amazing story is told by him in a National Public Radio programme, '*My lobotomy: Howard Dully's journey*', first broadcast on 6 November 2005. For details, see www.npr.org (accessed 11 December 2007).

24. H. Dully and C. Fleming (2007), *My Lobotomy: A Memoir.* New York: Random House.

25. Quoted in Whitaker (2002), op. cit.

26. D. B. Doroshow (2006), 'Performing a cure for schizophrenia: Insulin coma therapy on the wards', *Journal of the History of Medicine and Allied Sciences*, 62: 213–43. See also www.pbs.org/wgbh/amex/nash/index.html, a PBS website linked to a documentary film *A Brilliant Madness*, describing the life and treatment of John Forbes Nash, a Nobel Prize-winning mathematician who was diagnosed as suffering from schizophrenia, and who received the treatment (accessed 27 November 2007).

27. H. Bourne (1958), 'Insulin coma in decline', *American Journal of Psychiatry*, 114: 1015–17.

28. M. Tansella (2002), 'The scientific evaluation of mental health treatments: A historical perspective', *Evidence Based Mental Health*, 5: 4–5.

29. Freud, S. (1915), 'Introductory lectures on psychoanalysis', trans. J. Strachey, in *Collected Works*, London: Hogarth Press.

30. R. Leys (1981), 'Meyer's dealing with Jones: A chapter in the history of the American response to psychoanalysis', *Journal of the History of the Behavioural Sciences*, 17: 445–85.

31. See, for example, S. Freud (1933), *New Introductory Lectures in Psycho-analysis*, trans. J. Strachey, in *Collected Works*. London: Hogarth Press.

32. See S. Freud (1926/1959), *The Question of Lay Analysis: Conversations with an Impartial Person*, trans. J. Strachey, in *Collected Works*. London: Hogarth Press.

33. Shorter and Healy (2007), op. cit.

34. L. Johnson (2000), *Users and Abusers of Psychiatry*. Hove: Brunner-Routledge.

Chapter 3

1. T. Turner (2004), 'The history of deinstitutionalization and reinstitutionalization', *Psychiatry*, 3 (9): 1–4.

2. J. Geller (2000), 'The last half century of psychiatric services as reflected in *Psychiatric Services*', *Psychiatric Services*, 51: 41–67.

3. 'Insane hospital policies', *Guardian*, 22 May 1972; 'How many lost lives?', *Guardian*, 23 May 1972.

4. For discussion of some of these issues, see: A. Rogers and D. Pilgrim (2001), *Mental Health Policy in Britain*. Basingstoke: Palgrave; N. Crossley (2006), *Contesting Psychiatry: Social Movements in Mental Health*. London: Routledge.

5. A. Scull (1984), *Decarceration*. Englewood Cliffs, NJ: Prentice Hall.

6. Corporation for Public Broadcasting, 'The good war and those who refused

to fight it', http://www.pbs.org/itvs/thegoodwar (retrieved 10 January 2008).

7. E. Shorter (1997), *A History of Psychiatry*. New York: Wiley.

8. My account of the discovery of chlorpromazine is largely based on two sources: J. P. Swazey (1974), *Chlorpromazine in Psychiatry: A Study of Therapeutic Innovation*. Cambridge, Mass.: MIT Press; and D. Healy (2004), *The Creation of Psychopharmacology*. Boston, Mass.: Harvard University Press.

9. A. D. Smith (1995), 'Henri Laborit: In humanity's laboratory' (obituary), *Guardian* (14 June).

10. J. Moncrieff (2008), *The Myth of the Chemical Cure: A Critique of Psychiatric Drug Treatment*. London: Palgrave.

11. Healy (2004), op. cit.

12. H. Lehmann and D. Healy (1996), 'Psychopharmacotherapy' (interview), in D. Healy (ed.), *The Psychopharmacologists*. London: Chapman and Hall, pp. 159–86.

13. J. F. Casey et al. (1960), 'Drug therapy in schizophrenia: A controlled study of the relative effectiveness of chlorpromazine, promazine, phenobarbital, and placebo', *Archives of General Psychiatry*, 2: 210–20.

14. J. P. Leff and J. K. Wing (1971), 'Trial of maintenance therapy in schizophrenia' *British Medical Journal*, 3: 599–604.

15. D. J. Greenblatt and R. J. Shader (1971), 'Meprobamate: A study of irrational drug use', *American Journal of Psychiatry*, 127: 1297–1303.

16. The story of Kuhn's discovery is told in many places including: Healy (2004), op. cit.; S. H. Barondes (2003), *Better than Prozac: Creating the Next Generation of Psychiatric Drugs*. Oxford: Oxford University Press.

17. D. Healy (1997), *The Anti-depressant Era*. Cambridge, Mass.: Harvard University Press.

18. E. Shorter (1997), op. cit.

19. D. K. Routh (2000), 'Clinical psychology training: A history of ideas and practices before 1946', *American Psychologist*, 55: 236–41.

20. C. Hilton (2006), 'Mill Hill Emergency Hospital: 1939–1945', *Psychiatric Bulletin*, 30: 106–8.

21. M. Derksen (2001), 'Clinical psychology at the Maudsley', in G. C. Bunn, G. Richards and A. D. Lovie (eds.), *Psychology in Britain: Historical Essays and Personal Reflections*. Leicester: British Psychological Society, pp. 267–89.

22. L. T. Benjamine (2005), 'A history of clinical psychology in America', *Annual Review of Clinical Psychology*, 1: 1–30.

23. D. B. Baker and T. B. Ludy (2000), 'The affirmation of the scientist-practitioner: A look back at Boulder', *American Psychologist*, 55: 241–7.

24. Benjamine (2005), op. cit.

25. B. L. Hopkins (1970), 'The first twenty years are the hardest', in R. Ulrich, T. Stachnik and J. Mabry (eds.), *The Control of Human Behaviour*, volume 2: *From Cure to Prevention*. Glenview, Ill: Scott, Foresman & Co., pp. 358–65.

26. This was a position he developed throughout his life. See, for example, H. J. Eysenck and G. D. Wilson (eds.) (1973), *The Experimental Study of Freudian Theories*. London: Methuen; and also H. J. Eysenck (1985), *The Decline and Fall of the Freudian Empire*. Harmondsworth: Penguin.

27. H. J. Eysenck (1952), 'The effects of psychotherapy: An evaluation', *Journal of Consulting Psychology*, 16: 319–24.

28. J. B. Watson (1924), *Behaviorism*. New York: Norton.

29. P. Salkovskis (1998), 'Changing the face of psychotherapy and common sense: Joseph Wolpe, 20 April 1915–December 1997', *Behavioural and Cognitive Psychotherapy*, 26: 189–91.

30. J. Wolpe (1958), *Psychotherapy by Reciprocal Inhibition*. Stanford, Calif.: Stanford University Press.

31. B. F. Skinner (1948), *Walden Two*. New York: McMillan.

32. W. Isaacs, J. Thomas and I. Goldiamond (1960), 'Application of operant conditioning to reinstate verbal behaviour in psychotics', *Journal of Speech and Language Disorders*, 25: 8–12.

33. T. Ayllon and J. Michael (1959), 'The psychiatric nurse as behavioral engineer', *Journal of the Experimental Analysis of Behavior*, 2: 323–34.

34. For a recent case study which is remarkably similar to the report by Ayllon and Michael, see D. A. Wilder et al. (2001), 'Brief functional analysis and treatment of bizarre vocalizations in an adult with schizophrenia', *Journal of Applied Behavior Analysis*, 34: 65–8.

35. T. Ayllon and N. H. Azrin (1965), 'The measurement and reinforcement of behavior of psychotics', *Journal of the Experimental Analysis of Behavior*, 8: 365–85; T. Ayllon and N. H. Azrin (1968), *The Token Economy: A Motivational System for Therapy and Rehabilitation*. New York: Appleton-Century-Crofts.

36. A. E. Kazdin (1976), *The Token Economy: A Review and Evaluation*. New York: Plenum Press.

37. For a recent, up-beat assessment of this literature, see: S. Wong (2006), 'Behavior analysis of psychotic disorders: Scientific dead end or casualty of the mental health political economy?', *Behavior and Social Issues*, 15: 152–77. For a highly critical response to Wong, see J. C. Wakefield (2006), 'Is behaviorism becoming a pseudo-science? Power versus scientific rationality in the eclipse of token economies by biological psychiatry in the treatment of schizophrenia', *Behavior and Social Issues*, 15: 202–21.

38. G. L. Paul and R. J. Lenz (1977), *Psychosocial Treatment of Chronic Mental Patients: Milieu vs Social-learning Programs*. Cambridge, Mass.:

Harvard University Press. For a comprehensive and fairly positive review of controlled trials of token economy systems, see F. B. Dickerson, W. N. Tenhula and L. D. Green-Paden (2005), 'The token economy for schizophrenia: review of the literature and recommendations for future research', *Schizophrenia Research*, 75: 405–16.

39. My account of Rogers' life and work is largely taken from H. Kirschenbaum (2007), *The Life and Work of Carl Rogers*. Ross-on-Wye: PCCS Books.

40. J. Weizenbam (1966), 'ELIZA: A computer program for the study of natural language communication between man and machine', *Communications of the Association for Computing Machinery*, 9: 36–45.

41. A whole issue of the *Journal of Consulting Psychology* (volume 13, 1949) was devoted to papers describing research with these patients. Further studies were published in C. R. Rogers and R. Dymond (eds.) (1954), *Psychotherapy and Personality Change*. Chicago: University of Chicago Press.

42. C. R. Rogers (1956), 'Client centered therapy: A current view', in F. Fromm-Reichmann and J. Moreno (eds.), *Progress in Psychotherapy*. New York: Grune & Stratton, pp. 199–209.

43. C. R. Rogers (1957), 'The necessary and sufficient conditions of therapeutic personality change', *Journal of Consulting Psychology*, 21: 95–103.

44. C. R. Rogers et al. (eds.) (1967), *The Therapeutic Relationship and its Impact: A Study of Psychotherapy with Schizophrenics*. Madison: University of Wisconsin Press.

45. C. B. Traux (1966), 'Reinforcement and nonreinforcement in Rogerian psychotherapy', *Journal of Abnormal Psychology*, 71: 1–9.

46. R. D. Baker et al. (1977), 'Symptom changes in chronic schizophrenic patients on a token economy: A controlled experiment', *British Journal of Psychiatry*, 131: 381–93; J. N. Hall, R. D. Baker and K. Hutchinson (1977), 'A controlled evaluation of token economy procedures with chronic schizophrenic patients', *Behaviour Research and Therapy*, 15: 261–83.

47. E. Kruno and N. Asukai (2000), 'Efforts towards building a community-based mental health system in Japan', *International Journal of Law and Psychiatry*, 23, 361–73; K. J. Tsuchiya and N. Takei, 'Focus of psychiatry, in Japan', *British Journal of Psychiatry*, 184: 88–92.

48. A. S. Bellack (1986), 'Schizophrenia: Behavior therapy's forgotten child', *Behavior Therapy*, 17: 199–214.

49. Dickerson, Tenhula and Green-Paden (2005), op. cit.; Wong (2006), op. cit.

50. Wakefield (2006), op. cit.

51. D. L. Rosenhan (1973), 'On being sane in insane places', *Science*, 179: 250–58.

Chapter 4

1. A monograph by Hans Eysenck advocating a divorce between the two professions (H. J. Eysenck (1976), *The Future of Psychiatry*. London: Methuen) was soon followed by a review of clinical psychology working practices by the UK Department of Health (the Trethowan Report, published in 1977). Psychologists who were expecting that the status quo would be maintained were delighted when the report recommended that they should work independently in their own outpatient departments, where they would take referrals directly from family doctors. In the following years some psychiatrists flouted these recommendations by insisting to family doctors that they could only refer to psychologists patients who had first been assessed and recommended for psychological treatment by a psychiatrist (an obvious waste of everyone's time). Psychologists working in these areas found that they had to lobby health service managers to ensure that the new rules were followed; in some places this took many years.

2. R. D. Buchanan (2003), 'Legislative warriors: American psychiatrists, psychologists, and competing claims over psychotherapy in the 1950s', *Journal of the History of the Behavioural Sciences*, 39: 225–49.

3. D. Cooper (1967), *Psychiatry and Antipsychiatry*. London: Tavistock Press.

4. For sociological works that were highly critical of psychiatry, see: I. Goffman (1970), *Asylums*. London: Penguin Press; and T. Scheff (1966), *Being Mentally Ill: A Sociological Theory*. Chicago: Aldine. The French philosopher Michel Foucault is sometimes identified with the antipsychiatric movement following his historical study *Madness and Civilisation* (New York: Random House, 1961), which traced the development of ideas about mental illness from the Middle Ages to modern times.

5. For a discussion of this issue, see N. Crossley (2006), *Contesting Psychiatry: Social Movements in Mental Health*. London: Routledge.

6. My account of Laing's life is taken from J. Clay (1996), *R. D. Laing: A Divided Self*. London: Hodder and Stoughton.

7. R. D. Laing (1960), *The Divided Self*. London: Tavistock Press.

8. R. D. Laing and A. Esterson (1964), *Sanity, Madness and the Family: Families of Schizophrenics*. London: Tavistock.

9. For a detailed critique of Laing, which makes this point amongst others, see P. Sedgwick (1982), *Psychopolitics*. London: Pluto Press. Sedgwick was a left-wing activist and academic, who argued that we need more and better psychiatry rather than the loosely reasoned ideas of the antipsychiatry move-

ment. Sadly, he died (probably from suicide – his body was found in a canal) in 1983.

10. R. D. Laing (1967), *The Politics of Experience and the Bird of Paradise*. London: Penguin Press.

11. M. Barnes and J. Berke (1973), *Mary Barnes: Two Accounts of a Journey through Madness*. London: Penguin.

12. T. S. Szasz (1960), 'The myth of mental illness', *American Psychologist*, 15: 564–80; T. S. Szasz (1979), *Schizophrenia: The Sacred Symbol of Psychiatry*. Oxford: Oxford University Press. For an evaluation of Szasz's claims, see R. P. Bentall (2004), 'Sideshow?: Schizophrenia as construed by Szasz and the neoKraepelinians', in J. Schaler (ed.), *Szasz under Fire*. Chicago: Open Court, pp. 301–20.

13. T. S. Szasz (1960), op. cit.

14. H. Kirschenbaum (2007), *The Life and Work of Carl Rogers*. Ross-on-Wye: PCCS Books.

15. See, for example, Schaler (ed.) (2004), op. cit.

16. A. W. Clare (1980), *Psychiatry in Dissent*. London: Tavistock Press.

17. F. G. Glaser (1965), 'The dichotomy game: A further consideration of the writings of Dr Thomas Szasz', *American Journal of Psychiatry*, 121: 1069–74.

18. Clay (1996), op. cit.

19. G. B. Alermo (1991), 'The 1978 Italian Mental Health Law – a personal evaluation: A review', *Journal of the Royal Society of Medicine*, 84: 99–102.

20. L. Buti (2001), 'Italian psychiatric reform 20 plus years after', *Acta Psychiatrica Scandinavica*, 104 suppl. 410: 41–6.

21. For a detailed discussion of the little-recognized common ground between Szasz and biological psychiatrists, see Bentall, in Schaler (2004), op. cit. A problem with equating illness or disease with physical pathology is that it assumes that physical pathology is a morally unambiguous concept. However, even in physical medicine, abnormal (in the statistical sense) characteristics of the body are considered pathological only when they cause harm. If the only consequence of a swollen appendix was an immediate doubling of IQ, appendicitis would not be considered a disease.

22. P. Connell (1958), *Amphetamine Psychosis*. London: Chapman and Hall. Connell's observations were followed up by researchers in America, who asked medical students to take large doses of amphetamine so that they could observe the effects. See, for example, B. M. Angrist and S. Gershon (1970), 'The phenomonenology of experimentally induced amphetamine psychosis – preliminary observations', *Biological Psychiatry*, 2: 95–107.

23. P. Seeman et al. (1976), 'Antipsychotic drug dose and neuroleptic/dopamine receptors', *Nature*, 261: 717–19.

24. A. Coppen (1967), 'The biochemistry of affective disorders', *British Journal of Psychiatry*, 113: 1237–64.

25. For a detailed discussion of this issue, see J. Moncrieff (2008), *The Myth of the Chemical Cure: A Critique of Psychiatric Drug Treatment*. London: Palgrave.

26. J. R. Lacasse and J. Leo (2005), 'Serotonin and depression: A disconnect between the advertisements and the scientific literature', *PLoS Medicine*, 2: e392. J. Leo and J. R. Lacasse (2007), 'The media and the chemical imbalance theory of depression', *Society*, 45: 35–45.

27. S. Kety et al. (1976), 'Mental illness in the biological and adoptive families of adopted individuals who have become schizophrenic', *Behavior Genetics*, 6: 219–25; D. Rosenthal et al. (1971), 'The adopted away offspring of schizophrenics', *American Journal of Psychiatry*, 128: 307–11.

28. S. S. Kety (1974), 'From rationalization to reason', *American Journal of Psychiatry*, 131: 957–63.

29. E. C. Johnston et al. (1976), 'Cerebral ventricular size and cognitive impairment in chronic schizophrenia', *Lancet*, 2: 924–6.

30. American Psychiatric Association (1980), *Diagnostic and Statistical Manual of Mental Disorders*, 3rd edition. Washington, DC: American Psychiatric Association.

31. S. Guze (1989), 'Biological psychiatry: Is there any other kind?', *Psychological Medicine*, 19: 315–23.

32. G. L. Klerman (1978), 'The evolution of a scientific nosology', in J. C. Shershow (ed.), *Schizophrenia: Science and Practice*. Cambridge, Mass.: Harvard University Press, pp. 99–121.

33. N. C. Andreasen (1984), *The Broken Brain: The Biological Revolution in Psychiatry*. New York: Harper and Row.

34. D. Healy (1997), *The Anti-depressant Era*. Cambridge, Mass.: Harvard University Press.

35. G. L. Klerman (1990), 'The psychiatric patient's right to effective treatment: Implications of Osheroff v. Chestnut Lodge', *American Journal of Psychiatry*, 147: 409–18.

36. A. A. Stone (1990), 'Law, science and psychiatric malpractice: A response to Klerman's indictment of psychoanalytic psychiatry', *American Journal of Psychiatry*, 147: 419–27.

37. Klerman (1990), op. cit.

38. C. R. Rogers et al. (eds.) (1967), *The Therapeutic Relationship and its Impact: A Study of Psychotherapy with Schizophrenics*. Madison: University of Wisconsin Press.

39. P. R. A. May (1968), *Treatment of Schizophrenia: A Comparative Study of Five Treatment Methods*. New York: Science House.

40. A. H. Stanton et al. (1984), 'Effects of psychotherapy in schizophrenia: I. Design and implementation of a controlled study', *Schizophrenia Bulletin*, 10: 520–63; J. G. Gunderson et al. (1984), 'Effects of psychotherapy in schizophrenia: II. Comparative outcome of two forms of treatment', *Schizophrenia Bulletin*, 10: 564–98.

41. T. H. McGlashan (1984), 'The Chestnut Lodge follow-up study I: Follow-up methodology and study sample', *Archives of General Psychiatry*, 41: 575–85; T. H. McGlashan (1984), 'The Chestnut Lodge follow-up study II: Long-term outcome of schizophrenia and affective disorders', *Archives of General Psychiatry*, 41: 586–601.

42. B. Carey (2006), 'A career that has mirrored psychiatry's twisting path', *New York Times* (23 May).

43. S. A. Kirk and H. Kutchins (1992), *The Selling of DSM: The Rhetoric of Science in Psychiatry*. Hawthorne, NY: Aldine de Gruyter.

44. The debate about training psychologists to prescribe is ongoing, and can be accessed at many websites. My own view is mixed. One advantage of having a prescription pad would be that it would accord the psychologist un-prescribing rights (that is, the right to reduce medication when a patient is obviously receiving no benefit from it). My main worry is that prescribing psychologists might forget their roots in psychology, and become cheap psychiatrists who, like the expensive kind, resort to drugs at the first opportunity.

In the United States, arguments about psychologists prescribing have focused more on safety (psychiatrists claiming that prescribing psychologists might harm their patients) and access to mental health services (psychologists claiming that poor people living in rural areas have great difficulty obtaining psychiatric treatment). Both these arguments strike me as bogus. Nurses and ophthalmologists prescribe in most US states, and no one is arguing that they are dangerous because they have not been through medical school; besides, as we shall see in Chapter 9, there is plenty of evidence that psychiatrists are harming patients by their excessive reliance on drugs. As for access to mental health services in rural areas, I suspect that most American clinical psychologists, like psychiatrists, work in the large cities.

For a recent academic article discussing the pros and cons of this initiative, see: K. L. Lavoie and B. Silvana (2006), 'Prescription privileges for psychologists: A comprehensive review and critical analysis of current issues and controversies', *CNS Drugs*, 20: 51–66.

45. See, for example, D. Blazer (2005), *The Age of Melancholy: Major Depression and its Social Origins*. New York: Routledge; R. Muller (2007), *Doing Psychiatry Wrong: A Critical and Prescriptive Look at a Faltering Profession*. New York: Analytic Press. See also (written by two academic social workers who work closely with psychiatrists), A. V. Horwitz and J. C. Wakefield (2007), *The Loss of Sadness: How Psychiatry Transformed Normal Sorrow into Depressive Illness*. New York: Oxford University Press.

46. S. S. Sharfstein (2005), 'Big Pharma and American psychiatry: The good, the bad, and the ugly', *Psychiatric News*, 40: 3.

47. L. Slater (2004), *Opening Skinner's Box: Great Psychological Experiments of the Twentieth Century*. London: Bloomsbury.

48. R. McCabe et al. (2004), 'Engagement of patients with psychosis in consultation: Conversation analytic study', *British Medical Journal*, 325: 1148–51.

Chapter 5

1. G. L. Klerman (1978), 'The evolution of a scientific nosology', in J. C. Shershow (ed.), *Schizophrenia: Science and Practice*. Cambridge, Mass.: Harvard University Press, pp. 99–121.

2. World Health Organization (1992), *International Statistical Classification of Diseases and Related Health Problems*, 10th revision edition. Geneva: World Health Organization (*ICD-10*).

3. D. Healy (2004), *Let Them Eat Prozac: The Unhealthy Relationship between the Pharmaceutical Industry and Depression*. New York: New York University Press.

4. E. Bleuler (1911/1950), *Dementia praecox or the Group of Schizophrenias*, trans. E. Zinkin. New York: International Universities Press.

5. K. Schneider (1959), *Clinical Psychopathology*. New York: Grune & Stratton.

6. K. Leonhard (1957), *The Classification of Endogenous Psychoses*, 5th edition. New York: Irvington.

7. American Psychiatric Association (1980), *Diagnostic and Statistical Manual of Mental Disorders*, 3rd edition. Washington, DC: American Psychiatric Association (*DSM-III*).

8. R. L. Spitzer and J. L. Fliess (1974), 'A reanalysis of the reliability of psychiatric diagnosis', *British Journal of Psychiatry*, 123: 341–7.

9. J. E. Cooper et al. (1972), *Psychiatric Diagnosis in New York and London*, Maudsley Monograph, no. 20. Oxford: Oxford University Press. World Health Organization (1973), *International Pilot Study of Schizophrenia*. Geneva: World Health Organization.

10. For histories of *DSM-III* and the neo-Kraepelinian movement, see: R. K. Blashfield (1984), *The Classification of Psychopathology: NeoKraepelinian and Quantitative Approaches*. New York: Plenum; S. A. Kirk and H. Kutchins

(1992), *The Selling of DSM: The Rhetoric of Science in Psychiatry*. Hawthorne, NY: Aldine de Gruyter; H. Kutchins and S. A. Kirk (1997), *Making Us Crazy: DSM – the Psychiatric Bible and the Creation of Mental Disorders*. New York: Free Press. These issues are also dealt with in some detail in my book, R. P. Bentall (2003), *Madness Explained: Psychosis and Human Nature*. London: Penguin.

11. S. Hyler, J. Williams and R. Spitzer (1982), 'Reliability in the DSM-III field trials', *Archives of General Psychiatry*, 39: 1275–8. For a similar claim by another neo-Kraepelinian, see: G. Klerman (1986), 'Historical perspectives on contemporary schools of psychopathology', in T. Millon and G. Klerman (eds.), *Contemporary Directions in Psychopathology: Towards DSM-IV*. New York: Guilford Press.

12. R. L. Spitzer et al. (1992), 'The Structured Clinical Interview for DSM-III-R (SCID). I: History, rationale, and description', *Archives of General Psychiatry*, 49: 624–9.

13. S. R. Kay and L. A. Opler (1987), 'The Positive and Negative Syndrome Scale (PANSS) for schizophrenia', *Schizophrenia Bulletin*, 13: 507–18.

14. World Health Organization (1999), *Schedules for Clinical Assessment in Neuropsychiatry*. Geneva: World Health Organization.

15. R. L. Spitzer and J. L. Fliess (1974), 'A reanalysis of the reliability of psychiatric diagnosis', *British Journal of Psychiatry*, 123: 341–7.

16. Kirk and Kutchins (1992), op. cit.

17. P. D. McGorry et al. (1995), 'Spurious precision: Procedural validity of diagnostic assessment in psychotic disorders', *American Journal of Psychiatry*, 152: 220–23.

18. American Psychiatric Association (1987), *Diagnostic and Statistical Manual of Mental Disorders*, revised 3rd edition. Washington DC: American Psychiatric Association (*DSM-III-R*). American Psychiatric Association (1994), *Diagnostic and Statistical Manual for Mental Disorders*, 4th edition. Washington DC: American Psychiatric Association (*DSM-IV*). American Psychiatric Association (2000), *Diagnostic and statistical manual for mental disorders*, 4th edition – text revision. Washington DC: American Psychiatric Association (*DSM-IV-TR*).

19. World Health Organization (1992), op. cit.

20. I. Brockington (1992), 'Schizophrenia: Yesterday's concept', *European Psychiatry*, 7: 203–7.

21. Ibid.

22. J. van Os et al. (1999), 'A comparison of the utility of dimensional and categorical representations of psychosis', *Psychological Medicine*, 29: 595–606.

23. A. Jablensky (1995), 'Schizophrenia: The epidemiological horizon', in

S. R. Hirsch and D. R. Weinberger (eds.), *Schizophrenia*. Oxford: Blackwell, pp. 206–52.

24. F. K. Goodwin and K. R. Jamison (1990), *Manic-depressive Illness*. Oxford: Oxford University Press.

25. J. Kasanin (1933), 'The acute schizoaffective psychoses', *American Journal of Psychiatry*, 90: 97–126.

26. R. E. Kendell (1991), 'The major functional psychoses: Are they independent entities or part of a continuum? Philosophical and conceptual issues underlying the debate', in A. Kerr and H. McClelland (eds.), *Concepts of Mental Disorder: A Continuing Debate*. London: Gaskell, pp. 1–16.

27. L. N. Robins and B. Z. Locke (eds.) (1991), *Psychiatric Disorders in America*. New York: Free Press.

28. P. Tyrer (1990), 'The division of neurosis: A failed classification', *Journal of the Royal Society of Medicine*, 83: 614–16; C. Dowrick (2004), *Beyond Depression: A New Approach to Understanding and Management*. Oxford: Oxford University Press; D. Goldberg and I. Goodyer (2005), *The Origins and Course of Common Mental Disorders*. London: Routledge.

29. T. V. Moore (1930), 'The empirical determination of certain syndromes underlying praecox and manic-depressive psychoses,' *American Journal of Psychiatry*, 86: 719–38.

30. P. F. Liddle (1987), 'The symptoms of chronic schizophrenia: A reexamination of the positive-negative dichotomy', *British Journal of Psychiatry*, 151: 145–51.

31. V. Peralta and M. J. Cuesta (2001), 'How many and which are the psychopathological dimensions in schizophrenia? Issues influencing their ascertainment', *Schizophrenia Research*, 49: 269–85; J. Blanchard and A. S. Cohen (2006), 'The structure of negative symptoms within schizophrenia: Implications for assessment', *Schizophrenia Bulletin*, 32: 238–45.

32. See for example: R. Toomey et al. (1998), 'Negative, positive and disorganized symptom dimensions in schizophrenia, major depression and bipolar disorder', *Journal of Nervous and Mental Disease*, 186: 470–76; P. D. McGorry et al. (1998), 'The dimensional structure of first episode psychosis: An exploratory factor analysis', *Psychological Medicine*, 28: 935–47. For more details, see Bentall (2003), op. cit.

33. J. Allardyce, T. Suppes and J. van Os (2007), 'Dimensions of the psychosis phenotype', *International Journal of Methods in Psychiatric Research*, 16: S34–S40.

34. M. Tsuang, R. F. Woolson and J. A. Fleming (1979), 'Long-term outcome of major psychoses: I. Schizophrenia and affective disorders compared with psychiatrically symptom-free surgical conditions', *Archives of General Psychiatry*, 36: 1295–1301.

35. L. Ciompi (1984), 'Is there really a schizophrenia?: The longterm course of psychotic phenomena', *British Journal of Psychiatry*, 145: 636–40; Goodwin and Jamison (1990), op. cit.

36. N. Sartorius et al. (1987), 'Course of schizophrenia in different countries: Some results of a WHO comparative 5-year follow-up study', in H. Hafner, W. G. Gattaz and W. Janzarik (eds.), *Search for the Causes of Schizophrenia*, volume 16. Berlin: Springer, pp. 909–28.

37. T. Crow (1991), 'The failure of the binary concept and the psychosis gene', in Kerr and McClelland (eds.), op. cit., pp. 31–47.

38. R. E. Kendell and I. F. Brockington (1980), 'The identification of disease entities and the relationship between schizophrenic and affective psychoses', *British Journal of Psychiatry*, 137: 324–31.

39. E. C. Johnstone et al. (1988), 'The Northwick Park "functional" psychosis study: Diagnosis and treatment response', *Lancet*, 2: 119–25.

40. C. A. Tamminga and J. M. Davis (2007), 'The neuropharmacology of psychosis', *Schizophrenia Bulletin*, 33: 937–46.

41. M. Romme and A. Escher (1989), 'Hearing voices', *Schizophrenia Bulletin*, 15: 209–16.

42. J. Jaynes (1979), *The Origins of Consciousness in the Breakdown of Bicameral Mind*. London: Penguin.

43. A. Honig et al. (1998), 'Auditory hallucinations: A comparison between patients and nonpatients', *Journal of Nervous and Mental Disease*, 186: 646–51. In a recent study of a group of eighty adolescents hearing voices, Romme and Escher found that in approximately 60 per cent the hallucinations discontinued within a three-year period, and that only those who experienced their voices as intrusive or omnipotent tended to seek help. See S. Escher et al. (2002), 'Independent course of childhood auditory hallucinations: A sequential 3-year follow-up study', *British Journal of Psychiatry*, 181, Suppl. 43, s10–s18.

44. This issue has been addressed by a number of British clinical psychologists. See especially P. Chadwick and M. Birchwood (1994), 'The omnipotence of voices: A cognitive approach to auditory hallucinations', *British Journal of Psychiatry*, 164: 190–201; A. P. Morrison (2001), 'The interpretation of intrusions in psychosis: An integrative cognitive approach to hallucinations and delusions', *Behavioural and Cognitive Psychotherapy*, 29: 257–76.

45. The website for the British Hearing Voices Network can be found at www.hearing-voices.org (accessed 29 January 2009). The US Hearing Voices Network can be found at www.hva-usa.org (accessed 29 January 2009).

46. A. Y. Tien (1991), 'Distribution of hallucinations in the population', *Social Psychiatry and Psychiatric Epidemiology*, 26: 287–92.

47. J. van Os et al. (2000), 'Strauss (1969) revisited: A psychosis continuum in the normal population?' *Schizophrenia Research*, 45: 11–20.

48. J. Angst (1998), 'The emerging epidemiology of hypomania and bipolar II disorder', *Journal of Affective Disorders*, 50: 143–51; J. Angst (2005), 'The mood spectrum: Improving the diagnosis of bipolar disorder', *Bipolar Disorders*, 7: 4–12.

49. The continuum between normal functioning and psychosis has been much investigated by personality theorists, who have found that it is ridiculously easy to devise questionnaires that measure psychotic or 'schizotypal' experiences in ordinary people. Interestingly, factor analyses of these measures reveal that they break down into three main dimensions corresponding to the factors extracted when patients' symptoms are analysed: unusual experiences (corresponding to positive symptoms), introverted anhedonia (corresponding to negative symptoms) and cognitive disorganization. It has been found that individuals scoring high on these measures perform similarly to psychotic patients on a wide range of tests. For reviews of this research, see G. Claridge and C. Davis (2003), *Personality and Psychological Disorders*. London: Arnold; A. Raine (2006), 'Schizotypal personality: Neurodevelopmental and psychological trajectories', *Annual Review of Clinical Psychology*, 2: 291–326.

50. G. S. Claridge (1998), 'Creativity and madness: Clues from modern psychiatric diagnosis', in A. Steptoe (ed.), *Genius and the Mind*. Oxford: Oxford University Press. The link between creativity and psychosis is also discussed at length in Bentall (2003), op. cit.

51. J. Berkson (1946), 'Limitations of the application of the fourfold table analysis to hospital data', *Biometrics*, 2: 47–53. See also J. Schwatzbaum, A. Anders and M. Feychting (2003), 'Berkson's bias reviewed', *European Journal of Epidemiology*, 18: 1109–12.

52. N. Maric et al. (2004), 'Is our concept of schizophrenia influenced by Berkson's bias?', *Social Psychiatry and Psychiatric Epidemiology*, 39: 600–605.

53. E. J. Regeer et al. (in press), 'Berkson's Bias and the mood dimensions of bipolar disorder', *International Journal of Methods in Psychiatric Research*.

54. O. Yazici et al. (2002), 'Unipolar mania: A distinct disorder?', *Journal of Affective Disorders*, 71: 97–103; D. A. Solomon et al. (2003), 'Unipolar mania over the course of a 20-year follow-up study', *American Journal of Psychiatry*, 160: 2049–51.

55. M. Boyle (1990), *Schizophrenia: A Scientific Delusion*. London: Routledge.

56. R. P. Bentall, H. F. Jackson and D. Pilgrim (1988), 'Abandoning the

concept of schizophrenia: Some implications of validity arguments for psychological research into psychotic phenomena', *British Journal of Clinical Psychology*, 27: 303–24.

57. J. A. Lieberman and M. B. First (2007), 'Renaming schizophrenia: Diagnosis and treatment are more important than semantics', *British Medical Journal*, 334: 108.

58. M. First et al. (1995), *Structured Clinical Interview for Axis I DSM-IV Disorders*. Washington, DC: American Psychiatric Association Press.

59. H. S. Akiskal et al. (2005), 'Agitated "unipolar" depression reconceptualized as a depressive mixed state: Implications for the antidepressant suicide controversy', *Journal of Affective Disorders*, 85: 245–58. See also J. Cole, P. McGuffin and A. E. Farmer (2008), 'The classification of depression: Are we still confused?', *British Journal of Psychiatry*, 192: 83–5.

60. H. S. Akiskal et al. (2000), 'Re-evaluating the prevalence of and diagnostic composition within the broad clinical spectrum of bipolar disorders', *Journal of Affective Disorders*, 59, s5–s30.

61. Quoted in E. Shorter (1997), *A History of Psychiatry*. New York: Wiley. D. Double (1990), 'What would Adolf Meyer have thought of the neo-Kraepalinian approach?' *Psychiatric Bulletin*, 14: 472–4.

Chapter 6

1. Interview in the *Sunday Telegraph*, 16 February 1997. Watson shared the 1962 Nobel Prize with Francis Crick and Maurice Wilkin for working out the structure of DNA.

2. L. Ross (1977), 'The intuitive psychologist and his shortcomings: Distortions in the attribution process', in L. Berkowitz (ed.), *Advances in Experimental Social Psychology*, volume 10. New York: Academic Press, pp. 173–220.

3. A. F. Mirsky et al. (2000), 'A 39-year follow-up of the Genain quadruplets', *Schizophrenia Bulletin*, 26: 699–708; A. F. Mirsky and O. W. Quinn (1988), 'The Genain quadruplets', *Schizophrenia Bulletin*, 14: 595–611.

4. D. Rosenthal and O. W. Quinn (1977), 'Quadruplet hallucinations: Phenotypic variations of a schizophrenic genotype?', *Archives of General Psychiatry*, 34: 817–27.

5. R. Marshall (1990), 'The genetics of schizophrenia: Axiom or hypothesis?', in R. P. Bentall (ed.), *Reconstructing Schizophrenia*. London: Routledge, pp. 89–117.

6. E. F. Torrey et al. (1994), *Schizophrenia and Manic-depressive Disorder*. New York: Basic Books.

7. J.-E. Meyer (1988), 'The fate of the mentally ill in Germany during the Third Reich', *Psychological Medicine*, 18: 575–81; R. N. Proctor (1988), *Racial Hygiene: Medicine under the Nazis*. Cambridge, Mass.: Harvard University Press.

8. F. Kallmann (1938), *The Genetics of Schizophrenia*. New York: J. J. Angustine.

9. J. Read and N. Haslam (2004), 'Public opinion: Bad things happen and can drive you crazy', in J. Read, L. R. Mosher and R. P. Bentall (eds.), *Models of Madness: Psychological, Social and Biological Approaches to Schizophrenia*. London: Routledge, pp. 133–45.

10. For a compelling account of the search for the Huntington's gene, see S. H. Barondes (1998), *Mood Genes: Hunting for the Origins of Mania and Depression*. Oxford: Oxford University Press.

11. S. Rose, L. J. Kamin and R. C. Lewontin (1985), *Not in our Genes*. Harmondsworth: Penguin.

12. K. L. Jang (2005), *The Behavioral Genetics of Psychiatric Disorders*. Mahwah, NJ: Erlbaum.

13. S. S. Kety (1974), 'From rationalization to reason', *American Journal of Psychiatry*, 131: 957–63.

14. J. Joseph (2003), *The Gene Illusion: Genetic Research in Psychology and Psychiatry under the Microscope*. Ross-on-Wye: PCCS Books.

15. E. Turkheimer et al. (2005), 'Analysis and interpretation of twin studies including measures of the shared environment', *Child Development*, 76: 1217–33; E. Turkheimer et al. (2003), 'Socioeconomic status modifies heritability of IQ in young children', *Psychological Science*, 14: 623–8.

16. S. Rose (2001), 'Moving on from old dichotomies: Beyond nature-nurture towards a lifeline perspective', *British Journal of Psychiatry*, 178, suppl. 40: 3–7.

17. For an introduction to Freud's views about transference, see S. Freud (1915/1963), *Introductory Lectures on Psychoanalysis*, trans. J. Strachey, in *Collected Works*. London: Hogarth Press. For a more general review of ideas about transference and the relationship, see A. O. Horvath (2000), 'The therapeutic relationship: From transference to alliance', *Journal of Clinical Psychology*, 56: 163–73.

18. J. W. Ellason and C. A. Ross (1997), 'Childhood trauma and psychiatric symptoms', *Psychological Reports*, 80: 447–50; L. A. Goodman et al. (2001), 'Recent victimization in women and men with severe mental illness: Prevalence and correlates', *Journal of Traumatic Stress*, 14: 615–32; K. T. Mueser et al. (1998), 'Trauma and posttraumatic stress disorder in severe mental illness', *Journal of Consulting and Clinical Psychology*, 66: 493–9.

19. Y. Neria et al. (2002), 'Trauma exposure and posttraumatic stress

disorder in psychosis: Findings from a first-admission cohort', *Journal of Consulting and Clinical Psychology*, 70: 246–51.

20. For reviews, see: L. A. Goodman et al. (1997), 'Physical and sexual assault history in women with serious mental illness: Prevalence, correlates, treatment, and future research directions', *Schizophrenia Bulletin*, 23: 685–96; J. Read et al. (2005), 'Childhood trauma, psychosis and schizophrenia: A literature review and clinical implications', *Acta Psychiatrica Scandinavica*, 112: 330–50.

21. P. Bebbington et al. (2004), 'Psychosis, victimisation and childhood disadvantage: Evidence from the second British National Survey of Psychiatric Morbidity', *British Journal of Psychiatry*, 185: 220–26.

22. For example, T. Latasker et al. (2006), 'Childhood victimisation and developmental expression of non-clinical delusional ideation and hallucinatory experiences: Victimisation and non-clinical psychotic experiences', *Social Psychiatry and Psychiatric Epidemiology*, 41: 423–8.

23. I. Janssen et al. (2004), 'Childhood abuse as a risk factor for psychotic experiences', *Acta Psychiatrica Scandinavica*, 109: 38–45.

24. A. Honig et al. (1998), 'Auditory hallucinations: A comparison between patients and nonpatients', *Journal of Nervous and Mental Disease*, 186: 646–51.

25. E. Ensink (1993), 'Trauma: A study of child abuse and hallucinations', in M. Romme and S. Escher (eds.), *Accepting Voices*. London: Mind Publications, pp. 165–71; A. Kilcommons and A. P. Morrison (2005), 'Relationship between trauma and psychosis: An exploration of cognitive and dissociative factors', *Acta Psychiatrica Scandinavica*, 112: 351–9; J. Read et al. (2003), 'Sexual and physical abuse during childhood and adulthood as predictors of hallucinations, delusions and thought disorder', *Psychology and Psychotherapy: Theory, Research and Practice*, 76: 1–22; C. A. Ross, G. Anderson and P. Clark (1994), 'Childhood abuse and the positive symptoms of schizophrenia', *Hospital and Community Psychiatry*, 42: 489–91.

26. M. Shevlin, M. Dorahy and G. Adamson (2007), 'Childhood traumas and hallucinations: An analysis of the National Comorbidity Survey', *Journal of Psychiatric Research*, 41: 222–8.

27. P. Hammersley et al. (2003), 'Childhood trauma and hallucinations in bipolar affective disorder: A preliminary investigation', *British Journal of Psychiatry*, 182: 543–7.

28. J. Mirowsky and C. E. Ross (1983), 'Paranoia and the structure of powerlessness', *American Sociological Review*, 48: 228–39.

29. I. Janssen et al. (2003), 'Discrimination and delusional ideation', *British Journal of Psychiatry*, 182: 71–6.

30. T. Fuchs (1999), 'Life events in late paraphrenia and depression', *Psychopathology*, 32: 60–69.

31. G. Harrison et al. (1988), 'A prospective study of severe mental disorder in Afro-Caribbean patients', *Psychological Medicine*, 18: 643–57.

32. D. Bhugra et al. (1996), 'First contact incidence rates of schizophrenia in Trinidad and one-year follow-up', *British Journal of Psychiatry*, 169: 587–92; D. Bhugra et al. (1999), 'First-contact incidence rate of schizophrenia on Barbados', *British Journal of Psychiatry*, 175: 28–33.

33. J. B. Kirkbride et al. (2006), 'Heterogeneity in incidence rates of schizophrenia and other psychotic syndromes: Findings from the 3-center AESOP study', *Archives of General Psychiatry*, 63: 250–58. J.-P. Selten et al. (2001), 'Incidence of psychotic disorders in immigrant groups to The Netherlands', *British Journal of Psychiatry*, 178: 367–72.

34. J. Boydell et al. (2001), 'Incidence of schizophrenia in ethnic minorities in London: Ecological study into interactions with environment', *British Medical Journal*, 323: 1–4.

35. R. E. L. Faris and H. W. Dunham (1939), *Mental Disorders in Urban Areas*. Chicago: Chicago University Press.

36. J. van Os (2004), 'Does the urban environment cause psychosis?', *British Journal of Psychiatry*, 184: 287–8.

37. C. B. Pedersen and P. B. Mortensen (2001), 'Evidence of a dose-response relationship between urbanicity during upbringing and schizophrenia risk', *Archives of General Psychiatry*, 58: 1039–46.

38. Researchers have attempted to test this hypothesis, for example by analysing stored sera collected from children who later became psychotic, or from their mothers on the assumption that a maternal infection might have been passed across the womb to the foetus of the future patient. The results so far look mixed, with some studies apparently supporting the idea that viral damage to the brain might cause children to become psychotic (e.g. C. Dalman et al. (2008), 'Infections in the CNS during childhood and the risk of subsequent psychotic illness: A cohort study of more than one million Swedish subjects', *American Journal of Psychiatry*, 165: 59–65) and others finding no such effect (e.g. A. S. Brown et al. (2006), 'No evidence of relation between maternal exposure to herpes simplex virus type 2 and risk of schizophrenia?', *American Journal of Psychiatry*, 163: 2178–80).

39. Examples of this kind of theorizing are: G. Bateson et al. (1956), 'Towards a theory of schizophrenia', *Behavioral Science*, 1: 251–64; R. D. Laing and A. Esterson (1969), *Sanity, Madness and the Family: Families of Schizophrenics*, 2nd edition. London: Tavistock.

40. G. W. Brown, M. Carstairs, and G. Topping (1958), 'Post hospital adjustment of chronic mental patients', *Lancet*, 2: 685–9.

41. For example, G. W. Brown and M. Rutter (1966), 'The measurement of family activities and relationships: A methodological study', *Human Relations*, 19: 241–63; C. E. Vaughn and J. Leff (1976), 'The influence of family and social factors on the course of psychiatric illness: A comparison of schizophrenic and depressed neurotic patients', *British Journal of Psychiatry*, 129: 125–37; J. P. Leff and C. Vaughn (1980), 'The interaction of life-events and relatives' expressed emotion in schizophrenia and depressive neurosis', *British Journal of Psychiatry*, 136: 146–53.

42. For a systematic review of the very substantial research in this area, see R. L. Butzlaff and J. M. Hooley (1998), 'Expressed emotion and psychiatric relapse', *Archives of General Psychiatry*, 55: 547–52.

43. J. M. Hooley, J. Orley and J. D. Teasdale (1989), 'Predictors of relapse in unipolar depressives: Expressed emotion, marital distress and perceived criticism', *Journal of Abnormal Psychology*, 98: 229–37.

44. D. J. Miklowitz et al. (1988), 'Family factors and the course of bipolar affective disorder', *Archives of General Psychiatry*, 45: 225–31.

45. L. J. Yan et al. (2004), 'Expressed emotion versus relationship quality variables in the prediction of recurrence in bipolar patients', *Journal of Affective Disorders*, 83: 199–206.

46. D. L. Chambless and G. Steketee (1999), 'Expressed emotion and outcome for behavior therapy for agoraphobia and obsessive-compulsive disorder', *Journal of Consulting and Clinical Psychology*, 67: 658–65.

47. C. Barrowclough et al. (2003), 'Self-esteem in schizophrenia: The relationship between self-evaluation, family attitudes and symptomatology', *Journal of Abnormal Psychology*, 112: 92–9.

48. For example, E. Kuipers and D. Raune (2000), 'The early development of expressed emotion and burden in the families of first-onset psychosis', in M. Birchwood, D. Fowler and C. Jackson (eds.), *Early Intervention in Psychosis*. London: Wiley, pp. 128–40.

49. J. A. Doane et al. (1981), 'Parental communication deviance and affective style', *Archives of General Psychiatry*, 38: 679–85; M. J. Goldstein (1987), 'The UCLA high-risk project', *Schizophrenia Bulletin*, 13: 505–14; M. J. Goldstein (1998), 'Adolescent behavioral and intrafamilial precursors of schizophrenia spectrum disorders', *International Clinical Psychopharmacology*, 13, suppl. 1: 101.

50. W. L. Cook et al. (1989), 'Expressed emotion and reciprocal affective relationships in disturbed adolescents', *Family Process*, 28: 337–48.

51. M. T. Singer and L. C. Wynne (1965), 'Thought disorder and family relations of schizophrenics III. Methodology using projective techniques', *Archives of General Psychiatry*, 12: 187–200; M. T. Singer and L. C. Wynne

(1965), 'Thought disorder and family relations of schizophrenics IV. Results and implications', *Archives of General Psychiatry*, 12: 201–12.

52. P. Tienari et al. (2003), 'Genetic boundaries of the schizophrenia spectrum: Evidence from the Finnish adoptive family study of schizophrenia', *American Journal of Psychiatry*, 160: 1587–94.

53. K. E. Wahlberg et al. (2000), 'Thought disorder index of Finnish adoptees and communication deviance of their adoptive parents', *Psychological Medicine*, 30: 127–36.

54. M. Dozier and S. W. Lee (1995), 'Discrepancies between self- and other-report of psychiatric symptomatology: Effects of dismissing attachment strategies', *Development and Psychopathology*, 7: 217–26; P. Rankin et al. (2005), 'Parental relationships and paranoid delusions: Comparisons of currently ill, remitted and healthy individuals', *Psychopathology*, 38: 16–25.

55. M. L. Cooper, P. R. Shaver and N. L. Collins (1998), 'Attachment style, emotion regulation, and adjustment in adolescence', *Journal of Personality and Social Psychology*, 74: 1380–97; K. D. Mickelson, R. C. Kessler and P. R. Shaver (1997), 'Adult attachment in a nationally representative sample', *Journal of Personality and Social Psychology*, 73: 1092–1106.

56. L. Pickering, J. Simpson and R. P. Bentall (2008), 'Insecure attachment predicts proneness to paranoia but not hallucinations', *Personality and Individual Differences*, 44: 1212–24.

57. S. A. Medrick et al. (1987), 'The Copenhagen High-Risk Study', *Schizophrenia Bulletin*, 13: 485–95. J. Schiffman et al. (2001), 'Early rearing factors in schizophrenia', *International Journal of Mental Health*, 30: 3–16.

58. See, for example, C. Morgan et al. (2007), 'Parental separation, loss and psychosis in different ethnic groups: A case-control study', *Psychological Medicine*, 37: 495–503.

59. A. Myhrman et al. (1996), 'Unwantedness of pregnancy and schizophrenia in the child', *British Journal of Psychiatry*, 169: 637–40.

60. J. A. Egeland et al. (1987), 'Bipolar affective disorder linked to DNA markers on chromosome 11', *Nature*, 325: 783–7; R. Sherington et al. (1988), 'Localization of a susceptibility locus for schizophrenia on chromosome 5', *Nature*, 336: 164–7.

61. T. J. Crow (1997), 'Current status of linkage for schizophrenia: Polygenes of vanishingly small effect or multiple false positives?', *American Journal of Medical Genetics (Neuropsychiatric Genetics)*, 74: 99–103.

62. S. O. Moldin (1997), 'The maddening hunt for madness genes', *Nature Genetics*, 17: 127–9.

63. A. Elkin, S. Kalidini and P. McGuffin (2004), 'Have schizophrenia genes been found?', *Current Opinion in Psychiatry*, 17: 107–13.

64. H. Stefansson et al. (2002), 'Neuregulin 1 and susceptibility to schizophrenia', *American Journal of Human Genetics*, 71: 877–92.

65. P. J. Harrison and A. J. Law (2006), 'Neuregulin 1 and schizophrenia: Genetics, gene expression, and neurobiology', *Biological Psychiatry*, 60: 132–40.

66. A. R. Sanders et al. (2008), 'No significant association of 14 candidate genes with schizophrenia in a large European ancestry sample: Implications for psychiatric genetics', *American Journal of Psychiatry*, 165: 497–506.

67. E. K. Green et al. (2005), 'Operation of the schizophrenia susceptibility gene, Neuregulin 1, across traditional diagnostic boundaries to increase risk for bipolar disorder', *Archives of General Psychiatry*, 62: 642–8.

68. N. Craddock and M. J. Owen (2005), 'The beginning of the end of the Kraepelinian dichotomy', *British Journal of Psychiatry*, 186: 364–6.

69. M. J. Owen, N. Craddock and M. C. O'Donovan (2005), 'Schizophrenia: genes at last?', *Trends in Genetics*, 21: 518–25.

70. R. Raybould et al. (2005), 'Bipolar disorder and polymorphisms in the dysbindin gene (DTNBP1)', *Biological Psychiatry*, 57: 696–701.

71. R. Joober et al. (2002), 'Catechol-Omethytransferase Val-108/158-Met gene variants associated with performance on the Wisconsin Card Sorting Test', *Archives of General Psychiatry*, 59: 662–3; A. Rosa et al. (2004), 'New evidence of association between COMT gene and prefrontal neurocognitive function in healthy individuals from sibling pairs discordant for psychosis', *American Journal of Psychiatry*, 161: 1110–12.

72. S. J. Glatt, S. V. Faraone and M. T. Tsuang (2003), 'Association between a functional catechol-O-methytransferase gene polymorphism and schizophrenia: Meta-analysis of case control and family-based studies', *American Journal of Psychiatry*, 160: 469–76.

73. C. Henquet et al. (2005), 'The environment and schizophrenia: The role of cannabis use', *Schizophrenia Bulletin*, 31: 608–12; D. M. Fergusson et al. (2006), 'Cannabis and psychosis', *British Medical Journal*, 332: 172–5.

74. A. Caspi et al. (2005), 'Moderation of the effect of adolescent-onset cannabis use on adult psychosis by a functional polymorphism in the catechol-O-methyltransferase gene: Longitudinal evidence of a gene x environment interaction', *Biological Psychiatry*, 57: 1117–27.

75. Sanders et al (2008), op. cit.

76. T. J. Crow (2008), 'The emperors of the schizophrenia polygene have no clothes', *Psychological Medicine*, 38: 1679–80.

77. Reported in the *Independent*, 20 October 2007.

78. For a review, see J. Read et al. (2006), 'Prejudice and schizophrenia: A review of the "mental illness is an illness like any other" approach', *Acta Psychiatrica Scandinavica*, 114: 303–18.

79. S. Mehta and A. Farina (1997), 'Is being "sick" really better? Effect of the disease view of mental disorders on stigma', *Journal of Social and Clinical Psychology*, 16: 405–19; T. Lincoln et al. (2008), 'Can antistigma campaigns be improved? A test of the impact of biogenetic vs. psychosocial causal explanations on implicit and explicit attitudes to schizophrenia', *Schizophrenia Bulletin*, 34: 984–94.

Chapter 7

1. American Psychiatric Association (1994), *Diagnostic and Statistical Manual for Mental Disorders*, 4th edition. Washington DC: American Psychiatric Association (*DSM-IV*).

2. See, for example, D. Enoch (1991), 'Delusional jealousy and awareness of reality', *British Journal of Psychiatry*, 159, suppl. 14: 52–6; and M. D. Enoch and W. H. Trethowan (1979), *Uncommon Psychiatric Syndromes*, 2nd edition. Bristol: Wright.

3. E. C. Johnstone et al. (1976), 'Cerebral ventricular size and cognitive impairment in chronic schizophrenia', *Lancet*, 2: 924–6.

4. M. E. Shenton et al. (2000), 'A review of MRI findings in schizophrenia', *Schizophrenia Research*, 49: 1–52. See also I. C. Wright et al. (2000), 'Meta-analysis of regional brain volumes in schizophrenia', *American Journal of Psychiatry*, 157: 16–25.

5. S. Campbell et al. (2004), 'Lower hippocampal volume in patients suffering from depression: A meta-analysis', *American Journal of Psychiatry*, 161: 598–607.

6. C. McDonald et al. (2004), 'Meta-analysis of magnetic resonance imaging brain morphometry studies in bipolar disorder', *Biological Psychiatry*, 56: 411–17.

7. P. W. R. Woodruff and S. Lewis (1996), 'Structural brain imaging in schizophrenia', in S. Lewis and N. Higgins (eds.), *Brain Imaging in Psychiatry*. Oxford: Blackwell, pp. 188–214.

8. G. N. Smith and W. G. Iacano (1986), 'Lateral ventricular enlargement in schizophrenia and choice of control group', *Lancet*, 1: 1450.

9. C. McDonald et al. (2005), 'Regional volume deviations of brain structure in schizophrenia and psychotic bipolar disorder: Computational morphometry study', *British Journal of Psychiatry*, 186: 369–77; C. McDonald et al. (2006), 'Regional brain morphometry in patients with schizophrenia or bipolar disorder and their unaffected relatives', *American Journal of Psychiatry*, 163: 478–87.

10. C. McDonald et al. (2005), 'Regional volume deviations of brain structure

in schizophrenia and psychotic bipolar disorder: Computational morphometry study', *British Journal of Psychiatry*, 186: 369–77.

11. A. Vita and L. de Peri (2007), 'The effects of antipsychotic treatment on cerebral structure and function in schizophrenia', *International Review of Psychiatry*, 19: 431–8.

12. J. A. Lieberman et al. (2005), 'Antipsychotic drug effects on brain morphology in first-episode psychosis', *Archives of General Psychiatry*, 62: 361–70.

13. For example, C. Anderson et al. (2002), 'Striatal volume changes in the rat following long-term administration of typical and atypical antipsychotic drugs', *Neuropsychopharmacology*, 27, 143–51; L. McCormick et al. (2005), 'Effects of atypical and typical neuroleptics on anterior cingulate volume in schizophrenia', *Schizophrenia Research*, 80: 73–84.

14. Vita and de Peri (2007), op. cit.

15. T. Crow (1991), 'The failure of the binary concept and the psychosis gene', in A. Kerr and H. McClelland (eds.), *Concepts of Mental Disorder: A Continuing Debate*. London: Gaskell, pp. 31–47.

16. G. D. Pearlson et al. (1984), 'Lateral ventricular enlargement associated with persistent unemployment and negative symptoms in both schizophrenia and bipolar disorder', *Psychiatry Research*, 12: 1–9; R. Tandon et al. (2000), 'Phasic and enduring negative symptoms in schizophrenia: biological markers and relationship to outcome', *Schizophrenia Research*, 27: 191–201.

17. For general reviews of animal studies, see S. J. Suomi (1997), 'Long-term effects of different early rearing experiences on social, emotional, and physiological development in nonhuman primates', in M. S. Keshavan and R. M. Murray (eds.), *Neurodevelopment and Adult Psychopathology*. Cambridge: Cambridge University Press, pp. 104–16; J. Kaufman and D. Carney (2001), 'Effects of early stress on brain structure and function: Implications for understanding the relationship between child maltreatment and depression', *Development and Psychopathology*, 13: 451–71.

18. C. Nemeroff et al. (2006), 'Posttraumatic stress disorder: A state-of-the-science review', *Journal of Psychiatric Research*, 40: 1–21.

19. M. H. Teicher, A. Tomoda and S. L. Andersen (2006), 'Neurobiological consequences of early stress and childhood maltreatment: Are results from human and animal studies comparable?', *Annals of the New York Academy of Sciences*, 1071: 313–23; J. E. Downhill et al. (2000), 'Shape and size of the corpus callosum in schizophrenia and schizotypal personality disorder', *Schizophrenia Research*, 47: 193–208.

20. N. Kitayama, S. Quinn and J. D. Bremner (2006), 'Smaller volume of anterior cingulate in abuse-related posttraumatic stress disorder', *Journal of*

Affective Disorders, 90: 171–4; D. E. Job et al. (2002), 'Structural gray matter differences between first-episode schizophrenics and normal controls using voxel-based morphometry', *Neuroimage*, 17: 880–89.

21. J. Read et al. (2001), 'A traumagenic neurodevelopmental model of schizophrenia', *Psychiatry: Interpersonal and Biological Processes*, 64: 319–45.

22. K. Murugaiah et al. (1982), 'Chronic continuous administration of neuro-leptic drugs alters cerebral dopamine receptors and increases spontaneous dopaminergic action in the striatum', *Nature*, 296: 570–72.

23. P. J. McKenna (1994), *Schizophrenia and Related Syndromes*. Oxford: Oxford University Press.

24. D. F. Wong et al. (1986), 'Positron emission tomography reveals elevated D2 dopamine receptors in drug-naive schizophrenics', *Science*, 234: 1558–63.

25. L. Fadre et al. (1987), 'No D2 receptor increase in PET study of schizo-phrenia', *Archives of General Psychiatry*, 44: 671–2; Y. Okubo et al. (1997), 'Decreased prefrontal dopamine D1 receptors in schizophrenia revealed by PET', *Nature*, 385: 634–6.

26. G. D. Pearlson et al. (1995), 'In vivo D-sub-2 dopamine receptor density in psychotic and nonpsychotic patients with bipolar disorder', *Archives of General Psychiatry*, 52: 471–7.

27. D. F. Wong (2002), 'In vivo imaging of D2 dopamine receptors in schizophrenia', *Archives of General Psychiatry*, 59: 31–4.

28. M. Laruelle and A. Abi-Dargham (1999), 'Dopamine as the wind in the psychotic fire: New evidence from brain imaging studies', *Journal of Psychopharmacology*, 13: 358–71.

29. M. Laruelle, L. Kegeles and A. Abi-Dargham (2003), 'Glutamate, dopam-ine, and schizophrenia: From pathophysiology to treatment', *Annals of the New York Academy of Sciences*, 1003: 138–58.

30. K. C. Berridge and T. E. Robinson (2003), 'Parsing reward', *Trends in Neuroscience*, 9: 507–13.

31. W. Schultz, P. Dayan and P. Montague (1997), 'A neural substrate of prediction and reward', *Science*, 275: 1593–9.

32. S. L. Johnson et al. (2000), 'Increases in manic symptoms after life events involving goal attainment', *Journal of Abnormal Psychology*, 109: 721–7.

33. M. A. Ungless (2004), 'Dopamine: The salient issue', *Trends in Neuro-sciences*, 27: 702–5.

34. M. Pessiglione et al. (2006), 'Dopamine-dependent prediction errors underpin reward-seeking behaviour in humans', *Nature*, 442: 1042–5; M. Menon et al. (2007), 'Temporal difference modeling of the Blood-Oxygen Level Dependent response during aversive conditioning in humans: Effects of dopaminergic modulation', *Biological Psychiatry*, 62: 765–72.

35. J.-P. Selten and E. Cantor-Graae (2005), 'Social defeat: Risk factor for psychosis?', *British Journal of Psychiatry*, 187: 101–2.

36. M. Moutoussis et al. (2007), 'Persecutory delusions and the conditioned avoidance paradigm: Towards an integration of the psychology and biology of paranoia', *Cognitive Neuropsychiatry*, 12: 495–510.

37. D. Shakow and P. E. Huston (1936), 'Studies of motor function in schizophrenia: I. Speed of tapping', *Journal of General Psychology*, 15: 63–108.

38. A. S. Bellack et al. (1990), 'Remediation of cognitive deficits in schizophrenia', *American Journal of Psychiatry*, 147: 1650–55; M. F. Green et al. (1992), 'Wisconsin Card Sorting Test performance in schizophrenia: Remediation of a stubborn deficit', *American Journal of Psychiatry*, 149: 62–7. An interesting paper which uses a rather different technique to show the same effect in depressed patients is: A. Scheurich et al. (2007), 'Experimental evidence for a motivational origin of cognitive impairment in major depression', *Psychological Medicine*, 38: 237–46.

39. L. Davidson and D. W. Heinrichs (2003), 'Quantification of frontal and temporal lobe brain-imaging findings in schizophrenia: A meta-analysis', *Psychiatry Research: Neuroimaging*, 122: 69–87.

40. P. B. Jones and D. J. Done (1997), 'From birth to onset: A development perspective of schizophrenia in two national birth cohorts', in Keshavan and Murray (eds.), op. cit., pp. 119–36; P. B. Jones et al. (1994), 'Child developmental risk factors for adult schizophrenia in the British 1946 birth cohort', *Lancet*, 344: 1398–1402.

41. M. Davidson et al. (1999), 'Behavioral and intellectual markers for schizophrenia in apparently healthy male adolescents', *American Journal of Psychiatry*, 156: 1328–35.

42. S. Nasar (1998), *A Beautiful Mind*. London: Faber and Faber.

43. See R. P. Bentall (2003), *Madness Explained: Psychosis and Human Nature*. London: Penguin, chapter 5.

44. J. H. MacCabe et al. (2002), 'Do schizophrenic patients who managed to get to university have a non-developmental form of illness?', *Psychological Medicine*, 32: 535–44.

45. K. Nuechterlein et al. (1991), 'Information processing abnormalities in the early course of schizophrenia and bipolar disorder', *Schizophrenia Research*, 5: 195–6; M. R. Serper (1993), 'Visual controlled information processing resources and formal thought disorder in schizophrenia and mania', *Schizophrenia Research*, 9: 59–66; W.-C. C. Tam, K. W. Sewell and H.-W. Deng (1998), 'Information processing in schizophrenia and bipolar disorder: A discriminant analysis', *Journal of Nervous and Mental Disease*, 186: 597–603.

46. J. J. van Os et al. (1996), 'Developmental precursors of affective illness in a general population birth cohort', *Archives of General Psychiatry*, 54: 625–31.

47. M. F. Green (1998), *Schizophrenia from a Neurocognitive Perspective: Probing the Impenetrable Darkness*. Boston: Allyn and Bacon.

48. R. S. Keefe et al. (2006), 'Baseline neurocognitive deficits in the CATIE schizophrenia trial', *Neuropsychopharmacology*, 31: 2033–46.

49. R. M. G. Norman and A. K. Malla (1991), 'Dysphoric mood and symptomatology in schizophrenia', *Psychological Medicine*, 21: 897–903; N. M. Docherty (1996), 'Affective reactivity of symptoms as a process discriminator in schizophrenia', *Journal of Nervous and Mental Disease*, 184: 535–41.

50. I. Myin-Germeys, P. A. E. G. Delespaul and M. W. de Vries (2000), 'Schizophrenia patients are more emotionally active than is assumed based on their behaviour', *Schizophrenia Bulletin*, 26: 847–53.

51. I. Myin-Germeys et al. (2002), 'Are cognitive impairments associated with sensitivity to stress in schizophrenia? An experience sampling study', *American Journal of Psychiatry*, 159: 443–9.

52. M. F. Green and K. H. Nuechterlein (1999), 'Should schizophrenia be treated as a neurocognitive disorder?', *Schizophrenia Bulletin*, 25: 309–19.

53. C. Brett (2004), 'Anomalous experiences and cognitive processes in the development of psychosis', unpublished Ph.D. thesis, Institute of Psychiatry, King's College London.

54. R. P. Bentall (2003), *Madness Explained: Psychosis and Human Nature*. London, Penguin.

55. P. Jorgensen and J. Jensen (1994), 'Delusional beliefs in first admitters', *Psychopathology*, 27: 100–12; D. M. Ndetei and A. Vadher (1984), 'Frequency and clinical significance of delusions across cultures', *Acta Psychiatrica Scandinavica*, 70: 73–6; T. Stompe et al. (1999), 'Comparisons of delusions among schizophrenics in Austria and Pakistan', *Psychopathology*, 32: 225–34.

56. M. Moutoussis et al. (2007), op. cit.

57. G. Berrios (1991), 'Delusions as "wrong beliefs": A conceptual history', *British Journal of Psychiatry*, 159 suppl. 14: 6–13.

58. D. Freeman et al. (2005), 'Psychological investigation of the structure of paranoia in a non-clinical population', *British Journal of Psychiatry*, 186: 427–35.

59. L. C. Johns and J. van Os (2001), 'The continuity of psychotic experiences in the general populations', *Clinical Psychology Review*, 21: 1125–41.

60. P. Trower and P. Chadwick (1995), 'Pathways to defence of the self: A theory of two types of paranoia', *Clinical Psychology: Science and Practice*, 2: 263–78.

61. P. Chadwick et al. (2005), 'Phenomenological evidence for two types of paranoia', *Psychopathology*, 38: 327–33; R. P. Bentall et al. (2008), 'Paranoid delusions in schizophrenia and depression: The transdiagnostic role of expectations of negative events and negative self-esteem', *Journal of Nervous and Mental Disease*, 196: 375–83.

62. M. Fornells-Ambrojo and P. Garety (2005), 'Bad me paranoia in early psychosis: A relatively rare phenomenon', *British Journal of Clinical Psychology*, 44: 521–8.

63. S. Melo, J. Taylor and R. P. Bentall (2006), ' "Poor me" versus "bad me" paranoia and the instability of persecutory ideation', *Psychology & Psychotherapy – Theory, Research and Practice*, 79: 271–87.

64. S. Melo, R. Corcoran and R. P. Bentall (in press), 'The Persecution and Deservedness Scale', *Psychology and Psychotherapy: Theory, Research and Practice*.

65. S. Freud (1911/1950), 'Psychoanalytic notes upon an autobiographical account of a case of paranoia (Dementia Paranoides)', in *Collected Papers*, vol. 3. London: Hogarth Press, pp. 387–466.

66. K. M. Colby (1977), 'Appraisal of four psychological theories of paranoid phenomena', *Journal of Abnormal Psychology*, 86: 54–9.

67. E. Zigler and M. Glick (1988), 'Is paranoid schizophrenia really camoflaged depression?', *American Psychologist*, 43: 284–90.

68. H. M. Zullow et al. (1988), 'Pessimistic explanatory style in the historical record: CAVing LBJ, Presidential candidates, and East versus West Berlin', *American Psychologist*, 43: 673–82.

69. A. H. Mezulis et al. (2004), 'Is there a universal positivity bias in attributions? A meta-analytic review of individual, developmental and cultural differences in the self-serving attributional bias', *Psychological Bulletin*, 130: 711–47.

70. S. Kaney and R. P. Bentall (1989), 'Persecutory delusions and attributional style', *British Journal of Medical Psychology*, 62: 191–8.

71. P. Kinderman and R. P. Bentall (1997), 'Causal attributions in paranoia: Internal, personal and situational attributions for negative events', *Journal of Abnormal Psychology*, 106: 341–5.

72. C. L. Candido and D. M. Romney (1990), 'Attributional style in paranoid vs depressed patients', *British Journal of Medical Psychology*, 63: 355–63; C. F. Fear, H. Sharp and D. Healy (1996), 'Cognitive processes in delusional disorder', *British Journal of Psychiatry*, 168: 61–7.

73. L. Humphreys, and C. Barrowclough (2006), 'Attributional style, defensive functioning and persecutory delusions: Symptom-specific or general coping strategy?', *British Journal of Clinical Psychology*, 45: 231–46.

74. I. Janssen et al. (2006), 'Attributional style and psychosis: Evidence for

externalizing bias in patients but not individuals at high risk', *Psychological Medicine*, 27: 1–8; J. A. Martin and D. L. Penn (2001), 'Social cognition and subclinical paranoid ideation', *British Journal of Clinical Psychology*, 40: 261–5; J. A. Martin and D. L. Penn (2002), 'Attributional style in schizophrenia: An investigation in outpatients with and without persecutory delusions', *Schizophrenia Bulletin*, 28: 131–42; R. McKay, R. Langdon and M. Coltheart (2005), 'Paranoia, persecutory delusions and attributional biases', *Psychiatry Research*, 136: 233–45.

75. S. Jolley et al. (2006), 'Attributional style in psychosis: The role of affect and belief type', *Behaviour Research and Therapy*, 44: 1597–1607.

76. S. Melo, J. Taylor and R. P. Bentall (2006), ' "Poor me" versus "bad me" paranoia and the instability of persecutory ideation', *Psychology & Psychotherapy – Theory, Research and Practice*, 79: 271–87.

77. V. Thewissen et al. (2008), 'Fluctuations in self-esteem and paranoia in the context of everyday life', *Journal of Abnormal Psychology*, 117: 143–53. Viviane Thewissen has also been able to show that a relationship between self-esteem stability and paranoia exists at the population level. In the Dutch Nemesis study, in which 7,000 citizens were interviewed about psychiatric symptoms, self-esteem was measured three times, with two-year intervals between the assessments. Amazingly (to my mind) fluctuations in self-esteem between these measurement times were associated with paranoid symptoms in the sample. See V. Thewissen et al. (2007), 'Instability in self-esteem and paranoia in a general population sample', *Social Psychiatry and Psychiatric Epidemiology*, 42: 1–5.

78. P. A. Garety, D. R. Hemsley and S. Wessely (1991), 'Reasoning in deluded schizophrenic and paranoid patients', *Journal of Nervous and Mental Disease*, 179: 194–201; S. F. Huq, P. A. Garety and D. R. Hemsley (1988), 'Probabilistic judgements in deluded and nondeluded subjects', *Quarterly Journal of Experimental Psychology*, 40A: 801–12.

79. For a review, see R. E. J. Dudley and D. E. Over (2003), 'People with delusions jump to conclusions: A theoretical account of research findings on the reasoning of people with delusions', *Clinical Psychology and Psychotherapy*, 10: 263–74.

80. R. Corcoran, C. Cahill and C. D. Frith (1997), 'The appreciation of visual jokes in people with schizophrenia: A study of "mentalizing" ability', *Schizophrenia Research*, 24: 319–27; R. Corcoran, G. Mercer and C. D. Frith (1995), 'Schizophrenia, symptomatology and social inference: Investigating "theory of mind" in people with schizophrenia', *Schizophrenia Research*, 17: 5–13.

81. S. Baron-Cohen (1995), *Mindblindness: An Essay on Autism and Theory of Mind*. Cambridge, Mass.: MIT Press.

82. For recent reviews, see: M. Brune (2005). '"Theory of mind" in schizophrenia: A review of the literature', *Schizophrenia Bulletin*, 31: 21–42; L. Harrington, R. Siegert and J. N. McClure (2005), 'Theory of mind in schizophrenia: A critical review', *Cognitive Neuropsychiatry*, 10: 249–86.

83. P. Kinderman, R. I. M. Dunbar and R. P. Bentall (1998), 'Theory of mind deficits and causal attributions', *British Journal of Psychology*, 71: 339–49.

84. The results from this study are in the process of being reported in a series of papers, including: R. Moore et al. (2006), 'Misunderstanding the intentions of others: An exploratory study of the cognitive etiology of persecutory delusions in very late-onset schizophrenia-like psychosis', *American Journal of Geriatric Psychiatry*, 14: 410–18; N. Shryane et al. (2008), 'Deception and false beliefs in paranoia: Modelling theory of mind stories', *Cognitive Neuropsychiatry*, 13: 8–32; R. P. Bentall et al. (2008), 'Paranoid delusions in schizophrenia and depression: The transdiagnostic role of expectations of negative events and negative self-esteem', *Journal of Nervous and Mental Disease*, 196: 375–83; R. Corcoran et al. (2008), 'A transdiagnostic investigation of theory of mind and jumping to conclusions in paranoia: A comparison of schizophrenia and depression with and without delusions', *Psychological Medicine*, 38: 1577–83; R. P. Bentall et al. (2009), 'The cognitive and affective structure of paranoid delusions: A transdiagnostic investigation of patients with schizophrenia spectrum disorders and depression', *Archives of General Psychiatry*, 66: 236–47.

85. S. Kaney et al. (1997), 'Frequency and consensus judgements of paranoid, paranoid-depressed and depressed psychiatric patients: Subjective estimates for positive, negative and neutral events', *British Journal of Clinical Psychology*, 36: 349–64; R. Corcoran et al. (2006), 'Reasoning under uncertainty: Heuristic judgments in patients with persecutory delusions or depression', *Psychological Medicine*, 36: 1109–18; R. P. Bentall et al. (2008), 'Paranoid delusions in schizophrenia and depression: The transdiagnostic role of expectations of negative events and negative self-esteem', *Journal of Nervous and Mental Disease*, 196: 375–83.

86. For a detailed discussion of this idea, see M. Moutoussis et al. (2007), op. cit.

87. Ibid.

88. F. K. Goodwin and K. R. Jamison (1990), *Manic-depressive Illness*. Oxford: Oxford University Press.

89. J. Piaget (1926), *The Language and Thought of the Child*. London: Routledge and Kegan Paul.

90. L. S. V. Vygotsky (1962), *Thought and Language*. Cambridge, Mass.: MIT Press.

91. Most of the research demonstrating subvocalization during human

cognitive activity dates from some decades ago: for some reason psychologists have shown little interest in this phenomenon in recent years. A good but inevitably dated account of the voluminous literature predating the mid-1970s can be found in F. J. McGuigan (1978), *Cognitive Psychophysiology: Principles of Covert Behavior*. Englewood Cliffs, NJ: Prentice Hall. Slightly to my amazement, I have been unable to find a good review from the last ten years.

92. L. N. Gould (1948), 'Verbal hallucinations and activity of vocal musculature', *American Journal of Psychiatry*, 105: 367–72; L. N. Gould (1950), 'Verbal hallucinations and automatic speech', *American Journal of Psychiatry*, 107: 110–19.

93. For example, T. Inouye and A. Shimizu (1970), 'The electromyographic study of verbal hallucination', *Journal of Nervous and Mental Disease*, 151: 415–22; F. J. McGuigan (1966), 'Covert oral behavior and auditory hallucinations', *Psychophysiology*, 3: 73–80.

94. L. N. Gould (1949), 'Auditory hallucinations and subvocal speech', *Journal of Nervous and Mental Disease*, 109: 418–427. For a modern case study, in which the same finding was reported, see P. Green and M. Preston (1981), 'Reinforcement of vocal correlates of auditory hallucinations by auditory feedback: A case study', *British Journal of Psychiatry*, 139: 204–8.

95. P. W. R. Woodruff (2004), 'Auditory hallucinations: Insights and questions from neuroimaging', *Cognitive Neuropsychiatry*, 9: 73–91.

96. R. P. Bentall and P. D. Slade (1985), 'Reality testing and auditory hallucinations: A signal-detection analysis', *British Journal of Clinical Psychology*, 24: 159–69.

97. P. Rankin and P. O'Carrol (1995), 'Reality monitoring and signal detection in individuals prone to hallucinations', *British Journal of Clinical Psychology*, 34: 517–28; E. Barkus et al. (2007), 'Cognitive and neural processes in non-clinical auditory hallucinations', *British Journal of Psychiatry*, 191, suppl. 51: 76–81.

98. P. P. Allen et al. (2004), 'Misattributional of external speech in patients with hallucinations and delusions', *Schizophrenia Research*, 69: 277–87; L. C. Johns and P. K. McGuire (1999), 'Verbal self-monitoring and auditory hallucinations in schizophrenia', *Lancet*, 353: 469–70; L. C. Johns et al. (2001), 'Verbal self-monitoring and auditory hallucinations in people with schizophrenia', *Psychological Medicine*, 31: 705–15.

99. J. M. Ford and D. H. Mathalon (2004), 'Electrophysiological evidence of corollary discharge dysfunction in schizophrenia during talking and thinking', *Journal of Psychiatric Research*, 38: 37–46.

100. A. G. Gallagher, T. G. Dinin and L. V. J. Baker (1994), 'The effects of varying auditory input on schizophrenic hallucinations: A replication', *British*

Journal of Medical Psychology, 67: 67–76; A. Margo, D. R. Hemsley and P. D. Slade (1981), 'The effects of varying auditory input on schizophrenic hallucinations', *British Journal of Psychiatry*, 139: 122–7.

101. C. Brewin (2003), *Posttraumatic Stress Disorder: Malady or myth?* New Haven: Yale University Press.

102. See especially research conducted by my colleague Tony Morrison, for example: A. P. Morrison (2001), 'The interpretation of intrusions in psychosis: An integrative cognitive approach to hallucinations and delusions', *Behavioral and Cognitive Psychotherapy*, 29: 257–76; A. P. Morrison and C. A. Baker (2000), 'Intrusive thoughts and auditory hallucinations: A comparative study of intrusions in psychosis', *Behaviour Research and Therapy*, 38: 1097–106; A. P. Morrison and A. Wells (2003), 'Metacognition across disorders: A comparison of patients with hallucinations, delusions, and panic disorder with non-patients', *Behaviour Research and Therapy*, 41: 251–6.

103. D. M. Wegner (1994), *White Bears and Other Unwanted Thoughts: Suppression, Obsession and the Psychology of Mental Control*. New York: Guilford.

104. T. E. Goldberg and D. R. Weinberger (2000), 'Thought disorder in schizophrenia: A reappraisal of older formulations and an overview of some recent studies', *Cognitive Neuropsychiatry*, 5: 1–19.

105. See S. H. Jones and R. P. Bentall (eds.), *The Psychology of Bipolar Disorder*. Oxford: Oxford University Press.

Chapter 8

1. Freud's comment has been often misquoted, but the original (in J. Breuer and S. Freud (1895), *Studies on hysteria*, Standard Edition of the Complete Psychological Works of Sigmund Freud, volume 2. London: Hogarth Press) reads as follows: 'When I have promised my patients help or improvement by means of a cathartic treatment I have often been faced by this objection: "Why, you tell me yourself that my illness is probably connected with my circumstances and the events of my life. You cannot alter these in any way. How do you propose to help me, then?" And I have been able to make this reply: "No doubt fate would find it easier than I do to relieve you of your illness. But you will be able to convince yourself that much will be gained if we succeed in transforming your hysterical misery into common unhappiness. With a mental life that has been restored to health you will be better armed against that unhappiness."' I am grateful to Alan Elms of the University of California at Davis for reminding me of the original source.

2. R. Busse (2001), 'Expenditure on health care in the EU: Making projections

for the future based on the past', *Health Economics in Prevention and Care*, 2: 158–61.

3. D. R. Hoover et al. (2002), 'Medical expenditures during the last year of life: Findings from the 1992–1996 Medicare Current Beneficiary Survey', *Health Services Research*, 37: 1625–42. C. Alvarez-Dardet and M. T. Ruiz (1993), 'Thomas McKeown and Archibald Cochrane: A journey through the diffusion of ideas', *British Medical Journal*, 306: 1252–5.

4. T. McKeown (1979), *The Role of Medicine: Dream, Mirage or Nemesis?* Oxford: Blackwell.

5. R. Tallis (2007), *Longer, Healthier, Happier?*, Annual Sense About Science lecture. University College London.

6. A. L. Cochrane (1972), *Effectiveness and Efficiency: Random Reflections on Health Services*. London: Nuffield Provincial Hospital Trust.

7. D. L. Sackett, et al. (1996), 'Evidence based medicine: What it is and what it isn't', *British Medical Journal*, 312: 71–2.

8. P. J. Devereaux and S. Yusuf (2003), 'The evolution of the randomized controlled trial and its role in evidenced-based decision making', *Journal of Internal Medicine*, 254: 105–13.

9. Much of my information about Lind has been obtained from the James Lind Library (www.jameslindlibrary.org), which has been created by the Royal Society of Physicians of Edinburgh 'to help people understand fair tests of treatments in health care by illustrating how fair tests have developed over the centuries'. The website contains some fascinating documents, including facsimiles of Lind's own 'Treatise on Scurvy'.

10. J. Le Fanu (1999), *The Rise and Fall of Modern Medicine*. London: Little, Brown and Co.

11. P. J. Devereaux and S. Yusuf (2003), op. cit.

12. W. G. Thompson (2000), 'Placebos: A review of the placebo response', *American Journal of Gastroenterology*, 95: 1637–43; D. E. Moerman and W. B. Jonas (2002), 'Deconstructing the placebo effect and finding the meaning response', *Annals of Internal Medicine*, 136: 471–6; T. J. Kaptchuk et al. (2006), 'Sham device v. inert pill: Randomised controlled trial of two placebo treatments', *British Medical Journal*, 332: 391–7.

13. UK ECT Review Group (2003), 'Efficacy and safety of electroconvulsive therapy in depressive disorders: A systematic review and meta-analysis', *Lancet*, 361: 799–808.

14. I. Kirsch (2005), 'Placebo psychotherapy: Synonym or oxymoron?', *Journal of Clinical Psychology*, 61: 791–803.

15. K. F. Schulz et al. (1995), 'Empirical evidence of bias: Dimensions of methodological quality associated with estimates of treatment effects in controlled trials', *Journal of the American Medical Association*, 273: 408–12.

16. M. Marshall et al. (2000), 'Unpublished rating scales: A major source of bias in randomised controlled trials of treatments for schizophrenia', *British Journal of Psychiatry*, 176: 249–52.

17. R. Horton and R. Smith (1999), 'Time to register randomized controlled trials: The case is now unanswerable', *British Medical Journal*, 319: 865–6.

18. The trial was published as J. Scott et al. (2006), 'Cognitive behaviour therapy plus treatment as usual compared to treatment as usual alone for severe and recurrent bipolar disorders: A randomised controlled treatment trial', *British Journal of Psychiatry*, 118: 313–20.

19. T. Stephens and R. Brynner (2001), *Dark Remedy: The Impact of Thalidomide and its Revival as a Vital Medicine*. New York: Perseus.

20. I. Chalmers, C. Rounding and K. Lock (2003), 'Descriptive survey of non-commercial randomised controlled trials in the United Kingdom, 1980–2002', *British Medical Journal*, 327: 1–4.

21. I would like to acknowledge that the title of this section was borrowed from a now out-of-print book, A. Klass (1975), *There's Gold in Them Thar Pills: An Inquiry into the Medico-industrial Complex*. London: Penguin. Many years ago, this book first alerted me to the problems of evaluating the effects of drugs.

22. M. Angell (2004), *The Truth about Drug Companies: How they Deceive Us and What to Do About It*. New York: Random House.

23. J. Law (2006), *Big Pharma: How the World's Biggest Drug Companies Control Illness*. London: Constable and Robinson.

24. J. R. Lacasse and J. Leo (2005), 'Serotonin and depression: A disconnect between the advertisements and the scientific literature', *PLoS Medicine*, 2: e392.

25. T. M. Scott (2006), *America Fooled: The Truth about Antidepressants, Antipsychotics and How We've Been Deceived*. Victoria, Tex.: Argo Publishing.

26. E. F. Torrey (2002), 'The going rate on shrinks', *American Prospect*, 13 (13) (15 July).

27. A. Wazana (2000), 'Physicians and the pharmaceutical industry: Is a gift ever just a gift?', *Journal of the American Medical Association*, 283: 373–80.

28. See Senator Grassley's website at http://grassley.senate.gov/. Also, several articles relating to Grassley's work can be found on the *New York Times* website at http://www.nytimes.com/.

29. The details of the Borison case can be found in R. Whitaker (2002), *Mad in America: Bad Science, Bad Medicine and the Enduring Mistreatment of the Mentally Ill*. New York: Perseus Books.

30. J. Moncrieff (2003), *Is Psychiatry for Sale?* London: Institute of Psychiatry.

31. S. S. Sharfstein (2005), 'Big Pharma and American psychiatry: The good, the bad, and the ugly', *Psychiatric News*, 40: 3.

32. D. G. Altman et al. (2001), 'The revised CONSORT statement for reporting randomized trials: Explanation and elaboration', *Annals of Internal Medicine*, 134: 663–94.

33. I. Boutron et al. (2008), 'Extending the CONSORT statement to randomized trials of nonpharmacologic treatment: Explanation and elaboration', *Annals of Internal Medicine*, 148: 295–309.

34. C. Begg et al. (1996), 'Improving the quality of reporting of randomized controlled trials: The CONSORT statement', *Journal of the American Medical Association*, 276: 637–9.

35. M. L. Smith and G. V. Glass (1977), 'Meta-analysis of psychotherapy outcome studies', *American Psychologist*, 32: 752–60.

36. For an accessible introduction to effect sizes and meta-analysis, see B. E. Wampold (2001), *The Great Psychotherapy Debate: Models, Methods and Findings*. Mahwah, NJ: Laurence Erlbaum Associates.

37. J. Cohen (1988), *Statistical Power Analysis for the Behavioral Sciences*, 2nd edition. Hillside, NJ: Laurence Erlbaum Associates.

38. G. C. S. Smith and J. P. Pell (2003), 'Parachute use to prevent death and major trauma related to gravitational challenge: Systematic review of randomised controlled trials', *British Medical Journal*, 327: 1459–61.

39. A. Kazrin, J. Durac and T. Agteros (1979), 'Meta-meta analysis: A new method of evaluating therapy outcomes', *Behaviour Research and Therapy*, 17: 397–9.

40. The Cochrane collaboration, including summaries of systematic reviews of the effectiveness of treatments for various conditions, can be found at http://www.cochrane.org/ (accessed 29 January 2009).

41. J. E. Bekelman, Y. Li and G. P. Gross (2003), 'Scope and impact of financial conflict of interest in biomedical research: A systematic review', *Journal of the American Medical Association*, 289: 454–65; J. Lexchin et al. (2003), 'Pharmaceutical industry sponsorship and research outcome quality: Systematic review', *British Medical Journal*, 326: 1167–70.

42. The *American Journal of Psychiatry*, the *Archives of General Psychiatry*, the *Journal of Clinical Psychopharmacology* and the *Journal of Clinical Psychiatry*. R. Perlis et al. (2005), 'Industry sponsorship and financial conflict of interest in the reporting of clinical trials in psychiatry', *American Journal of Psychiatry*, 162: 1957–60.

43. S. Heres et al. (2006), 'Why olanzapine beats risperidone, risperidone beats quetiapine, and quetiapine beats olanzapine: An exploratory analysis of head-to-head comparison studies of second-generation antipsychotics', *American Journal of Psychiatry*, 163: 185–94.

44. Moncrieff (2003), op. cit.

45. National Center for Health Statistics (2006), *Health, United States, 2006, with Chartbook of Trends in the Health of Americans*. Hyattsville, Md.: US Government Printing Office.

46. P. D. Kramer (1993), *Listening to Prozac*. New York: Viking Press.

47. F. Song et al. (1993), 'Selective serotonin reuptake inhibitors: Meta-analysis of efficacy and acceptability', *British Medical Journal*, 306: 683–7.

48. I. Kirsch and G. Sapirstein (1998), 'Listening to Prozac but hearing placebo: A meta-analysis of antidepressant medication', *Prevention and Treatment*, 1: Art ID 2a (accessed at http://psychet.apa.org on 1 April 2008); I. Kirsch et al. (2008), 'Initial severity and antidepressant benefits: A meta-analysis of data submitted to the food and drug administration', *PLoS Medicine*, 2: e45 (accessed at http://medicine.plosjournals.org on 29 January 2009).

49. G. Parker (2009), 'Antidepressants on trial: How valid is the evidence?', *British Journal of Psychiatry*, 184: 1–3.

50. Quoted in D. Healy (2004), *Let Them Eat Prozac: The Unhealthy Relationship between the Pharmaceutical Industry and Depression*. New York: New York University Press.

51. Ibid.

52. I. Kirsch et al. (2002), 'The emperor's new drugs: An analysis of antidepressant medication data submitted to the U.S. Food and Drug Administration', *Prevention and Treatment* (accessed at http://journals.apa.org/prevention on 29 January 2009).

53. D. Healy and D. Cattell (2003), 'Interface between authorship, industry and science in the domain of therapeutics', *British Journal of Psychiatry*, 183: 22–7.

54. H. Melander, J. Ahlqvist-Rastad and B. Beerman (2003), 'Evidence b(i)ased medicine – selective reporting from studies sponsored by the pharmaceutical industry: Review of studies in new drug applications', *British Medical Journal*, 326: 1171–3.

55. E. H. Turner et al. (2007), 'Selective publication of antidepressant trials and its influence on apparent efficacy', *New England Journal of Medicine*, 358: 252–60.

56. The Wesbecker case and the trial that ensued are well documented. My account here is mainly taken from two sources: J. Cornwell (1996), *The Power to Harm: Mind, Murder and Drugs on Trial*. London: Penguin Books; Healy (2004), op. cit.

57. Potter *v.* Eli Lilly and Co., 926 S. N. 2d 449 (Ky. 1996).

58. D. Healy (2003), 'Conflicting interests in Toronto: Anatomy of a controversy at the interface of academia and industry', *Perspectives in Biology and Medicine*, 45: 250–63.

59. D. M. Fergusson et al. (2005), 'Association between suicide attempts and selective serotonin reuptake inhibitors: systematic review of randomised controlled trials', *British Medical Journal*, 330: 396–404.

60. A. Khan, H. A. Warner, and W. A. Brown (2000), 'Symptom reduction and suicide risk in patients treated with placebo in antidepressant clinical trials: An analysis of the Food and Drug Administration database', *Archives of General Psychiatry*, 57: 311–17; D. Gunnell, J. Saperia and D. Ashby (2005), 'Selective serotonin reuptake inhibitors (SSRIs) and suicide in adults: Meta-analysis of drug company data from placebo controlled, randomised controlled trials submitted to the MHRA's safety review', *British Medical Journal*, 330: 385–90.

61. M. Fink (1999), *Electroshock: Healing Mental Illness*. Oxford: Oxford University Press.

62. UK ECT review group (2003), 'Efficacy and safety of electroconvulsive therapy in depressive disorders: A systematic review and meta-analysis', *Lancet*, 361: 799–808.

63. I base this estimate on the results of a 24-week trial recently published as H. A. Sackheim et al. (2007), 'Continuation pharmacotherapy in the prevention of relapse following electroconvulsive therapy: A randomized controlled trial', *Journal of the American Medical Association*, 285: 1299–1307. Eighty-four per cent of patients receiving ECT alone relapsed during the follow-up period. Those receiving either ECT and an antidepressant (60 per cent) or ECT plus an antidepressant and lithium (39 per cent) did better but nonetheless had very high rates of relapse. The overall impression given by this and other studies is that ECT has a powerful effect on mood but that this does not last more than a few weeks. A psychiatric drug with effects that are just as temporary would be considered pretty useless, and it is not obvious to me why ECT should be considered differently.

With respect to ECT side effects, memory impairment is often reported, but objective measures of memory function suggest that these may not be serious and some authors have argued they are often symptoms of residual depression rather than evidence of neurological impairment (H. Brodaty et al. (2001), '"Side effects" of ECT are mainly depressive phenomena and are independent of age', *Journal of Affective Disorders*, 66: 237–45).

64. C. H. Kellner et al. (2007), 'Continuation electroconvulsive therapy vs pharmacotherapy for relapse prevention in major depression: A multisite study from the Consortium for Research in Electroconvulsive Therapy (CORE)', *Archives of General Psychiatry*, 63: 1337–44.

Chapter 9

1. R. J. Wyatt (1995), 'Early intervention in schizophrenia: Can the course of illness be altered?', *Biological Psychiatry*, 38: 1–3; R. J. Wyatt, M. F. Green and A. H. Tuma (1997), 'Long-term morbidity associated with delayed treatment of first-admission schizophrenic patients', *Psychological Medicine*, 27: 261–8.

2. M. Marshall et al. (2005), 'Association between duration of untreated psychosis and outcome in cohorts of first-episode psychosis: A systematic review', *Archives of General Psychiatry*, 62: 975–83.

3. R. J. Drake et al. (2000), 'Causes of duration of untreated psychosis in schizophrenia', *British Journal of Psychiatry*, 177: 511–15.

4. R. Warner (2002), 'Early intervention in schizophrenia: A critique', *Epidemiologia e psychiatrica sociale*, 11: 248–55; R. Warner (2005), 'Problems with early and very early intervention', *British Journal of Psychiatry*, 187: S104–S107.

5. A. Caspi et al. (2007), 'Premorbid behavioral and intellectual functioning in schizophrenia patients with poor response to treatment with antipsychotic drugs', *Schizophrenia Research*, 94: 45–9.

6. S. Friis et al. (2005), 'Effect of an early detection programme on duration of untreated psychosis: Part of the Scandanavian TIPS study', *British Journal of Psychiatry*, 187, suppl. 48: s29–s32.

7. I. Joa et al. (2008), 'The key to reducing duration of untreated first psychosis: Information campaigns', *Schizophrenia Bulletin*, 34: 466–72.

8. T. K. Larsen et al. (2006), 'Early detection of first-episode psychosis: The effect on one-year outcome'. *Schizophrenia Bulletin*, 32: 758–64; I. Melle et al. (2008), 'Prevention of negative symptom psychopathologies in first-episode schizophrenia', *Archives of General Psychiatry*, 65: 634–40.

9. M. G. Harris et al. (2008), 'Impact of a specialized early psychosis treatment programme on suicide: Retrospective cohort study', *Early Intervention in Psychiatry*, 2: 11–21.

10. A. R. Yung et al. (1998), 'Prediction of psychosis: A step towards indicated prevention of psychosis', *British Journal of Psychiatry*, 172, suppl. 33: 14–20.

11. J. Klosterkotter et al. (2001), 'Diagnosing schizophrenia in the initial prodromal phase', *Archives of General Psychiatry*, 58: 158–64. See also A. Bechdolf et al. (2005), 'Interventions in the initial prodromal states of psychosis in Germany: Concept and recruitment', *British Journal of Psychiatry*, 187, s45–48.

12. G. P. Amminger et al. (2006), 'Treated incidence of first-episode psychosis

in the catchment area of EPPICC: 1997–2000', *Acta Psychiatrica Scandinavica*, 114: 337–45.

13. A. Yung et al. (2006), 'Testing the Ultra High Risk (prodromal) criteria for the prediction of psychosis in a clinical sample of young people', *Schizophrenia Research*, 84: 57–66.

14. T. D. Cannon et al. (2008), 'Prediction of psychosis in youth at high clinical risk: A multisite longitudinal study in North America', *Archives of General Psychiatry*, 65: 28–37.

15. C. Pantelis et al. (2003), 'Neuroanatomical abnormalities before and after onset of psychosis: A cross-sectional and longitudinal MRI comparison', *Lancet*, 561: 281–8.

16. R. S. E. Keefe et al. (2007), 'A longitudinal study of neurocognitive function in individuals at-risk for psychosis', *Schizophrenia Research*, 88: 26–35.

17. C. Pantelis et al. (2003), op. cit.

18. D. Velakoulis et al. (2006), 'Hippocampal and amygdala volumes according to psychosis stage and diagnosis: A magnetic resonance imaging study of chronic schizophrenia, first-episode psychosis, and ultra-high-risk individuals', *Archives of General Psychiatry*, 63: 139–49.

19. Pantelis et al. (2003), op. cit.

20. B. Garner et al. (2005), 'Pituitary volume predicts future transition to psychosis in individuals at ultra-high risk of developing psychosis', *Biological Psychiatry*, 58: 417–23.

21. For a more detailed discussion of these issues, see R. P. Bentall and A. P. Morrison (2002), 'More harm than good: The case against using antipsychotic drugs to prevent severe mental illness', *Journal of Mental Health*, 11: 351–6.

22. O. Agid et al. (2003), 'Delayed-onset hypothesis of antipsychotic action: A hypothesis tested and rejected', *Archives of General Psychiatry*, 60: 1228–35.

23. J. F. Casey et al. (1960), 'Drug therapy in schizophrenia: A controlled study of the relative effectiveness of chlorpromazine, promazine, phenobarbital, and placebo', *Archives of General Psychiatry*, 2: 210–20.

24. M. Li, P. J. Fletcher and S. Kapur (2007), 'Time course of the antipsychotic effect and the underlying behavioural mechanisms', *Neuropsychopharmacology*, 32: 263–72.

25. B. J. Kinon, J. M. Kane and C. Johns (1993), 'Treatment of neuroleptic resistant relapse', *Psychopharmacological Bulletin*, 29: 309–14.

26. J. Kane (1989), 'The current status of neuroleptic therapy', *Journal of Clinical Psychiatry*, 50: 322–8.

27. J. de Leon et al. (2005), 'The CYP2D6 poor metabolizer phenotype may

be associated with risperidone adverse drug reactions and discontinuation',
Journal of Clinical Psychiatry, 66: 15–27.

28. J. Bray and C. Clarke (2008), 'Should we be "pushing meds"? The implications of pharmacogenomics', *Journal of Psychiatric and Mental Health Nursing*, 15: 357–64.

29. H. J. Coppens et al. (1991), 'High central D2-dopamine receptor occupancy as assessed with positron emission tomography in medicated but therapy-resistant patients', *Biological Psychiatry*, 29: 629–34.

30. For a comprehensive and accessible guide to all psychiatric drugs and their side effects, see D. Healy (2005), *Psychiatric Drugs Explained*, 4th edition. London: Elsevier.

31. T. Van Putten, S. R. Marder and J. Mintz (1990), 'A controlled dose comparison of haloperidol in newly admitted schizophrenic patients', *Archives of General Psychiatry*, 47: 754–758; J. P. McEvoy, G. E. Hogarty and S. Steingard (1991), 'Optimal dose of neuroleptic in acute schizophrenia: A controlled study of the neuroleptic threshold and higher haloperidol dose', *Archives of General Psychiatry*, 48: 739–45; A. Rifkind et al. (1991), 'Dosage of haloperidol for schizophrenia', *Archives of General Psychiatry*, 48: 166–70.

32. W. Shen (1999), 'A history of antipsychotic drug development', *Comprehensive Psychiatry*, 40: 407–14.

33. P. Bollini et al. (1994), 'Antipsychotic drugs: Is more worse? A meta analysis of the published randomized controlled trials', *Psychological Medicine*, 24: 307–16.

34. Royal College of Psychiatrists (1993), *Consensus Statement on the Use of High Dose Antipsychotic Medication (CR26)*. London: Royal College of Psychiatrists.

35. A. F. Lehman et al. (1998), 'Translating research into practice: The Schizophrenia Patient Outcomes Research Team (PORT) treatment recommendations', *Schizophrenia Bulletin*, 24: 1–10.

36. J. C. Day et al. (2005), 'Adherence with antipsychotic medication: The impact of clinical variables and relationships with health professionals', *Archives of General Psychiatry*, 62: 717–24.

37. For accounts of the development of clozapine, see D. Healy (2004), *The Creation of Psychopharmacology*. Boston, Mass: Harvard University Press; J. Crilly (2007), 'The history of clozapine and its emergence in the US market: A review and analysis', *History of Psychiatry*, 18: 39–60.

38. J. Kane et al. (1988), 'Clozapine for the treatment-resistant schizophrenic', *Archives of General Psychiatry*, 45: 789–96.

39. P. J. McKenna (1994), *Schizophrenia and Related Syndromes*. Oxford: Oxford University Press.

40. Healy (2004), op. cit.

41. Lehman et al. (1998), op. cit.

42. National Institute for Clinical Excellence (2002), *Schizophrenia: Core Interventions in the Treatment and Management of Schizophrenia in Primary and Secondary Care*. London: National Institute for Clinical Excellence.

43. S. M. Stahl and M. M. Grady (2006), 'High-cost use of second generation antipsychotics under California's Medicaid program', *Psychiatric Services*, 57: 127–9.

44. J. Day, P. Kinderman and R. P. Bentall (1997), 'Discordant views of neuroleptic side effects: A potential source of conflict between patients and professionals', *Acta Psychiatrica Scandinavica*, 97: 93–7.

45. S. E. Finn et al. (1990), 'Subjective utility ratings of neuroleptics in treating schizophrenia', *Psychological Medicine*, 35: 843–8.

46. K. R. Fontaine et al. (2001), 'Estimating the consequences of antipsychotic induced weight gain on health and mortality rate', *Psychiatry Research*, 101: 277–88.

47. J. Moisan et al. (2006), 'Exploring the risk of diabetes mellitus and dyslipidemia among ambulatory users of atypical antipsychotics: a population-based comparison of risperidone and olanzapine', *Pharmacoepidemiology and Drug Safety*, 14: 427–36.

48. W. A. Ray et al. (2001), 'Antipsychotics and the risk of sudden cardiac death,' *Archives of General Psychiatry*, 58: 1161–7.

49. C. H. Hennekens et al. (2005), 'Schizophrenia and increased risks of cardiovascular disease', *American Heart Journal*, 150: 1115–21.

50. J. L. Waddington, H. A. Youssef and A. Kinsella (1998), 'Mortality in schizophrenia: Antipsychotic polypharmacy and absence of adjunctive anticholinergics over the course of a 10-year prospective study', *British Journal of Psychiatry*, 173: 325–9; M. Joukamaa et al. (2006), 'Schizophrenia, neuroleptic medication and mortality', *British Journal of Psychiatry*, 188: 122–7.

51. S. Singh and E. Wooltorton (2005), 'Increased mortality among elderly patients with dementia using atypical antipsychotics', *Canadian Medical Association Journal*, 173: 252; L. S. Schneider, K. S. Dagerman and P. Insel (2005), 'Risk of death with atypical antipsychotic drug treatment for dementia: Meta-analysis of randomized-controlled trials', *Journal of the American Medical Association*, 294: 1934–43.

52. T. Van Putten et al. (1981), 'Subjective response to antipsychotic drugs', *Archives of General Psychiatry*, 38: 187–90; L. Voruganti and A. G. Award (2004), 'Neuroleptic dysphoria: Towards a new synthesis', *Psychopharmacology*, 171: 121–32.

53. K. C. Berridge and T. E. Robinson (2003), 'Parsing reward', *Trends in Neuroscience*, 9: 507–13.

54. T. J. MacMillan et al. (1986), 'The Northwick Park study of first episodes of schizophrenia III: Short-term outcome in trial entrants and trial eligible patients' prophylactic neuroleptic treatment', *British Journal of Psychiatry*, 148: 128–33.

55. N. R. Schooler (1994), 'Deficit symptoms in schizophrenia: Negative symptoms versus neuroleptic-induced deficits', *Acta Psychiatrica Scandinavica*, 89: 21–6.

56. C. Seale et al. (in press), 'Antipsychotic medication, sedation and mental clouding: An observational study of psychiatric consultations', *Social Science and Medicine*.

57. T. Miller and T. McGlashan (2003), 'The risks of not intervening in pre-onset psychotic illness', *Journal of Mental Health*, 12: 345–9.

58. P. D. McGorry et al. (2002), 'A randomized controlled trial of interventions designed to reduce the risk of progression to first-episode psychosis in a clinical sample with subthreshold symptoms', *Archives of General Psychiatry*, 59: 921–8.

59. T. H. McGlashan et al. (2006), 'Randomized, double-blind trial of olanzapine versus placebo in patients prodromally symptomatic for psychosis', *Archives of General Psychiatry*, 163: 790–99.

60. B. Carey (2006), 'A career that has mirrored psychiatry's twisting path', *New York Times* (23 May).

61. A. Rogers, D. Pilgrim and R. Lacey (1993), *Experiencing Psychiatry: Users' Views of Services*. London: Macmillan, in association with MIND Publications; J. Day and R. P. Bentall (1996), 'Schizophrenic patients' experience of neuroleptic medication: A q-methodological investigation', *Acta Psychiatrica Scandinavica*, 93: 397–402; M. A. Rettenbacher et al. (2006), 'Schizophrenia: Attitudes of patients and professional carers towards the illness and antipsychotic medication', *Psychopharmacology*, 37: 103–9.

62. S. K. Hoge et al. (1990), 'A prospective, multicenter study of patients' refusal of antipsychotic medication', *Archives of General Psychiatry*, 47: 949–56.

63. M. I. Herz et al. (1991), 'Intermittent vs maintenance medication in schizophrenia', *Archives of General Psychiatry*, 48: 333–9; A. G. Jolley et al. (1990), 'Trial of brief intermittent neuroleptic prophylaxis for selected schizophrenic outpatients: clinical and social outcome at two years', *British Medical Journal*, 301: 837–42.

64. A. Rogers et al. (1998), 'The meaning and management of neuroleptic medication: A study of people with a diagnosis of schizophrenia', *Social Science and Medicine*, 47: 1313–23.

65. E. C. Johnstone et al. (1988), 'The Northwick Park "functional" psychosis study: Diagnosis and treatment response', *Lancet*, 2: 119–25.

66. C. A. Tamminga and J. M. Davis (2007), 'The neuropharmacology of psychosis', *Schizophrenia Bulletin*, 33: 937–46.

67. J. R. Bola (2006), 'Medication-free research in early episode schizophrenia: Evidence of long-term harm?', *Schizophrenia Bulletin*, 32: 288–96.

68. J. Bola and L. Mosher (2003), 'Treatment of acute psychosis without neuroleptics: Two-year outcomes from the Soteria project', *Journal of Nervous and Mental Disease*, 191: 219–29.

69. L. Ciompi, H. P. Dauwalder and C. Maier (1992), 'The pilot project "Soteria Berne": Clinical experiences and results', *British Journal of Psychiatry*, 161: 145–53.

70. P. R. May et al. (1981), 'Schizophrenia: A follow-up study of the results of five forms of treatment', *Archives of General Psychiatry*, 38: 776–84.

71. W. Gaebel et al. (2002), 'First vs multiple episode schizophrenia: Two-year outcome of intermittent and maintenance medication strategies', *Schizophrenia Research*, 53: 145–59.

72. L. Wunderink et al. (2007), 'Guided discontinuation versus maintenance treatment in remitted first-episode psychosis: Relapse rates and functional outcome', *Journal of Clinical Psychiatry*, 68: 654–61.

73. S. Silvestri et al. (2000), 'Increased dopamine D_2 receptor binding after long-term treatment with antipsychotics in humans: A clinical PET study', *Psychopharmacology*, 152: 174–80.

74. J. Moncrieff (2006), 'Does antipsychotic withdrawal provoke psychosis? Review of the literature on rapid onset psychosis (supersensitivity psychosis) and withdrawal-related relapse', *Acta Psychiatrica Scandinavica*, 114: 3–13.

75. R. Whitaker (2005), 'Anatomy of an epidemic: Psychiatric drugs and the astonishing rise of mental illness in America', *Ethical Human Psychology and Psychiatry*, 7: 23–35.

76. J. Kane et al. (1988), op. cit.

77. T. Van Putten et al. (1993), 'Systematic dosage reduction in treatment-resistant schizophrenic patients', *Psychopharmacology Bulletin*, 29: 315–20.

78. J. Geddes et al. (2000), 'Atypical antipsychotics in the treatment of schizophrenia: Systematic overview and meta-regression analysis', *British Medical Journal*, 321: 1371–6.

79. S. Lewis and J. A. Lieberman (2008), 'CATIE and CUtLASS: Can we handle the truth?', *British Journal of Psychiatry*, 192: 161–3.

80. P. B. Jones et al. (2006), 'Randomized controlled trial of the effect on quality of life of second vs first generation antipsychotic drugs in schizophrenia: Cost Utility of the Latest Antipsychotic drugs in Schizophrenia Study (CUtLASS 1)', *Archives of General Psychiatry*, 63: 1079–87.

81. L. M. Davies et al. (2007), 'Cost-effectiveness of first vs second generation

NOTES

antipsychotic drugs: Results from a randomised controlled trial in schizophrenia responding poorly to previous therapy', *British Journal of Psychiatry*, 191: 14–22.

82. J. A. Lieberman et al. (2005), 'Effectiveness of antipsychotic drugs in patients with chronic schizophrenia', *New England Journal of Medicine*, 353: 1209–23.

83. D. D. Miller et al. (2008), 'Extra-pyramidal side-effects of antipsychotics in a randomised trial', *British Journal of Psychiatry*, 193: 279–88.

84. R. S. E. Keefe et al. (2007), 'Neurocognitive effects of antipsychotic medication in patients with chronic schizophrenia in the CATIE trail', *Archives of General Psychiatry*, 64: 633–47.

85. 'Comparing schizophrenia drugs', *New York Times* (21 September 2005), p. 24.

86. J. Moncrieff (2003), 'Clozapine v. conventional antipsychotic drugs for treatment-resistant schizophrenia: A re-examination', *British Journal of Psychiatry*, 183: 161–6.

87. S. W. Lewis et al. (2006), 'Randomized controlled trial of effect of prescription of clozapine versus other second-generation antipsychotics in resistant schizophrenia', *Schizophrenia Bulletin*, 32: 715–23.

88. J. P. McEvoy et al. (2006), 'Effectiveness of dozopine versus olanzapine, quetiapine, and respiradone in patients with chronic schizophrenia who did not respond to prior atypical anti-psychotic treatment', *American Journal of Psychiatry*, 163: 600–610.

89. H. Y. Meltzer et al. (2003), 'Clozapine treatment for suicidality in schizophrenia', *Archives of General Psychiatry*, 60: 82–91.

90. K. R. Fontaine et al. (2001), 'Estimating the consequences of antipsychotic induced weight gain on health and mortality rate', *Psychiatry Research*, 101: 277–88.

91. For modern discussions of this principle, see: R. Gillon (1985), *Philosophical Medical Ethics*. London: Wiley; T. L. Beauchamp and J. F. Childress (2001), *Principles of Biomedical Ethics*, 5th edition. Oxford: Oxford University Press.

92. W. O. Cooper et al. (2004), 'New users of antipsychotic medications among children enrolled in TennCare', *Archives of Paediatrics and Adolescent Medicine*, 158: 753–9.

93. I. C. K. Wong, D. Camilleri-Novak and P. Stephens (2003), 'Rise in psychotropic drug prescribing in children in the UK: An urgent public health issue', *Drug Safety*, 26, 1117–18.

94. M. Olfson et al. (2006), 'National trends in the outpatient treatment of children and adolescents with antipsychotic drugs', *Archives of General Psychiatry*, 63: 679–85.

95. A. Maslow (1966), *The Psychology of Science: A Reconnaissance*. New York: Harper & Row.

Chapter 10

1. G. L. Klerman (1990), 'The psychiatric patient's right to effective treatment: Implications of Osheroff v. Chestnut Lodge', *American Journal of Psychiatry*, 147: 409–18.

2. M. E. P. Seligman (1995), 'The effectiveness of psychotherapy: The Consumer Reports Study', *American Psychologist*, 50: 965–74.

3. B. E. Wampold (2001), *The Great Psychotherapy Debate: Models, Methods and Findings*. Mahwah, NJ: Laurence Erlbaum Associates.

4. C. R. Rogers (1957), 'The necessary and sufficient conditions of therapeutic personality change', *Journal of Consulting Psychology*, 21: 95–103.

5. A. O. Horvarth and B. D. Symonds (1991), 'Relation between working alliance and outcome in psychotherapy: A meta-analysis', *Journal of Counselling Psychology*, 38: 139–49.

6. See D. E. Orlinsky, K. Grawe and B. K. Parks (1994), 'Process and outcome in psychotherapy – noch einmal', in A. E. Bergin and S. L. Garfield (eds.), *Handbook of Psychotherapy and Behavior Change*, 4th edition. New York: Wiley, pp. 270–376.

7. L. Luborsky et al. (2003), 'The Dodo bird verdict is alive and well – mostly', *Clinical Psychology: Science and Practice*, 9: 2–12.

8. For a spectacularly ill-informed rant of this kind, see D. J. Nutt and M. Sharpe (2007), 'Uncritical positive regard? Issues in the efficacy and safety of psychotherapy', *Journal of Psychopharmacology*, 22: 3–6.

9. For a good introduction to these methods, see Wampold (2001), op. cit.

10. M. L. Smith and G. V. Glass (1977), 'Meta-analysis of psychotherapy outcome studies', *American Psychologist*, 32: 752–60.

11. Wampold (2001), op. cit.

12. M. L. Smith, G. V. Glass and T. I. Miller (1980), *The Benefits of Psychotherapy*. Baltimore: Johns Hopkins University Press.

13. See Luborsky et al. (2003), op. cit.; D. Chambless (2003), 'Beware the Dodo bird: The dangers of overgeneralization', *Clinical Psychology: Science and Practice*, 9: 13–16.

14. L. A. Robinson, J. S. Berman and R. A. Neimeyer (1990), 'Psychotherapy for the treatment of depression: A comprehensive review of controlled outcome research', *Psychiatric Bulletin*, 108: 30–49.

15. J. Horgan (1999), *The Undiscovered Mind: How the Brain Defies Explanation*. London: Weidenfeld and Nicolson.

16. The most famous exponent of this kind of model has been the American psychiatrist Jerome Frank; see J. D. and J. B. Frank (1991), *Persuasion and Healing: A Comparative Study of Psychotherapy*, 3rd edition. Baltimore: Johns Hopkins University Press; for a more recent, data-driven version of this account, see Wampold (2001), op. cit.

17. Wampold (2001), op. cit.

18. A. O. Horvath and L. Luborsky (1993), 'The role of the therapeutic alliance in psychotherapy', *Journal of Consulting and Clinical Psychology*, 61: 561–73; D. J. Martin, J. P. Garske and M. K. Davis (2000), 'Relation of the therapeutic alliance with outcome and other variables: A meta-analytic review', *Journal of Consulting and Clinical Psychology*, 68: 438–50.

19. S. Freud (1933), *New Introductory Lectures in Psychoanalysis*, trans. J. Strachey, in *Collected Works*. London: Hogarth Press

20. J. G. Gunderson et al. (1984), 'Effects of psychotherapy in schizophrenia: II. Comparative outcome of two forms of treatment', *Schizophrenia Bulletin*, 10: 564–98.

21. K. T. Mueser and H. Berenbaum (1990), 'Psychodynamic treatment of schizophrenia: Is there a future?', *Psychological Medicine*, 20: 253–62.

22. J. P. Leff et al. (1982), 'A controlled trial of intervention with families of schizophrenic patients', *British Journal of Psychiatry*, 141: 121–34.

23. R. I. Stanbridge et al. (2003), 'A study of families' satisfaction with family interventions in psychosis service in Somerset', *Journal of Family Therapy*, 25: 181–204.

24. S. Pilling et al. (2002), 'Psychological treatments in schizophrenia: I. Meta-analysis of family intervention and cognitive behaviour therapy', *Psychological Medicine*, 32: 763–82; G. Pitschel-Walz et al. (2004), 'The effects of family interventions on relapse and rehospitalization in schizophrenia: A meta-analysis', *Focus*, 2: 78–94.

25. G. Fadden (2006), 'Training and disseminating family interventions for schizophrenia: Developing family intervention skills with multi-disciplinary groups', *Journal of Family Therapy*, 28: 23–38.

26. A. T. Beck et al. (1979), *Cognitive Therapy of Depression*. New York: Guilford Press.

27. A. C. Butler et al. (2006), 'The empirical status of cognitive-behavioral therapy: A review of meta-analyses', *Clinical Psychology Review*, 26: 17–31.

28. R. Layard (2006), 'The depression report: A new deal for depression and anxiety disorders', pamphlet, The Centre for Economic Performance's Mental Health Policy Group, London School of Economics.

29. Speech given at the Improving Access to Psychological Therapies conference in London, 10 May 2007.

30. P. Chadwick and M. Birchwood (1994), 'The omnipotence of voices: A

cognitive approach to auditory hallucinations', *British Journal of Psychiatry*, 164: 190–201.

31. D. G. Kingdon and D. Turkington (1994), *Cognitive-behavioural Therapy of Schizophrenia*. Hove: Laurence Erlbaum Associates.

32. Examples include: E. Kuipers et al. (1998), 'London–East Anglia randomised controlled trial of cognitive-behavioural therapy for psychosis III: Follow-up and economic considerations', *British Journal of Psychiatry*, 173: 61–8; E. Kuipers et al. (1997), 'The London–East Anglia randomised controlled trial of cognitive-behaviour therapy for psychosis I: Effects of the treatment phase', *British Journal of Psychiatry*, 171: 319–27; T. Sensky et al. (2000), 'A randomized controlled trial of cognitive-behaviour therapy for persistent symptoms in schizophrenia resistant to medication', *Archives of General Psychiatry*, 57: 165–72; N. Tarrier (2000), 'Two-year follow-up of cogitive-behavioral therapy and supportive counselling in the treatment of persistent symptoms in chronic schizophrenia', *Journal of Consulting and Clinical Psychology*, 68: 917–22.

33. N. Tarrier et al. (2004), '18 month follow-up of a randomized controlled trial of cognitive-behaviour therapy in first episode and early schizophrenia', *British Journal of Psychiatry*, 184: 231–9.

34. A. P. Morrison et al. (2004), 'A randomized controlled trial of cognitive therapy for the prevention of psychosis in people at ultra-high risk', *British Journal of Psychiatry*, 185: 281–7.

35. T. Wykes et al. (2008), 'Cognitive behavior therapy for schizophrenia: Effect sizes, clinical models, and methodological rigor', *Schizophrenia Bulletin*, 34: 523–7.

36. A. Perry et al. (1999), 'Randomised controlled trial of efficacy of teaching patients with bipolar disorder to identify early symptoms of relapse and obtain treatment', *British Medical Journal*, 318: 149–53; F. Colom et al. (2003), 'A randomized trial on the efficacy of group psychoeducation in the prophylaxis of recurrences in bipolar patients whose disease is in remission', *Archives of General Psychiatry*, 60: 402–7; D. H. Lam et al. (2005), 'Relapse prevention in patients with bipolar disorder: Cognitive therapy outcome after 2 years', *American Journal of Psychiatry*, 162: 324–9.

37. J. Scott et al. (2006), 'Cognitive behaviour therapy plus treatment as usual compared to treatment as usual alone for severe and recurrent bipolar disorders: A randomised controlled treatment trial', *British Journal of Psychiatry*, 118: 313–20.

38. J. Scott, F. Colom and E. Vieta (2007), 'A meta-analysis of relapse rates with adjunctive psychological therapies compared to usual psychiatric treatment for bipolar disorders', *International Journal of Neuropsychopharmacology*, 10: 123–9.

39. National Institute for Clinical Excellence (2002), *Schizophrenia: Core Interventions in the Treatment and Management of Schizophrenia in Primary and Secondary Care*. London: National Institute for Clinical Excellence.

40. P. J. McKenna (2001), 'Cognitive therapy for schizophrenia', *British Journal of Psychiatry*, 178: 379–80. See also, the subsequent debate between McKenna and Douglas Turkington, published as D. Turkington and P. J. McKenna (2003), 'Is cognitive-behavioural therapy a worthwhile treatment for psychosis?', *British Journal of Psychiatry*, 182: 477–9.

41. E. Kuipers et al. (1998), 'London–East Anglia randomised controlled trial of cognitive-behavioural therapy for psychosis III: Follow-up and economic considerations', *British Journal of Psychiatry*, 173: 61–8; E. Kuipers et al. (1997), 'The London–East Anglia randomised controlled trial of cognitive-behaviour therapy for psychosis I: Effects of the treatment phase', *British Journal of Psychiatry*, 171: 319–27.

42. T. Sensky et al. (2000), op. cit.

43. S. Pilling et al. (2002), op. cit.

44. M. Birchwood and P. Trower (2006), 'The future of cognitive-behaviour therapy for psychosis: Not a quasi-neuroleptic', *British Journal of Psychiatry*, 108: 107–8.

45. P. Trower et al. (2004), 'Cognitive therapy for command hallucinations: Randomised controlled trial', *British Journal of Psychiatry*, 184: 312–20.

46. G. Haddock et al. (2003), 'Cognitive-behavioural therapy and motivational intervention for schizophrenia and substance misuse: 18-month outcomes of a randomised controlled trial', *British Journal of Psychiatry*, 183: 418–26.

47. G. Haddock et al. (2004), 'Cognitive-behaviour therapy for inpatients with psychosis and anger problems within a low secure environment', *Behavioural and Cognitive Psychotherapy*, 32: 77–98.

48. A. Gumley et al. (2003), 'Early intervention for relapse in schizophrenia: Results of a 12 month randomized controlled trial of cognitive behaviour therapy', *Psychological Medicine*, 33: 419–31.

49. P. Bach and S. C. Hayes (2002), 'The use of Acceptance and Commitment Therapy to prevent the rehospitalization of psychotic patients: A randomized controlled trial', *Journal of Consulting and Clinical Psychology*, 70: 1129–39.

50. S. C. Hayes, K. D. Strosahl and K. G. Wilson (1999), *Acceptance and Commitment Therapy: An Experiential Approach to Behavior Change*. New York: Guilford.

51. L.-G. Ost (in press), 'Efficacy of the third wave of behavioral therapies: A systematic review and meta-analysis', *Behaviour Research and Therapy*.

52. G. Dunn and R. P. Bentall (2007), 'Modelling treatment-effect hetero-geneity in randomized controlled trials of complex interventions (psycho-logical treatments)', *Statistics in Medicine*, 26: 4719–45.

53. J. C. Day et al. (2005), 'Adherence with antipsychotic medication: The impact of clinical variables and relationships with health professionals', *Archives of General Psychiatry*, 62: 717–24.

54. K. A. Weiss et al. (2002), 'Predictors of risk of nonadherence in outpatients with schizophrenia and other psychotic disorders', *Schizophrenia Bulletin*, 28: 341–9.

55. R. McCabe and S. Priebe (2004), 'The therapeutic relationship in the treatment of severe mental illness: A review of methods', *International Journal of Social Psychiatry*, 50: 115–28; S. Priebe and R. McCabe (2006), 'The therapeutic relationship in psychiatric settings', *Acta Psychiatrica Scandinavica*, 119, suppl. 429: 66–72; R. McCabe and S. Priebe (2008), 'Communication and psychosis: It's good to talk but how?', *British Journal of Psychiatry*.

56. The research addressing this topic really is in its infancy. See: E. Moore, R. A. Ball and L. Kuipers (1992), 'Expressed emotion in staff working with the long-term adult mentally ill', *British Journal of Psychiatry*, 161: 802–8; E. J. Finnema (1996), 'Expressed emotion on long-stay wards', *Journal of Advanced Nursing*, 24: 473–8. Also, for a review, see G. van Humbeeck and C. van Audenhove (2003), 'Expressed emotion of professionals towards mental health patients', *Epidemiolgia e psichiatria sociale*, 12: 232–7.

Chapter 11

1. T. McKeown (1979), *The Role of Medicine: Dream, Mirage or Nemesis?* Oxford: Blackwell.

2. C. M. Harding et al. (1987), 'The Vermont longitudinal study of persons with severe mental illness: II. Long-term outcome of subjects who retrospectively met DSM-III criteria for schizophrenia', *American Journal of Psychiatry*, 144: 727–35; C. M. Harding and J. H. Zahniser (1994), 'Empirical correction of seven myths about schizophrenia with implications for treatment', *Acta Psychiatrica Scandinavica*, 90: 140–46.

3. J. S. Strauss and W. T. Carpenter (1974), 'The prediction of outcome in schizophrenia: II. Relationships between predictor and outcome variables', *Archives of General Psychiatry*, 31: 37–42.

4. A. S. Bellack (2006), 'Scientific and consumer models of recovery in schizophrenia: Concordance, contrasts, and implications', *Schizophrenia Bulletin*, 32: 432–42.

5. L. Davidson (2003), *Living outside Mental Illness: Qualitative Studies of Recovery in Schizophrenia*. New York: New York University Press

6. L. Pitt et al. (2007), 'Researching recovery from psychosis: A user-led project', *Psychiatric Bulletin* 31: 51–60.

7. W. Anthony (1993), 'Recovery from mental illness: The guiding vision of the mental health service system in the 1990s', *Psychosocial Rehabilitation Journal*, 16: 11–23.

8. W. Anthony, E. S. Rogers and M. Farkas (2003), 'Research on evidence-based practices: Future directions in an era of recovery', *Community Mental Health Journal*, 39: 101–14.

9. New Freedom Commission on Mental Health (2003), *Achieving the Promise: Transforming Mental Health Care in America. Final Report*. Rockville, Md.: Department of Health and Human Services, publication SMA-03-3832.

10. N. Craddock et al. (2008), 'Wake-up call for British psychiatry', *British Journal of Psychiatry*, 193: 6–9.

11. J. Hamann et al. (2005), 'Do patients with schizophrenia wish to be involved in decisions about their medical treatment?', *American Journal of Psychiatry*, 162: 2382–4.

12. M. Paccaloni, T. Pozzan and C. Zimmerman (2004), 'Being informed and involved in treatment: What do psychiatric patients think?', *Epidemiologia e psichiatria sociale*, 13: 270–83; C. Goss et al. (2008), 'Involving patients in decisions during psychiatric consultations', *British Journal of Psychiatry*, 193: 416–21.

13. M. Hotopf et al. (2000), 'Changing patterns in the use of the Mental Health Act 1983 in England, 1984–1996', *British Journal of Psychiatry*, 176: 479–84.

14. M. Zinkler and S. Priebe (2002), 'Detention of the mentally ill in Europe: A review', *Acta Psychiatrica Scandinavica*, 106: 3–8.

15. S. K. Hoge et al. (1998), 'Family, clinician, and patient perceptions of coercion in mental hospital admission: A comparative study', *International Journal of Law and Psychiatry*, 21: 131–46; H. R. Kaltiala et al. (2000), 'Coercion and restrictions in psychiatric inpatient treatment', *European Psychiatry*, 15: 213–19; C. W. Lidz et al. (1998), 'Factual sources of psychiatric patients' perceptions of coercion in the hospital admission process', *American Journal of Psychiatry*, 155: 1254–60; B. G. McKenna, A. I. F. Simpson and T. M. Laidlaw (1999), 'Patient perception of coercion on admission to acute psychiatric services: The New Zealand experience', *International Journal of Law and Psychiatry*, 22: 143–53.

16. R. McCabe et al. (2004), 'Engagement of patients with psychosis in the

consultation: Conversation analytic study', *British Medical Journal*, 325: 1148–51.

17. E. B. Elbogen, J. W. Swanson and M. S. Swartz (2003), 'Psychiatric disability, the use of financial leverage, and perceived coercion in mental health services', *International Journal of Forensic Mental Health*, 2: 119–27; J. Monahan et al. (2005), 'Use of leverage to improve adherence to psychiatric treatment in the community', *Psychiatric Services*, 56: 37–44; J. Bindman et al. (2005), 'Perceived coercion at admission to psychiatric hospital and engagement with follow-up', *Social Psychiatry and Psychiatric Epidemiology*, 40: 160–66.

18. P. Deegan (1996), 'Recovery as a journey of the heart', *Psychiatric Rehabilitation Journal*, 19: 91–7.

19. R Gillon (1985), *Philosophical Medical Ethics*. London: Wiley.

20. World Medical Association Declaration of Helsinki on Ethical Principles for Medical Research Involving Human Subjects, adopted by the 18th WMA General Assembly, Helsinki, Finland, June 1964, and amended eight times, most recently at the 59th WMA General Assembly, Seoul, October 2008.

21. World Medical Association Declaration on the Rights of the Patient Adopted by the 34th World Medical Assembly, Lisbon, Portugal, September/October 1981, amended by the 47th WMA General Assembly, Bali, Indonesia, September 1995, and editorially revised at the 171st Council Session, Santiago, Chile, October 2005.

22. Committee of Ministers of the Council of Europe (1996), *Convention on Human Rights and Biomedicine*. Brussels: Council of Europe.

23. See Gillon (1985), op. cit.

24. O. O'Neill (2002), *Autonomy and Trust in Bioethics*. Cambridge: Cambridge University Press. See also G. M. Stirrat and R. Gill (2005), 'Autonomy in medical ethics after O'Neill', *Journal of Medical Ethics*, 31: 127–30.

25. The idea that normal functioning is associated with optimism, and that depression is associated with pessimistic beliefs about the ability to control what happens in the future, has a long history, but is often attributed to the work of Lyn Abramson and Martin Seligman. See: L. Y. Abramson, M. E. P. Seligman and J. D. Teasdale (1978), 'Learned helplessness in humans: Critique and reformulation', *Journal of Abnormal Psychology*, 78: 40–74; A. H. Mezulis et al. (2004), 'Is there a universal positivity bias in attributions? A meta-analytic review of individual, developmental and cultural differences in the self-serving attributional bias', *Psychological Bulletin*, 130: 711–47.

26. J. Mirowsky and C. E. Ross (1983), 'Paranoia and the structure of powerlessness', *American Sociological Review*, 48: 228–39; I. Janssen et al.

(2003), 'Discrimination and delusional ideation', *British Journal of Psychiatry*, 182: 71–6. See also Chapter 7.

27. S. Priebe and R. McCabe (2006), 'The therapeutic relationship in psychiatric settings', *Acta Psychiatrica Scandinavica*, 119, suppl. 429: 66–72.

28. A. Moore, W. Sellwood and J. Stirling (2000), 'Compliance and psychological reactance in schizophrenia', *British Journal of Clinical Psychology*, 39: 287–95.

29. S. Kisely et al. (2007), 'Randomized and non-randomized evidence for the effect of compulsory community and involuntary out-patient treatment on health service use: Systematic review and meta-analysis', *Psychological Medicine*, 37: 3–14.

30. T. Burns et al. (2007), 'Use of intensive case management to reduce time in hospital in people with severe mental illness: Systematic review and meta-regression', *British Medical Journal*, 335: 336–44.

31. For a compelling account of how this has happened, it is hard to beat Adam Curtis's documentary television series, *The Power of Nightmares: The Rise of the Politics of Fear* (originally aired in Britain on BBC2 between 20 October 2004 and 3 November 2004). Transcripts of the programmes are available at: http://www.daanspeak.com/TranscriptPowerOfNightmares1.html (accessed 31 October 2008).

32. G. Ward (1997), *Making Headlines: Mental Health and the National Press*. London: Health Education Authority.

33. D. Kahneman, P. Slovic and A. Tversky (1982), *Judgement under Uncertainty: Heuristics and Biases*. Cambridge: Cambridge University Press.

34. J. Shaw et al. (2006), 'Rates of mental disorder in people convicted of homicide: National clinical survey', *British Journal of Psychiatry*, 188: 143–7.

35. J. Bonta, M. Law and K. Hanson (1998), 'The prediction of criminal and violent recidivism among mentally disordered offenders', *Psychological Bulletin*, 123: 123–42; H. Stuart (2003), 'Violence and mental illness: An overview', *World Psychiatry*, 2: 121–4.

36. R. P. Bentall and J. Taylor (2006), 'Psychological processes and paranoia: Implications for forensic behavioral science', *Behavioral Sciences and the Law*, 24: 277–94; T. Stompe, G. Ortwein-Swoboda and H. Schanda (2004), 'Schizophrenia, delusional symptoms, and violence: The threat/control-override concept reexamined', *Schizophrenia Bulletin*, 30: 31–44.

37. P. S. Appelbaum, P. C. Robbins and J. Monahan (2000), 'Violence and delusions: Data from the MacArthur violence risk assessment study', *American Journal of Psychiatry*, 157: 566–72.

38. G. Szmukler (2000), 'Homicide inquiries: Do they make sense?', *Psychiatric Bulletin*, 24: 6–10.

39. M. Dolan and M. Doyle (2000), 'Violence risk prediction: Clinical and actuarial measures and the role of the Psychopathy Checklist', *British Journal of Psychiatry*, 177: 303–11; J. Monahan et al. (2000), 'Developing a clinically useful actuarial tool for assessing violence risk', *British Journal of Psychiatry*, 176: 312–19.

40. G. Szmukler (2001), 'Violence risk prediction in practice', *British Journal of Psychiatry*, 178: 84–5.

41. H. Peyser (2001), 'What is recovery? A commentary', *Psychiatric Services*, 52: 486–7.

42. F. J. Frese et al. (2001), 'Integrating evidence-based practices and the recovery model', *Psychiatric Services*, 52: 1462–8.

43. D. B. Fisher and L. Ahern (2002), 'Evidence-based practices and recovery', *Psychiatric Services*, 53: 632–3.

44. R. W. Heinrichs and K. K. Zakzanis (1998), 'Neurocognitive deficit in schizophrenia: A quantitative review of the evidence', *Neuropsychology*, 12: 426–45.

45. A. Lewis (1934), 'The psychopathology of insight', *British Journal of Medical Psychology*, 14: 332–48.

46. T. Trauer and T. Sacks (2000), 'The relationship between insight and medication adherence in severely mentally ill clients treated in the community', *Acta Psychiatrica Scandinavica*, 102: 211–16.

47. R. J. Drake et al. (2007), 'Insight as a predictor of the outcome of first episode non-affective psychosis', *Journal of Clinical Psychiatry*, 68: 81–6.

48. This claim was originally made several decades ago by the Harvard psychologist Brendan Maher on the basis of studies of the syllogistic (logical) reasoning of psychotic patients. See, for example, B. A. Maher (1988), 'Anomalous experience and delusional thinking: The logic of explanations', in T. F. Oltmanns and B. A. Maher (eds.), *Delusional Beliefs*. New York: Wiley, pp. 15–33. For a recent study which reaches the same conclusion using more realistic measures of reasoning, see R. Corcoran et al. (2006), 'Reasoning under uncertainty: Heuristic judgments in patients with persecutory delusions or depression', *Psychological Medicine*, 36: 1109–18.

49. A. Aleman et al. (2006), 'Insight in psychosis and neuropsychological function: Meta-analysis', *British Journal of Psychiatry*, 189: 204–12; M. A. Cooke et al. (2005), 'Disease, deficit or denial? Models of poor insight in psychosis', *Acta Psychiatrica Scandinavica*, 112: 4–17.

50. M. Birchwood et al. (1994), 'A self-report insight scale for psychosis: Reliability, validity and sensitivity to change', *Acta Psychiatrica Scandinavica*, 89: 62–7.

51. S. E. Taylor (1988), *Positive Illusions*. Basic Books: New York.

52. R. J. Drake et al. (2004), 'The evolution of insight, paranoia and

depression during early schizophrenia', *Psychological Medicine*, 34: 285–92.

53. P. H. Lysanker, D. Roe and P. T. Yanos (2007), 'Toward understanding the insight paradox: Internalized stigma moderates the association between Insight and social functioning, Hope, and self-esteem among people with schizophrenia spectrum disorders', *Schizophrenia Bulletin*, 33: 192–9.

54. J. Moncrieff (2008), *The Myth of the Chemical Cure: A Critique of Psychiatric Drug Treatment*. London: Palgrave.

55. S. Schachter and J. Singer (1962), 'Cognitive, social and physiological determinnts of emotional state', *Psychological Review*, 69: 379–99. There are also good theoretical reasons for doubting whether people can accurately report on internal states. See R. P. Bentall (2003), *Madness Explained: Psychesis and Human Nature*. London: Penguin, chapter 9.

56. J. C. Day et al. (1995), 'A self-rating scale for measuring neuroleptic side effects: Validation in a group of schizophrenic patients', *British Journal of Psychiatry*, 166: 650–53.

57. G. Jackson (2005), *Rethinking Psychiatric Drugs: A Guide to Informed Consent*. Bloomington, Ind.: Authorhouse; D. Healy (2005), *Psychiatric Drugs Explained*, 4th edition: London: Elsevier; J. Moncrieff (in press), *A Straightforward Guide to Psychiatric Drugs*. Ross-on-Wye: PCCS Books.

58. J. Law (2006), *Big Pharma: How the World's Biggest Drug Companies Control Illness*. London: Constable and Robinson.

59. B. Mintzes et al. (2002), 'Influence of direct to consumer pharmaceutical advertising and patients' requests on prescribing decisions: Two site cross sectional survey', *British Medical Journal*, 324: 278–9.

60. A. Herxheimer (2008), 'Relationships between the pharmaceutical industry and patients' organisations', *British Medical Journal*, 326: 1208–10.

61. National Institute for Clinical Excellence (2002), *Schizophrenia: Core Interventions in the Treatment and Management of Schizophrenia in Primary and Secondary Care*. London: National Institute for Clinical Excellence.

62. Department of Health (2007), *Improving Access to Psychological Therapies: Specification for the Commissioner-led Pathfinder Programme*. London: Crown Publications.

63. G. Fadden (2006), 'Training and disseminating family interventions for schizophrenia: Developing family intervention skills with multi-disciplinary groups', *Journal of Family Therapy*, 28: 23–38.

64. T. Lecomte and C. Leclerc (2007), 'Implementing cognitive behaviour therapy for psychosis: Issues and solutions', *Journal of the Norwegian Psychological Association*, 44: 588–97.

65. D. J. Nutt and M. Sharpe (2007), 'Uncritical positive regard? Issues in the efficacy and safety of psychotherapy', *Journal of Psychopharmacology*, 22: 3–6.

66. C. Evans et al. (2002), 'Towards a standardised brief outcome measure: Psychometric properties and utility of the CORE-OM', *British Journal of Psychiatry*, 180: 51–60.

67. F. Rohricht and S. Priebe (2006), 'Effect of body-oriented psychological therapy on negative symptoms in schizophrenia: A randomized controlled trial', *Psychological Medicine*, 36: 669–78.

68. N. Talwar et al. (2006), 'Music therapy for in-patients with schizophrenia', *British Journal of Psychiatry*, 189: 405–9.

69. M. D. Bell, J. Choi and P. Lysaker (2007), 'Psychological interventions to improve work outcomes for people with psychiatric disabilities', *Journal of the Norwegian Psychological Association*, 44: 2–14.

70. G. R. Bond et al. (2001), 'Does competitive employment improve non-vocational outcomes for people with severe mental illness?', *Journal of Consulting and Clinical Psychology*, 69: 489–501.

71. R. Warner (1985), *Recovery from Schizophrenia: Psychiatry and Political Economy*. New York: Routledge & Kegan Paul.

72. G. R. Bond (2004), 'Supported employment: Evidence for an evidence-based practice', *Psychiatric Rehabilitation Journal* 27: 345–59; T. Burns et al. (2007), 'The effectiveness of supported employment for people with severe mental illness: A randomised controlled trial', *Lancet*, 370: 1146–52.

73. M. D. Bell, J. Choi and P. Lysaker (2007), op. cit.

74. H. Tajfel et al. (1971), 'Social categorization and intergroup behaviour', *European Journal of Social Psychology*, 1: 149–78. For a review, see R. Brown (2000), 'Social identity theory: Past achievements, current problems and future challenges', *European Journal of Social Psychology*, 30: 745–78.

75. M. Rubin and M. Hewstone (1998), 'Social identity theory's self-esteem hypothesis: A review and some suggestions for clarification', *Personality and Social Psychology Revue*, 2: 40–62.

76. P. Herriot (2007), *Religious Fundamentalism and Social Identity*. London: Routledge.

77. N. Crossley (2006), *Contesting Psychiatry: Social Movements in Mental Health*. London: Routledge.

78. The website for the British Hearing Voices Network can be found at http://www.hearing-voices.org (accessed 29 January 2009). The US Hearing Voices Network can be found at www.hvn-usa.org (accessed 29 January 2009).

Index

Page references for illustrations and figures are in italics; those for endnotes contain the note number, e.g. 313n38

  Paul 148–51
symptoms *see* complaints
synapses 75–6
systematic desensitization 53
systematic review 203, 206–7, 208–9
Szasz, Thomas xvi, 69, 72–3, 72, 152,
    274
  and biological psychiatry 75, 302n21

Tajfel, Henri 285–6
tardive dyskinesia 223, 225
Tavistock Clinic 70
*Textbook of Psychiatry for Physicians
    and Students, A* (Kraepelin) 30,
    31
thalidomide 196
Thaw, Harry 32
theory of mind (ToM) 173–5
therapeutic alliance 60, 246, 249,
    259–60, 269
therapeutic relationship xix, 80,
    258–60, 265
  and coercion 274
  research 245–6
  Rogers 58–63
Thewissen, Vivianne 171–2, 323n77
thought disorder 7, 182
  and communication deviance 136–7,
    138
threats 175–6
Tienari, Pekka 136–7
time out from reinforcement 66
TIPS (Scandinavian Early Treatment
    and Intervention in Psychosis
    Study) 216, 233
token economy system 57, 58, 64, 65
Torrey, Fuller 199, 202
transference 60, 130, 245
trauma 131, 132, 138
  and auditory hallucinations 180–81
  see also post-traumatic stress disorder
Traux, Charles 62, 64
treatment *see* drug treatment;
    psychotherapy

treatment effectiveness 188–90, 274
  meta-analysis 205
  randomized controlled trials 190–97
  trial data 211–12
tricyclic antidepressants 48
Trower, Peter 168
tuberculosis 191
Tuke, Daniel Hack 89
Tuskegee 230
Twain, Mark 185
twin studies 119–20, 122, 124–5
typical antipsychotics *see* first-
    generation antipsychotics

unconditional positive regard 61
unipolar depression 7–8, 94
  and cognitive functioning 163
  international comparisons 20
  Kraepelin 31
United Kingdom *see* Britain
United States
  antidepressants 208
  antipsychotics 13, 47
  asylums 32, 34–5, 43
  clinical psychology 50–52, 83
  coercion 9
  cognitive behaviour therapy 253,
    258
  early intervention 215
  Epidemiological Catchment Area
    (ECA) study 101, 107
  extreme remedies 35–6
  number of mentally ill people 17–18
  pharmaceutical industry 197–8,
    201–2, 282–3
  psychiatric diagnoses 109, 110–11
  psychiatry 83–5, 96
  psychiatry and clinical psychology 69
  psychoanalysis 41
  psychosis 8
  recovery approach 266
  schizophrenia 19, 32, 96
  schizophrenia costs 9
  therapeutic employment 285
University College London 85–6